Volume 16

ISLAM AND THE POLITICAL
ECONOMY OF MEANING

ISLAM AND THE POLITICAL ECONOMY OF MEANING
Comparative Studies of Muslim Discourse

Edited by
WILLIAM R. ROFF

Routledge
Taylor & Francis Group

LONDON AND NEW YORK

First published in 1987

This edition first published in 2015
by Routledge
2 Park Square, Milton Park, Abingdon, Oxon, OX14 4RN

and by Routledge
711 Third Avenue, New York, NY 10017

Routledge is an imprint of the Taylor & Francis Group, an informa business

British Library Cataloguing in Publication Data
A catalogue record for this book is available from the British Library

ISBN: 978-1-138-78710-0 (Set)
eISBN: 978-1-315-74408-7 (Set)
ISBN: 978-1-138-81838-5 (Volume 16)
eISBN: 978-1-315-74496-4 (Volume 16)
Pb ISBN: 978-1-138-82018-0 (Volume 16)

Publisher's Note
The publisher has gone to great lengths to ensure the quality of this reprint but points out that some imperfections in the original copies may be apparent.

Disclaimer
The publisher has made every effort to trace copyright holders and would welcome correspondence from those they have been unable to trace.

Islam and the Political Economy of Meaning

COMPARATIVE STUDIES OF MUSLIM DISCOURSE

Edited by WILLIAM R. ROFF

CROOM HELM
London & Sydney

© 1987 Social Science Research Council, New York
Croom Helm Ltd, Provident House, Burrell Row,
Beckenham, Kent BR3 1AT
Croom Helm Australia, 44-50 Waterloo Road,
North Ryde, 2113, New South Wales

British Library Cataloguing in Publication Data

Islam and the political economy of meaning.
  1. Islam and politics
  I. Roff, William R.
  297'.1977   BP173.7

  ISBN 0-7099-4248-6

Printed and bound in Great Britain
by Billing & Sons Limited, Worcester.

Contents

Preface
Note on Transliteration
Editor's Introduction   1

Part One: The Political Economy of Religious Culture   11
1. Changing Interpretations of Islamic Movements
   Dale F. Eickelman   13
2. Islamic Movements: One or Many?
   William R. Roff   31
3. The Political Economy of Islamic Conversion in
   Modern East Java *Robert W. Hefner*   53
4. Structural Determinants of Urban Islamic Protest
   in Northern Nigeria *Paul M. Lubeck*   79

Part Two: Muslim Social Thought and the State   109
5. Revolution in Shi'ism *Said Amir Arjomand*   111
6. Islamic Arguments in Contemporary Pakistan
   Barbara D. Metcalf   132
7. Seduction and Sedition: Islamic Polemical
   Discourses in the Maghreb *Jean-Claude Vatin*   160
8. The Response of Muslim Youth Organizations to
   Political Change: HMI in Indonesia and ABIM in
   Malaysia *Muhammad Kamal Hassan*   180

Part Three: Change and the Individual Voice   197
9. Authority and the Mosque in Upper Egypt:
   The Islamic Preacher as Image and Actor
   Patrick D. Gaffney   199
10. Three Islamic Voices in Contemporary Nigeria
    Allan Christelow   226
11. An Islamic System or Islamic Values? Nucleus of
    a Debate in Contemporary Indonesia *A.H. Johns*   254

Glossary   281
Index   287

Preface

Earlier versions of most of the chapters in this book, together with some not appearing here, were prepared for a meeting held in New York City in May, 1984, sponsored by the Joint Committees on South Asia and on Southeast Asia of the American Council of Learned Societies and the Social Science Research Council. We should like to thank these committees for their hospitality and the committee on South Asia for its support of two earlier meetings in 1979 and 1983 which similarly set out to explore the 'indigenous conceptual systems' of Muslims.

A particular debt of gratitude is owed to David L. Szanton, of the Social Science Research Council's staff, whose intellectual contribution was quite as large as his administrative.

W.R.R.

Note on Transliteration

Any book that draws on materials in six major Islamic languages — Arabic, Persian, Urdu, Bengali, Malay, and Hausa, with some additional cognates such as Yoruba and Javanese — faces considerable problems of transliteration. The system employed here, with as much consistency as possible, has been to use for Arabic that given in the *Encyclopaedia Britannica* (1972: Vol. 2, 182-84), with other letters added to represent non-Arabic sounds in Persian, Urdu and Malay. Diacritics have been omitted, except in the Glossary, where they are given in full.

Arabic-derived terms occurring in languages other than Arabic are spelled in the way common in those languages (*mallam* rather than *mu'allam*, for example). So are personal (and some proper) names, which are given in locally preferred rather than artificially Arabicized forms (Usuman dan Fodio, and Abdurrahman, for example, rather than 'Uthman ibn Fudi, and 'Abd al-Rahman).

Editor's Introduction

The essays in this book seek to address one central question: How may we understand the nature, impulse, and dynamic of Muslim social and political action? More specifically, what are the relationships, direct or dialectical, between the prescriptions and requirements of Islamic belief, socially reproduced (of 'being Muslim', in short), and the economic, political, and social circumstances of the lives of actual Muslims? In trying to answer this question, the essays have as a shared premiss the assumption that 'what Muslims say' — and therefore the analysis of Muslim discourse about such matters — must have a central role in the enquiry.

In introducing the collection, however, which ranges very widely, from Nigeria and North Africa to Egypt, Iran, Pakistan, and Indonesia, and from the eighteenth century to the present, it might be as well to ask first a prior question. Why *should* we expect Muslims in such diverse contexts and from such different backgrounds to behave in ways shaped in any important, commonly identifiable fashion by an understanding of what it means to 'be Muslim', rather than, for example, by their shared peripheral relationship to the world capitalist order, by the demographics of rapid population increase, urban growth, and underemployment, or by statism and the rebirth-pangs of the post-colonial era? There can be little dispute that significant elements of a shared religious culture are in fact a feature of the social lives of Muslims from Dahomey to Doha and Dacca — among them, for example, a sacred text and set of symbols, a vocabulary of moral suasion, the practical knowledge associated with Islamic educational and juridical institutions, and the sodalities of the Sufi orders. It is therefore reasonable to enquire how elements of this shared culture, reproduced and given meaning anew in local terms from the Nejd to Nigeria, shape responses to (and are themselves shaped by) the harsh or subtle facts of political and economic life. How are the real or supposed imperatives of 'being Muslim' understood, and in what terms and by whom, and with what social implications are they expressed, conveyed, urged, argued, and acted upon?

Not all the contributors to this book would necessarily answer, or indeed address, these questions in the same way (and none, it must be emphasized, assumes a reified, essentialist 'Islam', divorced from real Muslims). What does distinguish them is a common recognition of the need to explore the reflexive relationships between Islamic

1

beliefs, ideas, ideologies, institutional forms, and prescriptive roles, socially reproduced by given groups of Muslims, and the political, economic, and other salient conditions under which these and other specifically situated Muslims live. It is this attempt to understand how Muslim 'discourses' about their lives are constituted, through the linking of symbolic or cultural analysis of what is said and done with analysis of the material and other conditions in which the saying and doing occur, that we intend when we refer to the 'political economy of meaning'. As Eickelman notes, in the essay that begins the book, an adequate political economy of meaning must rest on a proper balance between attention to the communication and development of complex systems of knowledge and practice, and the ways in which these systems inform and are informed by configurations of political domination and economic relations. Our primary aim has been to strive for and so far as possible to exemplify this balance, or at the very least to draw attention to the need for it and to the means of attaining it.

Listening to argument, then, and examining it as carefully as possible in context, is the principal intent of the essays presented here. What links them one with another (beyond the fact that they all deal with Muslims actively engaged in persuading Muslims) is less a theoretical perspective, despite our concern with the analysis of discourse, than a methodological and interpretative one. The essence of this perspective — contextual location of what Muslims say, with context denoting the archival repertoire of idea and sentiment available from within the Islamic tradition as well as actual socio-political circumstance — has already been indicated. Though what we mean by a 'discourse', namely the contextual written and spoken practice of given Muslims, has something in common with the current interest in the construction and deconstruction of discourses evidenced in many of the human and social sciences, we are more concerned to practise interpretation than to elaborate theory. It is sometimes argued that theory must precede practice, but if, as Paul Valéry is said to have remarked (and as much of Michel Foucault's writing implies), all theory is autobiography, it would be as curious to expect the practice of interpretation to be preceded by a theory of interpretation as to expect the lived life to be preceded by the examined life. The two must, indeed, proceed hand in hand, or perhaps more exactly dialectically, each informing and being informed by the other. It is recognition of this dialectical relationship between theory and action that prompts us, whatever our various individual 'theoretical' starting points, to turn our interpretative attention to the dialectic between prescription and circumstance in the lives of Muslim social actors, and to the discourses which reflect this dialectic.

The essays have been arranged in three sections, each reflecting a different emphasis or approach. The first four, on 'The Political Economy of Religious Culture', are concerned for the most part to raise the methodological and interpretative questions that confront us when contemplating the rhetoric of Muslim social and political action. Two of these essays deal, as it happens, with societies represented elsewhere in the book, Indonesia and Nigeria. Though something might have been gained by adopting an area rubric, and placing all the essays dealing with particular countries together, this would have worked against our main purpose, which has precisely not been to produce yet another volume of area studies but to focus in a comparative way on certain kinds of discourse and the circumstances of their production. This intention is made more explicit in the second section of the book, 'Muslim Social Thought and the State', which contains four essays reflecting situations — in Iran, Pakistan, the Maghreb, and Southeast Asia — in which the state may be perceived as the prime determinant of the dominant discourse in society, to which all alternative groups must necessarily respond. In the final section of the book, 'Change and the Individual Voice', the essays look at how individual Muslims may respond to change in political and economic circumstances, how they may seek to bring change and its management into congruence with their Islamic beliefs, and how they speak of this to other Muslims.

In the first section, Eickelman's discussion of 'changing interpretations of Islamic movements' starts by noting the way in which Western social science, with a prevailing view of 'religion' as a separable and separate domain of social thought and action increasingly irrelevant to the public life of modern and modernising societies, has been forced to come to grips with much evidence to the contrary — quite generally, but not least among Muslims. Though a recognition, in principle, of the interconnectedness of religious systems and their material and social contexts has re-emerged, the complex relationships between political economy and systems of knowledge and belief have more often been assumed than explored. Eickelman suggests, however, that certain shifts in disciplinary emphasis in the past two decades, notably among and between anthropologists and social historians, have helped to redirect analytical attention to how cultures and systems of meaning are reproduced, to the social and practical contexts in which knowledge is made available for reproduction, and to the varieties and levels of Muslim expression and discourse that result. He notes three significant focuses of attention characterizing such enquiries, all strongly present in the essays offered here; the historical specificity of change, the social scale of the community in which change occurs, and the internal social divisions reflected in the discourses that mark that change. It is the resulting debate within Muslim societies, he suggests, that, in conjunction with political and economic change, creates a continuous dialectic of self-renewal and social transformation.

In my own essay, 'Islamic movements: one or many?', I have emphasized the need to understand, within this debate, 'the intelligibility of Islamic imperatives for Muslims', and adopted an explicitly comparative approach. Arguing that Islamic precepts ('being Muslim') supply a major, sometimes determinative, part of the perceived objective conditions which direct or constrain social action, I examine the implications of such an assumption in the light of four of the so-called '*Wahhabi*' movements of the late eighteenth and early nineteenth centuries, in Central Arabia, West Sumatra, Bengal, and northern Nigeria. Though it may be concluded that simplistic evocations of 'Wahhabism' dissolve upon close inspection, and with them the implied claims they make to a special sort of *a priori* inherent universalism, they draw fresh attention, in virtue of the very specificity of the discourses that accompanied these social perturbations, to the ways in which Muslims may find meaning in, or create it from, a commonly shared, Islamically supplied, repertoire of imperatives to personal and social action.

The remaining two essays in this section, by Hefner and Lubeck, though similarly concerned to develop general interpretative arguments, do so in the contrasting circumstances of two closely observed contemporary societies — the highlands of central Java, and northern Nigeria. Hefner's paper is one of three in this volume dealing with Indonesians, each of which examines a different level of experience and social action within the world's most populous Muslim state. What it means to be, or become, or become more of, a Muslim in the remote villages of the previously non-Muslim highland Tengger, in the hot-house political life of the capital's Islamic youth movements, or in the perceptions of a single, thoughtful intellectual, produces distinctively different kinds of discourse. While at the local level, as Hefner shows, being or becoming a Muslim may acquire a new salience as a result of political and economic change, the problems of being a politically and personally committed Muslim in a Jakarta dominated by a statist regime unsympathetic to Islamic aspirations, and in an increasingly secular modern Indonesia, produces, as we shall see in the essays by Hassan and Johns, somewhat different

4

kinds of argument and debate.

Hefner's discussion of the particular situation of the *Buda* people in Besuki, in addition to making a significant contribution to studies of 'Islamization' in Indonesia, raises important general questions concerning the nature of 'traditional' and 'world' religious systems, and the conversion or intensification process that leads people from the former to the latter. In studying this kind of transition, he suggests, we need to take into account the cultural content of the religious discourses of both systems in relation to the scale, political and economic organization, and cultural diversity of the communities to which each appeals, and seek to discover how social and ideational realities cohere to form manageable systems of meaning.

The increasing failure to provide shared meanings for one particular segment of Muslim society in northern Nigeria — certain of the *gardawa* or peripatetic Qur'anic students and their *mallam* (teachers) — and the expression of their resulting discontent in the violent protest movement, known as 'Yan Tatsine, is the subject of Lubeck's paper. Arguing that ideas take form as social movements only when social and material conditions are present to sustain, recruit, and reproduce materially and ideologically the required support, he outlines the transformations of the Nigerian economy and state from the Sokoto period to the present. Islamic and Qur'anic networks that had functioned to integrate rural and urban areas, and to provide a meaningful existence to their participants, were restructured somewhat during the colonial-capitalist and early independence years, but remained an integral feature of northern Nigerian social life until the petroleum boom of the 1970s. The boom led to rapid urban-industrial growth and huge disparities of wealth, produced levels of corruption that severely damaged the social fabric, disrupted the balance of rural-urban relations, and contributed to a sharp increase in the power of the state. Full understanding of the 'Yan Tatsine reaction to these developments is possible, Lubeck suggests, only if one gives due weight to both the structural features of change and their cultural dimensions as expressed in the Islamic discourse of the most militant followers of the movement, the marginalized gardawa.

Implicit in several of the essays in the first section is the importance of the state as a primary determinant of Islamic discourses, either directly or by reaction. The second section of the book takes up this issue more explicitly. It contains four essays, which may conveniently be thought of in pairs, though they have overlapping concerns. In the first two, based on contemporary Iran and Pakistan, the ability of the authoritarian 'Islamic' state to establish the dominant terms of discourse is discussed, together with some of the consequences of this. In the second two, which relate to North Africa and Southeast Asia, primary attention is given to the 'Islamist' discourses (to use the now widely accepted French term) of social groups which are in certain ways at odds with state power, or forced to come to terms with it.

The revolution in Iran in 1979 has come to represent, for many in the world at large, the apparent political potency of aroused Islamic sentiment, and, as many of the papers in this volume testify (Vatin's on the Maghreb, for example, or Christelow's on Nigeria) it has indeed been a source of inspiration and enthusiasm for other Muslim communities. Arjomand's essay, 'Revolution in Shi'ism', however, demonstrates very clearly the specificity and particularity of the Iranian experience. As his title suggests, the revolution may be perceived as at least as much a revolution in Shi'i argument about the sovereignty of the *ulama* (*vilayat-e faqih*) as a revolution in the social order, though indeed the two are not wholly separable. The implications of this dual revolution, for society and Islamic institutions alike, remain to be worked out.

Metcalf, writing about 'Islamic arguments in contemporary Pakistan', is likewise concerned with a state that is undertaking wholesale 'islamization' of society, though in this instance through the agency of a military autocracy rather than a scholarly hierarchy. Tracing the development of views about the proper relationship between 'Islam and the state' from the foundation of Pakistan as 'a homeland for Muslims' in 1946 to the proclamation of the *nizam-i mustafa* ('system of the Prophet') by the Zia regime in 1977, she notes the relatively indirect role played throughout by ulama. Notwithstanding this, the ideas of the Jama'at-i Islam (an organization now formally banned, with all other political parties) and its founder Maududi underlie much of the activity of the present regime, which uses the institutions and resources of the state to alter or enact statute law to express the *shari'a*, and to promote social criticism of 'non-Muslim' life styles. The official discourse that results, with its twin emphases on the enactment of positive law and the state-sponsored islamization of social life, has resulted in, among other things, considerable argument about the position of women in society. Using this argument, and its various protagonists, as a lens through which to examine the larger process, Metcalf concludes that while islamization 'from the top down' plays a manifest role in preserving existing structures of society and maintaining an authoritarian regime in power, the ideology accompanying it is intensely appealing to certain segments of the population and must be understood in its own terms.

Social criticism of a kind familiar in both Iran and Pakistan — in particular, expressed discontent with Western-inspired forms in public and private life — is a marked feature of the Islamist movements discussed by Vatin, in his essay 'Seduction and sedition: Islamic polemical discourses in the Maghreb'. Quoting Maxime Rodinson's remark that it is hard to see the difference between those who seek power in order to apply Islam and those who use Islam to accede to power, Vatin examines two 'traditional-type' movements, one in contemporary Morocco and the other in Tunisia, which criticize the state and its social role while seeking to offer alternative visions of the ideal Islamic society, and then compares these with other, more 'progressive' movements there and in Algeria. In an essay of great richness of texture, in its account of the discourses recorded and the social bases of the groups espousing them, Vatin argues that the 'delegitimization' of the post-colonial state, as a result of its inability in the course of modernization to satisfy either the material or the moral demands of a large number of its members, has led both to state attempts to appropriate Islamic symbols and institutions in order to regain control over civil society, and to a wide range of Islamist claims to knowledge of competing systems that would better serve God and the needs of the Islamic *umma*. The result, in Vatin's terms, is an extensive interpenetration of the domains of religious and political discourse that reflects real divisions within Maghrebi society but has yet to provide any satisfactory reworking of the image of 'the Islamic city'.

Though the contest may not be as sharp in the major Islamic societies of Southeast Asia, it none the less lies at the heart of the politics described by Hassan, in his essay on 'The response of Muslim youth organizations to political change: *HMI* in Indonesia and *ABIM* in Malaysia'. Despite many elements of a shared indigenous culture and a not altogether dissimilar colonial past, the Indonesian and Malaysian states have adopted strikingly different attitudes to recent Islamic and islamizing movements. The authoritarian military regime in Indonesia, a country in which 90 per cent of the population of 165 million declares itself to be Muslim, has since the early 1970s sought to depoliticize Islam and elevate to ideological primacy the statist doctrine known as Pančasila. Malaysia, a parliamentary democracy with a very large non-Muslim minority (nearly half of the population of 15 million), has during the same period sought for the most part to accommodate, and increasingly to co-opt, the rather broad range of movements that respond to the *da'wa* (call) of Islamic revitalization. In Indonesia, Hassan notes, the response of the important group

of young Muslim intellectuals, HMI, has moved from initial acceptance of the secular modernizing state, combined with personal commitment to a 'renewed' (and modernized) Islamic faith, to a more
holistic (and potentially more political) view of Islam as a complete
way of life that must make demands upon the state apparatus. In
Malaysia, by contrast, the corresponding shift in stance and discourse
exemplified by the ABIM youth movement has been in the opposite
direction relative to the state, from a largely rejectionist da'wa to a
more pragmatic effort to attain the substance of social reform in
Islamic directions, with the state itself (and the Malay nationalism
that underlies it) seemingly prepared to accommodate such pressures
and to adopt Islamic symbols and forms of discourse.

The three essays in the final section of the book shift the focus
somewhat, from states and movements to individual actors, and to
some of the ways in which individual Muslims — preachers and propa-
gandists, judges and journalists — have sought from within the Islamic
tradition to argue the need for change and renewal.

Gaffney, in 'Authority and the mosque in Upper Egypt: the Islamic
preacher as image and actor', places at the center of his essay the
social arena which is a locus for a major part of all Islamic discourses,
the mosque of general assembly. Taking as his starting point two contrasting preachers — a traditional, Azhar-trained scholar in a long-
established, state-funded mosque associated with the *baraka* (blessing) of a notable saint, and a layman in an independent mosque founded
and supported by a local social welfare association — he examines
the construction of their respective Friday *khutba*s (sermons). Each
employs a common, indeed shared, flexible repertory of symbols
invested with meaning at different levels of social and cultural
reference. In their separate ways, and with contrasting rhetorical
styles, they unite, says Gaffney, 'communities of ritual' with 'communities of action', representing in their persons an exemplary unity
of image and actor, at once the symbolic articulators of fixed and
sacred ideas and, by virtue of their own mundane roles in society,
models for ordinary conduct in a changing human world. Their
efficacy as leaders depends, Gaffney suggests, on their capacity to
maintain the dialectic inherent in and crucial to this double role.

Allan Christelow, writing about the northern Nigeria whose under-
class has already been described in Lubeck's discussion of the 'Yan
Tatsine movement, supplies a careful delineation of three individual
spokesmen for different Islamic tendencies among the elite. To give
voice to their views and to address the Nigerian umma all three employ
the modern media, especially the weekend press and the radio. They

8

are Abubakar Mahmud Gumi, a proponent of various kinds of *status quo*, whose background is the mosque and a 'Wahhabi-like' moral reform movement, but who is above all a noted radio speaker in Hausa (reminding us of the Moroccan identification, referred to in Eickelman's essay, of 'radio Islam' with 'official Islam'); Ibraheem Sulaiman, a lecturer in administration at Ahmadu Bello University, an ex-student leader who still writes, in English, for a mainly student audience, promoting an Islamic ideology for the nation as a whole; and Abdulmalik Bappa Mahmud, chief *qadi* (judge) in one of the state courts, who writes in both Hausa and English on the relevance of Islam for law and authority. What is noteworthy about all three men is that in the circumstances of Nigeria's secular state and multi-cultural political life (with Muslims a bare majority, as in Malaysia), Islamic discourses, insofar as they enter the national arena, do so not through formal, well-organized movements or parties, but in the voice of individuals, dependent as individuals upon private employment, contributions from followers, and the interest (and state tolerance) of the media.

The strongly individual voice presented by Johns, in his essay 'An Islamic system or Islamic values? Nucleus of a debate in contemporary Indonesia', finds expression in an extraordinary document that has become the center of much debate and controversy in Indonesia since its publication in 1981. It is the diary of a young, Western-educated journalist, a deeply committed Muslim, and one-time leading member of Hassan's HMI, Ahmad Wahib. In the last years of his life (he died in a traffic accident in 1973, aged 30 or 31), Wahib recorded in detail and at length his reflections on a wide range of questions concerning Islam, the individual, and society in present-day Indonesia. In the diary we see him struggling with problems relating to the authority of the ulama to translate the message of the Qur'an to others, the proper responsibilities of the Muslim intellectual to self and society, the relationship of freedom of thought to transcendentally revealed truth, and that of 'private' to 'public' Islamic belief and practice, and the relative force of the Qur'anic utterance and the example of the Prophet Muhammad for behavioral imperatives. These internal discussions are seen to exist not *in vacuo* but in the immediate context of the issues of the day, of politics and culture, economic modernization, student life, the idea of the Islamic State, and the coexistence within Indonesia of other religious traditions. Few of Wahib's speculations, Johns says, are especially new, or unfamiliar in other Muslim contexts, though they are expressed in a fresh and often moving way. What they do testify to, however, as does the energy of the very mixed reception given to the diary, ranging from enthusiasm to anger, is the way in which an individual voice may seem to speak to the present situation of countless Indonesian Muslims.

The essays in this book, taken together, illustrate a broad spectrum of Muslim discourse and practice, and help us to consider how we may best 'read' such discourse in context, and understand and interpret the social and political action that accompanies it. They help to make us aware of some of the ways in which Muslims, as acceptors of the shari'a, perceive the human condition and its particularities, and find meaning in or give meaning to the Islamic precepts by which they see themselves as enjoined.

William R. Roff

Part One

The Political Economy
of Religious Culture

1

Changing Interpretations of Islamic Movements

Dale F. Eickelman

The Iranian revolution signalled a major turning point in understanding Islam among both scholars and believers. Until 1979, many scholars dismissed Islamic intellectuals and leaders as elderly men without replacements in younger generations, and regarded popular Islamic movements as incapable of generating sustained support for specific political goals. This view was shared by some of the elite of Muslim countries, who considered Islam as a political force to be a receding phenomenon. Turkey, Indonesia, the Soviet Union, India, and even Iran were variously cited as indicators of the trend toward the relegation of religion to a compartmentalized, private sphere. Only exceptionally did studies break with the prevailing assumption of Islam's declining political significance (e.g., Kessler, 1978) or admit the possibility of new forms of Islamic leadership emerging, as had often occurred in earlier eras (e.g., Hammoudi, 1981)

In particular, the notion of religion receding as a political force was accepted both by many members of the Western-educated technocratic elite throughout the Muslim world and by scholars accepting the common assumptions of modernization theory prevalent in the 1950s and 1960s. Local setbacks notwithstanding, religion was seen as a force to be invoked in the preamble to constitutions or on formal occasions, rather than as a politically significant element of ideology, practice, and organization.

Political trends in Egypt have often been regarded as a bell-wether for the Arab Muslim world. Thus, Egypt's experience was thought to exemplify the prevailing assumption of the political decline of religious movements. The massive reaction among Egyptian Muslims and Copts to reports of the apparition of the Virgin Mary over a Coptic church in a Cairo suburb in April 1968, certified as authentic by the Coptic Patriarch of Egypt and All Africa (Nelson, 1974: 253–66), suggests the continuing depth of religious sentiment, with political implications ranging well beyond the limits of state control. None the less, the disappearance in 1954 of the Muslim Brotherhood as a formal political force in Egypt was until recent years cited as an example of religion's declining significance. The Brotherhood, possibly Egypt's one genuine twentieth-century mass political movement, never fully recovered from the crippling wave of mass arrests and imprisonment instigated by Nasser.

Whenever religious interpretations, organizations, or practices are officially repressed or held in disfavor, official estimates of susceptibility to their message or goals must be regarded with extreme caution. For this reason, it is often easier to know the religious attitudes of earlier eras than those of the present. As Kepel (1985) observes, the arrest of suspected Muslim Brothers in the 1950s created an oppressive environment, which was ideal for instigating more radical religious interpretations and for recruiting a younger generation of radicalized militants unwilling to compromise with the existing state authorities. The prisons and prison camps became vivid metaphors for the moral bankruptcy of existing government. *Jahil* is a Qur'anic term evoking the state of ignorance, violence, and self-interest which existed prior to the revelation of the Qur'an and which continues to hamper realization of a full Islamic community. Islamic 'militants' and many other Muslims consider existing state organizations 'barbaric' (*jahili*) because they do not govern in accordance with Islamic principles.

The tactics of Sadat's assassins, who justified themselves by asserting the jahili nature of Sadat's rule, may have had limited popular support. But the existence of six mosques in Egypt independent of government control for every authorized one as of 1981 (Ansari, 1984: 129) suggests the extent to which Islam is considered to be both a vehicle for expression and a potential organizing force for significant elements of the population. The formal separation of religion and politics has not fared well outside of elite circles.

In many parts of the Muslim world, Islamic political activism is in part encouraged by what is perceived as the practical realization of Islamic rule in Iran. As a consequence, both voices of opposition and established authorities now seek to co-opt the popular slogans of Islamic militancy. In an effort to co-opt the left in the 1970s, the Moroccan monarch's 'Revolution of the King and the People' emulated the former Shah's 'Revolution of the Shah and the People'. In Morocco it is now the language of militant Muslims that is co-opted in an effort to enhance monarchic authority (Tozy, 1984: 413;

Eickelman, in press).

At the near antipodes of the Muslim world, early interpretations of Indonesia's post-1966 'New Order' suggested that the political elite sought to depoliticize Islam and promote instead the Pančasila, the official, pan-religious national ideology (McVey, 1983; 199). More recent analysis (Hefner, 1985a; cf. Geertz 1972: 81–84) suggests a more complex political process in which the 'New Order' seeks to encompass a multitude of shifting local-level coalitions and ideological orientations. The government party, GOLKAR, has managed to embrace Islamic symbols in such a manner as to sustain a guided dialogue between a variety of 'local' cultures and the nation state. The government seeks to communicate the message that religion is an important component of national development, and that local understandings of the process of development are important considerations. Hence there have been quiet but pervasive programs for upgrading the quality and training of village preachers, with parallel developments in Javanese Hindu communities (Hefner 1985b; 239–65). By allowing for such local participation and the fusion of religious symbols, especially Islamic ones, with national goals, the Indonesian government may be changing the local political balance by creating a more uniform Islamic community. For the moment, Indonesia appears to provide an example of the successful fusion of state development progams with a variety of local religious understandings.

The Indonesian case notwithstanding, many analyses of 'resurgent' Islamic movements suggest a deep Western bias against any valid role for religion in contemporary politics. As Piscatori (1983: 1) writes, Muslims are thought to become 'politically active out of an excess of zeal rather than with clearly defined goals'. Islam is associated with fanatical opposition, aimless revolution, anti-Westernism and anti-modernism, so that the widespread evidence of interpretations of Islam and Islamic movements facilitating major social transformations is downplayed or ignored. Many Muslims none the less consider that Islam should play a central and pervasive role in politics and economics. For this reason alone, Islamic ideas and practices assume a major significance.

TOWARD A POLITICAL ECONOMY OF ISLAM

Islamic doctrine, tradition, and practice have been elaborated, understood, and transmitted to successive generations and new communities in different historical, political, and economic contexts throughout the world. Recognition of these transformations has become, at least in principle, a familiar part of the intellectual landscape. In practice, however, most studies assume, rather than explore, the complex, multi-dimensional relationships between political economy, on the one hand, and belief systems, on the other (Kessler, 1978: 20; cf. Eickelman, 1982: 6–8). A 'political economy of meaning' (Eickelman, 1979) contrives to achieve a balance between concern with the communication and development of complex belief systems and how these systems shape and in turn are shaped by configurations of political domination and economic relations among groups and classes in societies of different levels of complexity. In itself, this goal is not unique. Indeed, it is one of the central concerns of classical social thought. None the less, advocates of the political economy approach have often remained primarily at the level of theoretical exposition or implicit assumption. The elaboration of such concepts in the context of specific comparative studies has become common only in the last few years.

Of course, studies of Islam form part of broader intellectual currents and consequently reflect wider debates. In recent years there has been a shift away from emphasis upon an almost exclusive concern with symbolic forms, often devoid of a clear representation of economic and political activities, toward discerning how systems of meaning are transmitted and reproduced. Ortner (1984; see also Cohn, 1981) argues that the reintroduction into anthropology of a political economy approach in the 1960s contributed to the discipline's belated 'rediscovery' of history after a long interval of prior neglect. Anthropologists interested in political economy have for the most part concerned themselves with larger regional processes, instead of the highly localized studies of an earlier era in which broad economic and political trends were evoked only peripherally. Since the 1960s there has been a growing effort to link these trends with their consequences for particular social groups and classes, effects which are also traced over time (e.g., Hopkins, 1983). On the negative side, self-identified studies of political economy by anthropologists have tended to emphasize economic factors above all others, in part perhaps to compensate for their earlier neglect. They have also tended to present a highly capitalism-centered view of the world. But these shortcomings are not inherent in the approach. 'Meanings' not founded in Western notions of politics and economics motivate people and have major consequences for social and political action. A renewed attention to the political economy of meaning seeks to alter the prior disregard

16

of how understandings of Islam shape political and economic perceptions and activity.

PREDECESSORS

The development of a political economy of meaning in the study of religious tradition and discourse has distinguished antecedents in some respects, although in others it constitutes a significantly new point of departure. Ernest Troeltsch (1976 [orig. 1911]), for example, characterized the history of Christianity as one of progressive shifts between compromise and non-compromise with the social world: the delineation of 'intrinsic' sociological ideas of Christianity, the influence of Christian doctrine upon the social world, what he termed the 'reflex' influence of these conditions upon the ideas of Christianity themselves, and the 'inner' reality of religion (Troeltsch, 1976: 34). Despite his insistence upon the 'briefest possible presentation' (1976: 25), the fact that his study is over a thousand pages in length suggests the challenge of elaborating sociological hypotheses richly informed by attention to social history. Troeltsch's magisterial study admittedly left vague many key concepts (e.g., Christianity's 'inner' reality), but it none the less constituted, together with the earlier work of W. Robertson Smith (1956 [orig. 1889]), a pioneering effort to link the development of religious concepts with social and economic conditions.

In the last two decades, studies with a more sharply delineated historical compass have begun to offer a more precise understanding of how religious identities and concepts are differently elaborated within varied social classes and categories, and often change their significance when taken up by novel contexts or new groups. Merad (1967) shows the intimate and necessary interrelationship between the reformist ideology and its carriers in Algeria during the 1920s and 1930s, the resistance to the reformist movement from rural notables and the heads of religious orders, and the importance of understanding the prevailing assumptions of Islamic belief and practice to which the reformists were opposed. An indirect consequence of Algerian reformism was to disseminate a rationalist conception of Islam which inadvertently set religious doctrines and practice apart from other aspects of social life. More recent studies have dealt with such diverse topics as changing interpretations of Islam in local contexts (Eickelman, 1976), support for reformist thought (Metcalf, 1982), and the changing implications of conversion to Islam according to period, social category, and context (Bulliet, 1979).

The study of a world religion as it has been realized in various times and places implies what from some perspectives is obvious: the ideologies and practices associated with it are elaborated, understood, and subsequently reproduced in particular places and at particular moments. Even eternal truths are necessarily revealed in a specific language and setting. Revelation 'in Arabic, that ye may be understood' (Qur'an, 12: 2) has significantly different implications for a seventh-century Arabian merchant, a nineteenth-century Bengali peasant, a Turkish *Gastarbeiter* in Bonn, and a twentieth-century Malaysian university student.

The main challenge for the study of Islam is to describe how its universalistic or abstract principles have been realized in various social and historical contexts without representing Islam as a seamless essence on the one hand or as a plastic congeries of beliefs and practices on the other. To this end, the prevalent earlier conceptual dichotomy of 'great' and 'little' traditions can retrospectively be viewed as a significant first step. As initially employed in the late 1940s, this conceptualization contained an historical component and was used to explore the possible relationships between religious traditions, as known through the texts and exegeses of a cultural elite on the one hand, and the religious expressions and interpretations prevalent in village of 'folk' contexts, on the other. Unlike the earlier doctrine of 'survivals', which presumed that folk traditions were vestiges of earlier civilizations and less permeable to change than 'high culture', the notion of great/little tradition made no gratuitous assumptions concerning the historical precedence of some civilizational elements over others. Yet as ordinarily reported, great and little traditions were more often juxtaposed than used as the basis for analysing their complex interrelationships. Literate traditions were taken to be closer to orthodoxy, and 'local' ones were variously assumed to be misinterpretations of the 'vulgar' or even 'pre-Islamic' vestiges, rather than indications of the key points at which the Islamic tradition is continuously undergoing an internal dialectic of adaptation and self-renewal.

For Marshall Hodgson, one of the most sensitive interpreters of the Islamic tradition of the 1950s and 1960s, there was an awareness of the capacity for self-renewal within the Islamic tradition at all levels. His explicit concern was with 'high' culture in the 'primary milieu of Islam', which to him was constantly renewed and transformed by the dialogues of successive generations of intellectuals who grasped the formative ideals of their civilization. Unlike other scholars, Hodgson acknowledged that the traditions of 'peasants or even non-lettered peoples' share substantially the same dynamics of change, but he explicitly left aside any detailed description of such changes or how they may have been interrelated to those of the 'high' culture (Hodgson, 1974: 1,80). It has been argued that this notion of the dialogue between successive generations of 'piety-minded Muslims' on Islam's formative ideals comes close to an essentialist vision. It minimizes some aspects of the historical context in a manner which Hodgson himself deplored in the work of other scholars (Burke, 1979: 261–62). None the less, Hodgson's history of Islamic civilization, unlike others, was not unduly centered upon the Arab Middle East, and depicted in detail the changing forms and contexts in which Islamic ideals were expressed. Moreover, the recognition at least in principle of equivalent transformations occurring among peasants and the non-lettered was a major achievement.

Of equal importance were anthropological efforts in the 1950s to represent the full complexity of religious tradition in specific localities. The enduring strength of *The Religion of Java* (Geertz, 1960) is not its theoretical framework, which by design takes second place to ethnographic exposition, but its descriptive portrayal of religion in a highly complex civilizational tradition. The argument that the three principal 'orientations' of Javanese religious beliefs and practices refract an underlying cultural unity (Geertz, 1960: 324; cf. Roff, 1985) may be questioned, but the text offers a practical ethnograpic exemplar for representing the culture and social organization of a complex, highly differentiated religious tradition in which there are only partial and shifting correspondences between the social characteristics of the carriers of the various 'sub-traditions'.

An antithetical but productive reaction to the essentialist tradition, inspired by the heyday of structuralist studies in the 1960s, was the suggestion that the term *Islam* be replaced by *islams*. This approach emphasizes the multiplicity of Islamic expression and asserts that in all historical and social contexts the islams of elite and non-elite, literate and illiterate, theologians and artisans, tribesmen and peasants, are equally valid expressions of a fundamental, unconscious (in the structuralist sense) set of principles (Zein, 1974: 172; 1977: 227–54; *Hérodote* 1984).

The islams approach can thus be seen as a reaction against both the orientalist search for an ahistorical Islamic 'essence' and the somewhat parallel venture of Muslim fundamentalists who declare their own beliefs and practices to be 'Islamic' in opposition to the jahili practices of other Muslims, Ironically, by considering all expressions of Islam as transformations based upon a single set of principles, the conceptual end-product of the islams approach likewise reduces Islamic tradition to an essentialist, ahistorical core. The islams approach also disregards the fact that most Muslims quite consciously hold that their religion possesses central, normative tenets and that these tenets are critical to an understanding of Islamic belief and practice. Further, ideas and practices take on radically different meanings depending upon who introduces, advocates and supports them. Some understandings of Islam are more highly valued than others because of their identification with certain carriers and groups. The islams approach neglects this important social dimension of the transmission and reproduction of ideas and organizations (Eickelman, 1985; Hefner 1985b). The islams approach, like that of cultural 'orientations', falls short of accounting for the historical conditions which favor the emergence of particular institutional arrangements or cultural notions over alternative, coexisting ones.

CONJUNCTURES: TIME, SCALE, AND INTERNAL DEBATE

Three conceptual elements are necessary for a full realization of a political economy of religious culture: a renewed attention to historical transformations, including recognition of varied rates of change; a recognition of the implications of differences in scale for forms of religious understanding and organization; and an intensified concern with differences of religious understanding within particular societies.

Times and rates of change

An historical approach necessarily implies a concern with individual actors and specific institutions. Every society contains conflicting or alternative ideas and institutional arrangements, some of which come to the foreground only because of a conjuncture of favorable events and of persons disposed to their advocacy and support. Whether these individuals are central or peripheral to their communities, and capable of realizing the implications of new ideas, institutions, or opportunities, also makes a significant difference. None the less, the understanding of historical change in the West has often been conceived in terms of global periodizations based upon events presumed to have an overarching significance: the establishment of colonial rule or its termination, a significant economic or military event, or similar considerations. For specific purposes such periodizations are highly useful, provided that they are recognized as scholarly artifacts essential for explanation. For such complex cultural constructs as religion, the notion of unitary periodizations becomes strained.

Fernand Braudel (1975) offers an alternative conceptualization of intersecting levels of historical change. *La longue durée* is the most durable and slow-changing, and is complemented by those of the medium term (*conjoncture*) and the short term (*évènement*). These interrelated levels are best invoked as explanatory approximations and guides, not as separable levels of reality. Implicit religious understandings, such as those tied up with the highly localized maraboutic shrines and descent groups in North Africa (Eickelman, 1977: 5–7) or what one scholar terms the 'local religion' or shrines and regional sanctuaries in Catholic Spain (Christian, 1981), are so resilient that they are best considered in terms of *la longue durée*. Such implicit local understandings can have as much contemporary political significance as those engendered by more short-term transformations.

An important medium-term form of transformation is generational in Mannheim's (1952: 276–320) sense of the term. For Mannheim, each succeeding social group, or cohort, is defined by shared common perceptions and experiences. It makes 'fresh contact' with its political and cultural heritage and reassesses its content. Thus a younger generation of educated Moroccans with experience of the colonial era only as children, or none at all, is in the vanguard of those who express discontent with existing political arrangements. It is with this group that susceptibility to militant Islamic doctrines has been most intensive. This generation has benefited from the massive educational expansion of the post-colonial era, but is also the first to recognize that formal education in the last two decades has conferred fewer benefits than it did in earlier eras when it was a scarce commodity. Although the time-scale differs, similar developments have occurred elsewhere in the Muslim world and are not confined to it. Having experienced 'tradition' in significantly different economic and political contexts than an earlier generation, its meaning is necessarily altered.

Attention to contextual shifts in the 'mix' between various styles and levels of religiosity is an especially significant component in a political economy of meaning. The Moroccan monarchy as an institution remains linked to durable, pervasive local interpretations of Islam, not all of which coincide with Islam as interpreted by traditionally educated Muslim scholars, reformists, and modernists. The religious attitudes of the educated and the political elite, sometimes called 'radio Islam' by the non-elite in rural Morocco because 'official' Islam is identified with the state-controlled media, are more readily discerned than those of the non-elite. None the less, 'commoner' (*'ammi*) practices and attitudes directly inform popular notions of legitimacy and social justice, thus placing implicit limits upon the range of political actions of the elite. More so than the spokesmen for Morocco's political parties or of militant Islamic groups, Morocco's monarch implicitly recognizes the importance of such popular beliefs.

In Morocco as elsewhere, including Indonesia (e.g., Nakamura, 1983: 140–83), reformist movements appear more immediately sensitive to economic and political shifts than long-term, underlying patterns of religious belief. It is useful to consider carefully which aspects of belief and practice are subject to rapid change and which are not. For the highland Javanese community of recent converts to Islam described by Hefner in this volume, there was a significant historical shift in how its mythological traditions were interpreted. As he writes, the prevalent anthropological notion that myths 'reflect' social values fails to note that myths speak to certain critical realities while ignoring others, and that the nature of the 'critical realities' and of the Javanese interpretation of the mythical tradition has changed significantly from the late nineteenth century to the present, the period of his concern. Hefner's discussion of the reinterpretation of mythological tradition represents an important development in what Martin (1985: 364) calls speech-act or discourse analysis, in which the content of shared discourse is integrally related to the context in which it takes place, a dimension largely absent from earlier discussions of 'symbol systems'.

Roff's essay, in this volume, illustrates the importance of controlled historical comparisons in discerning these long-term shifts in ideology, politics, and economy. His analysis of partially parallel religious movements in the eighteenth and nineteenth centuries offers a useful counterpoint to the proliferation of studies on contemporary Islamic movements that have appeared since the Iranian revolution. Roff uses the term 'Wahhabi-like' at one point to explain seeming parallels, and recognizes, but does not assign an overriding importance to, the importance of networks of communication established through Muslim scholars and the pilgrimage to Mecca. Disruptive economic transformations appear in every case to have created a fertile ground for the rise of these movements to political prominence, but there are important differences in each of the cases. In Bengal, the interests of global capitalism appear most directly responsible for the social dislocation and impoverishment of peasants and weavers, the groups most susceptible to the message of the Fara'idi movement. Within a decade of the movement's beginning in 1821, it was embraced by an estimated one-sixth of the peasant population. In contrast, the growing export trade for highland *Arabica* coffee in central Sumatra fostered the emergence of new groups of producers, traders, and carriers, who formed the core of the reformist Padri movement. The vanguard of this movement was constituted by prosperous traders who gradually displaced an older merchant elite and their royal patrons, who were associated with the declining trade in pepper and gold. An understanding of reformist movements in both Bengal and central Sumatra hinges largely upon internal divisions already present in society, and the response of specific groups to changes in ideologies, political circumstances, and economic opportunity.

Scale

The emergence of larger political and economic formations facilitates certain types of religious movements more than others. Roff's essay suggests the importance of eighteenth and nineteenth century Islamic movements for state formation and for the intensified control by states over their hinterlands. Along these lines, many contemporary Islamic movements challenge the nature of existing state organizations. Even if they do not propose clear specific alternatives to existing state rule, as Vatin demonstrates, they raise basic issues concerning the limits and popular legitimacy of existing state authority.

Johnson (1982) provides a provocative hypothesis involving the issue of scale in an analysis of the role of Islam in the emergence of Palestinian nationalism during the 1920s and 1930s. He argues that during this period a major shift occurred from a fragmented, locality-centered politics of notables to a society-wide populist revolt under Islamic aegis. Appeals to the sacred by populist Islamic leaders calling for a reordering of society and polity were particularly effective because such appeals 'not only allow one to take up a cause, they imply that it can be no other way' (Johnson, 1982: 32). Cut to its essentials, Johnson's suggestion that the erosion of 'prevailing edifices of power and meaning' facilitates the appearance of new social movements coalescing about 'ambiguous condensed symbolic forms' (Johnson, 1982: 102) merely states the obvious: that new social movements cannot easily emerge where they are effectively suppressed or find no fertile ground for recruits. But his study of the specific implications of the major transition of scale (and of appeal to new social groups) in forms of popular religious authority in Palestine is an original contribution to the politics of meaning.

Johnson's study indicates a new trend in anthropological studies of meaning. Until recently, the anthropological tradition has been more concerned with the study of religion in small-scale communities that could be represented as autonomous rather than with complex ones transcending sharply defined boundaries. This emphasis upon religion and world-view in small-scale, 'primitive' societies was encouraged less by parochialism than by the promise, in the best Durkheimian tradition, of discerning basic social and symbolic regularities. Such an approach sidesteps the significances of both differences and changes in scale. In small-scale, relatively isolated societies, it is difficult to formulate a definition of religion independent from common-sense assumptions toward life.

World religions also encompass parochial elements, which indeed provide them with an important depth of shared local experience, but they have more abstract components as well. The full substance of tradition in 'world' religions cannot be conveyed in face-to-face encounters, as is the case in the religions of small-scale societies. However interpreted locally, their adherents are aware at least in principle of a diversity of practice and interpretation that ranges well beyond the confines of localized, face-to-face communities. Recognizing the varieties of 'religion' in small-scale societies, Weber (1968: 399) explicitly refrained from providing a formal definition of religion. He saw no utility in formulating a definition so broad as to encompass the wide diversity of behaviour labelled as 'religious' by actors in various societies. In many contexts 'religion' is more often implicit than explicit.

For those components of world religious traditions amenable to abstract formulation, it is possible to delineate a distinctly 'religious' sphere, even if it does not account for all aspects of religious experience. But as Hefner brilliantly demonstrates in this volume, the intellectual preoccupations prevalent in world religious traditions differ significantly in form from those of many small-scale societies, at least until they are intensively caught up in wider social and political currents. Embedded local understandings often cannot be generalized and made to appear meaningful in other cultural contexts. Just as it is inconceivable to think of Nuer religion among the Dinka, to use Hefner's example, it is difficult to imagine a proliferation of Moroccan maraboutic practices in Java. Such localized practices derive their strength from being deeply enmeshed in local social contexts and cannot be abstracted to others. So when such communities experience formal conversion to a 'world' religion, 'The peculiar dilemma of life in the "macrocosm" is not so much the expansion of one's field of social experience, but the distinctive problems of morality and identity brought about by that expansion' (Hefner, this volume). Adherents to the 'great/little' tradition approach recognized some aspects of the importance of scale for types of intellectual formulations, but did not consider the political contexts of ideas and their carriers as systematically as contemporary studies seek to do.

Internal debate

The importance of recognizing divisions within societies has already been discussed in the context of historical change and the predisposition for accepting and propagating new religious interpretations. Earlier anthropological studies of small-scale communities and history-of-religion studies of world religious traditions tended to assume a unity of vision throughout any given society or tradition. Contemporary studies pay much more attention to the social location of actors participating in religious movements and elaborating particular interpretations of religious ideology. Class, social category, generation (in Mannheim's sense), and status all provide different conjunctions from which ideas and practices are learned, valued, transmitted, and reproduced.

The essays in this volume emphasize the diversity of social and political contexts in which knowledge and practice are selected and made available for reproduction. In Hefner's case, conversion to Islam in the Javanese highlands in the late nineteenth century entailed conversion from one religion to another. Thus it had an entirely different meaning from contemporary 'conversion', which usually occurs within the Islamic community and implies acceptance of a more 'purified' version of Islam. As Hefner states, religion is not just an individual matter but a moral and political one in which the social location of individuals converted or adhering to a particular religious tradition assumes major sociological importance. In light of an earlier tradition that treated 'symbol systems' as disembodied from their economic and political contexts, it cannot be sufficiently emphasized that ideologies and practices are fundamentally dependent upon the social institutions through which they are communicated and reproduced. Some meanings are shared, others are denied, and most are consciously or implicitly altered in the process of transmission.

The implications of major changes in political and economic

forms and in the intellectual technology of how ideas are reproduced and disseminated are just beginning to be explored in the context of Islamic studies. Jack Goody (1977) discusses the impact of literacy upon historically known and contemporary societies and the sociological consequences of the introduction of such a new intellectual technology. Such major innovations have major consequences for religious belief and practice, for they affect how individuals think about their social and spiritual universe and manage to act within it.

Goody's (1977: 152–62) account of the more nuanced problem of the shift from restricted to generalized literacy, from literacy possessed by a minority specialist elite to that accessible to wider elements of the population, occupies only the last ten pages of his book. This form of transformation has major implications for dominant styles of religious authority, for it changes the relationship among various social categories.

As Mardin (1982) points out in his study of the Turkish fundamentalist leader Said Nursi (1873–1960), the growth of the movement was made possible by the spread of literacy throughout Turkey and new forms of communication, including newspapers. Earlier religious movements depended upon personal bonds between Sufi leaders and their followers. From the movement's origins in the 1920s, Said Nursi and his disciples learned to work with 'modern' ideas and materials, emphasizing the dynamic quality of the Qur'anic message and its compatibility with scientific understanding and the modern world. At the outset, the movement's mix of modern and traditional concerns appealed especially to the newly educated cadres of small towns in western Turkey, to which Said Nursi was exiled by the Republican government. The movement subsequently expanded its appeal.

Of equal importance was the movement's innovative organizational structure. Other Sufi movements emphasized the importance of the persons of their leaders and personal ties to them. The Nursi movement emphasized the 'message' of its founder, designed like newspapers and magazines to appeal to the 'presumed shared rationality' of its followers (Mardin, 1982: I,13). Said Nursi lacked the claims to authority of traditional men of learning (ulama) whose forms of discourse were largely confined to other persons with similar training and relied upon elaborate chains of authority. Said Nursi's message appealed directly to his audience, thus creating a qualitatively different relationship with them. Similarly, the collapse of traditional institutions of learning and the rise to prominence of other educational forms has brought about shifts in what Moroccans consider to be religious knowledge and in its appropriate carriers at both the popular level and that of religious specialists (Eickelman 1985).

A strong case can be made for linking the rise of militant Islamic associations, especially among educated youth, in particular those from social categories with minimal access to education in earlier generations, to long-term changes in styles of religiosity, especially those made possible by the greatly increased access to schooling over the last three decades. In the past, traditional men of learning were recognized as religious authorities by nearly all Moroccans. Younger militants now appeal to the Qur'an and to essays on Islam by militant leaders for their authority. More so than in the past, the members of these movements use their own faculties to assess the merits of arguments, rather than relying upon established authorities. Those who have received education in modern state institutions appear most susceptible to this form of Islamic appeal, again indicating the importance of social differentiation (and generational specificity to some extent) to determine the appeal of such movements.

Changes in basic patterns of thought and religiosity are often evident only in retrospect. Marc Bloch (1964: 148) writing of the 'great transformation' of the emergence of feudalism in Europe, wrote that

> these generations of men had no conscious desire to create new social forms, nor were they aware of doing so. Instinctively each strove to turn to account the resources provided by the existing social structure and if, unconsciously, something new was eventually created, it was in the process of trying to adapt the old.

Full realization of a political economy of Islam will encompass not only attention to the internal divisions of contemporary and historically known Muslim societies, but also an integration of these divisions and their implications with varied, intersecting rates of historical transformations and differences in scale at various times and places. This vision of political economy depends largely upon a depth of interpretative experience in perceiving conjunctures of internal debate over self-renewal and transformation, and not upon the postulation of a 'superstructure' that more or less automatically follows shifts in the 'hard surfaces' of politics and economics.

NOTE

I wish to thank Robert W. Hefner, Ward Keeler, and William R. Roff

27

for comments on a draft of this paper. An earlier version of several passages appeared in Eickelman (1982).

REFERENCES

Ansari, Hamied N. (1984), 'The Islamic Militants in Egyptian Politics', *International Journal of Middle East Studies* 16: 123–44.

Bloch, Marc (1964), *Feudal Society*, tr. L.A. Manyon. Chicago: University of Chicago Press.

Braudel, Fernand (1975), *The Mediterranean and the Mediterranean World in the Age of Philip II*, tr. Sian Reynolds. New York: Harper and Row.

Bulliet, Richard W. (1979), *Conversion to Islam in the Medieval Period: An Essay in Quantitative History*. Cambridge and London: Harvard University Press.

Burke, III, Edmund (1979), 'Islamic History as World History: Marshall Hodgson, "The Venture of Islam" ', *International Journal of Middle East Studies* 10: 261–2.

Christian, Jr., William A. (1981), *Local Religion in Sixteenth-Century Spain*. Princeton: Princeton University Press.

Cohn, Bernard S. (1981), 'Anthropology and History in the 1980s,' *Journal of Interdisciplinary History* 12: 227–52.

Eickelman, Dale F. (1976), *Moroccan Islam: Tradition and Society in a Pilgrimage Center*. Austin and London: University of Texas Press.

—— (1977), 'Ideological Change and Regional Cults: Maraboutism and Ties of "Closeness" in Western Morocco', in Richard P. Werbner (ed), *Regional Cults*. New York and London: Academic Press, 3–28.

—— (1979), 'The Political Economy of Meaning', *American Ethnologist* 6: 386–93.

—— (1982), 'The Study of Islam in Local Contexts', *Contributions to Asian Studies* 17: 1–16.

—— (1985), *Knowledge and Power in Morocco: The Education of a Twentieth Century Notable*. Princeton: Princeton University Press.

—— (In press), 'Religion in Polity and Society', in I. William Zartman (ed.), *The Political Economy of Morocco*. New York: Praeger.

Geertz, Clifford (1960), *The Religion of Java*. New York: The Free Press.

—— (1972), 'Religious Change and Social Order in Soeharto's Indonesia', *Asia* 27 (Autumn): 62–84.

Goody, Jack (1977), *The Domestication of the Savage Mind*. Cambridge and New York; Cambridge University Press.

Hammoudi, Abdellah (1981), 'Aspects de la mobilisation populaire à la campagne vus à travers la biographie d'un mahdi mort en 1919', in Ernest Gellner and Jean-Claude Vatin (eds), *Islam et politique au Maghreb*. Paris: Centre National de la Recherche Scientifique, 47–55.

Hefner, Robert W. (1985a), 'Islamizing Java? Religion and Political-Economic Change in New Order East Java', Paper presented at the American Anthropological Association Annual Meeting, Washington D.C., December 5.

—— (1985b), *Hindu Javanese: Tengger Tradition and Islam*. Princeton:

Princeton University Press.

Hérodote: Revue de Géographie et Politique, 35 (1984). Special issue. 'Géopolitique des Islams'.

Hodgson, Marshall G.S. (1974), *The Venture of Islam*. Chicago and London: University of Chicago Press.

Hopkins, Nicholas S. (1983), *Testour ou la transformation des campagnes maghrebines*. Tunis: Cérès Productions.

Johnson, Nels (1982), *Islam and the Politics of Meaning in Palestinian Nationalism*. London and Boston: Kegan Paul International.

Kepel, Gilles (1985). *The Prophet and Pharaoh: Muslim Extremism in Egypt*, tr. Jon Rothschild. London: Al Saqi Books.

Kessler, Clive S. (1978), *Islam and Politics in a Malay State: Kelantan 1838-1969*. Ithaca and London: Cornell University Press.

McVey, Ruth (1983), 'Faith as the Outsider: Islam in Indonesian Politics', in James P. Piscatori (ed.), *Islam in the Political Process*. London and New York: Cambridge University Press, 199-225.

Mannheim, Karl (1952), *Essays on the Sociology of Knowledge*. London: Routledge and Kegan Paul.

Mardin, Serif (1982), 'Bediüzzaman Saïd Nursi: Preliminary Approaches to the Biography of a Turkish Muslim Fundamentalist Thinker'. Manuscript cited with author's permission.

Martin, Richard C. (1985), 'Understanding the Qur'an in Text and Context', *History of Religions* 21: 361-84.

Merad, Ali (1967), *Le réformisme musulman en Algérie de 1925 à 1940*. Paris and the Hague: Mouton.

Metcalf, Barbara Daly (1982), *Islamic Revival in British India: Deoband, 1860-1900*: Princeton: Princeton University Press.

Nakamura, Mitsuo (1983), *The Crescent Arises Over the Banyan Tree*. Yogyakarta: Gadjah Mada University Press.

Nelson, Cynthia (1974), 'Religious Experience, Sacred Symbols, and Social Reality', *Humaniora Islamica* 2: 253-66.

Ortner, Sherry B. (1984), 'Theory in Anthropology since the Sixties', *Comparative Studies in Society and History* 26: 126-66.

Piscatori, James P. (1983), 'Introduction', in James P. Piscatori (ed.), *Islam in the Political Process*. London and New York: Cambridge University Press, 1-11.

Roff, William R. (1985), 'Islam Obscured? Some Reflections on Studies of Islam and Society in Southeast Asia', *Archipel* 29: 7-34.

Smith, W. Robertson ([1889] 1956), *Lectures on the Religion of the Semites*, second edition. New York: Meridian.

Tozy, Mohamed (1984), 'Champ et contre champ politico-religieux au Maroc', Thesis for the *doctorat d'état* in Political Science, presented to the Faculté de Droit et de Science Politique d'Aix-Marseille.

Troeltsch, Ernest (1976), *The Social Teaching of the Christian Churches*, tr. Olive Wyon. (Midway Reprint) Chicago: University of Chicago Press. (Original 1911.)

Weber, Max ([2nd edn 1925] 1968), *Economy and Society*, ed. Guenther Roth and Claus Wittich, New York: Bedminster Press.

el-Zein, Abdul Hamid M. el- (1974), *The Sacred Meadows: A Structural*

Analysis of Religious Symbolism in an East African Town. Evanston: North-western University Press.

—— (1977), 'Beyond Ideology and Theology: The Search for the Anthropology of Islam', *Annual Review of Anthropology* 6: 227–54.

2

Islamic Movements: One or Many?

William R. Roff

Let me try to phrase the problem addressed in this essay as a series of linked questions. Does 'Islam' constitute social relations in Muslim societies? If so, does it do so in ways that are common to all or most Muslim societies? If so, how can we best inquire into and understand the processes involved?

My own answer would be something like the following. All social action by Muslims, *acting as Muslims* (acceptors of the *shari'a*), is constrained by the objectively invariant prescriptions of 'Islam', known to the believer first from the Qur'an and secondly (if more questionably invariant) the *sunna*. Though these prescriptions (and their elaboration by those learned in the shari'a) must be interpreted and applied by historically situated individuals (or collectivities), and hence do not exist outside of time or social context, it can be argued that they supply a major, sometimes determinative, part of the perceived objective conditions which direct or constrain action. Further, the common need to persuade, urge, teach, command, or reason with one's fellows in pursuit of proper Muslim action ensures the frequent iteration of prescription and its embodiment in argument and discourse. It is to this discourse, then, in all its complexity, and subject to its own rules, that we must turn in order to determine (if we care to) anything like common principles of Muslim social action. That all such discourse necessarily takes place in contingent and highly variable circumstances requires that the context and levels of the discourse, and *their* cultural and material constraints and determinants, be adequately discerned and understood. It is our apprehension of the simultaneous operation of the prescriptive and circumstantial conditions of action that may permit us to speak with some validity of a specifically Islamic constitution of social relations that can reasonably be held to apply to most if not all of 'the Muslim world'.

In a critical review not long ago of Ernest Gellner's *Muslim Society*, Jacques Berque wrote (1981: 1433) that '[the life of Muslim societies] is ordered — or disordered — in a perpetual debate between their principle and their reality, and any study of them which neglects one of these terms will lack either realism or intelligibility — by which I mean an intelligibility conceived in the same mode as the subject itself'. It is this 'intelligibility in the same mode as the subject itself' that must be our principal concern.

The answer to the question 'Islamic movements, one or many?' plainly is (to my mind): both. That they are many is self-evident; that they should be perceived as one in any useful, interpretative sense, however, is much more problematic. It is easy to find unhelpful examples of what this perception can result in, whether it is constituted by orientalists about 'the other'; stems from the ideologically formed views of political persuaders (be they Pan-Islam-fearful imperialists or wishful-thinking Khilāfatists); or is the fruit of post-Marxist reflections on ideology and utopia (such as those of Russell (1920: 118–19) or Rodinson (1972: 154–6). Though each of these positions, and their simulacra, would doubtless yield something to *verstehen* analysis, they are alike unhelpful in adopting or assuming a congealed and reified notion of 'Islam' that takes little account either of real context or of the ways in which, starting from prescription, Muslims actually do construct, evoke, deploy, and accept the 'Islam' from which they act, see themselves as acting, or argue that action should flow.

Historical or social enquiry based on examination of Muslim argument about these matters may well appear to reveal a plurality of Islams (see, for example, el-Zein, 1977: 228, 242ff; Eickelman, 1982:1), but it seems clear that these Islams manifest in turn a shared repertory of principles of individual and collective action, of a kind that encourages us to explore not merely the intelligibility of Islamic imperatives for Muslims, but the comparability of the social dynamics that (notwithstanding the specificity of circumstance) result. Or to put the thing the other way round, though the real world (but note that just as there may be said to be many 'Islams', there are many 'real worlds' too) impinges on all human actors, not excepting Muslims — through social formations and relations of production that are at any particular moment given, through state systems and refractions of state power, and in other determinative (and overdeterminative) forms — we may observe Muslims acting in ways for which they derive, and to which they give, force and meaning through a wide range of common, Islamically supplied (or enjoined) wellsprings of behavior and response.

One of the principal means of access we have to understanding of this response and its social dynamic is through the discourse of Muslims about (as Lenin put it from within another prescriptive tradition) 'What is to be done?' It is therefore of primary importance to take seriously and in its own terms what Muslims, acting as Muslims, say, and not suppose that what they say 'really' signifies something else. Though doing this doubtless does not rule out Derridan or other semiotic approaches to 'the text' of what is being transacted, I intend here simply the desideratum that, at the outset at least, what is said be taken at face value and in terms of its own intelligibility system, making the assumption that once familiar with much Muslim discourse, in many contexts, we can have fairly direct access to what and how it 'means' for its utterers and auditors.

There is a tendency, not confined to studies of the Muslim world, to suppose that what the natives say is part of an innocent pathology, of an unknowing and essentially self-deceptive symptomology, to which only the trained observer-analyst can have the diagnostic key. This seems dubious, and indeed interpretatively unwise and impermissible if it involves disaggregation (rather than deconstruction) of the discourse, into parts or according to schema derived in extra-discourse terms. Lewis Hyde (1983; McGilchrist, 1984; 77), in his recent book *The Gift*, contrasts the circulation of gifts among 'primitive' peoples with the hoarding of those same gifts when they passed into the hands of the first anthropologists and were sent to the museums of the great universities. Much the same treatment has often been accorded to the conceptual currency of Muslims (and others), save that it has ended up on fixed deposit in the pages of anthropological (or, to be fair, Islamicist) monographs. If anyone should ask (as well they might, given the supposed nature of the category) why no '*abangan*' Muslims have been discovered in India (or if it comes to that, in Malaysia or much of Indonesia), the simplest answer is surely that Clifford Geertz did his field-work in central Java. Not that that would end the matter.

Let me return, however, to the question of how we may usefully, at times, see the Muslim world whole, and find Islamic movements in some sense one. Or to phrase the matter as I did at the outset, in what ways can it make sense to see 'Islam' as constituting social relations in Muslim societies. If Muslim discourse, and the perceptions of constraint, moral imperative, and proper action that it embodies, is in fact central to any such enquiry, then one method of pursuing it might be to examine the discourse across a range of seemingly comparable, if in fact discretely various, historical circumstance. For instance, though there seems still to be a presumption among scholars that something called 'Wahhabism' played a significant part in violent social upheavals occurring in many scattered regions of 'the Muslim world' in the late eighteenth and early nineteenth centuries, it is actually not at all clear what, if anything, they truly had in common, in either impulse or content. What can one learn from looking at them in a comparative way, from the standpoint of the discourse among their Muslim protagonists — as well, obviously, as from whatever else we can know of the circumstances in which they occurred?

It is not hard to find idealist postulations of the wide significance of the movement described by its opponents as 'Wahhabiya' and by its participants as *al-da'wa ila al-tawhid*; it is less easy to learn what precisely 'Wahhabism' could have meant (and how) in local terms in places as diverse as the Nejd itself, West Sumatra, the Hausa states, and Bengal. To take only one recent if summary expression of the idealist view, Ali Merad (1977: 113), writing in a special issue of *Cultures* devoted to 'Islam: The Perenniality of Values', and claiming that 'the Wahhabis greatly contributed to restore the confidence of Muslim peoples and the dynamism they lacked', speaks of 'the regenerating wind of Wahhabism . . . [sweeping] through the entire Muslim community', and sees 'the Wahhabian impulse' as (quoting Iqbal) 'the first pulsation of life in modern Islam'. What can such an appeal to idea and sentiment possibly mean when examined in the immediate circumstances of peoples' lives across half the surface of the globe? Attempts to address this question have taken several forms, none of them (I think) wholly satisfactory.

On the assumption that it is the idea and its articulation that counts, but that (in good Islamic, not to say historiographical, fashion) the *isnad* (chain of authority) must be known, some effort has been made to reconstruct the intellectual milieu of late eighteenth and early nineteenth century Arabia (to which so many Muslims went to perform the *hajj* and to study), and to establish something substantial about the teachers and the taught and their links with a wider Muslim world. John Voll's essay on Muhammad Hayya al-Sindi and Muhammad ibn 'Abd al-Wahhab in eighteenth-century Madina is an important contribution in this respect, as is A. H. Johns' discussion of Ibrahim ibn al-Kurani (father of one of al-Sindi's principal teachers) and Ahmad al-Qashashi (Ibrahim al-Kurani's teacher), who through their student 'Abd al-Ra'uf al-Singkeli provide a connection with a somewhat earlier Sumatra (Voll, 1975: 32–9; Johns, 1978: 469–85). Both Voll and Johns help to provide a much clearer picture of the scholarly community of the late seventeenth and early eighteenth century Hijaz, drawn from many scattered parts of the world from the Maghreb to Persia, India, and Acheh, and linked by learning and *turuq* affiliation alike. Some of the ideational emphasis that emerge — among them a strong emphasis on *hadith* studies and on a purified Sufism associated perhaps mainly with the Naqshbandiya *tariqa* — certainly assist in establishing the lineaments of the dominant discourse that is being shaped.

THE NEJD

But useful as this kind of study (and its necessary extension to more detailed examination of the writings and teachings of those involved) unquestionably is in elucidation of the intellectual matrices from which so much late eighteenth century Muslim social thought seems to have sprung, it is a task that remains largely to be accomplished. For as Voll notes (1975: 38–9), though many attempts have been made to portray the wider influence of 'Wahhabi' ideology, 'less has been done in analyzing the context out of which Wahhabism itself grew'. Plainly, that context is not simply the cosmopolitan world of Mecca and Madina in the first half of the eighteenth century, but paramountly the more remote world of warring segmentary tribal lineages among the pastoral nomads of inner Arabia in the latter part of the century. For it was here, initially in the Nejd, that Muhammad 'Abd al-Wahhab, gripped by his own sense of the gap between prescription and social reality in the lives of Bedu and townsmen alike, began to preach the kind of strict constructionism (an entirely appropriate term) to which in due course the eponym *Wahhabi* became attached, and found a patron and extender in Muhammad ibn Sa'ud, *amir* of the tribal group centered on the oasis settlement of Dir'iya.

The principal doctrinal elements of al-Wahhab's teachings, and their expression in social and political institutions within the domains of the *muwahhidun* (unitarians), are tolerably well-known and understood, having been described (and to some extent set out) almost contemporaneously and often discussed since.[1] So also are the successful territorial campaigns of the Sa'uds, from the long struggle with Riyadh at the outset to the extension of Sa'udi influence over most of the peninsula up to Syria and the occupation of the Hijaz from 1803 to 1814. What we mainly lack, however, or so it seems to me, is any serious analysis of the dynamic of muwahhidun argument in the context of those social groups, institutions and processes that characterized eighteenth and early nineteenth-century Arabia, from tribal organization, war and affiliation, to pastoral nomadism and settlement, trade and territory, and the politics of claimed Ottoman hegemony. The Wahhabi-Sa'udi conquest of Arabia was, of course, to a considerable degree a matter of warfare and submission, but it was warfare invested with moral argument, that made moral claims, and carried moral teaching. And it was teaching, one must assume, of a kind that carried meaning in terms of the time, place and context, timeless though its origins and *modus operandi* might claim to be, based on the seeking of God's will for man as set out in the revelation. *How* this teaching meant is likely to elude us unless we can apprehend both the circumstantial context in which it operated and the discourse that accompanied its contestation and acceptance.

These arguments are obvious enough, and offered not as in themselves any addition to interpretative understanding of 'Wahhabism', but rather as an exemplification of the way in which interpretative understanding must proceed, and through which some comprehension of the social dynamic of Islamic argumentation may be obtained. When we move beyond Arabia, exactly the same considerations arise. But first let us look briefly at what is known about the substantive links between the Arabia of this time and the immediately relevant other parts of the Muslim world. Mervyn Hiskett (1962: 593) has said of the Fulani *jihad*ists, 'it is impossible that they can have remained unaware of the "innovations" in Arabia in their day', and we are quite familiar in a general way with the networks of communication which, through the hajj, peripatetic students and teachers, and affiliation with turuq, ensured a constantly renewed reportage of ideas and events from the Ivory Coast to Mindanao. More specifically, however, with respect to the 'Wahhabi' movements we are considering here, the outbreak of the 'Padri' revolt in Minangkabau has long been associated (with what validity may appear) with the 'three hajjis' who returned there from Mecca in 1803, and the Fara'idi movement in East Bengal with the return of Hajji Shariat Allah from twenty years in the Hijaz in 1818. And even in Hausaland (usually thought to be the most dubious of the cases) the return from his second hajj in 1786/87 of the Qadiriya Shaykh Jibril b. 'Umar, Usuman dan Fodio's most influential teacher, was followed by a marked intensification of dan Fodio's personal revelation and preachings, culminating in the *hijr* and jihad of 1804.

By themselves, however, such connections can be little more than inferential — in the real sense 'accidental' — and indeed further enquiry readily shows that in all cases (especially perhaps those of Minangkabau and the Fulani) the apparent crucial moment turns out to be itself part of a somewhat longer local experience of social perturbation expressed in Islamic ways. Nor, from the standpoint of interpretative interest, is happenstance the point, any more than are calendrical occasion and the messianic expectations said to have been widely prevalent among Muslims at the turn of the hijri century in 1785 (as again in 1882, and some would say 1979). That there should be connections — between people and places, or times and events — is, of course, not without consequence, and their nature must where possible be accounted for and their ramifications explored. But the principal task remains that of trying to understand how, when invoked, Islamic imperatives come to have (or give) meaning for those involved.

THE PADRI MOVEMENT

The most careful and detailed examination that I know of the economic, social, and political context for a 'Wahhabi' movement of the late eighteenth and nineteenth centuries is the study of the Padri movement recently published by Christine Dobbin, *Islamic Revivalism in a Changing Peasant Economy: Central Sumatra, 1784–1847.*[2] The part of central Sumatra known as Minangkabau consists of an extensive and well-populated highland massif, falling away abruptly to a narrow coastal strip on the west, and wandering off through swampy, riverine lowlands to the Malacca Strait in the east. Settled by agriculturalists cultivating wet and dry rice in the valleys and on the hill slopes of the massif, it had been connected to the outside world since at least the fifteenth century by a valuable trade in gold, mined in the highlands and taken out through west coast ports. Control of gold workings and trade routes (and from the sixteenth century, participation in the cultivation and marketing of export pepper) provided the basis for the Minangkabau state and underwrote one of the main forms of social differentiation. Another derived from the coexistence of two major principles of social organization, each with its own system of *adat* (Ar. *'ada*): that associated with the royal family, patrilineal in emphasis, and the 'republicanism' of the majority of the population, expressed in non-territorial but land-owning matriclans. Minangkabau probably became Muslim in the course of the sixteenth century, initially through the west coast ports and those most involved in the commerce in gold (notably the royal family and traders), later among the generality of peasant agriculturalists through lineage Islamic functionaries and, at the village level, through the institution of the *surau* (young and unmarried men's houses), which increasingly became the focus of Sufi *turuq* and schools.

The decline of the gold workings in the latter half of the eighteenth century, accompanied by a collapse of the pepper market, placed great strains on Minangkabau economy and society, loosening political ties, aggravating regional imbalances, and assisting the penetration of society by forces associated with the rapid growth of a new export crop, *Arabica* coffee (itself perhaps introduced, coincidentally, by returned Mecca pilgrims). Coffee did best on marginal land, on hill slopes above the previously more prosperous lineage-controlled *sawah* (wet rice) lands. Its cultivation brought into being new wealth, creating tensions between sawah lineages and land-short coffee growers, as well as between villages competing for boundary land. It fostered the entry into commercial activity of new groups of intermediate traders and carriers, distinguished from the old gold route trading elite and their royal family patrons. Market centers established in the highlands became the locus not simply of new wealth but of forms of economic and social behavior not previously manifested or sanctioned, from a cruder individualism to banditry, rampant gambling, and associated evils. In these circumstances, Dobbin (1983: 126) argues, it was the surau that emerged as an alternative to lineage institutions for regulating society's affairs, especially with respect to dispute settlement and with an altogether new emphasis on the shari'a rather than adat as the supplier of codes of conduct.

The first Islamic 'renewal' in Minangkabau dates from about 1784, when the Shattariya surau of Tuanku Nan Tua, in the Agam district, began to function as a major source for the teaching of a revived Islamic jurisprudence in the practical context of conflict over trading and land matters among neighboring villages, to the extent that by the 1790s Nan Tua had become known as 'the patron of the traders' (Dobbin, 1983: 127). Similar developments are documented for elsewhere in the region, as is a marked increase in the pilgrimage to Mecca by those benefitting from the new wealth. One of the famous 'three hajjis' who returned in 1803, Haji Miskin, had been involved in Tuanku Nan Tua's renewal movement before his departure, and now proceeded to teach what Dobbin terms 'Wahhabi' doctrines in one of the newly prosperous coffee-producing villages, urging adherence in all respects to a shari'a derived solely from the Qur'an, requiring the substitution of plain white clothing (and the veiling of women) for native dress, strict performance of the *salat* and other *'ibadat*, and the prohibition of cock-fighting, tobacco and opium smoking, and *tuak* (rice wine) drinking. Subsequently, under the patronage of another major Shattariya teacher, Tuanku Nan Rinceh, the local struggle was extended in a more general 'jihad', accompanied by

38

much violence, to spread these teachings, and the adoption of the shari'a, administered by specially appointed *qadis*, to regulate all matters of property and commerce. The civil strife that resulted in Agam persisted for six years, and was later replicated in other major areas of Minangkabau, until involvement by the Dutch in the 1820s altered the whole character of the affair.

One might, perhaps, do more than Dobbin has chosen to do to disinter the detail of the discourse among Muslims that accompanied the Padri movement. Though the materials are limited, it is clear that there was much debate, much appeal to authority of varying sorts within the Islamic tradition itself, much discussion of proper *modus operandi*, and the argument might with advantage be treated somewhat more coherently in its own terms, and less derivatively. But her account comes a great deal nearer than most (whether of this movement or others) to situating the discourse in a closely examined context of socio-economic change, and to taking seriously the dialectic that results. While it may not be necessary (and at times perhaps not even helpful) to see the movement as 'Wahhabi', there can be little doubt that despite the great contextual differences it was remarkably similar to that of the muwahhidun in its impulses and argument, in its capacity to create and convey meaning for its followers through Islamic imperatives, and can best be understood, in a comparative way, in such terms.

THE FARA'IDI MOVEMENT

Can one say the same of Hajji Shariat Allah's *Fara'idi* movement in East Bengal, launched in 1821? It may be worth noting at the outset — for again the contexts are very different — that where Tuanku Nan Tua became known to his supporters as 'the patron of the traders', Hajji Shariat Allah was derided by his opponents as 'the *pir* of the *julahas*' (spiritual mentor of the [poor] weavers) (Ahmad Khan, 1965: 86). The establishment of East India Company control over Bengal in the 1770s, and the introduction of a British-devised system of administration in place of the supplanted Mughal one, had profound effects especially on land tenure and revenue collection, transforming the basis of the state from what may be termed a tributary mode of production to a rentier capitalist one. In brief, the Mughal *zamindars* (ideally, the revenue collecting agents of the state, though with certain accrued hereditary rights over land as well) became, through the 'permanent settlement' of 1793, proprietors of the land, liable only for regular and fixed payments to the state. Furthermore, in the space of a few decades only, with the Mughal upper class (for the most part non-Bengali in origin, and Persian and Urdu-speaking, but Muslim) pushed aside and much of their lands resumed, the zamindars were drawn increasingly from among Calcutta-based, Hindu merchant collaborators with the Company, set thereby over a largely Muslim peasantry reduced to the status of tenants-at-will. Two further economic changes greatly affected the condition of the predominantly Muslim poorer classes of the delta, peasant and artisan. The loss of Britain's colonies in the Americas led at the turn of the century to the emergence of East Bengal as a major center for the cultivation of indigo by British plantation interests, with oppressive effects on land use and tenant conditions; and metropolitan policies concerning the manufacture, import and export of cloth goods led to the rapid decline and eventual extinction of the Bengal cotton- and silk-weaving craft industry. The net effect of half a century of Company rule was the impoverishment of the poorer classes of Muslims, especially in the delta areas of East Bengal, and the erosion of social ties between the peasantry and the erstwhile (now much reduced) Muslim official and landowning classes.[3]

Shariat Allah had been born into a *taluqdar* (petty landowning) family in the delta district of Faridpur in 1781. In 1799, at the age of 18, he went to Mecca with his Calcutta teacher of Persian and Arabic, Mawlana Basharat 'Ali, who, it is said, had become 'disgusted with the British regime and decided to emigrate to the holy city' (Ahmad Khan, 1965: 3). He remained in the Hijaz for nineteen years (save for two years at al-Azhar), became a student in most of the Islamic sciences of Shaykh Tahir al-Sunbal al-Makki (of whom little is known), and was initiated by him into the Qadiriya tariqa. He returned briefly to Bengal in 1818, and then in 1821 for good. Appalled at the state of Muslim belief and practice in his native land, with its emphasis on shrine worship and pir veneration and its adulteration by Hindu and other custom and ritual, he began to preach a renewed Islam purified of *bida'* and insistent upon proper performance of the fundamental duties of the faith (*fara'id*, hence the name by which the movement became known). His following is said contemporaneously to have grown rapidly, embracing by the 1830s about one-sixth of the rural population (Taylor, 1840, cited in Ahmad Khan, 1965; 12). At the same time, it brought him into conflict with the Hindu zamindars, over non-paymnent of 'idolatrous' taxes, and with more traditional Muslim leaders on a variety of issues, not least his proscription of pir veneration (he claimed for himself only the title *ustaz*, teacher) which undercut the basis of much rural spiritual authority. Where specifically state power was concerned, Shariat Allah's requirement of his followers that Friday congregational (*juma'*, *jam'*) and *'Id* (festival) prayers not be held in villages and towns in a Bengal effectively stripped under Company rule of its legitimating Islamic authority (amir and qadi) can be seen as having political implications, though there is some difference of opinion over whether it was directed more against the British or against a local Muslim leadership perceived as errant or absent.

The transformation of the Fara'idis from communities of personally purified Muslims based on repentance (*tawba*), observance of the fara-id, and strict avoidance of *shirk* (polytheism), into a more direct and militant expression of economic and social discontent of a kind quickly characterized as 'Wahhabi' was largely the work of his son, Muhammad Muhsin al-Din Muhammad (better known as Dudhu Miyan), who returned from some five years in Mecca in 1836 (four years before his father's death), and proceeded to supply the movement with organization and structure which transcended its original impulse. Building on the first, local level *panchayats* (village councils) set up by his father as teaching centers, and on the idea of a solidary community of believers, he established an elaborate network of authority, with himself as Ustaz (after 1840) and a hierarchy of advisory *khalifas* (deputies) at the center, superintendent khalifas at district level, and unit khalifas in village and town ward. Authority was expressed through both *siyasa* and *dini* structures, the former to recruit fighting groups through which to assert directly the rights of cultivators and artisans against zamindars and forced-contract indigo planters, the latter to govern fara'idi communities, with unit khalifas acting as imams and qadis, overseeing *zakat* and *'ushr* collection, and responsible for the provision of community *astanas*, used among other things for visiting teachers and for the regular performance of Qadiriya *dzikr*. In the course of the twenty years from Dudhu Miyan's return to Bengal and the outbreak of the 'Indian Mutiny', the Fara'idis grew considerably in numbers, and were increasingly involved in organizing and channelling agrarian protest throughout East Bengal, continually coming before the British on charges of public violence and luddism, and perceived as having established among themselves to a threatening degree an *imperium in imperio*.

Any brief summary of the kind given above must do violence to the complexity of social reality. The Fara'idis were by no means the only Muslim renewal movement to become resoundingly active (and to be labelled Wahhabi) in early ninteenth-century Bengal, and the later set debates (*bahas*) between these several tendencies, together with the *puthi* literature that reflects them (perceptively discussed by Rafiuddin Ahmed (1981) for the second half of the century), was plainly an important part of a larger 'Islamization' process that was under way. Similarly, the Hindu context of social action was altogether more subtle than this summary can convey, and the sharpening of boundaries between Hindus and *sabiqi* Muslims (traditionalists, 'syncretists' — read 'abangan'?) is obviously more than a matter of emerging conflict between the poorer (not solely Muslim) classes and the zamindars (not all of whom were Hindu). Much remains to be known, too, in a sociological way, about the Fara'idi leadership, as well as that of similar movements.

My present concern, however, is simply to raise the question, not to my mind yet answered by the literature, of how, for the Fara'idis, leaders and followers, fara'idi prescription operated within the given socio-economic and cultural circumstances, and, from the outset of Shariat Allah's mission, to enjoin and to give meaning to personal and social action in such a way as to render comprehensible in its own terms the social dynamic that resulted. This question certainly cannot be answered by application of the term 'Wahhabi', but it is not very satisfactorily addressed either by predominantly materialist or instrumental interpretations of the movement, persuasive as these may be as glosses after the fact, pointing to the attraction of a textually validated Islamic equalitarianism for caste-like (and out of work) weavers; to the appeal of the Qur'anic *ayat*, 'Whatever is in the heavens and in the earth belongs to Allah', (Qur'an 2: 129 and 4: 131; cf. Ahmad Khan, 1965: 114) as a charter for oppressed peasants; or to the interests served by social mobilization for ousted elites suffering from relative deprivation.[3a] What one needs, it may rather be maintained, is to know more of the discourse that accompanied, and formed the burden of, fara'idi prescription. In fact, this may not be very easily supplied. The most detailed and carefully argued discussion of the Fara'idis, that by Muin-ud-Din Ahmad Khan, is able to reproduce very little of it, especially from the early period, having to rely largely on later emanations from the movement (in the form of *fatawa, puthi* literature, hagiographies and the like), together with some contemporary report and the counterblasts of such prominent opponents as Mawlana Karamat 'Ali. But the question is worth addressing, and could with profit be pursued.

THE FULANI JIHAD

Turning, briefly, to the last of my examples, what is perhaps most striking about the Fulani jihad, in contrast to the Padri and Fara'idi movements (or that of the Nejdi muwahhidun) is the abundance of contemporary documentation produced by its protagonists. One of the consequences of this is that it has been possible for students of the movement to produce descriptive and interpretative accounts which draw heavily, indeed rely considerably, on the writings of those who took part. Not surprisingly, such accounts tend to see and explain the jihad in substantially local, though not thereby wholly *sui generis*, terms. One might be inclined to think that, had this been possible for the Padri and Fara'idi movements, they would less often be labelled 'Wahhabi' and more readily discussed in terms of their explicit impetuses. No doubt overmuch should not be made of this, for the jihadists too had significant links with the Sufi and Hijazi intellectual circles of the time (and they too were aware of the turn of the Islamic calendar), but it comes as a useful corrective.

The Fulbe (Hausa: Fulani) of the central Sudan in the eighteenth century were a mainly transhumant pastoralist, clan-organized people, speaking the Fulfulde language, who, tracing their origins to the western reaches of the medieval Saharan kingdom of Mali (where they claimed a measure of Berber descent), had migrated from the fifteenth century on into the Hausa-speaking country east of the middle Niger. Here on the scrubby savannah lands of the Sahel, they grazed their cattle and moved among the settled agriculturalist population, owning at least nominal allegiance to the Hausa chiefs of more than a dozen principalities, half of which were in some sense Muslim and half not. The Islamic religion, and with it a substantial measure of Arab culture (not least the Arabic language among the learned), seems to have been strongly present in the central Sudan from about the early sixteenth century, associated especially with traders seeking gold and slaves and (in due course) with literati seeking patronage at Hausa courts. Nuclei of Islamic communities existed in the walled towns of the region, from which some influence extended to the surrounding 'mixed' communities, and there was in addition a constant traffic through the region of Muslim scholars, students and teachers, seeking each other, going on and returning from the hajj, engaged to some degree in trans-Saharan trade, affiliated from the eighteenth century with one or another Sufi tariqa, and teaching wherever they could. The Islamic presence, like the population generally, may thus be said to have had its settled and its peripatetic components.

43

Among the Fulani, many but not all of whom were Muslim, was one clan or sub-clan that had a particular association with and commitment to Islamic learning. These were the *Torodo* (pl. *Torodbe*), originally from Futa Toro in western Senegambia, where their kinsmen had been involved in earlier West African jihads against non-Muslim hosts or neighbors, establishing state-like Imamates in Futa Toro, Bondo and Futa Jalon in the early and late eighteenth centuries. The Torodo Fulani who had migrated a thousand miles to the east in the fifteenth century, centering themselves on the northern Hausa kingdom of Gobir, lived both settled and peripatetic lives, as scribes, counsellors, and teachers at the court and in the towns, and as itinerant scholars (*mallams*) living from time to time in smaller settlements and villages but constantly on the move. Though their primary constituency, outside the towns, was among the Muslim cattle-Fulani nomads, they had some following also among those of the Hausa peasantry who had become in a measure Muslim, and an often (though not always) close association with the nomadic Tuareg of the northern marchlands, especially the latter's *Ineslemen* (mallam) lineages.

There are some indications that in the late eighteenth century endemic, incipient, or potential systemic stresses between the several groups comprising the Gobir (and other Hausa) polities were in process of exacerbation. Fulani nomadic pastoralists, despite a tendency to concentrate in the outer reaches of the Hausa kingdoms, were always liable to conflict with the settled Hausa peasantry over access to grazing land and water supplies. Subjected to state cattle taxes seen as burdensome (and to the mallam Islamically improper), their problems in this respect were certainly less than those of the Hausa cultivators, the objects of frequently discriminatory and oppressive taxes on land and produce by their rulers. Fulani and Hausa alike were prey to slave raiding, an immemorial problem given fresh edge in the late eighteenth century by the acquisition of firearms by the court-sanctioned raiders. Tuareg nomadic herdsmen, growing in number, felt increasingly impelled to move from the northern Sahel to better southern pastures. As one historian (Waldman, 1965: 344) has said, 'At the end of the eighteenth century, Hausaland was filled with people dissatisfied with the Hausa order' and ready to join movements of protest. In this context, it was the Fulani, and especially the Torodo Fulani mallams, who were best able to find both ideology and structure for such protest: ideology through an Islamically argued need for change, structure through their own and associated clan solidarities and their network of long-distance teaching and exchange.

The course of the movement brought into being by Usuman dan Fodio ('Uthman b. Muhammad Fudi), and his brother Abdullahi and son Muhammad Bello, has been frequently and well described,[4] and will not be set out at any length here. Usuman, son of a learned (Ful., *fudiye*) Torodo mallam, was born in a village in northern Gobir in 1754. Educated into the tradition by his father and uncles, he later (1779) became the student of the militantly rigorist Tuareg Shaykh Jibril b. 'Umar al-Aqdasi, not long returned from Mecca and Cairo, who initiated him into probably three Sufi turuq, notably the Khalwatiya and Qadiriya, both then part of the purified Sufi response to muwahhidun strictures on excesses (and the latter the tariqa of the fara'idi Shariat Allah).[5] Among other teachers of consequence were his cousin (or maternal uncle) Muhammad al-Raj, who taught him al-Bukhari, having studied hadith in Madina with 'Abu'l Hasan al-Sindi, a pupil of the Muhammad Hayya al-Sindi who had taught 'Abd al-Wahhab ('Abdullah ibn Muhammad Fodio, 1963: 95). In 1774, aged 20, Usuman dan Fodio began his own peripatetic teaching, first in Gobir and then in neighboring states, both among the Muslim Fulani and among those, Hausa as well as Fulani, who had not yet 'smelt the scent of Islam'. Encouraged by wide success as a teacher, and an extirpator of laxity among the 'mixers', he sought out the nominally Muslim ruler of Gobir, 'to [explain] to him the true Islam and [order] him (to observe it) and to establish justice in his lands' (ibid: 86). Some years later (in 1787 or 1788) he and numerous other mallams confronted the ruler at the *'Id al-Adha* festival, and obtained from him a list of promised concessions to Muslim subjects of the state. He continued to teach, to travel, and to win a following. From 1789 (1204) onwards, Usuman was vouchsafed a succession of personal visions, in which first the Prophet Muhammad appeared before him, and then, in 1794, 'Abd al-Qadir al-Jailani, founder of the Qadiriya order, who gave him a green robe embroidered with the *shahada* and a 'sword of truth' to unsheath against the enemies of Allah.[6] Relations between a new and less secure Gobir ruler (acceded 1796) and the Muslims deteriorated until, in 1804, modelling himself on the Prophetic tradition, Usuman dan Fodio declared a hijr to the borders of the kingdom, from whence was launched the jihad, led in the field by his brother Abdullahi and son Muhammad Bello, that several years later resulted in the establishment of what became known as the Sokoto caliphate or empire. Though the kernel of the jihad forces were drawn from the mallams, the rank and file support, as it accumulated, was extremely heterogeneous, from Fulani (and Hausa) Muslims to previously non-Muslim groups which for many and diverse reasons became caught up in the struggle.

Usuman dan Fodio throughout much of his life from the early 1790s (he died in 1817) committed a great deal of his teaching and argument to writing, a corpus of materials added to by Abdullahi dan Fodio, Muhammad Bello and others of his Companions (as well as by those court-appointed mallams with whom he debated), so that we have an extraordinary quantity of Muslim discourse on which to base understanding of the imperatives claimed by the movement, and how they spoke to those who became its adherents.[7] Though most of Usuman's writings were in Arabic, he wrote also (especially in verse) in Fulfulde and possibly also in Hausa, presumably to reach a wider audience. The works ranged from emotional Sufi poems and simply expressed teachings of the *'aqa'id* to carefully argued expositions of his theological beliefs and political views. They extend in time from his *Ihya al-sunna wa ikhmad al-bid'a* (Revivification of the *sunna* and extinction of innovation), which in a largely non-polemical way set out in 1792 to correct the practice of Muslims in his own place and time, through the *Masa'il muhimma* (Important matters) of 1803, which presaged the need for hijr and jihad, to the 1806/7 *Bayan wujub al-hijra 'ala'l 'ibad* (Explanation of the obligation of hijr for the worshippers) and *Kitab al-farq bain wilayat ahl al-Islam wa bain wilayat ahl al-kufr* (Book of the difference between the government of the people of Islam and the government of the unbelievers) in the post-jihad period, together with discussions in poems and elsewhere (notably in the 1811/12 *Siraj al-ikhwan* [Lamp of the brethren]) of himself not as *Mahdi* but as the calendrical *Mujaddid* (Renewer), and of the crucial distinction (in the context of any argument for jihad) between sinners and apostates or unbelievers.[8]

THE DIALECTIC

Faced with this mass of detailed, socially embedded Muslim discourse — to which must be added the biographical accounts and didactic writings of Abdullahi and others, and the contemporary histories — simplistic evocations of 'Wahhabism' necessarily dissolve. But as they dissolve, and with them the implied claims they make to a special sort of *a priori* inherent universalism, they draw fresh attention, in virtue of the very specificity of the discourse and its circumstance, to the *modus operandi* by which particular Muslims, utterers and auditors, find meaning in or create meaning from a commonly shared, Islamically derived repertoire of imperatives to personal and social action. It is in the intricate analysis of the dialectic between any given, historically evolved set of structural relations — be they those of the Nejdi muwahhidun, Padris, Fara'idis, or Fulani — and the transcendental prescriptions as understood by those involved (a dialectic accessible through, and only through, what the natives say) that the oneness of Islamic movements may at times be usefully discerned. It is a oneness residing not in any supposed essential features of 'Islam' (for in this sense it has none, and must be construed) but in the logic of relations between the meanings given to prescription and those given to circumstance; between, for Muslims, as Berque suggested, their principle and their reality.

I have tried in this paper to address these questions by looking at some of the roughly contemporaneous movements often described as 'Wahhabi'. One might equally well, I suppose, have taken the 'Salafiya' movements of a century later, or, if it comes to that, something nearer our own day. My argument, if it has any validity at all, is not dependent upon cases. The 'Muslim world' today is at least as various as it was at the end of the eighteenth century (and is, of course, not only, or always, the Muslim world, but part of the 'capitalist periphery', of the 'Third World', of 'post-colonial state systems', and much else, depending on the lens one chooses). It is quite as interconnected as it was then, and presumably much more so. The hajj, Sufi turuq, learning in Mecca and Madina and at al-Azhar, have not been supplanted, but they have had added unto them, magnified by the explosion of communications to which we have all been subjected, International Islamic Universities in at least three other countries, international da'wa organizations, the Organisation of the Islamic Conference, the Islamic Development Bank, Qaddafi's secret legions, and a lot more. The context of Muslim discourse (in the sense in which I have been speaking of it) and its external constraints have as a result become infinitely more complex. But the task and the challenge of understanding and interpreting that discourse remain, it seems to me, much the same, as do the means of undertaking the task.

I shall end with a reflection that may or may not be pertinent, and is commonplace enough in its way. Not long ago I found myself sitting one Friday at mid-day in the garden outside the Badshahi Mosque in Lahore, waiting for a friend. Because he was late, I was able to sit there throughout the *juma'* prayer, and in due course to listen to the *khutba*. My knowledge of Urdu is negligible, but I found it was not hard to follow, in general terms, what the *khatib* was saying, and how he was saying it, in an address concerned largely with the

Soviet occupation of Afghanistan, and with what must, by Muslims, be done. I could follow what he was saying for several reasons. First of all, because the shape of the khutba and its rhetorical style were familiar; secondly, because as in all such addresses the speaker illustrated his argument by frequent quotation from the Qur'an, given in Arabic and then translated into the vernacular; and thirdly, because, though I was outside the mosque and could see nothing of what was going on, I was acutely aware that I was present at a performance in which the speaker, and an audience vocal in response, were together engaged in an exercise the general drift of which did not elude me. Obviously, had I understood Urdu, or indeed had better Arabic, had I been present in the mosque and been able to observe, and had I known something about the khatib, his own background, his relation to his parishioners and to the state (and all the other things that Patrick Gaffney is looking at so carefully in his essay), I should have been rather better able to 'analyze the discourse'. My capacity to analyze it at all, however, is not the point, but rather the certain fact that it might equally well have been taking place (on whatever subject, or indeed on Afghanistan) in Jakarta, Kuala Lumpur, Dacca, Delhi, Qum, Cairo, or Kano, and that Muslims from any or all of these places would have grasped its import much more readily than I. If there is not an 'Islamic world', perhaps at times not even a 'Muslim world', there is an evident world of Muslims, to whom Muslim discourse speaks.

NOTES

1. See, especially, O'Kinealy, 1874:66–82; Burckhardt, 1831:96–357 (esp. 131–62 on government, administration of justice, and revenue collection); Brydges, 1834:II, 7–164ff. (esp. 115–27 on administration of justice); Raymond, 1925; Niebuhr, 1792:II, 130–36. The principal secondary account is presumably Rentz, 1948; but cf. also Rentz, 1972:54–56. Materials in Arabic unavailable to me include 'Abd al-Wahhab, n.d. (cited in Al-Yassini 1982:83); 'Abd al-Wahhab, 1955 (cited in Zaharuddin 1979:156); Al-'Uthaymayn, n.d.; and *Majmu'ah al-rasa'il*, 1928–31 (the last two cited in Voll, 1982:361).

2. Dobbin, 1983. See also Hollander, 1857:Vol. 5 (being an account in Malay by a participant, with Dutch translation); de Stuers, 1849–50, 2 vols.; and Stein Parvé 1855:245–78. Cf. also Cuisinier, 1959: 70–88; and Abdullah 1966: 1-24.

3. For an account of this process, see Mallick, 1961 (esp. Chap. II); and cf. also Kaviraj, 1982 (esp. Chap I).

3a. For an interpretation of this kind see, e.g., W.C. Smith, 1963:178; and the recent study by Samad, 1983.

4. The principal accounts are Last, 1967: Part I, 1–62; Hiskett, 1973;

Martin, 1976:13–35. Cf. also Waldman, 1965:333–55; M.G. Smith, 1966:408–20; and the useful short account in Hiskett, 1976:131–51.

5. Martin, 1976, provides the best discussion of the Sufi background; and cf. also Martin, 1972:300–5.

6. Hiskett, 1973:66, quoting Usuman's late-written *Wird*; and cf. also the earlier Fulfulde verse, translated into Arabic by Abdullah ibn Muhammad Fodio, 1963:105–7.

7. For lists, finding aids, and descriptive accounts of this literature, a large part of which exists only in manuscript, see Last, 1967:xxv–lvii, 236–54; Balogun, 1975:177–83; Tapiero, 1963:49–88. The general bibliographies in Last, 1967 and Hiskett, 1973 contain details of most of the material that has been published or translated. Cf. Also Hiskett, 1975; and Bivar and Hiskett, 1962:104–48.

8. Usuman's *Ihya' al-sunna*, published in Cairo in 1962, is summarized and in part translated in Balogun, 1975:49–81; his *Kitab al-farq* is published in translation, with parallel text, in Hiskett 1960:558–79. Hiskett, 1973, contains numerous and extended passages of translation from Usuman's writings; cf. also 'Abdullah ibn Muhammad Fodio, 1963. Usuman's own account of his life, written originally in Fulfulde, is published in translation, with a photocopy of the text and a transliteration, in al-Masri, Adeleye, and Hunwick, 1966:1–36. Cf. also Arnett, 1922, which contains a paraphrase and in parts a translation of the *Infaku'l Maisuri* of Sultan Muhammad Bello. On the specific question of the argument for jihad, see Martin, 1967:50–97; and cf. Willis, 1967:395–415.

REFERENCES

'Abd al-Wahhab , Muhammad Ibn (1955), *Kitab al-tawhid*. Cairo.

'Abd al-Wahhab, Muhammad ibn (n.d.), *Mu'alafat al-shaykh al-imam Muhammad ibn 'Abd al-Wahhāb*. Riyadh: Islamic University of Imam Muhammad Ibn Sa'ud. 12 vols.

'Abdullah ibn Muhammad Fodio (1963), *Tazyin ak-waraqat* (ed. and transl. by M. Hiskett, with parallel Arabic text). Ibadan: Ibadan University Press.

Abdullah, Taufik (1966), 'Adat and Islam: An examination of conflict in Minangkabau', *Indonesia*, 2:1–24.

Ahmad Khan, Muin-ud-Din (1965), *History of the Fara'idi Movement in Bengal (1818–1906)*. Karachi: Pakistan Historical Society.

Ahmed, Raffiuddin (1981), *The Bengal Muslims, 1871–1906: A Quest for Identity*. Delhi: Oxford University Press.

Arnett, A.J., (1922), *The Rise of the Sokoto Fulani, being a paraphrase and in some parts a translation of the Infaku'l Maisuri of Sultan Muhammad Bello*, Kano.

Balogun, Ismail A.B. (1975), *The Life and Works of 'Uthmān dan Fodio*. Lagos: Islamic Publications Bureau.

Berque, Jacques (1981), 'The popular and the purified', *Times Literary Supplement*, 11 December 1981:1433.

Bivar, A.D.H. and M. Hiskett (1962), 'The Arabic literature of Nigeria to 1804: a provisional account', *Bulletin of the School of Oriental and African*

Studies, 25:104-48.

Brydges, H.J. (1834), 'A brief history of the Wahauby', in his *Account of His Majesty's Mission to Persia in the years 1807-11*. London: James Bohn, Vol. II, 7-164ff.

Burckhardt, J.H. (1831), *Notes on the Bedouins and Wahabys*. London.

Cuisinier, Jeanne (1959), 'La guerre des Padris (1803-1838-1845)', *Archives de Sociologie des Religions*, 7:70-88.

Dobbin, Christine (1983), *Islamic Revivalism in a Changing Peasant Economy: Central Sumatra, 1784-1847*. London: Curzon Press.

Eickelman, Dale F. (1982), 'The study of Islam in local contexts', *Contributions to Asian Studies*, 17:1-16.

Hiskett, Mervyn (1960), '*Kitab al-farq*: A work on the Habe kingdoms attributed to 'Uthmān dan Fodio', *Bulletin of the School of Oriental & African Studies*, 23:558-79.

Hiskett, Mervyn (1962), 'An Islamic tradition of reform in the western Sudan from the sixteenth to the eighteenth century', *Bulletin of the School of Oriental & African Studies*, 25:577-96.

Hiskett, Mervyn (1973), *The Sword of Truth: The Life and Times of Shehu Usuman dan Fodio*. New York: Oxford University Press.

Hiskett, Mervyn (1975), *A History of Hausa Islamic Verse*. London: School of Oriental and African Studies.

Hiskett, Mervyn (1976), 'The nineteenth century *jihāds* in West Africa', in *The Cambridge History of Africa*. Cambridge: University Press, Vol. 5, 131-51.

Hollander, J.J. (1857), 'Hikajat Sjech Djilal Eddin Tuanku Samiang; verhaal van den aanvang der Padri-onlusten op Sumatra', in his (ed.) *Maleisch Leesboek voor Eerstbeginnenden en Meergevorderen*. Leiden: Brill, Vol. 5.

Hyde, Lewis (1983), *The Gift: Imagination and the Erotic Life of Property*. New York: Random House.

Johns, A.H. (1978), 'Friends in grace: Ibrāhim al-Kūrānī and 'Abd al-Ra'ūf al-Singkeli' in S. Udin (ed.), *Spectrum: Essays Presented to Sutan Takdir Alisjahbana on his Seventieth Birthday*. Jakarta: Dian Rakyat, 469-85.

Kaviraj, Narahari (1982),*Wahabi and Farazi Rebels of Bengal*. Delhi: Peoples' Publishing House.

Last, Murray (1967), *The Sokoto Caliphate*. London: Longman.

McGilchrist, I.A. (1984), Review of Lewis Hyde, *The Gift: Imagination and the Erotic Life of Property*, *Times Literary Supplement*, 27 January 1984:77.

Majmu'ah al-rasā'il (1928-31), *Majmu'ah al-rasā'il wa musā'il al-Najdiyyah*. Cairo: Matba'ah al-Manar. 4 vols.

Mallick, Azizur Rahman (1961), *British Policy and the Muslims in Bengal, 1757-1856*. Dacca: Asiatic Society of Pakistan.

Martin, B.G. (1967), 'Unbelief in the western Sudan: Uthman dan Fodio's *Ta'līm al-ikhwān'*, *Middle Eastern Studies*, 4:50-97.

Martin, B.G. (1972), 'A short history of the Khalwati order of dervishes', in N. Keddie (ed.), *Scholars, Saints, and Sufis*. Berkeley, Cal.: University of California Press, 275—305.

al-Masri, F.H., R.A. Adeleye, and J.O. Hunwick (1966), '*Sifofin Shehu:* An autobiography and character study of 'Uthmān b. Fūdī in verse',

Research Bulletin, Centre of Arabic Documentation (Ibadan), 2:1–36.
Merad, Ali (1977), 'Reformism in modern Islam', *Cultures*, 4:108–27.
Niebuhr, M. (1792), 'Of the new religion of a part of Nedsjed', in his *Travels through Arabia*, Edinburgh: R. Morison & Son, 130–6.
O'Kinealy, J. (1874), 'Translation of an Arabic pamphlet on the history and doctrines of the Wahhābis, written by 'Abdullah, grandson of 'Abdul Wahhāb, the founder of Wahhābism', *Journal of the Asiatic Society of Bengal*, 1:66–82.
Raymond, Jean (1925), *Mémoire sur l'origine des Wahabys, sur la naissance de leur puissance et sur l'influence dont ils jouissent comme nation. Rapport de Jean Raymond daté de 1806 . . .* Cairo: Societé Royale de Géographie d'Égypte.
Rentz, George S. (1948), 'Muhammad ibn 'Abd al-Wahhāb (1703/04 – 1792) and the beginnings of unitarian empire in Arabia.' Berkeley, Cal.: University of California, Berkeley. (Unpubl. Ph.D. dissertation).
Rentz, George S. (1972), 'Wahhabism and Saudi Arabia' in D. Hopwood (ed.) *The Arabian Peninsula: Society and Politics*. London: Allen & Unwin, 54–66.
Rodinson, Maxime (1972), *Marxisme et Monde Musulman*.Paris: Ed. du Seuil.
Russell, Bertrand (1920), *Bolshevism: Practice and Theory*. New York: Harcourt, Brace & Rowe.
Samad, Abdus (1983), 'Dynamic of ascriptive politics: A study of Muslim politicization in East Bengal'. New York: Columbia University. (Unpubl. Ph.D. dissertation).
Smith, M.G. (1966) 'The *jihād* of Shehu dan Fodio: Some problems', in I.M. Lewis (ed.), *Islam in Tropical Africa*. London: Oxford University Press, 408–20.
Smith, W.C. (1963), *Modern Islam in India: A Social Analysis*. London: rev. ed. 1946, repr. Lahore: Ashraf.
Stein Parvé, H.A. (1855), 'De secte der Padaries (Padries) in de bovenlanden van Sumatra', *Tijdschrift voor Indische Taal-, Land- en Volkenkunde*, 3:245–78.
de Stuers, H.J.J.L. Ridder (1849–50), *De Vestiging en Uitbreiding van de Nederlanders ter Westkust van Sumatra*. Amsterdam: Van Kampen. 2 vols.
Tapiero, N. (1963), 'Le grand shaykh Peul 'Uthmān ibn Fudi (Othman dan Fodio) . . . et certaines sources de son Islam doctrinal', *Revue des Études Islamiques*, 21:49–88.
Taylor, James (1840), *A Sketch of the Topography and Statistics of Dacca*. Calcutta.
al-'Uthaymayn, 'Abdallāh al-Sālih (n.d.), *Al-shaykh Muhammad ibn 'Abd al-Wahhāb, hayyātuhu wa fikruhu*, Riyadh: Dar al-'Ulūm.
Voll, John (1975), 'Muhammad Hayyā al-Sindi and Muhammad ibn 'Abd al-Wahhāb: An analysis of an intellectual group in eighteenth century Madina', *Bulletin of the School of Oriental and African Studies*, 38:32–9.
Voll, John (1982), *Islam: Continuity and Change in the Modern World*. Boulder, Col.: Westview Press.
Waldman, Marylin (1965) 'The Fulani *jihād*: A reassessment', *Journal of African History*, 6.
Willis, John R. (1967), '*Jihād fi sabīl Allāh*: Its doctrinal basis in Islam and some aspects of its evolution in nineteenth century West Africa', *Journal*

of African History, 8:395–415.

al-Yassini, Ayman S. (1982), 'Saudi Arabia: The Kingdom of Islam', in C. Caldarola (ed.), *Religion and Societies: Asia and the Middle East*. Berlin: Mouton, 61–84.

Zaharuddin, M.Z. (1979) 'Wahhābism and its influence outside Arabia', *Islamic Quarterly*, 23:146–57.

el-Zein, Abdul Hamid (1977), 'Beyond ideology and theology: The search for an anthropology of Islam', *Annual Review of Anthropology, 1977.*

3

The Political Economy of Islamic Conversion in Modern East Java

Robert W. Hefner

In 1966, while much of the rest of rural Java was preoccupied with the horrifying violence which accompanied the destruction of the Indonesian Communist Party, some 150 *Buda* households in the East Javanese mountain community of Besuki[1] reached an agreement with their Islamic village chief on an issue which had polarized the community since Indonesian independence. He would allow the non-Islamic villagers to continue to celebrate *Karo*, the most important annual Buda festival, if they agreed from that point on to identify themselves publicly as Muslim rather than Buda. The Buda villagers would not be required to attend Islamic study classes, nor would they be obliged to pray in the village mosque. They were asked simply to go along with the chief's wish to list them as 'Muslim' in government statistics, and to tolerate the perfunctory Islamic religious instruction their children would receive for a few minutes each day in the village elementary school.

Representing just one-fourth of the village's residents, Besuki's Buda leaders agreed only reluctantly to the chief's demand. Similar religious developments in neighboring communities had convinced the leaders that Buda religion was no longer viable. Besuki was in fact the last in a series of settlements in this mountain region which, since the end of the last century, had progressively restricted Buda rites in favor of Islam. Buda villagers had consistently protested against these measures, insisting that the traditions of the region had been instituted by its first-founding ancestors (*cikal bakal*) and were thus vital to its religious well-being. Muslim leaders had retorted that such local traditions were not 'religious' in any genuine sense, and that it was time for people of the region at any rate to 'act like other Javanese'. It was improper, they said, to worship ancestral spirits, and foolish to think that God could be honored by rites including drinking and dancing. Muslims took particular offense, however, at the fact that such ritual was conducted by a Buda priest (*dukun Buda*) rather than Islamic *modin*. The *dukuns* in this mountain region were different from specialists of the same name found elsewhere in Java (Geertz, 1960:86). They specialized not in curing, sorcery, and magic, but in the celebration of a formal liturgy once known throughout East Java's Tengger massif. They made no pretense of being Muslim, instead professing a faith they called 'Buda religion', the liturgies of which were claimed to have originated in the Javanese kingdom of Majapahit before the coming of Islam.[2]

The conspicuously non-Islamic nature of the Besuki region's Buda traditions had made them the focus of Muslim criticism since the beginning of the century. Besuki's Muslim leaders pointed out that, in allowing the continued celebration of the Karo rite, they were making a greater concession to Buda interests than had been the case in many neighboring communities. As I was told when I visited Besuki in 1979, however, the implicit understanding among Muslim leaders at the time was that, with the passing of another generation, support for Buda ritual would die. Their prognosis appears to have been accurate. The elderly Buda priest whom I met during the same visit confessed that Buda was 'wrecked' and, when he died, so too would Besuki's liturgical heritage.

In this essay I want to explore the cultural and historical background to Besuki's Islamization. My reason for doing so is, first and most simply, to extend our understanding of Islam and Islamization in Java. As Ricklefs (1979:100) has recently emphasized, Java's Islamization has been an ongoing process over the past six centuries, and in many ways it is still incomplete. Besuki's conversion is of special interest in this connection because it has occurred a full two centuries after the period conventionally cited as that during which the last pockets of Hindu-Buddhist population in Java were at least nominally Islamized. Studies of Islamization in Java have neglected this region because it lies outside of the Central Javanese heartland most often examined in historical and anthropological studies, and because the people of this East Javanese mountain territory have often been mistakenly identified as non-Javanese. As I have discussed elsewhere (1983a; 1985), however, the residents of this region refer to themselves as Javanese, and the Buda faith to which they are heirs was once part of a popular Sivaite tradition earlier found throughout rural East Java and Bali. This region's recent Islamization is thus quite relevant for our understanding of Islam and non-Islam in Java.

My second goal in this essay is to raise broader questions

concerning the nature of 'traditional' and 'world' religions,[3] and the conversion process which leads people from the former to the latter. Religious developments in Besuki were directly related to larger politico-economic developments which had shaken this mountain territory since the early nineteenth century. The non-Islamic ritual heritage and the identity with which it was linked had both been well adapted to the cultural terrain of these isolated highland communities, with their subsistence economies and community-oriented notions of status and consumption. The increasing incorporation of the region into a national polity and economy, however, eroded the tradition's social supports, and created conditions favorable to the ascendance of a less parochial religious idiom, and a village elite committed to its promotion. The example suggests that in studying the transition from locally-based faiths to 'world' religion we need to examine the cultural content of both religious discourses in relation to the social scale, political organization, and cultural diversity of the communities to which each would appeal. Among other things, such an approach requires us to recognize that in all religious and ideological discourse there is a dual economy of knowledge, in which explicit doctrinal knowledge is informed by and mutually informs a less discursive, tacit knowledge constructed in a wider social experience. From this perspective, the distinction between traditional and world religions is best understood not in terms of a Weberian contrast between 'traditionalism' and 'rationalization', but in terms of the primary cultural diversity of each religious community, and the shared tacit knowledge its idioms can assume.

BESUKI IN HISTORY

Part of the reason Central Javanese models of Islam must be qualified in speaking of developments in Besuki has to do with the community's peculiar location and history. Besuki lies in densely populated hill country 30 kilometers to the east of the city of Malang, and 20 kilometers to the southwest of Mt Bromo, a volcano which marks the center of the Tengger highlands. The mountain terrain as a whole lies within the eastern fifth of the island of Java, an area which begins around Mt Kawi and the city of Malang and extends almost 200 kilometers east to the straits separating Java from Bali. Known as the 'Eastern Salient' (*ujung timor, oosthoek*), the location and social history of this region have profoundly influenced the course of Islam in the area.

It was in this region, just 28 kilometers from modern Besuki, that the powerful Hindu-Buddhist kingdom of Singasari was established in the thirteenth century. Two of the kingdom's most impressive funerary temples (*candi* Jago and Kidal) still stand today in the region, monuments to the distinctively Javanese blend of Hinduism and Buddhism for which Singasari and its dynastic successor, Majapahit, were famous (Ensink, 1978; Pigeaud, 1962:IV, 3; Rassers 1959). Although Majapahit eventually relocated its capital closer to the north coast (Robson, 1981), historical evidence indicates that the valley and hill communities of this region were major centers of religious activity in the fourteenth and fifteenth centuries, when East Javanese kingdoms dominated the political life of much of the Indonesian archipelago (Pigeaud, 1962:IV, 479; Hefner, 1985).

After Majapahit's collapse in the sixteenth century political hegemony in Java shifted to Muslim principalities on the island's north coast. By the end of the century, however, Java's political center moved inland again to Central Java's wet-rice heartlands. The shift to the interior greatly influenced the development of classical Javanese Islam (Geertz, 1968; Ricklefs, 1979; De Graaf, 1970). Although the Central Javanese court of Mataram oversaw the dismantlement of Java's Hindu-Buddhist ecclesiastical domains, it none the less preserved a strongly Indic style in the arts and in the political pageantry of the court. It also controlled and, at times, violently suppressed independent-minded Muslim leaders, and cultivated a sufi-influenced and relatively inexclusive form of Islam. Large portions of the countryside remained only nominally Islamic. The rise of a revitalized reformist Islam in the nineteenth century, however, served to draw even many rural Javanese to a more orthodox, scripturalist Islam.

Cultural circumstances were different in the Eastern Salient in the centuries following Majapahit's collapse. Although Central Javanese armies devastated population centers and prevented the rise of real courtly rivals in most of the region, no Muslim kingdom ever managed to establish effective control over the entire eastern territory. From the sixteenth to the eighteenth centuries, Muslim principalities — first from Java's north coast, later from inland Mataram — launched repeated attacks on the few small Hindu principalities which survived in isolated areas. One such Hindu principality survived in the extreme east of the island (across the straits from Bali) into the middle of the eighteenth century, when its court was captured and its royalty Islamized (Ricklefs, 1981:96). In hillsides and valleys around Besuki, no such Hindu principality appears to have survived beyond the late sixteenth century, but a non-Islamic rural population did. The region's political instability was a major factor in their survival. Anti-Mataram rebels used the Tengger mountains as hideouts, beginning first in the late seventeenth century, when Trunajaya rebels took refuge there (Jasper, 1926), and then again at the beginning of the eighteenth century, when followers of the famous anti-Dutch and anti-Mataram rebel Surapati (Kumar, 1976) retreated to the mountains after the collapse of their lowland strongholds (Jasper, 1926; Ricklefs, 1981:84). For three-quarters of a century afterward descendants of the Surapati rebels continued to use the mountains as centers of anti-Dutch and anti-Mataram resistance, collapsing only in the face of repeated Dutch incursions into the region. Mataram's failure to control the rebels, and its reliance on Dutch power to aid in their final suppression, were among the reasons the Central Javanese court was forced to cede the entire Eastern Salient to the Netherlands Indies Company (VOC) in 1743 (Ricklefs, 1981:89).

It was only under Dutch authority that a regional administration was finally re-established throughout the Eastern Salient. Some two centuries of regional warfare, however, had taken a grim human toll. Whole territories were without population (ibid.:95); where populations survived, they were scattered about in isolated rural pockets preserving popular rather than courtly traditions. Many of the aggressively populist styles of speech, art, and social interaction still today characteristic of the Eastern Salient can no doubt be traced back to these distinctive historical circumstances. So too can the survival of Java's only regionally-based, explicitly non-Islamic Buda priesthood.

Dutch economic penetration into rural areas of the Eastern Salient began toward the end of the eighteenth century and would eventually contribute to the demise of the Tengger highlands' Buda heritage. The first Dutch visitors to the mountain region noted its rich volcanic soil, and lamented the lack of population to take good commercial advantage of it (Jasper, 1926:11). Coffee was not yet cultivated in the area (Rouffaer, 1921:301). Economic activity in the region focused on swidden cultivation of maize. Throughout Indonesia, the colonial administration regarded swidden terrains as 'waste lands' (Geertz, 1963:58) since their populations were usually too sparse and too mobile to allow for lucrative commercial exploitation. Wherever possible, therefore, swidden cultivators were restricted to small plots of land so as to free the remaining land for commercial enterprise. In Java, this became a particularly effective strategy after the Dutch discovered that coffee flourished in mountain uplands. At the end of the eighteenth century, the Dutch had implemented their first program of forced coffee cultivation in West Java's Priangan highlands. The experiment proved so successful that it soon 'spread to the mountainside areas of the still sparsely settled East Hook' (ibid.) In the Tengger highlands such a coffee program was still hampered by a shortage of local population; in resolving this problem, however, the Dutch had Java's demographic circumstances on their side.

Java's population began a period of spectacular increase in the last half of the eighteenth century and continued to grow steadily throughout most of the nineteenth century (Carey, 1979:46; Geertz, 1963:69). The extension of Dutch colonial power occurred throughout the same period, igniting rebellion in Central Java from 1825 to 1830 and twenty years later provoking famines in which tens of thousands of people died. These latter developments only slightly reduced the pace of population growth; more importantly in the present discussion, they set in motion a century-long movement of population from Central Java to the Eastern Salient. Folk histories from modern Besuki speak of the coming of these migrants. The village itself was founded, local legend says, by a man from Mataram (said to be fleeing political unrest) and a woman from the Tengger highlands. They married and raised many children. Although the man was Central Javanese, he and his wife are said to have been Buda, not Muslim, and they sponsored priestly rites like those celebrated in other Buda communities of the Tengger highlands.

Later migrants are said to have come from the island of Madura off East Java's north coast. In the first decades of the nineteenth century, large areas of the lowlands around Tengger were leased by the Dutch to Chinese landlords; the lands were then cultivated by a 'supply of landless peasants . . . available from the well-populated but *sawah*-less Madura' (Geertz, 1963:59).[4] In the Besuki region, the Madurese originally came as migrant workers on Dutch-owned estates, moving from village to village in a seasonal fashion common throughout areas of the Eastern Salient (Carey, 1979:50). Eventually, however, many of the migrants were awarded sections of the region's swidden 'waste lands' and thus settled in the area. The Madurese in areas to the north and east of the Tengger highlands settled in such large numbers that today they form the majority population in most of those areas' communities. They formed only a minority population in Besuki, and their numbers were even sparser in communities in the Tengger highlands above 1200 meters, since above that altitude coffee does not flourish. Not coincidentally perhaps, today the only remaining non-Islamic communities in the Tengger highlands all live above 1300 meters.

Folk histories from contemporary Besuki provide us with a fascinating picture of the immigrant Madurese population. The Madurese are said to have formed two groups: a small class of wealthy entrepreneurs, who acted as labor managers and coffee agents for the Chinese and Dutch, and a much larger class of landless laborers to work the region's coffee tracts. The Madurese lords enjoyed a legal monopoly on collection of the area's coffee harvest, which they turned over to government agents in exchange for a share of its total value. Besuki's folk histories also take note of an even more curious fact. The landless laborers, it is said, were known as *santri*, and to work on another person's lands in this fashion was known as to *nyantri*. In modern Java, of course, the term *santri* commonly refers to anyone who faithfully adheres to the ritual tenets of Islam (Geertz, 1960a:5-6). Besuki villagers insist that the term originally had no such religious connotation in their village, but referred to what was, in effect, a relationship of dependency or patron-clientship previously unseen in the area.[5]

The Madurese may not have been *santri* according to the term's modern usage, but its religious reference does not appear to have been entirely irrelevant. Folk histories from Besuki also note that the Madurese were the first villagers to pray 'Arab-style', to gather for services on Friday, and to perform the *pasa* fast each year during Ramadan. Even strict Muslims in modern Besuki concede that earlier Javanese immigrants to the community had tended to identify themselves as Buda.[6] One Central Javanese immigrant who became village chief in the mid-nineteenth century, for example, is said to have been such a champion of the Buda faith that he eventually left Besuki because of the influx of Muslims to take up residence in a more exclusively Buda community higher in the Tengger mountains. His successor, an East Javanese immigrant from Singasari, is reported (again even by Muslim apologists today) to have been so vigorously anti-Islamic that on his death bed in the 1860s he asked that his body be cremated (a practice unknown even in Buda villages) in the local spirit shrine rather than buried. After his death, however, local Muslim leaders prevailed against his wish, burying his body and giving the local Buda population his clothes for cremation.

Other facts from late nineteenth-century Besuki similarly suggest a slow decline in Buda influence. By that time, the settlement had begun to take on its modern pattern, Buda people congregated in the upper hamlet and Muslims in a separate hamlet one kilometer below. The Islamic population continued to grow substantially throughout the nineteenth century, largely as a result of a government policy giving land titles to both the coffee lords and their previously landless dependents. The policy was designed to establish a permanent labor force for the coffee industry in the region, and inevitably altered the political balance between the two religious communities in the area. The Buda hamlet in Besuki, for example, was poor by comparison with its kindred Muslim hamlet. The introduction of coffee in the area had not only changed the village's ethnic and religious composition, but had also introduced a new mode of production in which the Buda population was at a distinct disadvantage. The earlier system of swidden cultivation had primarily been subsistence-oriented, with only a small portion of each household's lands devoted to vegetable cash crops to be sold in lowland markets. By contrast, sale of the region's primary cultigen, maize, was (and still is today) forbidden by tradition. The use of wage-labor for maize cultivation was similarly taboo, as was the rental or sale of land to people from outside the community. These and other economic constraints restricted the formation of a genuine native landlord class, and for most of the nineteenth century the communities in the Tengger highlands were renowned throughout Java for their only modest internal differentiation, and for their residents' aggressively egalitarian social and linguistic styles.

As I have discussed elsewhere (Hefner, 1983b), differences of wealth and status were found in these communities, but they were linked to a system of ritual consumption which channelled most surplus wealth into lavish ritual festivals. All adult villagers were obliged to participate in a system of ritual credit and exchange, through which an individual (or a husband-wife couple) would lend large amounts of money and materials to relatives and neighbors sponsoring large ritual festivals. No-one of any social standing could avoid this responsibility, and no other social event rivaled the prestige of the resulting ritual festivals. Once given, however, the value of goods could be recalled by its donor only when she or he planned a similar festival event. When returned, moreover, the goods always came with a value surplus — several kilos of rice, for example, in excess of the amount originally received — intended not as interest on the earlier payment, but as a loan establishing a new debt so that the 'siblingship was not broken' and future exchanges would occur. An individual usually had a large number of such exchange partners, a greater number involving larger amounts of wealth for people of higher social standing and more abundant economic means. The system thus linked wealth, status, and ritual piety, and through it whole communities were in effect drawn into a festival circuit of which the Buda priesthood was a vital part. No festival could occur without the priest's prior invocation of ancestral and guardian deities, for whom, in theory, the festival was really intended. The economic organization of the festival system did not really 'level' economic differences as such, but ensured that an enormous portion of the wealth produced by more successful peasants was consumed in non-productive activities which muted economic differentiation while enhancing differential status. The ritual economy thus had a distinctly self-absorbed communitarian focus.

The social world gradually constructed by Besuki's later immigrants had a far less parochial focus. Buda and Muslim villagers alike were obliged to market their coffee harvests through the local coffee lords, and the latter maintained extensive ties outside the community. These same men were the first to control large tracts of village land and to hire laborers for its cultivation. Oral histories in modern Besuki agree that these men were the first to pay agricultural wages, and the first to control land without themselves cultivating it. The coffee lords devoted their energies to commerce, including not only the marketing of coffee, but the purchase and sale of vegetable crops, and the hiring of coolies for their transport to urban markets. Marketing enterprises became particularly important around 1880, when rail lines were constructed linking the nearby market town of Tumpang to the major urban center of Malang.

Besuki's later immigrants also held themselves aloof, it is said, from the village's traditional system of ritual exchange. While they at first tolerated celebration of Buda-style village festivals, they did not support Buda household and life-passage rites; hence they did not get involved with the local ritual exchange system. Instead they celebrated Islamic rites of life passage, without the lavish feasting and drinking of Buda festivities. They invested their wealth in land and commercial enterprises, and built larger, urban-style homes. Even the poorer Madurese immigrants to Besuki reportedly had little interest in Buda styles of household festivity. Many of these men and women maintained active ties with relatives back in Madura or in nearby areas of East Java. For these people, the social focus of ritual, status, and consumption lay far less singularly in the village.

The cultural balance between Buda and Islam reached a critical turning point in 1872, when villagers elected their first Muslim chief, a man by the name of Haji Muhammed Saleh. Muhammed Saleh was widely regarded as a compromise candidate capable of bridging the two religious communities in Besuki. A wealthy entrepreneur and the first villager ever to make the *hajj* pilgrimage, he was none the less Javanese and a native son of Besuki, from one of the first local families to break into the coffee industry previously monopolized by Madurese. According to modern reports, moreover, Muhammed Saleh defended Buda ritual as a 'village tradition' (*adat desa*) which did not necessarily conflict with Islam. He is said to have been a believer in a moral tale which rose to prominence in Buda communities of the Tengger highlands in the last decades of the nineteenth century. The tale spoke of an ancient non-aggression pact between the prophet Muhammad and a Javanese culture hero by the name of Ajisaka, and enjoined tolerance between the followers of the two leaders.

AJISAKA AND THE COMING OF ISLAM

In Central Javanese traditions, Ajisaka is said to have been an Indian prince who came to Java almost 2000 years ago, expelled the island's demonic king, and imposed a peaceful and prosperous Hindu civilization (Poerwadhie, 1957). The Ajisaka of the Besuki tale wears a somewhat different garb. Here too he is a bearer of civilization, but his is a curious mixture of animism, Hinduism, and Islam. Aji, the story begins, was an orphan raised by the mighty world serpent, Antaboga, a creature associated in Southeast Asian mythology with the physical anchoring of the world. The Antaboga taught Aji a wonderful array of magical powers, including how to fly through the air, render bullets and daggers ineffectual, and be invisible to one's foes. One day, however, the Antaboga realized that Aji had learned everything the wonderful serpent had to teach. Hence it decided it was time for Aji to go to study with an even more powerful teacher, the prophet Muhammad in Mecca.

Aji traveled to distant Arabia, joining Abu Bakar, Usman, Umar, and Ali as students of the great prophet. Aji quickly established himself as Muhammad's most celebrated student. One day the prophet sent him off on an important mission to the *zam-zam* spring to help divine how the prophet could stop a fearsome plague sweeping the land. En route, an archangel appeared to Aji and, taking him aside, taught him powers which not even the prophet Muhammad could know. Aji then returned to Mecca and appeared before Muhammad. Without hearing a word, the prophet realized that Aji had experienced a wonderful transformation, and was now ready to leave Arabia and become his own teacher of men. Aji thus politely took leave of Muhammad, saying that he had to return to Java to teach knowledge of true religion. It was through this series of events that Aji, a curious student of the prophet Muhammad, brought religion to the eastern island.[7]

Arriving in Java, Aji realized that he had left his dagger (*keris*) with the prophet Muhammad in Mecca. He quickly dispatched his servant to fetch it, warning him to allow no-one else to take possession of it. Meanwhile, back in Mecca, the prophet Muhammad came across Aji's dagger and, realizing Aji's error, sent off his own servant to return it to Aji, warning the servant to give it to no-one but Aji himself. A predictable catastrophe thus unfolded. The two servants met mid-route. 'Faithful to his master's command', each demanded to take the dagger, and in the ensuing struggle the two servants killed each other. Days passed, and the two masters grew worried. Each eventually set out on the trail of his servant. They met mid-route, at the site of their servants' clash, and immediately recognized the cause of the tragedy: the servants had been overzealous in obedience to their masters' commands. Muhammad and Aji thus reached an agreement: so that the followers of Aji would never again fight with those of Muhammad, the people of Java should celebrate the Karo festival, or festival of 'two' or 'both'. Before departing, Muhammad and Aji affirmed their pact with the following declaration: when Aji is day, Muhammad will be night; when Muhammad is day, Aji will be night. When Muhammad is male, Aji will be female; when Aji is male, Muhammad will be female. Such is the truth of life. The two of Karo cannot exist independently of each other. Buda and Islam must co-exist as one. Such is the truth of fertility and balance. It is this which is celebrated in the Karo festival.

What is one to make of this tale? Historical evidence from the Tengger highlands indicates that the Aji account became popular only after the 1860s, a time which neatly coincides with the region's politico-economic transformation. My own ethnographic research indicated that the tale was popular even in lowland communities outside of the Tengger highlands. In the Malang and Turen area still today, for example, there are two separate shrines which are supposed to contain the remains of the two slain servants. The caretaker at one such burial shrine (*punden*) explained to me that pilgrims regularly flocked to the area prior to the massacres of 1965–66. This and other evidence indicates that the Ajisaka tale played a role in some areas of the Eastern Salient equivalent to that played by the legendary Sunan Kalijaga in Central Java (Geertz, 1968:25). In both tales, mythical biography provides a metaphor for a society's religious transformation. In keeping with the Eastern Salient's distinctive social history, however, Ajisaka's relationship to Islam is much more tenuous than that of Sunan Kalijaga. Indeed Aji's conversion to Islam is far from clear. Whereas in the Central Javanese tale Islamization is presented as a product of 'an inner change of heart brought on by . . . yoga-like psychic discipline' (ibid.:29), it is questionable in the Aji tale that any conversion has even taken place. Aji is a student of Muhammad, but he has his own ideas as well.

Ajisaka was perhaps a suitable symbol of cultural compromise for a community as complex as nineteenth-century Besuki. The tale is interesting, however, not only for what it says, but for what it neglects to say. Karo had been a ritual tradition in the Tengger highlands long before the appearance of the Aji tale. Indeed, religious leaders in some more exclusively Buda communities always rejected the tale, insisting that it was in effect a tool for conversion to Islam. The Karo liturgy itself, they pointed out, makes no mention of Ajisaka. The rite is instead directed toward guardian and ancestral spirits, thought to play a vital role in the annual renewal of a village's fertility and blessing. The 'two' of Karo, these leaders insisted, refers not to Muhammad and Ajisaka, but to male and female, the living and the dead, water and land — all dualities which are the source of life.

To say then that the Ajisaka tale 'reflected' social reality is to fail to note that it spoke to certain critical realities of nineteenth-century society while ignoring others. It is, of course, just this selective focus which is so fascinating. We see in it the efforts of a localized tradition to come to terms with a rapidly changing social environment. The tale is in a very real sense a document of cultural rationalization, or, at least, attempted rationalization. The circumstances to which it addressed itself were those influenced by political developments in larger Java. The period was characterized by increasing colonial penetration into Java's hinterlands, a spectacular growth in religious schools and Sufi *tarekat* brotherhoods, and the ascendance of Islam to the forefront of efforts to forge an anti-Dutch and anti-aristocratic movement (Carey, 1979:99; Geertz, 1960b; Kartodirdjo, 1972:112). In the light of these developments, the Ajisaka tale bears remarkable testimony to the resilience of Buda tradition in this corner of the Eastern Salient, and the relatively retarded advance of Islam. Even in the final quarter of the nineteenth century, this region had no *pesantren* religious schools, no mosques and no prayer houses (*langgar*). The nearest mosque was in the town of Tumpang, about 15 kilometers away. Even as Muslim a figure as Haji Muhammed Saleh continued to endorse the truths of the Aji tale throughout his administration as village chief, from 1872–87.

By the beginning of the twentieth century, however, Buda influence was in precipitous decline. The changing balance in political culture was sometimes signaled in a curious fashion. In the first decade of the new century, for example, village leaders in Besuki launched a campaign against what they called 'Tengger' pronouns and speech styles. Among other things, the leaders encouraged villagers to learn and use the status-sensitive language levels so important for expressing social position and deference in standard (Central) Javanese speech, but absent or unelaborated in the traditional dialect of the Tengger highlands. Leaders exhorted their people to adopt the more differentiating speech styles by saying, 'You are not Tengger, but Javanese, so why should you speak like Tengger?' Everyday usage of the traditional dialect finally died out in the 1950s.

Other developments were of a more directly religious nature. Leaders in the nearby village of Kembar (6 kilometers from Besuki) voted in 1900 to replace the annual Karo festival — still celebrated up to that time by a Buda priest — with an annual village rite to be celebrated by an Islamic *modin*. Village leaders argued that the Karo festival was too expensive, and that it was important to perform rituals in a 'Javanese fashion'. Despite the wishes of many in the community, the leaders' initiative was possible because a decade earlier the Dutch had brought about an administrative reorganization of villages in the area, the practical result of which was that several previously autonomous Buda communities were made hamlets in larger reorganized communities with majority Muslim populations. Ten years later an event shook the Buda community even further. A wealthy Madurese merchant from Kembar — famous still today because he was the only native in Dutch times ever to own an automobile — hired laborers to erect the region's first mosque. Twelve years later (circa 1922) Besuki's Muslim population followed suit, choosing a former ancestral shrine as the site for the building. Buda residents of the community were shocked. Did these acts not violate the Karo pact?

By this time, however, social change in the region was no longer primarily the product of local social alignments. In the 1930s, Muhammadiyah reformists from the city of Malang launched a program of religious education in Besuki and several neighboring communities; the villages were chosen in part because of their well-known Buda past. The Muhammadiyah effort does not appear to have met with widespread success among popular sectors of the community, but it had a greater influence on village leaders. For the first time in the region's history, leaders in the Muslim community began to collect the annual *zakat* tax. Buda priests were barred from celebrating funerary services. All villagers from this point on were required to be married before an Islamic modin, although those who desired to celebrate Buda wedding services afterwards were allowed to do so.

In several communities adjacent to Besuki, the Buda priest was barred from celebrating the most important of all household rites, the post-mortem purification of family dead, a rite necessary for the souls of one's ancestors to ascend to heaven.

The final period of Buda decline began during the Indonesian independence struggle. Besuki and other mountain communities in this region were important centers of anti-Dutch national resistance. Besuki's own village chief was a leader in a Muslim militia which at one point engaged in a fierce fight with Dutch forces in which 30 Besuki men died. Shortly thereafter, the Dutch intervened directly in the community and replaced the rebel chief (who fled from the village) with a puppet administrator. After independence in 1949, however, the chief triumphantly returned to his village and was reinstalled as village leader. A devoted modernist Muslim and a progressive administrator, this man launched road-building programs, a drinking water project, a program for co-operative home reconstruction — and religious reforms. Around 1955 he banned public consumption of alcohol, public dancing, and the recitation of the Ajisaka tale. He appealed to villagers to stop wasting their wealth in ritual exchange and festivity, and to set their minds to modernizing their village. As a concession to the village's Buda population, however, he continued to allow celebration of the Karo festival, insisting however, that it was not 'religious' but merely a 'village custom'.

The political fortune of the Buda population was finally wiped out in the aftermath of the events of 1965–66. Since Besuki had had no active communist organizers, there was no physical violence in the community. On nearby coffee and tea estates where the Communist Party had been effective in organizing large numbers of rural workers, however, the violence occurred on a horrifying scale. In its aftermath, word spread throughout the region that persons not professing a recognized religion (Islam, Christianity, or Balinese 'reformed' Hinduism) could be accused of being communist. These were the circumstances in which the Besuki chief made his compromise offer to the village's Buda population: if they agreed to identify themselves as Muslim, he would continue to allow celebration of the Karo rite. They would be protected and still be able to preserve something of their tradition.

It has been documented that in many areas of post-1966 Java there was a resurgence of non-Islamic religious organization in response to the excesses of the 1965–66 tragedy. In areas of Central Java, for example, there occurred a significant increase in conversion to Christianity and Hinduism (Geertz, 1972:69, Ricklefs, 1979:124).

Judging by the evidence of the Besuki region, however, we should be careful not to assume too quickly that a similar recession in rural Islamization occurred throughout the island. In the communities around the Besuki area, Islamic social, educational, and political institutions have thrived in the aftermath of 1965–66 while the Buda heritage has died. Although 'Javanist' and mystical religious organizations remain active in urban areas, they have had virtually no influence in the countryside around Besuki. The continuing effectiveness of Muslim organization in the countryside is no clearer than in Besuki itself. A new village chief was elected in 1968. Since taking office, he has overseen the construction of a new mosque, eight new prayer houses, and an Islamic elementary school. He has also launched an ambitious program of Islamic education. There are four religious study groups in the community (two for men and two for women), each of which meets three times a week. Each night their prayers are broadcast into the village through a battery-powered loudspeaker. Having successfully finished his building program, in 1978 the village chief led a company of eight villagers on pilgrimage to Mecca. A year later, the chief pointed out to me that now only 80 of 500 households in the community bothered to prepare the ritual offerings required to invoke ancestral spirits during Karo. In another generation, the chief predicted, the Buda tradition would have disappeared.

Besuki's Buda priest confirmed the chief's prognosis. A frail man in his 70s, the priest will have no successor. Schooled in lowland towns, his sons showed no interest in studying the priestly liturgies. They explained to me that they now considered themselves Muslims, although they noted that they were Muslims the 'Buda way', which is to say that they do not perform *solat* (daily, fixed prayers), fast, or pay the zakat tax. What was the point of preserving their father's faith, they asked? 'Javanese people are Muslims. In your country there are Christians, in India maybe there are Hindus. But to be Javanese means to be Muslim.'

CONVERSION AND WORLD RELIGION

Conversion is a troublesome problem in the anthropology of religion, in part because it so effectively obliges us to reflect upon our assumptions as to the relationship of society and religion, and in part because, at least in instances of conversion on a scale like that here in Besuki, the conversion process itself is inherently multi-layered and uneven. Not everyone in this East Javanese community has been swept away with a Paulist faith in a life-changing religion. Remnant institutions remain from the old. None the less a fundamental reorientation is clearly occurring, and it is in some compelling sense related to a wider range of political, economic, and cultural developments. To speak of the Besuki case as relevant for our understanding of Javanese Islam or conversion in general, however, requires a more self-conscious consideration of the relationship of religious ideas to social process. Does religious belief 'reflect' or 'replicate' some more primary social field? Or is it itself a primary ingredient in social process, an autonomous social force? Does the conversion process reveal anything distinctive about the organization and ideology of world religions? At issue here is the familiar problem of sociocultural integration, or how social and ideational realities cohere to form some kind of 'system', and it is on this point that the Besuki example is of some interest.

In reflecting on the conversion process in Besuki, the first fact which strikes us is that the process occurred a full two centuries after the at least nominal conversion of Central Java to Islam, and that, when it did occur here in the Tengger highlands, it seems to have taken what is by Javanese standards a rather orthodox turn. The two facts are no doubt related. The community's late conversion insured that it was drawn into Java's Islamic community at the same time that Islam throughout the island was experiencing profound revitalization. Equally importantly, here there was no well-entrenched body of courtly religious officials, as in Central Java, to check or challenge Muslim reformist organization. The terms of the religious debate in the Besuki region were thus quite different from those of Central Java or North Sumatra during the same period.[8] They focused not on competing definitions of *adat* and Islam, but on two very different religious traditions. Moreover, five centuries after the fall of Hindu Majapahit, the one tradition had in effect been reduced to the status of a regionally-based village tradition, unable to look to any urban or courtly counterpart, and lacking the educational and organizational tools necessary for responding to the challenge of the national era. By contrast, Islam provided the ready-made terms for a far less parochial idiom, and could look to an already well-tested national organization.

There is none the less clear evidence that the Buda community sought to come to terms with its collapsing social world. Ajisaka — prime character in this community's turn-of-the-century ideological appeal — was a pan-Javanese culture hero, after all, identified in the Aji tale with all of Javanese society rather than with the territory and ancestry of the Tengger highlands. Aji was for 'Javanism', the tale hoped to show, what Muhammad was for Islam. The discontinuity between the pan-Javanese appeal of the myth and the local focus of the Buda community illustrates the unevenness of the community's cultural rationalization. The tale's effort at cultural legitimation, moreover, was fatally flawed from the start. A student of Muhammad, Ajisaka was a compromised culture hero who only postponed a more rigorous Islamic challenge. This may not have been apparent in nineteenth-century Besuki, when even the community's *hajji* chief affirmed that Buda and Islam should live as one. In what we call 'world' religions, however, the full substance of tradition need not be conveyed in the simple face-to-face interaction so important in the religions of small-scale societies. The development and dissemination of cultural ideas is no longer strictly confined to a neatly bordered local community. This heightened receptivity to cultural influence need not be apparent at the time of initial conversion, as the past five centuries of Javanese Islam show so well. Its full realization presumes the development of lines of communication between otherwise 'primordial' social communities.

One could hypothesize, of course, that, had Besuki's Buda people had more time, the changes set in motion with the region's incorporation into a wider social order might eventually have resulted in a rationalized and revitalized Buda. Clifford Geertz (1973) has traced the course of just such a development in nearby Hindu Bali. In the West African context, Robin Horton (1971; 1975a; 1975b) has similarly discussed the emergence of Aladura 'African Churches' in light of a similar process of cosmological rationalization. Horton (1971:102) invites us to consider just what might have been the changes in West African cosmology had the region experienced the past three centuries of socioeconomic change 'without the concomitant influx of Islamic and Christian proselytizers'. He suggests that such distinctive attributes of world religion as belief in a supreme being would probably have developed anyway. Arguing from a modified intellectualist position, Horton believes that traditional religious thought serves (among other things) to provide a theoretical framework for the 'explanation, prediction, and control of space-time events' (ibid.:94). Since most people in small-scale societies spend their lives in restricted, relatively close-knit communities, their religious ideas tend to be more closely adjusted to local circumstances than to the 'macrocosmic' horizons emphasized in world religion. The spirits invoked to explain and control natural and social events thus tend to be local figures — ancestral spirits, nature deities, territorial guardians. Traditional peoples may have a concept of a Supreme Being, Horton asserts, but that deity acquires real intellectual import only when people are drawn from their small communities out into the affairs of a large social macrocosm, where familiar spirit concepts no longer have a sufficiently encompassing explanatory range. It is important to point out that Horton acknowledges that religion is not concerned with explanation and control alone; it also has a 'communion' aspect. Most of the major Christian churches he believes have moved away from the early Church's concern with *both* religious communion and explanation-prediction-control to a more exclusive concern with communion, having ceded the control function to science.

From the perspective of a general theory of conversion, Horton's 'experiment' is interesting for two reasons. First, it leads him to postulate that variations in 'the cult of the supreme being are correlated with variations in the extent to which the macrocosm impinges on the life of the individual' (ibid.:101). People who live in the larger world tend toward more generalized doctrines and cosmology. Second, it suggests that 'acceptance of Islam and Christianity is due as much to development of the traditional cosmology in response to other features of the modern situation as it is to the activities of missionaries'. The world religions are, in a word, 'catalysts — i.e. stimulators and accelerators of changes which were "in the air" anyway' (ibid.:103).

This intellectualist approach to conversion and cosmological change provides one model whereby we might understand, first of all, just why traders, voyagers, and wandering students in the Muslim world are so often associated with a more rigorously monotheistic or, minimally, universalistic style of Islam. They live, Horton would suggest (1975b:391), 'on a more unambiguously international plane', and have 'virtually no residual commitments to the defence of microcosmic boundaries'. Similarly, here in the Besuki region, it provides an explanation of just why village leaders, merchants, and Madurese migrant laborers may have been the first attracted to a more orthodox Islam. They too spent more of their social lives in the macrocosm. The same theory can be applied to developments in the Buda camp. It suggests that the cultural motive for the emergence of the Ajisaka cult was the disruption of local communities, and the sudden expansion of peoples' existential horizons. The principle underlying Horton's argument, we should note, is not a Durkheimian one. Cosmological change does not occur because religion and cosmology are symbolic 'replicators' of some more primary social field, but because, in moving out into an expanded world, people confront a whole host of intellectual problems for which the old cosmology, tailored to the demands of a familiar small-scale society, is no longer sufficient. Only a less particular, more generalizable cosmology is capable of meeting the intellectual challenge of daily life.

I find Horton's analysis of conversion and cosmological change of interest for two more general reasons as well. First, it draws our attention to what is I believe a generally consistent difference between (to overdichotomize once again) small-scale and world religions: that the cosmology of the former tends to devote much more attention to local, ancestral, and territorial spirits (we might call this a 'low cosmology' bias), while that of the latter tends more consistently to emphasize more encompassing or overarching supreme deities (a 'high cosmology' bias). The second thing about Horton's model that I find compelling is its implicit argument that religious ideas in traditional faiths are quite capable of meeting practico-intellectual challenges in a systematically coherent fashion. This argument, I believe, is more consistent with the findings of ethnographic studies of religion than is the view, put forth in at least some Weberian and philosophical treatments of 'primitive' religion, that sees traditional faiths as intellectually stifled by the heavy hand of 'custom'.

Certain aspects of the conversion process here in Besuki, however, suggest that, while Horton's intellectualist model has sensitized us to some of the problems involved in understanding religious change, it has neglected others. Its first limitations, I believe, lie not in its assertion of the practico-theoretical capabilities of traditional religious ideas, but in its implicit suggestion that the 'intellectual' preoccupations of traditional and world religions are fundamentally the same, differing only in the scale of the field to which they are applied. The Besuki example suggests, I think, that when a small society is drawn into the larger 'macrocosm' it is obliged to confront a qualitatively different intellectual — or more precisely, 'moral' — problem. The Ajisaka myth illustrates this qualitative shift in cultural preoccupations. The tale is from a region in the throes of social change, and it shows the quite deliberate effort of a people to come to terms with the challenge of the surrounding society and its religious culture. The concern of the tale is with a kind of moral problem which usually cannot so preoccupy people in a more autonomous small community: self-definition and cultural legitimation in a plural social universe of which this people is now irreversibly part. The cultural 'other' here must to some degree be accommodated within the terms of this people's social identity, rather than in opposition to them. A rival religious culture cannot be dismissed simply as something found only in another society. The peculiar dilemma of life in the 'macrocosm', in other words, is not so much the expansion of one's social horizons alone, but the distinctive problems of morality and self-definition that expansion brings.

It is on this point that one can perhaps appreciate Clifford Geertz's (1973:174) comments (building from Max Weber) on the 'rise to consciousness of the problem of meaning in explicit form' characteristic of modern world religion. This development takes place, Geertz suggests, as a result of a thorough shaking of the foundations of social order. In its wake the challenge brings a fundamental change in the kind of religious questions men and women ask, and the cultural responses they devise. The distinctive cosmological characteristic of this change, Geertz writes, is that the 'sense of sacredness' is 'gathered up' and removed from the everyday world, so as to be 'concentrated in a nucleate (though not necessarily monotheistic) concept of the divine'. The suggestion here resembles that made by Horton — that world religions involve a shift toward high cosmology, and a relative de-emphasis of a low cosmology centered on cults of territorial and ancestral spirits. Again following Weber, however, Geertz uses this point on the 'disenchantment' of the post-traditional world to explain the rationalization of rites and doctrines so often seen in world faiths:

> With this tremendous increase in 'distance,' so to speak, between man and the sacred goes the necessity of sustaining the ties between them in a much more deliberate and critical manner. As the divine can no longer be apprehended *en passant* through numberless concrete, almost reflexive ritual gestures strategically interspersed throughout the general round of life, the establishment of a more general and comprehensive relationship to it becomes, unless one is to abandon concern with it altogether, imperative. (ibid.)

It is in response to this cultural dilemma, Geertz argues, that world religions develop doctrines and beliefs which are 'more abstract, more logically coherent, and more generally phrased' (ibid.:172). They respond to problems of meaning in a 'sweeping, universal, and conclusive manner', so as to 'maintain . . . a sense of a meaningful tie between man and the removed divine'. Traditional religious concepts, by contrast, take a 'piecemeal' approach to the problem of meaning; they are 'discrete and irregular' in the formulas they provide, because they are 'inextricably bound up with secular custom in an almost point-for-point manner' (ibid.:171).

This analysis raises important issues, but it leaves unanswered the question as to just why the 'disenchantment' of the world through the removal of the divine should occur at all. Geertz seems to suggest that it occurs as an inevitable consequence of the shaking of the social order. His own fascinating analysis of Balinese efforts to formalize a body of religious doctrine where before there was 'almost no interest in doctrine' (ibid.:177) provides little evidence that this effort occurred because of a general loss of faith in localized divinities; indeed more recent reports from Bali indicate that, even as Balinese religion changes, ancestral and territorial cults remain strong (Boon, 1779:288). Geertz's beautiful descriptions of events in Bali here prove more faithful to the complex reality of things, to my mind, than does the Weberian theory he borrows. The descriptions clearly indicate that the drive for doctrinal elaboration in Bali has more to do with the island's incorporation into the Indonesian nation state than with the removal of the divine:

> The emergence of the unitary Republic and the enclosure of Bali as a component within it has brought modern education, and modern governmental forms, and modern political consciousness to the island. Radically improved communications have brought increased awareness of, and contact with, the outside world, and provided novel criteria against which to measure the worth both of their own culture and that of others. (Geertz, 1973:182).

It is from this perspective of sociocultural incorporation, I believe, that we can best begin to understand the peculiar problems faced by populations like the Buda community in Besuki, and the powerful appeal of world religions. The small-scale religions customarily studied by anthropologists are so fundamentally integrated into the political, economic, and cultural fabric of a community that it is in some sense impossible to conceive of them in another society. The adherents of such religions, moreover, frequently have the same difficulty: they find it unattractive or impossible to speak of Nuer religion among the Dinka, or Hopi religion among the Sioux. An analyst can trace common themes, styles, and beliefs, but in a more general sense these religions are not 'designed' to be abstracted from the network of institutions with which they are interwoven. They do not try to bridge tribal or ethnic boundaries. It is this quality more than any other, I believe, which explains their distinctive style of cultural appeal. These traditional faiths say 'less' — or say what they say in a less explicitly doctrinaire fashion — because they can assume more. A depth of shared experience ensures that ritual acts and moral issues can be evaluated against the background of unspoken cultural intuitions. The 'functional' burden of doctrinal tuition is borne here by shared socialization.

It is thus misleading to see in this style of cultural appeal evidence of an inherently 'piecemeal' approach to problems of meaning, or, by implication, an absence of rationality. If we take religious rationalization to mean the reordering of 'one's belief in a new and more coherent way to be more in line with what one knows and experiences' (Peel, 1968, cited in Horton, 1971:98), the evidence from Besuki and many other societies indicates that their religions often adapt quickly and intelligently to changing social conditions, particularly where doctrines are not frozen in fixed literary forms preserved by powerful religious hierarchies. What is at issue here is not non-rationality, but a style of rationality which can build its appeals on a much richer and largely unspoken body of shared experience and intuition.

'World' religions, by contrast, are faiths which in some sense span a variety of local social terrains. This almost trivially apparent aspect of their social organization is, to my mind, a more revealing point of departure for their comparison with traditional religions than is their characterization in Weberian analysis as more 'rational'. The problem with the latter approach — besides the obvious fact that 'rationality' and 'rationalization' are ideologically loaded terms in Western intellectual tradition, and they are by no means free of such bias in Weber's usage — is that it confuses a different style of rational appeal with the absence of rationality. In this sense, the Weberian characterization is similar to the views of certain sociolinguists, criticized by Labov (1972), who see the condensed styles of 'restricted' speech found in small speech communities as inherently less rational, rather than rationally elaborated in a different fashion. Whatever the larger limitations of his intellectualist framework, Horton rightly emphasizes that religious beliefs in small-scale societies can be used by their believers in an intelligent and coherent fashion to interpret events in the world; the complexity of such beliefs, and the multiplicity of spirits they address, cannot automatically be taken as signs of intellectual incoherence.

The social organization of world religions thus importantly influences their style of rational elaboration; the analysis of cultural form cannot be separated from the communicative constraints imposed by social organization. A world religion is in a certain sense a kind of secondary community built above and between those given by local social circumstances. The precise nature of that religious community, and the content of its ideological appeal, can, of course, vary significantly and act as a force in its own right. Islam and Theravada Buddhism, for example, frequently adopt a very different stance toward popular belief in ancestral and territorial spirits, and this doctrinal difference can result in quite different religious programs. However, world religions share this one vital social characteristic: bridging more primordial social communities, they cannot assume the same depth of shared experience reflexively verified in the day-to-day interactions of a small society. It is in response to these circumstances that those religions which have succeeded in ascending to world prominence tend to be 'more abstract, more logically coherent, and more generally phrased' (Geertz, 1973:172). Their cultural logic is shaped by the peculiar circumstances of their dissemination. Their frequent concern with formal education, the written word, abstract ethical codes, universal prophets, and holy lands for all of humankind serves to elevate their appeal above more restricted social terrains. They provide the discourse for the elaboration of a secondary moral and ideological identity beyond that given in the immediacy of local groupings.

A tension remains none the less, for, whatever their ideological appeal, the fact remains that knowledge of these faiths is always transmitted in particular communities, each with its own history, identity, and political circumstances. The sometimes tenuous relationship of Javanese Islam to more directly Middle Eastern forms of Islam shows the reality of this tension. The recent history of Javanese Islam also shows that this tension can prove explosive when abstract allegiance to a world faith confronts the substantive reality of that faith's multiple expressions. As the Besuki example shows, however, the same developments which allow for the recognition of such cultural discontinuity can also create conditions favorable to the emergence of a religious idiom less exclusively confined to local circumstances. From this perspective, the 'hallmark of modern consciousness' is not always the 'increasing diversification of individual experience' (Geertz, 1968:15). Whether one speaks of Besuki's Islamization or the rise of orthodox reformism in the modern Arab world, there is a contrary development as well, as more people are drawn into a political process which, by creating similar circumstances in different regions, creates an environment congenial to the adoption of common social idioms and shared political ideals.

To return then to the earlier question, why did Besuki's non-Muslim population not develop a rationalized Buda faith capable of drawing them into modern Indonesia? The obvious answer to this question is that the Indonesia into which they were drawn is itself largely Islamic. But a more compelling answer to this question requires that we attend once again to religion in the 'local context' (Eickelman, 1981). The fact is that in the higher-lying, more homogeneously non-Islamic communities of the Tengger highlands a successful movement for Hindu religious reform has developed (Hefner; 1985). That this did not occur in Besuki indicates another way in which the intellectualist approach to conversion is insufficiently attentive to sociological concerns. For over one hundred years this community has been the site of an ongoing struggle over religion and a people's self-definition. Village leadership played a key role in that struggle, and eventually Muslim leaders were able to regulate and even abolish certain Buda practices. The example points to a fundamental truth: cosmological ideas are not adopted and changed according to an individual's intellectual criteria alone. Religion is not simply a matter of individual belief. At some point it is also a social institution which, like all institutions, depends upon a particular social and political configuration for its reproduction.[9] To speak then of conversion simply from the perspective of an individual's involvement in the 'macrocosm' risks overlooking the fact that the conversion of some people or classes of people is more sociologically significant than others. Surely this was the case in Besuki. The political economy of religious culture ensured that conversion was not simply a matter of individual evaluation, but a social problem, related to the construction of political institutions under which some meanings would be shared and others denied.

NOTES

1. All the village names (but not towns or cities) in the present article have been changed so as to preserve the privacy of villagers.
2. This non-Islamic liturgical tradition is discussed in Hefner 1983a, 1983b; and 1985. The term Buda, one should note, is consistent with usage in other areas of Java. As Pigeaud has noted (1962:IV), the pre-Islamic religion of Java included both Buddhist and Hindu religious orders. Although Hinduism seems to have enjoyed greater court patronage for much of the Hindu-Buddhist era, the religion of old Java has, in Islamic times, been popularly referred to as Buda religion. It is historically unclear just why the Buda designation was adopted rather than a Hindu term. The liturgical tradition of the Tengger highlands, one might add, is descended from a form of popular Sivaism and contains no Buddhist influences.
3. I am using these terms in a loosely contrastive way to cover what is in fact a wide variety of religious forms. Much of what I have later to say concerning 'traditional' religions could, one should note, be applied to

local communities professing world faiths but in fact little involved in the social community of that larger world faith.

4. *Sawah* is wet rice land.

5. Linguistic evidence seems to confirm villagers' claims that the term *santri* can be used without a religious denotation. W.J.S. Poerwadarminta's (1939) Javanese dictionary includes in its listings under *santri* the following 'regional usage': 'batur lanang, batur sing ngupakara rajakaya', or, roughly, a male servant who cares for another person's livestock or productive property.

6. Interestingly, the term *abangan*, used in many areas of Java to refer to people of nominal Islamic persuasion (cf. Geertz, 1960), is rarely used in Besuki. Villagers consider the term derogatory. Non-Muslims traditionally referred to themselves as Buda, while nominal Muslims have preferred to call themselves 'Javanese-' or 'Buda-Muslims'.

7. Myths rarely come in one form, and not surprisingly there are other versions of this portion of the Aji tale which cast a different light on the origins of his special knowledge: the spirit who took Aji aside, some Muslim informants explained to me, was an *iblis* devil, not an archangel.

8. Cf. Siegel, 1969 on North Sumatra and Abdullah 1966 on West Sumatra.

9. Cf. Eickelman, 1978; Hefner, 1983a on cultural reproduction and social theory.

REFERENCES

Abdullah, Taufik (1966), 'Adat and Islam: An Examination of Conflict in Minangkabau', *Indonesia*, 2:1–24.

Boon, James A. (1979) 'Balinese Temple Politics and the Religious Revitalization of Caste Ideals', in A.L. Becker and Aram A. Yengoyan (eds.), *The Imagination of Reality*, Norwood (New Jersey): Ablex Publishers, 271–91.

Carey, P.B.R. (1979), 'Aspects of Javanese history in the nineteenth century', in Harry Aveling (ed.), *The Development of Indonesian Society*, Queensland (Australia): University of Queensland Press, 45–105.

De Graaf, H.J. (1970), 'Southeast Asian Islam to the eighteenth century', in P.M. Holt, Ann K.S. Lambton, and Bernard Lewis (eds.), *The Cambridge History of Islam*. Volume 2: Cambridge: Cambridge University Press, 123–54.

Eickelman, Dale F. (1978), 'The art of memory: Islamic education and its social reproduction', *Comparative Studies in Society and History*, 20:485–516.

Ensink, Jacob (1978), 'Siva-Buddhism in Java and Bali', in Heinze Bechert (ed.), *Buddhism in Ceylon and Studies on Religious Syncretism in Buddhist Countries*. Gottingen: Vandenhoeck and Ruprecht, 179–98.

Geertz, Clifford (1960a), *The Religion of Java*. Glencoe (Il.): The Free Press.

—— (1960b), 'The Javanese *kijaji*: the changing role of a cultural broker', *Comparative Studies in Society and History*, 2:228–49.

—— (1963), *Agricultural Involution*. Berkeley: University of California Press.

—— (1968), *Islam Observed*. Chicago: University of Chicago Press.

—— (1972), 'Religious change and social order in Soeharto's Indonesia', *Asia*, 27–62–84.

—— (1973), '"Internal conversion" in contemporary Bali', in *The interpretation of Cultures*. New York: Basic Books, 170–89.

Hefner, Robert W. (1983a), 'Ritual and cultural reproduction in non-Islamic Java', *American Ethnologist*, 10:665–83.

—— (1983b), 'The problem of preference: economic and ritual change in highlands Java', *Man* (n.s.), 18:669–89.

—— (1985), *Hindu Javanese: Tengger Tradition and Islam*. Princeton: Princeton University Press.

Horton, Robin (1971), 'African conversion', *Africa*, 41:85–108.

—— (1975a), 'On the rationality of conversion: part I', *Africa*, 41:219–35.

—— (1975b), 'On the rationality of conversion; part II', *Africa*, 46:373–99.

Jasper, J.E. (1926), *Tengger en de Tenggereezen*. Batavia: Druk Van G. Kolff.

Kartodirdjo, Sartono (1972), 'Agrarian radicalism in Java: its setting and development', in Claire Holt (ed.), *Culture and Politics in Indonesia*. Ithaca: Cornell University Press, 70–125.

Kumar, Ann (1976), *Surapati: Man and Legend*. Leiden: E.J. Brill.

Labov, William (1972), 'The logic of non-standard English', in P.P. Giglioli (ed.), *Language and Social Context*. Baltimore: Penguin, 179–215.

Peel, J.D.Y. (1968), *Aladura: A Religious Movement among the Yoruba*. London: Oxford University Press.

Pigeaud, Th. G. Th. (1962), *Java in the 14th Century* (4 vols.). The Hague: Martinus Nijhoff.

—— (1967), *Literature of Java* (3 vols.). The Hague: Martinus Nijhoff.

Poerwadarminta, W.J.S., (1939). *Bausastra Jawa*. Batavia: J.B. Wolters.

Poerwadhie, Atmohihardjo (1957), 'Adjisaka sanes babad utawi sedjarah', *Djaja Baja*, 11:20: 18–30.

Rassers, W.H. (1959), *Panji, The Culture Hero: A Structural Study of Religion in Java*. The Hague: Martinus Nijhoff.

Ricklefs, M.C. (1979), 'Six centuries of Islamization in Java', in Nehemia Levtzion (ed.), *Conversion to Islam*, New York: Holmes and Meier, 100–128.

—— (1981), *A History of Modern Indonesia*. Bloomington: Indiana University Press.

Robson, S.O. (1981), 'Java at the crossroads', *Bijdragen tot de Taal-, Land-, en Volkenkunde*, 137:259–92.

Rouffaer, G.P. (1921), 'Tenggereezen', *Encyclopaedie van Nederlandsche-Indie*, pp. 298–308. Leiden: Brill.

Siegel, J.T. (1969), *The Rope of God*. Berkeley: University of California Press.

4

Structural Determinants of Urban Islamic Protest in Northern Nigeria: A Note on Method, Mediation and Materialist Explanation

Paul M. Lubeck

By way of introduction it may be helpful to the reader to know that consideration of the problem discussed in this essay originated in numerous discussions with colleagues about proper methods of analyzing Islamic social movements. The conference at which earlier versions of the papers in this volume were first presented made an effort to address this problem but, as often occurs at academic conferences, an interesting methodological debate had to give way to organizational constraints. At the same time, however, I believe that social scientific analysis of Islamic social and political movements will be advanced if the methodological debate over the respective roles of *material conditions* and *culture* is taken up again in this essay. I would be less than candid if I were to suggest that I have no position on this question, or that my position is typical of scholars who study Islamic social movements. But this is just the problem that I believe constrains 'Islamic studies' from explaining rather than merely describing one of the most dynamic social forces in the contemporary Third World/periphery.

The problem is not just to describe Islamic social movements but to explain why they occur when and where they do. In my view, one of the major obstacles facing those who wish to explain militant Islamic social movements lies in their weak understanding of materialist method broadly understood, their unfamiliarity with the innovations of neo-Marxists during the past two decades, and, of course, the long standing preference of many Islamic scholars for cultural and idealist explanations that focus on the alleged unity and essentialism of Islamic societies.[1]

Having restated the standard materialist critique of orthodox Islamic studies, let me emphasize how important I believe cultural factors are in any religious-based social movement. None the less, my assumption is that Muslims are like the rest of us. Like Catholics, for example, they possess a scriptural tradition that is believed to be transcendentally inspired, and a complex web of institutions that maintain purity and reproduce beliefs among the believers for generation after generation. Yet Catholicism is in turmoil, especially in Latin America, over the application and interpretations of these time-honored beliefs. Indeed, the theology of liberation is transforming the bottom of a once authoritarian hierarchical system, a transformation that is inseparable from the agony and misery of the Latin American popular classes.[2] So dramatic is the transformation of the lower orders of the Catholic and other established Christian churches that the editors of the *Monthly Review*, one of America's oldest and most influential Marxist journals, recently wrote:

> It is now becoming clear — in what may turn out to be one of history's most startling reversals — that what nearly everyone believed was simply not true. A widespread rapprochment between religion and the left is actually taking place. Exactly when and where it started may be difficult to establish, but that by now it is a reality cannot be doubted. (*Monthly Review*, 1984:2)

The relevance of the Christian and Marxist rethinking of their respective dogmas to the methodology of Islamic studies is not that the three discourses are textually based, but rather that analysts of the first two have reconsidered their object of inquiry in the light of historical change and from the perspective of the popular classes rather than elites.[3]

Before turning to an analysis of two Islamic social movements in northern Nigeria, and how materialist method may explain divergent outcomes, I want to articulate some rules that guide my interpretation of the relationship of material conditions and social structures to cultural institutions and ideas. To begin, the relevance of my reference to Catholic liberation theology and the Marxist discovery of revolutionary Christian movements to the debate over the proper method of analyzing Islamic social movements concerns the *choice of interpretation* by the social scientist. Obviously, if the Marxist editing the *Monthly Review*, or the founders of the theology of liberation, chose to select and focus upon the most rigid and mutually antagonistic statements existent in their respective texts, then the scintillating and creative products of their discourse could never have appeared. If one were to apply their example to a possible dialogue between neo-Marxist social scientists and Islamic scholars in the cultural-interpretative tradition, then it is necessary for the former to take Islamic culture and ideas seriously and for the latter to examine Marxist methodological texts that allow for cultural determination at many levels and instances. Since the intended audience for this argument is Islamic scholars rather than neo-Marxist social scientists, I shall center attention on the problem of choice in Marxist texts.

One of the ways one can advance this proposed discourse is to acknowledge the diversity of interpretations available in Marx's classical writings. While one may *choose* to emphasize, as is so often the case in polemical writings, the most rigid interpretation of the relationship between material conditions and social structure of cultural institutions and ideas, it is always a conscious choice of the interpreter. For example, the most commonly cited of Marx's statements on this question is taken from *A Preface to a Critique of Political Economy* where the founder of historical materialism describes the formation of his method:

> The general conclusion at which I arrived and which, once reached, continued to serve as the leading thread in my studies, may be briefly summed up as follows: In the social production which men [sic] carry on they enter into definite relations that are indispensable and independent of their will; these relations of production correspond to a definite state of development of their material powers of production. The sum total of these relations of production constitutes the economic structure of society — the real foundation, on which rise legal and political superstructures and to which correspond definite forms of social consciousness. The mode of production in material life determines the general character of the social, political and spiritual process of life (Marx, 1904:II).

One would be hard pressed to rebut charges that Marx was a vulgar economic determinist if this text were his sole statement on this methodological point. Fortunately, while the text was hegemonic, especially among orthodox Marxist-Leninists, two other relevant texts, *The German Ideology* and the *Grundrisse*, offer a more dialectical and autonomous role for culture. In the first, Marx argues that one must expound the real process of production and see this mode of production:

> . . . as the real basis of all history; and to show it in its actions as State, to explain all the different theoretical products and forms of consciousness, religion, philosophy, ethics, etc., etc., and trace

their origins and growth from that basis; by which means, of course, the whole thing can be depicted in its totality (and therefore, too, the reciprocal action of these various sides on one another) (Marx, 1970:58).

For our purposes the emphasis he places on the 'reciprocal action of these various sides on one another' differs from the first quotation from the *Preface*, as does the following quote from the *Grundrisse* where he attacks vulgar economism:

Reduced to their real meaning, these commonplaces express more than their preachers know, namely, that every form of production creates its own legal relations, forms of government, etc. The crudity and the shortcomings of the conception lie in the tendency to see only an accidental reflective connection in what constitutes an organic union (McLellan, 1977:349).

Now it is obvious that the choice of one of the three quotations, a conscious interpretative decision by any scholar, would virtually determine one's understanding of Marxist materialist method. All three are textual and therefore valid expressions of the author's perspective. But other than for polemicists or professional anti-Marxists, of what use is it to emphasize the rigid and determinist writings rather than the latter two, which allow a more flexible, dialectical and reciprocal interpretation of the relationship between material conditions and ideas?

My own methodological position relies on the latter two quotations. My assumption is that culture and material-social structures are in a dialectical and reciprocal relationship with each other. And the notion that ideas are an inert, accidental reflection of a material base, without the weight of history and the tensions exerted by previous modes of production and their associated cultures, seems to be extremely crude. Equally important, if one chooses to accept the vulgar materialist determinism of the *Preface*, one not only ignores the latter two texts, but eliminates the creative dialogue that forms the basis of the theology of liberation and the reassessment promised by the *Monthly Review*.

At the same time, I do not believe that Islamic culture in and of itself can explain the rise of Islamic social movements, for there are always plenty of ideas around that promise to resolve any social problem or crisis. It is the notion of an organic union, that is, a situation where concrete material and social conditions correspond to a particular set of ideas in a particular time and social setting, that best explains the rise and trajectory of a particular social movement, be it Islamic, Christian or Marxist. Nor does the analytical process end once one discovers the 'fit' between concrete material and social conditions that sustain and reproduce a social movement with a corresponding and appropriate social consciousness. Instead, mediating organizations like the state must be evaluated with regard to their capacity to rationalize, to co-opt or to repress an Islamic social movement once the fit between ideology and material circumstances crystallizes into an active movement. Again, if the ideas advocating jihad, Mahdist rebellion or any other anti-institutional social movement inspired by Islamic culture were determinant, then such upheavals would occur daily in all states with Islamic populations. But they do not. Hence, scholars must analyze both the social and material conditions as well as the discourses and texts that provide the ideologies for anti-institutional social movements. If not, one can never explain the when, where and why of any Islamic social movement.

Advocating that scholars investigate the 'fit' between material social conditions and the ideas that inspire an Islamic social movement does *not* mean assuming *a priori* a functionalist linkage, without contradictory and historically particular elements. The application of the concept of 'organic union' means that in order for a society to exist in relative stability and to reproduce itself materially, socially, and culturally, there must be some correspondence among economic, political and culture institutions. This does not mean that historically prior institutions, practices and beliefs are not present in any situation, but rather that they must be subordinated to the dominant mode or else the society is thrown into great tension, resulting in social upheaval and even social revolution, as in the Iranian case. Even if the historically prior mode is subordinated to a newer dominant mode, a tension usually exists such that social actors often legitimate their cause by referring to traditional rights enjoyed under the historically prior mode.

In the contemporary Muslim world virtually no society has escaped the effects of industrial capitalism in its transnational form, especially since the petroleum boom. The two modes — Islamic prebendal-feudal and transitional industrial capitalist — are joined in a complex, dialectical whole, where each constrains the other and where the struggle for dominance sometimes takes the form of Islamic social movements. Yet, history is crucial. And historically generated institutions, elites and status groups are seminal mediators of the dialectical tension between the Islamic mode and the industrial capitalist mode. At the same time, it is erroneous to interpret the rise of Islamic social movements as the unmediated product of the petroleum boom. Ironically, this appears to be the position of the neo-conservative historian, Daniel Pipes (1980:41):

> The evidence suggests that the oil boom is primarily responsible for the surge in Islamic political activities during the seventies. It brought Muslims three things missing in their modern history: a sign of Islam's validity; centers of Islamic power; and a charismatic leader. Oil thus increased receptivity to Islam, provided the means to further it, and produced a model Muslim movement to inspire others.

Again, this is an example of vulgar economism, one that ignores the particular, concrete historical process underlying diverse Islamic social movements and, most egregiously, the reciprocal effect of mediating institutions such as the state or the legitimacy of the socio-economic system in the eyes of the popular classes. Such over-generalized conceptions of Islamic actors, coupled with an explicitly unmediated economic determinist interpretation of the relationship between the oil boom and the production of 'a model Muslim movement', is a useless and bankrupt intellectual exercise. Where is the autonomy of cultural and political institutions in this mechanical schema? What of the role of the Islamic discourse on questions of social justice, external alliances and the corrupt extravagances of the ruling groups?

In the following section I intend to show how mediating structures — factory management and state organization — intervene among members of the same social stratum with a particular social status, that of Qur'anic student, so as to orient them toward particular interpretations of an ongoing and historically rooted Islamic discourse. But before moving to the situation of Qur'anic students in northern Nigerian cities, I want to refer back to the problem of interpretation of texts and the importance of flexible and open interpretations of founding texts. Compare the following quotation from Marx (*Capital* Vol. III, no less!) with that, above, of the historian Pipes, with regard to the importance of mediating factors between economic structures and socio-cultural phenomena. After describing the mode of surplus extraction by the dominant class from the direct producers and its relationship to the political institutions and the 'specific form of the state', Marx qualifies this often quoted statement (1982:927):

This does not prevent the same economic basis — the same in its major conditions — from displaying endless variations and gradations in its appearance, as the result of innumerable different empirical circumstances, natural conditions, racial relations, historical influences acting from outside, etc., and these can only be understood by analysing these empirically given conditions.

To summarize: while material factors structure what is possible to exist and be reproduced as a social form (e.g., social democracy, or female liberation in an industrial capitalist society), the relatively autonomous and reciprocal effect of mediating institutions and historically formed cultures specifies the concrete, empirically existent phenomena which one observes as an Islamic social movement.

ORGANIZATIONAL MEDIATION, ISLAMIC CULTURE AND POPULAR SOCIAL MOVEMENTS

The task at this stage is to apply the method that I have advocated to the Muslim city of Kano, Nigeria, which is a center of both Muslim scholarship and economic activity for the northern region of Nigeria. Since Allan Christelow, in his essay below, provides a general background to Nigeria and Islam, I shall move directly to the problem of Islamic social movements among the popular classes (the *talakawa*, or commoners) of the Hausa-speaking cities of northern Nigeria, of which Kano is both the largest (*circa* 1.5 million) and most politically volatile, especially since the onset of the petroleum boom. My objective is to show how talakawa-origin migrants to the city, many of whom enter the labor market through peripatetic Qur'anic student networks, employ Islamic concepts of social justice, legitimate rebellion and, in one instance, Mahdist ideology, in order to cope with new forms of social inequality in a city undergoing the turbulent transition to semi-industrial capitalism.[3]

The argument is relatively simple. There are two categories of laborers *cum* Qur'anic students: industrial workers who remain integrated into Qur'anic school networks, and a more occupationally diverse group who are often laborers but are defined in the local Islamic discourse as *gardawa*, meaning a youth or adult who is unmarried, who wanders from community to community begging for subsistence and marginal laboring opportunities while, at the same time, assuming the status of a Qur'anic student or minor *mallam* (teacher). A significant proportion of the Hausa-speaking, Muslim industrial workers entered the labor market as gardawa, as did the marginalized, perhaps lumpen, laborers who continue to pursue Islamic studies and attach themselves to the leading Islamic scholars. From the beginning of the 1960s at the earliest a group of gardawa attached themselves to one Alhaji Mohammed Marwa, known locally as *Maitatsine* (literally, the one who damns). The latter is said to have declared himself a prophet, perhaps the Mahdi, sometime during 1979, and in December 1980 instigated a millenarian insurrection lasting ten days, in which his gardawa occupied sections of the old city (Birni) and held off the Nigerian security forces until the army intervened with heavier weapons. Maitatsine was killed and a section of the city was destroyed, along with five to ten thousand of his followers, hostages and innocent bystanders. The Maitatsine insurrection represented the most devastating urban social upheaval since the 1966 communal riots that presaged the Nigerian civil war. Nor was Kano the last insurrection; for with great regularity, his followers have revolted against both religious and secular authorities on at least four subsequent occasions: Kaduna (1982), Bulum-Ketu near Maiduguri (1982), Jimeta near Yola (1984) and Gombe (1985). (The last case is so recent that it should be coded as tentative, for any Islamic protest against the authorities could be rationalized, and repressive force justified, merely by defining it as 'Yan Tatsine (the followers of Maitatsine.)

What do all of these millenarian eruptions have in common? First, all occurred during the dry season, from December to April. Secondly, in virtually every case the 'Yan Tatsine attacked the police and the local population only after confrontations with the authorities, the threat of exile, or an attempt by the police to arrest the local leader and remove him from the separate community that they had formed. And finally, members of the sect are almost always described as gardawa, and/or performers of menial tasks such as watercarriers, houseboys or shoemakers. In the case of Kano, a member of a declining occupation, that of gatekeeper to one of Kano's many gates, is said to be a member of the sect.

In order to analyze this movement and compare it to the activities of Muslim industrial workers, who also employed Islamic symbols, rationale and leadership in their struggle with employers over pay and working conditions, I shall limit this discussion to the insurrection that occurred at Kano. Note that although many industrial workers (e.g., 13.8 per cent of Hausa-Fulani workers surveyed) (Lubeck, 1986) were drawn from gardawa networks, neither the official reports of inquiry nor my own research indicated any participation by industrial workers in the 'Yan Tatsine movement. And further, what is it about the empirical circumstances and modes of mediation between structural experience and Islamic consciousness that orients one group of gardawa toward reformist class conflict at the factory, while the other, more marginalized gardawa join the millenarian insurrection of Maitatsine?

In order to answer this question, one should view the gardawa and their Qur'anic networks in historical perspective, and especially the role that the gardawa played in the 'moral economy' of pre-colonial and pre-capitalist northern Nigeria. In the following sections I shall describe the material, social and cultural basis of gardawa networks from the nineteenth century through the colonial-mercantile capitalist period until the onset of the petroleum boom. Then the organizational situation of industrial workers and their use of Islamic culture, leadership and tactics will be compared to that of Maitatsine's marginalized gardawa. In social science language, the difference between the Islamic orientation and actions of the two groups is determined by their differing relationship to the Nigerian state and the labor process of industrial production. While both groups recruit many of their members from the gardawa, the industrial situation and the role of the state mediated in such a way as to direct the industrial workers toward reform along more quietist Islamic lines, while directing the marginalized gardawa toward the millenarian insurrection of Maitatsine.

QUR'ANIC SCHOOLS AND ISLAMIC NETWORKS IN NINETEENTH-CENTURY KANO

While Islamic networks in the peripatetic tradition pre-date the jihad of Usuman dan Fodio (1804), it is convenient to begin with the era of the Sokoto Caliphate because, as a Muslim empire, Islamic networks and Qur'anic schools were integral to the expansion, reproduction, and ideological integration of the pre-capitalist social formation. One should note that dan Fodio was a wandering Qur'anic student in his youth. The dominant class, an urban-resident, office-holding Muslim aristocracy, legitimated its domination and exploitation of the peasantry through the ideology of Muslim law. Whatever position one might take on the relationship of nineteenth-century practice to the ideals of the shari'a, it is certain that the leaders of the jihad encouraged the expansion of Islamic learning and scholarship. For the peasantry, moreover, Islamic learning offered one of the few routes, together with trade, for achieving upward mobility as a mallam, as a scribe or as a minor official in the state's patrimonial bureaucracy.[5]

While the Islamic state and ideology integrated this pre-capitalist social formation, it was for economic and ecological reasons that the peripatetic tradition took the form of seasonal migration of youths from the countryside to the centers of commerce and handicraft industry, located in both rural and urban areas. Situated in a harsh environment where rainfall was uncertain, and even when abundant fell only during four months of the year, the peripatetic tradition related harmoniously to the needs and risks of the peasant household economy. At harvest time, and especially among the rural Hausa, grain is put aside and conserved to feed active farming members of the household during the next rainy season. To fail to do so would risk the survival of the household. Children and youths, while of critical importance during the periods of planting and harvesting, become a drain on household grain supplies during the months following harvest and up until the rains of the planting season. Given this ecological constraint on household security, the tradition of the peripatetic mallam offered a positive economic benefit in that it lowered the household's risk of famine and even enhanced the skills of the child, while formally serving the ideological goal of expanding and deepening the knowledge and practice of Islam within the Sokoto Caliphate. Children and youths sent wandering with a mallam are said by parents to obtain the discipline and isolation that is believed necesssary for success in Islamic scholarship. Although mallams often took their dependents to rural areas where they farmed for the mallam, many also migrated to the cities and centers of commerce located on the trade routes of the Sokoto Caliphate. Here the practice called for youths and children to beg for alms in the more affluent centers of the Muslim state, to study the Qur'an or more advanced texts and, at the same time, to engage in productive labor either for their mallam or for wages as in the case of the indigo dyeing industry. According to Shea (1975), the latter industry often required infusions of labor in order to dye cloth for passing caravans whose orders exceeded a merchant's standing supply. Because Qur'anic students were strangers in these communities, they were ideally suited for casual wage laborers in the export-oriented cloth trade that was a pillar of Kano's economy during the nineteenth century. Furthermore, Shea notes an instance where a Kano mallam built dye pits in the city expressly for Qur'anic students to support themselves during the dry season migration to the city.

Within the confines of the pre-capitalist Muslim social formation, therefore, the peripatetic tradition worked in harmony with the ecological constraints, the ideological goals and the economic needs of the situation. It is clear that the gardawa and peripatetic Qur'anic schools extended Islamic belief among the talakawa. Therefore, these institutions played an important role in the ideological, political, and, to a degree, the economic reproduction of pre-capitalist society. More importantly, the ethics and status-honor norms of the pre-capitalist society made it necessary that Qur'anic students receive alms in the form of food and shelter. Given the relief from peasant grain consumption which Qur'anic migration from rural to urban areas necessarily entails, the institution of Qur'anic schools is actually a form of redistribution of wealth from the more affluent urban dwellers to the sons of rural dwellers under the norms of Islamic charity. Further, wandering Qur'anic students also learned valuable craft and commercial skills during their urban sojourns and many were probably absorbed into the households of their urban patrons.

In return for feeding, housing, and perhaps clothing the students of a mallam, the head of the household could take advantage of the scholarly and ritual services of the mallam. Usually, the peripatetic mallams lived in the entry-room of an urban compound, thus the term was coined 'mallamin soro' (literally, 'entry-way mallam'). Sons often followed the relationship that had been established between their fathers and a patron; rural-urban linkages reduced the domination of the city over the countryside; and new ideas both religious and secular, were disseminated from urban centers to the countryside.

Both ecological and economic factors provided the material basis of the gardawa and the peripatetic tradition's contribution to political and cultural integration in the Sokoto Caliphate. Shea (1983) notes that the peripatetic gardawa constituted a 'floating labor pool' in craft centers, that they probably worked for less than 'settled family men' and that they were directed by their more knowledgeable Qur'anic teachers, whose information networks enabled them to direct gardawa to economic centers demanding seasonal unskilled labor. It is important to stress the interrelationship of ecology, economy, and ideology when evaluating the role of the gardawa. Because most were seasonal in that they returned home to farm when the rains came, they were an ideal labor category for the handicraft industry, which was dominated by Muslim mercantile capitalists. For they were mobile and available, yet their temporary residence enabled their employers to avoid the expense of a permanent client relationship, except when it was their choice.

To conclude, Islamic and Qur'anic networks functioned to

integrate both ideologically and socially separated rural and urban areas of the pre-capitalist social formation. In reproducing the ideological and political conditions for the maintenance of the Islamic Hausa social formation, the peripatetic Qur'anic school network reduced the burdens of a peasantry who existed in a precarious relationship within a harsh and uncertain environment. Qur'anic students residing in urban areas not only were the recipients of urban charity and social redistribution but they also provided an additional source of labor for craft and commercial enterprises. Finally, it is noteworthy that peripatetic Qur'anic schools thrived because they were supported by the dominant class that controlled the state and because they were positively integrated into the economic needs of the urban economy.

QUR'ANIC NETWORKS, COLONIAL RULE, AND MERCANTILE CAPITALISM

Colonial rule did not interfere with Islamic practice in the Sokoto Caliphate. In fact, 'indirect rule' created an alliance between a faction of the Muslim aristocracy and the colonial state in which foreign trading firms, acting through layers of agents, linked the pre-existing peasant household and market sectors to the capitalist world economy. In this sense, colonial mercantile capitalism, though subordinated to industrial capitalism located in western Europe, was articulated on to the pre-existing Islamic Hausa social formation. Because neither white settlers, nor mining capital, nor foreign plantations accompanied British overrule, capitalism did not completely penetrate the peasantry or the rural economy, except through trade, credit and new items of consumption. True, this process gradually eroded the autonomy and security of the household and its material security, but it took several decades to complete. In urban centers, such as Kano, foreign firms employed seasonal wage laborers only during the evacuation of peasant-produced staples such as groundnuts and cotton. Hence, capitalism at the level of production either in agriculture, mining, or industry was not introduced to any significant degree during the colonial period. As a result, a backward, colonial form of capitalism was articulated on to a pre-capitalist social formation. This process strengthened the technical domination of the ruling class over the peasantry, reinforced and even extended the influence of Islamic institutions, in part as a result of Muslim resistance, and deepened the penetration of market and commodity relations into areas not previously governed by Muslim mercantile capitalism. Clearly, the

90

contradictions of this articulation expressed themselves as tensions in the state apparatus: there were too few colonial officers to correct traditional abuses of the now-salaried Muslim officeholders *cum* colonial bureaucrats; an urban land market and any technical development of agrarian production were resisted by colonial officials; and, most importantly, authoritarian rule on the part of the Emir was enhanced further because the traditional checks on centralized power had been removed by the British (Watts, 1983; Fika, 1978).

Colonial Kano was one of the few pre-capitalist cities to benefit from the railhead, the groundnut trade, and the colonial infrastructural investments made by the state from indirect taxation of peasant production. Again, there was no reason for the seasonal Qur'anic migrations to Kano to end, since the peasant village and the pre-capitalist Muslim city remained intact. Indeed, the development of motor roads probably increased the flow of Qur'anic students through cities like Kano, for the advent of railway and motor transport reduced the number and economic importance of urban centers along caravan routes and increased the importance of those that were located on rail and motor roads. Hence, wandering gardawa fortunate enough to receive charity in the form of transportation followed the new colonial transportation network which led to cities like Kano. One could argue, moreover, that the *Pax Britannica*, by ending slave raiding and interstate warfare, actually increased the opportunities for Qur'anic students to migrate either permanently or seasonally to cities like Kano. In general, therefore, Islamic networks and the institutions of Qur'anic schools did not decline and probably increased among the talakawa as a reaction to colonial conquest by Christians, the historical enemy of the Muslim community.

QUR'ANIC STUDENTS AND THE LABOR MARKET PRIOR TO THE PETROLEUM BOOM

Prior to 1974–75 when the effects of the petroleum revenues accelerated capitalist growth, state centralization, and inflation of the costs of subsistence, or means of consumption, Qur'anic students continued to relate harmoniously to the urban economy and were even absorbed into Kano's industrial labor force. It is noteworthy that among Hausa and Fulani workers enumerated in an industrial survey during 1971, 13.8 per cent responded to an open-ended question that, initially, they had migrated to Kano in order to pursue Qur'anic studies (Lubeck, 1986). Clearly, much of the historical pattern of seasonal peripatetic migration from the rural areas to urban Kano continued and was articulated first to the urban labor market and from there to the industries which were stimulated by the production needs arising from the Nigerian civil war.

If one examines the daily life of a Qur'anic student, one discovers that they rise early in the morning to pray and to study their lessons until mid-morning. Then it is customary for them to pursue casual labor or handicrafts. These involve diverse activities such as sewing multi-colored and distinctly Muslim caps, sewing buttons on garments for their mallams, dyeing cloth in the traditional style, or, for older students, repairing dried mud houses during the dry season. Within the public markets the Islamic institutional influence of the bazaar economy is structured so that, traditionally, Qur'anic students are given the right to carry packages for shoppers. To support Qur'anic students, therefore, is a form of almsgiving for the Muslim shopper. Examples abound of the way in which Qur'anic students, especially during the dry season, fulfil the need for casual labor services in the Muslim cities of northern Nigeria. On a more permanent basis, the seclusion of married women creates a need for children to transport raw materials and finished products from one household to another and from the household to the market: women who do not have suitable children often rely on Qur'anic students to do this.

It is also of interest to note that the status of Qur'anic students exists as an objective category in the minds of youths who migrate to cities purely for economic reasons. This was apparent when I interviewed several factory workers regarding their adjustment to the city. Youths who were new to the city and who lacked patronage or other support actually *assumed* the status of Qur'anic students so that they could subsist on the alms, usually food, distributed by urban dwellers in the evening to students who chanted Qur'anic verses in front of each household. In this sense, the status of Qur'anic student functions as a pre-capitalist subsistence institution, a kind of socially defined absolute level of subsistence that assures minimal survival for youths migrating to the city. Moreover, the fact that this subsistence institution is Islamic means that it resists the penetration of capitalism better than most pre-capitalist institutions.

Given the introduction of capitalist production in the form of import-substitution industries during the late 1950s and the 1960s, how did Qur'anic networks relate to the urban labor market and industrial wage labor? Of course, the stated origins and purposes of both activities are opposed to each other: on the one hand, Qur'anic students seek casual wage labor in order to pursue Islamic learning and thus to reproduce, as much as is historically possible, the pre-capitalist institutions that gave rise to Islamic society. And on the other hand, the urban labor market acts to allocate labor especially to factories, whose ultimate purpose is to accumulate capital and to expand capitalist industrialization. Curiously, the two activities — Qur'anic schooling and industrial wage labor — were both harmonious and antagonistic to each other. Interviews with industrial workers indicate that when Qur'anic students carried packages at the market or participated in casual labor, they gradually became absorbed into the urban labor market. Factory managers often recruit temporary industrial labor at the public markets or at transportation centers where a large and competitive pool of labor is readily available. It is at such a site that the two institutions, Qur'anic student networks and the urban labor market, socially intersect (i.e. articulate) in such a way that both Qur'anic school students *and* industrial workers state that they freely choose to enter industrial labor because of their need to fulfil desires for new material objects of consumption, or because they wish to marry and need a steady income to support their wives.

ISLAMIC PROTEST AND ORGANIZATIONAL MEDIATION: THE PROCESS OF RATIONALIZATION

Throughout the 1970s industrial production and industrial workers increased until, by 1982, there were about 50,000 industrial workers employed in Kano State. While the increase began during the Nigerian civil war in response to the foreign-exchange crisis and the demands of a war economy, the petroleum boom was a decisive stimulant to industrialization and investment by multinational corporations, indigenous Hausa merchant capitalists and Levantine entrepreneurs who were being eased out of the retail and wholesale trade.

The question of significance for this essay is: what influence did Islamic culture, leadership and practice have upon the consciousness and actions of Kano's Muslim factory workers, many of whom emigrated to Kano as gardawa? Throughout the decade and even earlier it is certain that their resistance to industrial discipline and industrial inequality contained an Islamic element, one that I argue articulated with an emerging class consciousness. The key issue was the conflict between Islamic timing and discipline and the rationality and timing necessary for industrial production. In structured interviews and in informal field data, complaints about the refusal of management to allow prayer at 2 p.m. were voiced by the experienced and the neophyte and in international as well as indigenous firms. Many also voiced a demand that the factory management should build a mosque for industrial workers, that the unsanitary toilet facilities (a source of ritual pollution) be repaired and that Muslim culture be respected in other diverse ways. Indeed, the struggle over prayer time led to the founding of one of the first industrial trade unions in Kano by a Qur'anic mallam who was punished for praying at the correct time by the European factory manager of an indigenously-owned textile firm. Here the Islamic discourse is the key to the formation of the trade union. According to the worker-mallam, he met with fellow workers to decide on industrial action:

> I told them that we should not agree to the ruining of our religion by this company, we must do something about it. I told them that the Koran and the Hadith of Bukari instructed us to come together in order to help each other (Lubeck, 1975).

Just how typical the relationship between Islamic status, gardawa-origin and Islamic consciousness was in militant class consciousness became the next problem of my research on Kano's industrial working class. A survey of industrial workers was conducted in Kano's three largest factories. Tables 4.1 and 4.2 present the relationship between Qur'anic school participation and five indicators of class consciousness. Table 4.2 controls for the effect of urban residential experience. The statistical data confirm the findings from field data: workers who participated in Qur'anic schools, usually as gardawa, were significantly more likely to support strikes, to believe that Islam agrees with striking for a fair reason and support organizational participation in trade unions and political activities as workers. Table 4.2 is interesting because it shows that militancy, as measured by the indicators of class consciousness, is strongest among those who have lived in the city longest, thus eliminating the Durkheimian and Parsonian thesis that social protest is strongest among those least socially integrated and thus most anomic. Indeed, it is contact with industrial capitalism of the dependent, transnational variety that stimulates class consciousness, especially on the organizational indicators pertaining to 'organizing at the factory level' and 'political engagement', among workers with high levels of Qur'anic school participation. (Date of survey: 1972).[6]

The next question is: what happened to Islamic issues in subsequent industrial protests during the petroleum boom, when trade

Table 4.1: Class consciousness and Qur'anic school participation

Dimension of consciousness	Variable years of Qur'anic schooling	Positive or Agree	N =	Statistics
Agrees that pay is unfair	High number of years[a]	(21) 47.7%	(44)	Gamma = .08 $P < .82$ Corrected x^2 = .05
	Low number of years[b]	(40) 44.0%	(91)	
Adebo strike support	High number of years[a]	(30) 66.7%	(45)	Gamma = .40 $P < .04$ Corrected x^2 = 4.29
	Low number of years[b]	(44) 46.3%	(95)	
Islamic approval of fair strike	High number of years[a]	(30) 66.7%	(45)	Gamma = .44 $P < .02$ Corrected x^2 = 5.58
	Low number of years[b]	(41) 43.6%	(94)	
Agreement with organizing at the factory level	High number of years[a]	(27) 67.5%	(40)	Gamma = .54 $P < .00$ Corrected x^2 = 3.36
	Low number of years[b]	(34) 38.2%	(89)	
Agreement with workers engaging in politics	High number of years[a]	(22) 51.2	(43)	Gamma = .48 $P < .01$ Corrected x^2 = 6.49
	Low number of years[b]	(23) 26.7%	(86)	

Notes: [a]Eight years or more (upper third).
[b]Seven years or less.

unions were reorganized by the state and when, during the period of civilian rule (1979–83), a radical Islamic populist government, the People's Redemption Party (PRP), ruled Kano state? Management soon learned that the prayer and mosque issues were too intense to resist. Prayer time was allowed and mosques were usually built on factory sites. When the PRP took office, the debate over Islamic issues among factory workers ended, precisely because the state now supported the Islamic protest of the workers and because the parties wished to

95

Table 4.2: Class consciousness and Qur'anic school participation

With high urban residential experience

Dimension of consciousness	Variable years of Qur'anic schooling	Positive or Agree	N =	Statistics
Adebo strike support	High number of years[a]	(22) 68.8%	(32)	Gamma = .16 $P < .\ 65$ Corrected x^2 = .21
	Low number of years[b]	(30) 61.2%	(49)	Total N = 81
Islamic approval of fair strike	High number of years[a]	(24) 75.0%	(32)	Gamma = .36 $P < .20$ Corrected x^2 = 1.67
	Low number of years[b]	(28) 58.3%	(48)	Total N = 80
Agreement with organizing at the factory level	High number of years[a]	(23) 74.2%	(31)	Gamma = .52 $P < .04$ Corrected x^2 = 4.32
	Low number of years[b]	(23) 47.9%	(48)	Total N = 79
Agreement with workers engaging in politics	High number of years[a]	(19) 61.3%	(31)	Gamma = .54 $P < .02$ Corrected x^2 = 5.42
	Low number of years[b]	(15) 31.9%	(47)	Total N = 78

With low urban residential experience

Dimension of consciousness	Variable years of Qur'anic schooling	Positive or Agree	N =	Statistics
Adebo strike support	High number of years[a]	(8) 61.5%	(13)	Gamma = .57 $P < .08$ Corrected x^2 = 2.97
	Low number of years[b]	(14) 30.4%	(46)	Total N = 59
Islamic approval of fair strike	High number of years[a]	(6) 46.2%	(13)	Gamma = .37 $P < .38$ Corrected x^2 = .78
	Low number of years[b]	(13) 28.3%	(46)	Total N = 59
Agreement with organizing at the factory level	High number of years[a]	(4) 44.4%	(9)	Gamma = .37 $P < .52$ Corrected x^2 = .41
	Low number of years[b]	(11) 26.8%	(41)	Total N = 50
Agreement with workers engaging in politics	High number of years[a]	(3) 25.0%	(12)	Gamma = .13 $P < .94$ Corrected x^2 = .01
	Low number of years[b]	(9) 20.5%	(39)	Total N = 51

Notes: [a]Eight years or more (upper third).
[b]Seven years or less.

incorporate trade unions and industrial workers into their respective coalitions.

In the case of gardawa who became industrial workers, Islamic protest was effectively mediated by management and the state in such a way that the crude insensitivity of earlier European managers was rationalized by the incorporating strategies of management and the state elite. Hence, there was little interest shown by industrial workers, and no participation, in the millenarian insurrection of Maitatsine. Let us examine how the situation of the gardawa changed during the petroleum boom so as to orient them toward the millenarian promise of Alhaji Mohammed Marwa Maitatsine.

THE STRUCTURAL DETERMINANTS OF THE 'YAN TATSINE: THE DECLINE OF THE MORAL ECONOMY

The argument and evidence presented hold that the gardawa are rooted in a non-capitalist moral economy; that they are a self-conscious Islamic status-honor group who perceive themselves as fulfilling an Islamic obligation; and that this obligation requires that they take political and social action to correct injustice and to institutionalize Islamic norms of social justice. Further, the diverse network of Qur'anic schools and their mallam patrons function in urban centers as socializing institutions where an indigent youth, assuming the status of a *gardi* (singular), receives shelter and food until he is able to support himself. What is also clear from the survey data and from my own observations is that Qur'anic schools socialize ignorant rural youths into the political perspective of the urban talakawa, one that is visible in the two institutionalized political parties of the talakawa. Yet, whereas in the First Nigerian Republic, the talakawa's opposition party, the Nigerian Elements Progressive Union (NEPU), never assumed power at the regional or state level, by 1979 Kano State was administered by the heir of NEPU, the People's Redemption Party, which in typical populist fashion engaged in many of the corrupt practices and abuses associated with the aristocratic and capitalist elites. Kano, moreover, was dependent upon federal revenue from petroleum rents, and federal policy limited any major structural reforms that might have ameliorated the misery of the rural and urban lower classes. Thus, for the urban lower classes, the triumph of the PRP has not transformed their material and social existence, nor has the trend toward corruption and the internationalization of consumption been halted. The elite shifted but the class structure remained the same.

97

The reforms introduced by the federal military government (FMG) were intended to eliminate the patrimonial bureaucrats of the authoritarian Native Authority system. Police, courts and many regional functions were allocated to the federal level. In place of the ward-based patrimonial system, a new, western-educated administrative elite now presided over the Local Government Authority. Typically, the new administrative elite did not live in the old city where Maitatsine preached and recruited his gardawa; rather they resided in the elite areas once occupied by colonial administrators, managers of international firms and others of wealth and elite status. It seems clear to this observer that the patrimonial Native Authority bureaucrats would have had better intelligence regarding the intentions and practices of Maitatsine than the new administrative elite, if only because they reside in the same urban milieu. Recall that he had been expelled in 1962 for slander by the Native Authority officials. The relevant point here is that the reform of the state reduced the capacity of the local officials to control and to mediate between Maitatsine and his followers.

A final point concerns the Nigerian police who manage the floating urban population of the cities. By 1980, public fear and hatred of the police reached explosive levels because of corruption, physical abuse and manipulation by the Shagari government. It is not surprising that the ideology of the 'Yan Tatsine defined the police as representatives of the devil, for they abused their authority without restraint. The state apparatus, therefore, was increasingly illegitimate by 1980 and its mediation between the structural position of the gardawa and Islamic culture stimulated support for Maitatsine.

GARDAWA, QUR'ANIC NETWORKS, AND SEMI-INDUSTRIAL CAPITALISM

The magnitude of the change in the Nigerian economy brought about by the rise in petroleum prices during the 1970s can be assessed from the following statistic: in 1970 total federal revenue, including earnings from all export commodities, was approximately $1 billion; by 1980 it was approaching $23 billion. What were the consequences of this massive infusion of wealth, as mediated by state institutions, for a northern Muslim city such as Kano? To begin with, one must understand that the influx of petroleum revenue occurred at the same time as a severe drought, so that the balance of rural-urban relations was undermined by both natural and socio-economic factors. Whereas an increase in world economic demand for agricultural commodities produced by smallholders would distribute profit evenly across regional and social strata in a decentralized way, the OPEC-determined rise in Nigeria's petroleum revenues resulted in state centralization. Thus the economic status of the local Muslim aristocracy and the Kano state government came to depend on the price and demand for petroleum in the world market. Petroleum rents and state centralization at the federal level determined that access to state revenues in the form of state contracts, loans, and gross corruption became the unrivaled route to capital accumulation among the northern merchant-industrial and petty bourgeoisie., Accordingly, the state bureaucratic bourgeoisie allocated billions for urban infrastructural projects (e.g., new modern roads through the old city of Kano), and, of course, major office buildings; the petty bourgeoisie responded by investing in office buildings and in housing for professionals, salaried and wage workers. And industrial production increased, though not in proportion to the demand for wage employment among migrants.

For these reasons construction was the dynamic industry during the oil boom. One of its features is that it demands large numbers of unskilled workers for temporary periods but at comparatively high wages. Because the price of labor increased enormously after the Udoji (1975) wage increases and after the rapid rise in urban food prices, modern cement construction replaced traditional mud construction, which was labor-intensive — a technique, one should stress, in which rural-origin gardawa were proficient, while modern cement construction was usually unknown. Furthermore, modern state infrastructure in the form of roads, industrial estates, new housing areas situated on land confiscated from the densely-settled peri-urban peasantry, and new commercial and state educational institutions (e.g., Bayero University), radically altered the physical form and spatial relations of metropolitan Kano. Moreover, since compensation to the peasantry (whenever paid) was not allocated at the market rate but rather as a disturbance fee for improvements, the physical expansion, which was led by the state sector, was perceived by many of its victims and their supporters as wholly illegitimate. Note that during the Second Republic (1979–83), 'spontaneous' fires destroyed Kano's land transaction records at the Ministry of Works and Surveys and the Kano Metropolitan Planning Authority. Just as in the federal capital, Lagos, most observers interpreted these fires as arson designed to cover up the corrupt land transactions among state officials and their cronies which led to the demise of the peri-urban peasantry, who often participated as gardawa in the complex Qur'anic school networks.

Finally, the physical form of the city was transformed by the process of 'gentrification', whereby areas once allocated to the laboring poor like Tudun Wada became prime targets of speculators who razed the existing structures and replaced them with modern cement structures.

The next major transformation was the internationalization of consumption. To be sure, prior to the civil war and the petroleum boom, great social and economic inequality existed, but its expression, and its public consumption, was restrained, generally following the norms of Muslim dignity. Moreover, great wealth was confined to the merchant-industrial class and their allies, the Muslim office-holding aristocracy. To document the transition to the internationalization of consumption, one could cite the lavish homes of the wealthy, the proliferation of video and stereo sets, or the fast transnational lifestyle of the newly rich who 'hop on flights' to London to shop; but the ideal indicator, from the perspective of the gardawa, is the rise in automobile ownership. The new roads are designed for this object of elite consumption, and, since the state subsidized purchase by means of cheap loans for civil servants, automobile ownership mushroomed during the petroleum boom: e.g., in 1970 new registration of passenger cars in Kano numbered 693, or 18.2 per cent of all registrations, but by 1976 the number had increased to 5,595, or 24.8 per cent of all registrations for an increase of 707.4 per cent (Frishman, n.d.). Finally, as anyone who has driven in Kano knows, nowhere is the tension of rapid and uneven development more prevalent than on the motorways where rivalry and recklessness slaughter thousands yearly.

Before discussing the effects of semi-industrial capitalism during the petroleum boom on Kano's gardawa, the effect of the unequal and often illegitimate pressure of petroleum wealth on the social fabric in general requires discussion. Note the changes: urban growth probably averaging 7 or 8 per cent per annum, massive increases in income and consumption for individuals who cannot legitimately explain its origin, confiscation of land from the peri-urban peasantry which is allocated by state officials to themselves and to rentier capitalists, a rise in the number of hajj pilgrims (circa 100,000) often for corrupt ends (e.g., drugs, smuggling, and foreign exchange), ownership of shares in indigenized companies by brotherhood leaders who mediate between individual capitalists, and an unprecedented and spectacular rise in the level of urban crime and urban violence. Although it is difficult to measure the increase in income inequality, virtually all sources, including Bienen and Diejomaoh (1981), agree that the gap between rich and poor has widened according to official statistics which, since so much income is obtained illegally, vastly understate the widening gap. A study by the World Bank (Sarly, 1981) estimates that 52 to 67 per cent of Kano's urban population remain at the 'absolute poverty level', i.e. less than $472 per capita per annum (Frishman, 1981). Additional examples abound describing the material deprivation, the decline in sanitation, since Kano is without sewers, and the virtually endless reports of massive official corruption in the face of equally massive human misery. And finally, note that the conservative (pro-National Party of Nigeria) faction of the populist People's Redemption Party does not deviate from this pattern: according to *West Africa* (30 January 1984), when the home of the PRP governor Alhaji Sabo Bakin Zuwo was searched by the new military government, N3.4 m. ($5.1 m.) was found 'stacked up'.

MATERIAL CONSTRAINTS ON THE SOCIAL REPRODUCTION OF THE URBAN GARDAWA

Now let us move to the micro-level in order to illustrate how the transformation of state structures, the urban economy, and the undermining of community life have threatened the ability of the gardawa to reproduce themselves as they had for centuries. Income opportunities were not eliminated but new capital-intensive innovations certainly undermined their traditional petty income activities. The consequences flowing from the reduction of mud construction in favor of cement construction on the gardawa's opportunities have already been noted. Furthermore, the banning of hand-pushed carts by the local government authorities — though an invidious occupation associated with drug consumption — eliminated an income opportunity for older, more proletarianized gardawa. And finally, the generalized competitive pressure on independent commodity producers — craftsmen, petty traders, and small-scale producers — reduced income opportunities for gardawa because changes in taste, as in the example of tailoring, reduced the demand for their traditional skills.

As noted earlier, in addition to petty income opportunities, the gardawa depended upon charity in the form of housing in the entry-ways of houses (i.e., mallamin soro). Several changes reduced the availability of this resource. First, inflation and population growth created a greedy class of rentier capitalists who accumulated capital by building housing in elite as well as working-class areas of the city. It was common to build a second story even on mud constructed houses, which excluded an entry-way. Secondly, building plots

101

allocated by the state became very expensive: for example, whereas one could purchase a plot in the working-class area of Tudun Wada for two or three hundred Naira in 1970, by 1978 the price had risen to over seven thousand Naira. Hence new construction for housing new migrants often did not contain the traditional entry-way in order to maximize the return on investment in urban space. Thirdly, another housing constraint for the gardawa was the increased use of iron grids and bars over existing entry-ways in order to secure the house from thieving and armed robbery, a growth industry in contemporary Nigeria. Fear of theft coupled with increased income inequality, moreover, created understandable anxiety among the propertied and middle-income groups which was expressed as a fear that they would be robbed by the gardawa who, of course, were quite impoverished and shabby in personal appearance. Hence, over the decade of the petroleum boom, the gardawa, a social category that once reproduced the ideology of the Islamic state and served as an opportunity for gaining merit by engaging in Islamic charity, became redefined by the newly wealthy classes as a dangerous and immoral social category. Later the effect of state educational policy marginalized them even further. Needless to say, four major urban insurrections of the 'Yan Tatsine have only confirmed in the minds of the upper income groups that the gardawa are a dangerous social group.

One of the rituals that punctuate Kano's dusk and early evening is the sound of Qur'anic students chanting outside residences for surplus food, and, traditionally, households prepare enough food to distribute to the wandering gardawa. Of course, prior to the petroleum boom when food was domestically produced and cheap relative to urban wages, the Islamic norms of charity corresponded to the consumption needs of the gardawa. But by the time Marwa incited his gardawa to seize control of the 'Yan Awaki ward of Kano's Birni, the urban food economy had been dramatically transformed. In large part due to the distortions introduced into the rural labor market by the high wages paid to rural-origin laborers during the urban construction boom between 1970 and 1978, Nigeria's real food output per capita fell by 1.5 per cent per annum. By 1980 the cost of total food imports exceeded $2.9 billion, with the federal government alone having imported N1.5 billion worth of cereals, a figure that contrasts with N46.4 m. for total imports in 1965 (Watts, 1983:ch.8). Through corruption, wage increases designed to shore up political support among civil servants, and general economic mismanagement, inflation galloped at an estimated rate of at least 20 per cent annually. Table 4.3 presents food costs from 1971 to 1980 as compared to the

Table 4.3: Food prices and industrial wages in Kano, 1971 to 1980[a]

Item	November 1971	November 1975	Increase 1971-5[b]	November 1978	Increase 1971-78[b]	December 1980	Increase 1971-80[b]
Millet (measure)	.17	.50	(1.94)	1.10	(5.47)	1.20	(6.05)
Rice (measure)	.83	1.60	(0.92)	2.50	(2.01)	5.50	(5.62)
Sorghum (Guinea Corn) (measure)	.21	.50	(1.38)	1.00	(3.76)	1.00	(3.76)
Beet (kg)	.93	—	—	2.50	(1.68)	3.50	(2.76)
Palm oil (beer bottle)	.17	.70	(3.11)	1.55	(8.11)	1.00	(4.88)
Groundnut oil (beer bottle)	.25	.85	(2.40)	1.25	(4.00)	.70	(1.80)
Pepper (measure)	.33	—	—	1.00	(2.03)	3.50	(9.60)
Starting wage for industrial worker	.87	1.75	(1.01)	2.25	(1.58)	3.85	(3.43)

Notes: [a]Wages and Prices in Naira (one Naira = approximately $1.65)

[b]Rate of Increase = $\dfrac{\text{(Price at given year)} - \text{(Price November 1971)}}{\text{(Price November 1971)}}$

starting wage for industrial workers who, one must emphasize, are the privileged members of the urban lower stratum, for the gardawa possess only a fraction of the income of the industrial worker. By 1980, therefore, real wages had declined in relation to the cost of foodstuffs, which increased by over 600 per cent in the case of millet. Note that rice increased only slightly in comparison to industrial wages until 1980, when the price increase far exceeded increases in the starting wage rate for industrial workers. The reason, of course, was that rice imports were determined by the distribution of import licenses, which, in turn, were distributed by the Shagari regime to reward their financial and political supporters. Thus a 50 Kg bag costing anywhere from N17 to N20 to land at Lagos could cost N80 to N100 in the markets of the interior, depending on the season. Hence, from the perspective of the gardawa and other low-income groups, not only were the inflation and the contradictions of the petroleum economy undermining the institutional basis for their sub-sistence, but the villains were the political elite and the food merchants who hoarded and speculated in foodstuffs in order to reap windfall profits.

The final contradiction which undermined the peripatetic gardawa and their mallams was located in the decision by the northern Muslim elites to support the Universal Primary Education Program (UPE). The restructuring of the state since the civil war is crucial to the rise of the 'Yan Tatsine. For, in order for the northern Muslim elites to exercise hegemony as they have since Murtala Mohammed through the Shagari and Bukari regimes, they must reduce the technical and educational imbalance between the northern and southern states in Nigeria. Hence, the petroleum boom enabled the federal state to initiate an ambitious UPE program. Prior to this program there was little state investment in primary school education in the northern states except in urban centers. For example, in the early years of the 1970s less than 10 per cent of primary-school-aged children in Kano State attended primary school. Moreover, most of this enrolment was in urban centers, and the degree of primary school enrolment in rural areas was negligible. Over the long term, the consequences of the UPE are certain to accelerate the rural-urban drift which has already overburdened urban services and strained the subsistence institutions that sustain the peripatetic Qur'anic schools. Yet, in the case of the UPE, an even more important social change, that is, the reduction of cultural resistance to Western education, has occurred, which will affect both the wandering mallam and his gardawa.

THE CONTRIBUTION OF CULTURE AND ISLAMIC TRADITION

Thus far I have argued that a structural crisis in the urban economy, the legitimacy of the Nigerian state, and the subsistance ethic that sustained the gardawa provided the material basis for the recruitment of the gardawa into the fold of Maitatsine. But tradition and ideology played their role also. Neither Maitatsine's public statements nor his ideology, nor his follower's claims, associated him directly with the Mahdi. The insurrection of 1980, however, fell close to the beginning of a new century in the Muslim calendar, when Islamic tradition in the Western Sudan holds that a Renewer will appear. Furthermore, newspaper reports during the 1980 insurrection at Kaduna suggested that Maitatsine was taken by his followers to be a prophet for Africans, hence for an indigenous African religion. Such reports are difficult to confirm, since the imprisoned gardawa allegedly refuse to discuss their beliefs with the police authorities who are, for them, the personification of the devil. But the rituals of the 'Yan Tatsine, e.g., praying three rather than five times a day and in any direction rather than toward Mecca, the use of tattoos, juju, drug potions, and invincible 'magic sand' to protect them from police bullets, suggest a syncretist rather than an orthodox Mahdist movement.

Obviously, any analysis that purports to explain the social and material basis of a millenarian movement must consider carefully the anti-materialist content of Maitatsine's ideology. Not only did he curse the extravagance, corruption and decadent consumption practices of the newly rich, he also instructed his followers to avoid modern consumption items themselves — watches, bicycles, and automobiles — and he further instructed them to possess only enough money to carry them through the next day. Clearly, the intent of these beliefs is to assert the moral superiority of the material deprivation experienced by the gardawa in the face of the mindless consumption of these same Western-origin items by the wealthy and powerful classes.

At the same time, Maitatsine appears to have endeavored to provide for the material needs of his followers, at least during the insurrection when mass preparation of food (rice) was organized for them. Moreover, just prior to the insurrection at Kano, a vernacular newspaper (*Meganar Kano*, 19 December 1980) published an account of his activities in 'Yan Akawi and Kofar Wombai wards. According to this source, residents complained that Marwa and his followers built houses on others' plots saying, 'All land (plots) in this world belong to Allah and that he does not have to ask permission of anyone before building on any plot'. The same source quoted the residents' accusation that the 'Yan Tatsine took over for their private use a public lavatory and expelled the caretaker, a clear reference to the needs of a homeless class of vagabonds which this group of gardawa had become. The merchants of Kofar Wombai market were also expelled from their shops by the 'Yan Tatsine, only for them to become centers of armed strife with the police. While I am not arguing that the 'Yan Tatsine represent a purely Lumpenproletarian movement, there is a clear class antagonism to their ideology.

CONCLUSION: NOTES ON METHOD AND MEDIATION

To return to the problem of base and superstructure, to use the Marxist language, the two examples developed here illustrate how industrial organization and the role of the state as well as questions of legitimacy and Islamic ideology reciprocally influence each other in such a way that radically different Islamic social movements emerge from the same ideological and historical source and from the same urban social stratum. There is no need to repeat the arguments made earlier that the two examples reflect the importance of organizational and institutional mediation between the material situation and ideological outcomes expressed as a social movement. The next problem for research in this area should center on the possibilities of channeling the energy expressed by the millenarian fantasies of the 'Yan Tatsine toward a social movement or alliance capable of ameliorating the misery and deprivation of the gardawa of northern Nigeria.

NOTES

1. For a discussion of materialist method and a critique of essentialism see Turner, 1978.
2. For a review of this dialogue and discourse see Berryman, 1984.
3. For a discussion of Islamic society, culture and politics see Paden, 1973.
4. For survey and ethnographic material on Kano's industrial workers see Lubeck, 1986
5. For a discussion of Qur'anic studies in the nineteenth century see Last, 1967, and for the twentieth century see Chamberlin, 1975.
6. The complete survey results are found in Lubeck, 1986: Chapter Seven.

REFERENCES

Berryman, Phillip (1984), *The Religious Roots of Rebellion: Christians in Central American Revolutions*. Ossining, N.Y.: Orbis Books.

Bienen, Henry and V.P. Diejomaoh (1981), *The Political Economy of Income Distribution in Nigeria*. New York: Holmes & Meier.

Chamberlin, John (1975), 'The development of Islamic education in Kano City, Nigeria'. Unpub. Ph.D. dissertation, Columbia University, New York.

Fika, Adamu (1978), *The Kano Civil War and British Overrule, 1882–1940*. Ibadan: Oxford University Press.

Frishman, Alan (1981), 'Urban transportation decisions in Kano'. Geneva and New York. Unpub. ms.

Last, Murray (1967), *The Sokoto Caliphate*. London: Longman.

Lubeck, Paul (1975), 'Unions, workers and consciousness in Kano, Nigeria', in R. Sandbrook and R. Cohen (eds), *The Development of an African Working Class*. London: Longman.

——. (1986), *Islam and Urban Labor in Northern Nigeria: the Making of a Muslim Working Class*. Cambridge: Cambridge University Press.

McLellan, David, (1977), *Karl Marx: Selected Writings*. Oxford: Oxford University Press.

Marx, Karl ([1859] 1904), *A Contribution to the Critique of Political Economy*. Chicago: Charles Kerr.

——. ([1932]1970). *The German Ideology*. New York: International Publishers.

Marx, Karl ([1867]1982), *Capital*. New York: International Publishers.

Monthly Review, The (1984), 'Preface: religion and the left'. Vol. 36, No. 3, July-August, pp. 1–8.

Paden, John (1973), *Religion and Political Culture in Kano*. Berkeley, Cal.: University of California Press.

Pipes, Daniel (1980), 'This world is political: The Islamic revival of the seventies', *Orbis* (Spring 1980): 9–41.

Sarly, R. (1981), 'Urban Development Strategy in Metropolitan Kano', Washington, DC: World Bank. Unpublished.

Shea, Philip (1975), 'The development of an export-oriented dyed cloth industry in Kano emirate'. Unpub. Ph.D. dissertation, University of Wisconsin, Madison

——. (1983), 'Approaching the study of production in rural Kano', in Bawuro Barkindo (ed.), *Studies in the History of Kano*. Ibadan: Heinemann.

Thompson, Edward (1963), *The Making of the English Working Class*. Harmondsworth: Penguin Books.

Turner, Bryan S. (1978), *Marx and the End of Orientalism*. London: Allen & Unwin.

Watts, Michael (1983), *Silent Violence*. Berkeley, Cal.: University of California Press.

Part Two

Muslim Social Thought and the State

5

Revolution in Shi'ism

Said Amir Arjomand

The nature of the state, and of state authority, in Iran, and the character of the dominant discourse there, are intimately connected. The Islamic revolution of 1979, however, was led by the Shi'ite ulama in order to defend and preserve Shi'ism, with the state as their vehicle. They acted as the custodian of a religious tradition they considered threatened with corruption, if not disappearance. Paradoxically, however, their attempt to restore and revitalize the Shi'ite tradition has constituted a true revolution in Shi'ism. In a paper prepared for a SSRC-ACLS conference in 1981 (Arjomand, 1984a:Ch. 10), I characterized the movement led by Ayatollah Khomeini as 'revolutionary traditionalism'. I still consider the Islamic revolution in Iran as the first traditionalist revolution in modern history (Arjomand, 1985). It should be emphasized, however, that the Islamic revolution in Iran has not only been a political revolution but equally a religious revolution. Shi'ite revolutionary traditionalism in Iran has brought about a revolution *in* Shi'ism.

The concern for the restoration of the pure and authentic Islam is evident in the Preamble to the Constitution of the Islamic Republic of Iran. It states that after the earlier political movements of the present century — the movements against autocracy (1905–11) and the nationalization of oil (the late 1940s and early 1950s) — became stagnant *'because of their deviation from authentic Islamic positions'*, 'the wakeful conscience of the nation, under the leadership of the esteemed *marja'-e taqlid*, His Eminence Grand Ayatollah Imam Khomeini, perceived the necessity of pursuing the line of the *authentic doctrinaire* [*maktabi*] and Islamic movement'. It is stated further that the Constitution lays the foundation of the sovereignty of the jurist 'in order to act as a guarantee *against deviation* of various organizations from their *authentic Islamic functions.*'[1] In a similar vein, the textbook for the third grade of high schools in the chapter on Islamic government states

> the leader of Islamic government must have a comprehensive view of these plans [of the enemies of Islam for cultural penetration], must recognize all the deviant and syncretic (*elteqati*) lines and Satanic plots, and must lead the Islamic *umma* to the correct path with competence and statesmanship so as to lead it to victory over all the enemies of Islam. (Vezarat-e Amuzesh va Parvaresh, 1983:127).

In their relentless *Kulturkampf* against Westernized intellectuals and the 'syncretic' thought of the Islamic modernists, Iran's ruling clerics have claimed legitimacy as the authoritative interpreters of Islam in general and of the Shi'ite tradition in particular. Yet, they have radically deviated from the Shi'ite tradition by creating an Islamic *ideology* whose cornerstone is a novel theory of theocratic *government*. This major innovation has far-reaching ramifications. It has set in motion a profound transformation of the Shi'ite political ethic which constitutes a watershed in the history of Shi'ism and will undoubtedly continue for decades to come.

In what follows I shall briefly analyze the motives of Khomeini and the militant Shi'ite clerics in initiating such a transformation, and the broad outline of the changes in the Shi'ite political ethic.

THE SHI'ITE ULAMA AND THE POLITICAL REVOLUTION OF 1979

An essential precondition of modern revolutions is the modernization and centralization of the state. Without the existence of a centralizing (Britain) or centralized (France, Russia, Germany, Iran) state, rebellions and movements of protest cannot take the form of modern popular revolutions.

The centralization of the state necessitates the concentration of coercive material and symbolic resources and thus entails the dispossesion of certain privileged strata (Eisenstadt, 1978). Baechler (1975:139) identifies the reaction of the autonomous centers of power against the expansion of the state as 'a major source of revolutionary phenomena'. The reaction of the dispossessed strata is therefore of crucial importance and can produce a revolution (Goldstone, 1982:194-5); the early phase of the English revolution, the Fronde and the aristocratic pre-revolution of 1787–8 in France (Cobban, 1968:23, 68–82, 97) readily come to mind. One might equally think of the Japanese and the Prussian landlords who had no institutional base for challenging the central monarchical bureaucracy. Here, the *independence* of the Iranian religious elite, of the Shi'ite hierarchy from the state assumes crucial importance. In contrast to the Iranian landowning class which was liquidated by the Shah's land reform in the 1960s and was unable to react, the partially dispossessed Shi'ite clerical estate retained its autonomous religious authority and its control over appreciable resources independently of the state bureaucracy (Arjomand, 1981). It could react and did so.

The independence of the ulama from the state in Iran was a distinctive feature of Shi'ite Islam in contrast to Sunnism. Norms of authority in religion contain crucial implications both for religious ranking and for political stratification. Shi'ism contains several norms of authority, which have the potential for such an impact. All of these are ultimately deducible from the theory of Imamate or infallible leadership of the community of believers. The Akhbari (Traditionalist) conception of Imamate, which was dominant before the eleventh century and was revived in the seventeenth, was hostile to all extension of the authority of the Imams after the concealment of the twelfth Imam, which is believed to have taken place in the ninth century, and conceded *de facto* religious authority only to the compilers of their Traditions. Indirectly, however, it enhanced the stratification of the Shi'ite community into ordinary believers and the *sayyids*, descendants of the Prophet, who could claim to partake of the charisma of the lineage of the Imams. The Sayyids' charisma of descent from the Prophet and the Imams thus became a source of legitimacy for their privileges under the Safavids (1501–1722) and enhanced their socio-political domination in the seventeenth and early eighteenth centuries. Thus, the Akhbari orientation indirectly encouraged the fusion of religious and political authority and militated against the consolidation of differentiated religious authority.

A second historically important norm of authority in Shi'ism is the mahdistic tenet — the belief in the return of the twelfth Imam as the Mahdi or the rightly-guided (messianic) leader at the End of Time. This chiliastic norm of authority, when successfully activated by a claimant to Mahdihood — the founder of the Safavid empire was one such claimant — immediately instituted a charismatic structure of domination in which religious and political authority was fused in the person of the supreme leader (Arjomand, 1984b:Ch.2).

Lastly, we have the Shi'ite norm of the juristic authority of the specialists in religious learning. In contradistinction to the previous two norms, the juristic principle enhances differentiated religious authority and creates a basis on which hierocratic authority can be established alongside political authority *and independent of it*. This last norm of religious authority emerged with the rise of the Shi'ite science of jurisprudence (*usul al-fiqh*) in the eleventh century and assumed its final form in the division of the Shi'ite community into *mujtahids* (jurists), the most important of whom were the *maraji'-e taqlid* (sources of imitation), and *muqallids* (followers) in the nineteenth century.

The autonomy of the Shi'ite hierocracy has assured its survival despite the relentless pressure from the state during the twentieth century. The modernisation of the state did entail a drastic diminution of the institutional prerogatives and social power of the hierocracy. However, it did not impair the legitimacy of the exclusive hierocratic authority of the ulama, which had become definitively established in the early nineteenth century, and which assured the continued financial independence of the hierocracy, and consequently its survival and virtually exclusive control over religious learning and over the authoritative interpretation of Shi'ite Islam. Owing to this continued autonomy, the Shi'ite hierocracy, unlike its Ottoman counterpart, did not disintegrate with the collapse of the monarchical state. On the contrary, it emerged as the decisive institution during the paralysis of the state in 1978, and succeeded in subjugating the latter after the collapse of the monarchy the following year.

Khomeini had been preparing the Shi'ite ulama for such a takeover for a decade, and had enlisted the loyalty of many of the ablest and most energetic among them by the late 1970s. The militant Shi'ite ulama had rallied behind him on a platform which was staunchly traditionalist and frankly clericalist: Western cultural domination threatened Islam with corruption if not extinction, and the Shah's policies threatened the hierocracy and its *madrasas* (schools) with liquidation. The ulama were enjoined to live up to their responsibility as the custodians of the Shi'ite tradition, and to unite in order to remove the danger and preserve Islam. To do so, they had to overthrow the monarchy and set up an Islamic theocratic *government*. The historical moment had come when the Shi'ite hierocracy was to subjugate the state from which it had secured its independence in the early years of the nineteenth century.

The official historian of the Islamic revolution, in a work written in the mid-1970s, claims that Khomeini has trained 500 Shi'ite doctors (*mujtahids*) throughout his long teaching career, and that 12,000 students took his courses in the years immediately preceding his exile (Ruhani, 1982:42–50). The leading personalities among the militant clergy who now occupy the highest positions of power in the Islamic Republic are, with rare exceptions, first and foremost Khomeini's former students, and secondly, his collaborators in the agitations of the 1960s. Socially, they are in all likelihood from the traditional urban background typical of the Shi'ite clergy in the second half of the nineteenth and first half of the twentieth century. They were keenly aware of the dispossesion of the Shi'ite clergy by the Pahlavi regime and bent on the recovery of lost historical privileges. The younger clergy, on the other hand, are heavily drawn from humbler rural and small-town backgrounds. For them, the Islamic revolution has created avenues of rapid upward social mobility. However, the ideological weapon of the ranking militant Ayatollahs for the recovery of their lost privileges is the same as that of the younger clerics for safeguarding their rapid social ascent: Khomeini's theory of theocratic government or *velayat-e faqih*.

TRANSFORMATION OF THE SHI'ITE THEORY OF AUTHORITY

There has been remarkable consensus among the Shi'ite jurists throughout the centuries regarding the interpretation of the 'authority verse' of the Qur'an (IV:59). The major Shi'ite Qur'an commentaries, al-Tusi's (d. 1067) *Tibyan* (al-Tusi, 1957:II, 236–7), al-Tabrisi's (d. 1153 or 1158) *Majma' al-Bayan* (al-Tabrisi, 1970/71:V, 202–3), and Muqaddas Ardabili's (d. 1585) *Zubdat al-Bayan* (Muqaddas Ardabili, 1966:687) assert that 'those in authority' (*ulu 'l-amr*) are neither the secular rulers (*amirs*) nor the ulama — none of whom is immune from error and sin — but rather the infallible (*ma'sum*) Imams, 'Ali and his eleven descendants. The Shi'ite consensus on the interpretation of the authority verse continued to hold until our own time and up to the onset of Khomeini's formulation of a new Shi'ite political theory. It is worth quoting the most influential contemporary Qur'an commentary, Tabataba'i's *Tafsir al-Mizan* (written in the 1950s and 1960s) on verse IV:59:

> The conclusion is that it would not make sense to take the verse *'ulu 'l-amr minkum'* to refer to 'the people of binding and loosening' as a social sodality, in whatever sense. Therefore 'those in authority' must refer to the individuals from the *umma* who are infallible [*ma'sum*], whose recognition depends on the explicit

designation of God or his messenger, and to whom obedience is incumbent. All this corresponds only to what has been related from the Imams of the House of the Prophet, may peace be upon them, as 'those in authority'.

As for the assertion that 'those in authority' are the rightly-guided caliphs, the lords of the swords (*amirs*), or the '*ulama*' who are followed in their sayings and views, *it can be completely refuted* in two ways: firstly, the verse indicates the infallibility of 'those in authority' and there is undoubtedly no one who is infallible in any of the above categories (except for 'Ali, may peace be upon him, according to Shi'ite belief); secondly, there is no evidence to support any of these three opinions.[2]

The Shi'ite notion of authority implied in the above interpretations of the authority verse was not confined to Qur'an commentaries but also informed Shi'ite jurisprudence. Shayhk Murtaza Ansari (d. 1865), the towering jurist of the second half of the nineteenth century, for instance, in his discussion of authority sought, firstly,

> to demonstrate how absurd it is to reason that because the Imams should be obeyed in all temporal and spiritual matters, the *faqih* are also entitled to such obedience; and second . . . that in principle no individual, except the Prophet and the [infallible] Imam, has the authority to exert *wilaya* over others. (Enayat, 1982:162)

As has been pointed out, the *Usuli* movement finally established the religious and juristic authority of the ulama on behalf of the Hidden Imam. As a consequence, a number of highly specific functions of the Imam covered in the medieval treatises in jurisprudence such as the Muhaqqiq al-Hilli's (d. 1277) *al-Mukhtasar al-Nafi'* under the rubric of *Wila' al-Imama* (al-Muhaqqiq al-Hilli, 1864:273) were now said to devolve, during the Occultation, upon the Shi'ite jurists by virtue of their collective office of 'general viceregency' (*niyabat 'amma*). By the 1960s, the *wilaya* transferred from the Imam to the jurists had highly specific and well-delineated connotations:

> The *velayat* of the fully qualified *faqih*, according to indubitable evidence, is the authority over the affairs of those minors who have no specific parents, and over the insane, so that he may manage their affairs according to expediency, and also authority over the wife of a person who has disappeared as regards maintenance and divorce . . . and the supervision of those *awqaf* which are without

a specific administrator, and the upholding of the *hudud* and judgeship and ruling according to the Sacred law (*hukumat*) and resolution of hostilities and investigation of claims and upholding of rights, and the like (Naseri, 1972:4–5)

In his bid to overthrow the Shah from exile in early 1970, Khomeini took a bold step by asserting that the *velayat-e faqih* went beyond these specific types of authority and included a general right to rule. The velayat-e faqih thus assumed the meaning of the sovereignty of the jurist. Khomeini extended the arguments of the early *Usuli* jurists, which were designed to establish the *legal* authority of the ulama on the basis of a number of Traditions from the Prophet and the Imams, to eliminate the duality of religio-legal and temporal authority altogether. Having firmly rejected the idea of the separation of religion and politics as instilled by imperialist plotters, Khomeini argues that during the Occultation of the Imam, sovereignty devolves upon the qualified ulama.

This formulation still preserved the Shi'ite juristic pluralism, as *velayat* was presented as the collective prerogative of all Shi'ite jurists or at least all the *maraji'-e taqlid*. About a year later, Khomeini attempted to reduce this juristic pluralism to a unitary theocratic leadership to be installed by an Islamic revolution. Having reaffirmed that the ulama 'possess with respect to government all that the Prophet and the Imams possessed' (Khomeini, 1971), Khomeini maintains that:

> *wilaya* falls to *al-faqih al-'adil*. Undertaking a government and laying the foundation of the Islamic state (*al-dawlat al-Islamiyya*).
> *If one such succeeds in forming a government it is incumbent on the others to follow him. If the task is not possible except by their uniting, they must unite to undertake it*. If that were not possible at all, their status would not lapse, though they would be excused from the founding of a government. (Calder, 1982:14, emphasis added).

In less than a decade, Khomeini's theory was embodied in the Constitution of the Islamic Republic of Iran. On the basis of a revolutionary reinterpretation of *velayat-e amr* and an equally revolutionary reinterpretation of Imamate as the principle of continuous (*mustamarr* — i.e. uninterrupted by the Occultation of the twelfth Imam) theocratic leadership, the sovereign jurist is identified as the *valiy-e amr* and his supreme office is interchangeably defined as '*Imamate*' and 'leadership' (*rahbari*). The Constitution defines the Islamic Republic as 'an order based on the belief in: 1) the one God (there is no god but God) and the restriction of sovereignty and legislation to Him, and the necessity of submission to His command . . . ; 5) Imamate and continuous leadership, and its fundamental role in the perpetuation of the Islamic revolution' (Clause 2). Clause 5 asserts that during the Occultation 'velayat-e amr and the Imamate of the umma is upon the just and pious . . . jurist'. A commentator on the Constitution unabashedly declares: 'the *ulu'l-amr* refers equally to the Imam and the Deputy (*na'ib*) of the Imam, and the Deputy of the Imam is the jurist who is installed in this position with the necessary conditions' (Madani, in *Sorush*, 1983).

The clerical ideologues have sought to link the Islamic revolution irrevocably to the establishment of supreme clerical sovereignty. In the words of the late Ayatollah Motahhari, 'the analysis of this revolution is not separable from the analysis of the leadership of the revolution'. Or, as another Islamic ideologue has remarked more recently:

This revolution is the integration of religion and politics, or better put, it is the refutation of the colonialist idea of 'separation of religion from politics'. In other words, this revolution is the acceptance of the servitude of God for deliverance from the servitude of non-God, and the acceptance of the sovereignty of God for salvation from the domination of *taghut*, a sovereignty which is realized through obedience to the Prophet and the infallibles and obedience to the learned and just ulama. (Haddad 'Adil, in *Ettela'at*, 1983)

Incidentally, it is interesting to note that no mention is made of the principle of consultation (*shura*) or democracy as a defining characteristic of the Islamic Republic. The principle of shura makes its appearance only in Clause 7. Madani's commentary (*Sorush*, 175, 1983) explains the subsidiary role of consultation. The principle of consultation is accepted but as a subsidiary to the principle of Imamate. 'Islamic consultation is only possible when Imamate is dominant. In other words, consultation is at the service of Imamate.' The Qur'anic verse III: 153 (*wa shawirhum fi'l-amr* etc.) is said to imply that the actual decision-maker is the Prophet who is also the Imam. The commentator adds that the advocates of the shura during the drafting of the Constitution either did not firmly believe in Islam or were contaminated by 'syncretic' thinking, and were trying 'to link the shura to the principle of national sovereignty'.

As we have seen, Khomeini's theory of theocratic government

extends the Shi'ite norm of juristic authority as elaborated in the nineteenth century into a new sphere previously not covered by it: government. Rival theories of government such as democracy and sovereignty of the nation apart, Khomeini's theory of the Mandate or the Sovereignty of the Jurist is open to two forceful objections. The first is that the mandate or authority of the Shi'ite ulama during the Occultation of the twelfth Imam cannot be extended beyond the religio-legal sphere to include government. The second objection is that the mandate in question refers to the *collective* religio-juristic authority of *all* Shi'ite jurists and cannot be restricted to that of a single supreme jurist nor, by extension, to a supreme council of three or five jurists (as envisaged in the Constitution of the Islamic Republic). The above doctrinal objections to velayat-e faqih have been voiced by the Grand Ayatollahs Kho'i and Qumi and the late Shari'at-madari and a number of other Ayatollahs.[3]

As is well known, the Grand Ayatollahs Khomeini and Shari'at-madari presented a united front against the Shah during the last months of his reign. Differences between them surfaced soon after the revolution, and resulted in serious violent clashes between their supporters in Tabriz before the end of 1979. Against this background, the first obstacle to be removed to pave the way for the universal acceptance within Shi'ism of theocratic government, velayat-e faqih, and then of the designation of a successor to Khomeini, was the removal of Shari'at-madari. In April 1982, in a move unprecedented in Shi'ite history, some 17 out of the 45 professors of the Qum theological seminaries were prevailed upon to issue a declaration 'demoting' him from the rank of Grand Ayatollah. In May-June 1982, the leading pro-Khomeini clerics further decided on a purge of the pro-Shari'at-madari ulama and of other 'pseudo-clerics' reluctant to accept velayat-e faqih. The Society of Militant Clergy was put in charge of 'confirming' the 'true' clerics.

Hand in hand with the demotion of Shari'at-madari and the silencing of clerical opposition went a sustained effort to promote the theory of velayat-e faqih. Ayatollah Khaz'ali, who presided over a series of seminars convened for the discussion of *velayat*, would confirm the principle that 'the Jurist (*faqih*) is the lieutenant of the lieutenant of the lieutenant of God, and his command is God's command' (March 1982).

In the previous section of this paper, three Shi'ite norms of authority were identified: the Mahdistic (millenarian), the juristic, and the Akhbari (traditionalist). The last norm was discarded in the nineteenth century and has not been revived since the revolution. In fact, the term *Akhbari* is used only as a pejorative label to designate the apolitical, 'stagnant' and 'superstitious' orientation of those clerics who do not subscribe to the politicized and ideological Islam of the militant ulama and who reject the concept of velayat-e faqih. As has been pointed out, velayat-e faqih consists in the extension of the Shi'ite juristic norms of authority from the religious to the political sphere and thus the addition of the claim to political rule to the prerogatives of the Shi'ite ulama. In addition, however, the Islamic revolution has also revived the Mahdistic (millenarian) Shi'ite norm of authority, albeit in an implicit and modified form.

The acclamation of Khomeini as 'Imam' by his followers in the 1970s was an unprecedented event in Shi'ite history. The connotation of 'Imam' in the mind of the believers as a divinely-guided leader has undoubtedly worked to enhance Khomeini's charisma. Already in 1978 with Khomeini's meteoric advent on the Iranian political arena, there were debates, especially among the uneducated, as to whether he was in fact the Mahdi or merely his 'Forerunner'. Millenarian yearnings and expectations were strengthened by the coincidence of the Islamic revolution in Iran with the turn of the fifteenth Islamic century. On at least one televised occasion, Khomeini was asked by a Majlis deputy from Tehran, with a confirmed habit of comparing Khomeini with Abraham and other prophets, whether or not he was in fact the Mahdi. Khomeini conveniently observed a noble silence. In 1982, side by side with the advocacy of velayat-e faqih and the campaign against dissident clerics, the tendency to attribute supernatural qualities to Khomeini was intensified. The influential late Ayatollah Sadduqi of Yazd, for instance, reported a miracle performed by Khomeini many years earlier (in the form of creating a spring in the middle of the desert under the scorching sun).

Khomeini opted for the milder claim and let currency be given to the idea that he was the forerunner of the Mahdi. There is political wisdom in this decision — and a historical precedent. The founder of the Safavid empire in the sixteenth century had claimed Mahdihood and used the Mahdistic tenet for the purpose of the millenarian mobilization of the tribes he led in the battlefield. Having completed the conquest of Iran, he presumably recognized the inconvenience of political volatility stemming from millenarianism, and modified his claim to that of being the forerunner of the Mahdi. Safavid scribes and historians subsequently attenuated the claim still further to the formula that the rule of the Safavid dynasty would continue until the Advent of the Mahdi (Arjomand, 1984b). A strikingly similar development has occurred in Iran in the past two years, this time with a modern revolutionary twist. The most frequently chanted slogan in demonstrations organized by the followers of the 'Line of the Imam' has for some time been the following: 'O God, O God, keep Khomeini until the Revolution of the Mahdi'. In November 1982, the intellectual journal of the followers of the 'Line of the Imam', *Sorush*, published an astonishing — though not untypical — article on 'The Connectedness of the Two Movements' (those of Khomeini and the Mahdi) in which the above slogan was recommended to the reader as a constant prayer. The article referred to an interview published in the journal in June of the same year in which a man wounded on the war front reported seeing the Mahdi and talking to him. The Mahdi reportedly told him 'your prayer, "O God, O God, keep Khomeini until the Revolution of the Mahdi", has expedited my Advent by a few hundred years'. In September 1982, a clerical deputy of the Majlis predicted the imminent Advent of the Mahdi in Jerusalem and cited Traditions of the Sixth Imam in support of this prediction.

Khomeini seemingly realizes that, although millenarian expectations can motivate young believers to fight courageously and court martyrdom at the front, they are not a stable basis for the consolidation of his regime in Iran. Consolidation requires the institutionalization of clerical rule, which can only be achieved on the basis of the extension of the Shi'ite juristic norm of authority. Khomeini's charisma cannot be transferred to his successor without 'routinization' and institutionalization into the office of the supreme jurist, or to that of a council of supreme jurists. Therefore, the legitimacy of theocratic government has to be established as a new article of Shi'ite faith, and procedural mechanisms for the selection of a 'Jurist' or a 'Council of Jurists' to succeed Khomeini brought into existence. As both these objectives are novel and without precedent in Shi'ite history, their attainment probably requires all the weight of Khomeini's authority and the efficacy of his unique charisma. At any rate, the realization that the resolution of the problems of legitimization and succession is much more difficult after the death of Khomeini than in his lifetime has prompted Khomeini and the militant clergy to take a series of concerted measures with uncompromising determination.

After the 'demotion' of Shari'at-madari, propaganda on the question of velayat-e faqih was stepped up in the government-controlled media. One interesting means of promoting the theory was the publication of the wills of the 'martyrs' of the war. Throughout May and June 1982 (and subsequently), the newspapers would regularly publish the martyrs' profession of faith in velayat-e faqih and their praise for the Imam and the militant clergy. Statements to the effect that

121

obedience to the ulama as 'those in authority' is incumbent upon the believer as a religious duty, were often excerpted from the wills and made into headlines in bold letters.

The *Imam Jom'ehs* have incessantly preached the doctrine of velayat-e faqih and have enjoined their congregations to obey the ulama as a matter of religious obligation. A headline on the front page of the daily *Ettela'at* in the early days of December 1983, can be taken to represent the culmination of this trend. It was a statement by the Prosecutor General and referred to Khomeini as *vali-ye faqih* (the sovereign jurist) — an astonishing phrase in view of the fact that, as we have seen, the term *vali* has never been used in the Shi'ite tradition in this general sense except to refer to the twelve Imams. But the most important measure taken to enshrine the novel doctrine of theocratic government has been to teach it in the schools. Velayat-e faqih is now taught in schools throughout the country as part of the compulsory course on Islamic ideology from the first grade of high schools onwards.

Since August 1983, numerous conventions organized by revolutionary foundations and Islamic associations have been in the habit of passing resolutions endorsing and pledging full support to the concept of velayat-e faqih, and declaring obedience to the faqih a religious obligation.

It should be evident that Khomeini's attempt to subordinate juristic pluralism, in the form of the voluntary submission of the Shi'ite believers to the Grand Ayatollahs as *marja'e taqlid*, has been at the expense of the latter.[4] The relationship between the interpretation of the new supreme leadership as velayat-e amr and the old positions of marja'-e taqlid remains a thorny theoretical issue.[5] Khomeini himself could not put forward any juristic argument and justified his position on the purely pragmatic grounds of the necessity of the maintenance of order in society. Recent discussions have not gone beyond Khomeini's pragmatic justification of the superiority of one faqih over the others. Madani, for instance (*Sorush* 177, 1983), conceives of the relationship between the supreme leadership and the *marja'iyyat* as one between the general and the particular: the supreme leader has to be a marja'-e taqlid but not every marja'-e taqlid can undertake the supreme leadership. Furthermore,

> the maintenance of order in society necessitates that when the Leader or the Leadership Council is accepted, all should obey a single authority in the social and general problems of the country within the framework of the Islamic Constitution. Such obedience

is implied in the title of 'valiy-e amr' and 'Imamate of the umma' and applies to all members of society without exception, and in this respect the mujtahid and the non-mujtahid, the marja' and the non-marja' are in an equal situation.

Despite this accommodation, however, the future of the institution of marja'iyyat is in question. Doubts have been raised as to the legitimacy of individual as distinct from collective *ijtihad* now that, for the first time in the history of Shi'ism, an Islamic order has been created. One need only draw out the implications of this typical passage to understand that the institution of marja'iyyat has a dark future (Haddad 'Adil in *Ettela'at*, 1983):

> With the establishment of Islamic government marja'iyyat, in practice and officially, took the form of leadership and rule over society; and the velayat-e faqih, which in past history had almost never been applied from the position of government, and had always been realized in a defective and incomplete manner, with this revolution reached perfection in practice and occupied its true station.

The militant ulama who followed Khomeini in the 1960s and 1970s sought to defend and revitalize the Shi'ite tradition through a political revolution. To secure the leadership of this political revolution for themselves, they have revolutionized the Shi'ite political ethos whose distinctive mark had been the secularity of temporal rule and the desacralization of political order (Arjomand, 1984b). To establish and propagate their new conception of authority, the clerical rulers of Iran have incessantly insisted on the sacred character of all authority and thus the throughgoing sacralization of the political order. Here are four examples. In a lecture on the newly-established Islamic order, the late Ayatollah Motahhari emphatically maintained that in Islamic government, authority is sacred (*muqaddas*). This is so because the offices of government and judgeship devolve upon the ulama.[6] Ayatollah Rabbani Amlashi, the temporary imam jom'eh of Tehran, would accordingly tell his congregation:[7]

> Obedience to the velayat-e faqih is an incumbent duty (*wajib*). In the Islamic Republic obedience to the law is incumbent like the daily prayer and fasting, and disobeying it is like disobeying the Islamic Sacred Law.

Ayatollah Meshkini, the imam jom'eh of Qum, takes a step in a different direction to sacralize politics:[8]

> Political activity is an incumbent (shar'i) duty. Today, one of the
> most important acts of devotion ('*ibadat*) is political activity because
> without politics our religiosity (*diyanat*) will not last.

Finally Ayatollah Mo'men, member of the Council of the Guardians
of Constitution, takes a further step to sacralize *all* authority, legal
and political:[9]

> The legitimacy and legality of whatever is done and whatever insti-
> tutions exist are due to the fact that they are buttressed by the
> velayat-e faqih. As the velayat-e faqih is at the head of all affairs
> and the main guarantor of the current laws of the country, it is
> the *divinely-ordained duty of all the people* to follow every law
> which is passed and given to the Islamic government for execu-
> tion . . . Disobeying such a law is forbidden (*haram*) as drinking
> wine is forbidden by Islam.

The paradox of the actual insignificance of the political ethics in
the Shi'ite sacred law — the paucity of political provisions which
reflects the age-old secularity of political authority and the political
order in Shi'ism — against the claim of the Islamic militants that Islam
is a total way of life and a total ideology, which is above all political
and activistic, has struck some observers. The clerical rulers of Iran
have sought to resolve this paradox by making a distinction between
the 'primary commandments' (*ahkam awwaliyya*) and 'secondary
commandments' (*ahkam thanawiyya*). The first are said to derive from
the sources of the Shari'a, the second from expediency and the necessity of the maintenance of order and the avoidance of chaos. Both
categories are said to be binding on the believer as a religious obligation. Thus, for the first time in Shi'ite history, sacrality is claimed
for a category of 'secondary commandments' which are derived *not*
from the juristic competence of the Shi'ite ulama *but from their alleged
right to rule*.

OTHER CHANGES IN THE SHI'ITE POLITICAL ETHIC

Despite the theoretical permanence and immutability of the Shari'a,
its provisions have been subjected to change, either imperceptibly or
as a result of heated juristic controversy. The function of leading the

Friday congregational prayer was one of the functions of the Imam which the early Shi'ite jurists declared in abeyance during the Occultation. In a treatise on practical jurisprudence written with a view to its implementation in the local Shi'ite state of Sarbidaran in northeastern Iran, Makki al-'Amili, the First Martyr (d. 1384) ruled that the congregational prayer should be led by the deputy of the Imam even if the latter were a jurist (Calder, 1979; Arjomand, 1984b:71). With the establishment of the Shi'ite empire by the Safavids, the decisive majority of the Shi'ite jurists ruled in favor of holding the congregational prayer during the Occultation of the twelfth Imam (Ashraf, 1983). During the Qajar period, the Friday congregational prayer lost much of its socio-political significance because the prayer leaders (singular, imam jom'eh) were among the very few religious functionaries appointed by the Shah, and therefore had an ambiguous relationship with the autonomous Shi'ite hierocracy headed by the mujtahids. Since the revolution, the Friday congregational prayer has been vigorously revived and fully institutionalized as one of the main pillars of the Islamic theocratic state.[10] The media regularly cover the Friday congregational prayers which are routinely described as 'the unity-creating and enemy-smashing congregational prayer' held in 'the meeting-place of the lovers of God'. The Friday sermon (khut-ba), in Tehran as well as in the remotest towns, has emerged as an important political instrument for announcing governmental policies and mobilizing popular support for them.

Hajj, another cardinal practical tenet of Islam, has been given a pronounced political interpretation. In a typical remark, the imam jom'eh of Rasht has asserted: 'the political dimension of hajj is higher than its devotional dimension'.[11] Consistently with this political re-emphasis, Khomeini has in recent years, to the great chagrin and alarm of the Saudi authorities, repeatedly enjoined the Iranian pilgrims to turn hajj into a forum of protest against imperialism, and to raise the cry of the 'disinherited' of the earth against the world-eating taghut and the Great Satan, namely the United States.

Not surprisingly, there has been an emphatic renewed emphasis on the incumbency of 'enjoining the good' and 'forbidding the evil' since the Islamic revolution. Al-'Urwat al-Wuthqa of Muhammad Kazim Tabataba'i Yazdi (d. 1919) which has served as the model for all the subsequent treatises on practical jurisprudence (these are required to establish Shi'ite doctors as marja'-e taqlid) contains no specific section on jihad, 'enjoining the good' and 'forbidding the evil'. The treatise appeared in 1912/1330 and, in addition to conforming to the Shi'ite traditions, it perhaps also reflects the disillusion of

125

the leading Shi'ite religious authorities of the period with clerical political activism during the Constitutional Revolution of 1905–11. Tabataba'i Yazdi's de-emphasis of political ethics set the tone for the authoritative interpretations of the practical requirements of Shi'ism in the subsequent half century. This de-emphasis was dramatically reversed with the onset of traditionalist clerical activism in the 1960s. Not only did the topic receive considerable attention but a major qualification in Shi'ite jurisprudence for 'enjoining the good' and 'forbidding the evil' — i.e. that their performance entail no harm to the person carrying out these duties — came under heavy attack. Hand in hand with this emphatic insistence on the enjoining of the good and forbidding of the evil went a critical reinterpretation of the Shi'ite tenet of *taqiyya* (dissimulation of faith) which clearly makes for quietism and non-assertiveness. Taqiyya has been generally denounced and declared impermissible whenever it entails 'a corruption of religion' (Enayat, 1982:178–81). Since the 1960s, jihad has also been predictably brought to the foreground in the discussions of political ethics. It is interesting to note, however, that the basic Shi'ite interpretation of the incumbency of jihad has so far remained unchanged: it remains restricted to defensive war during the Occultation of the twelfth Imam (Rajaee, 1983:88–91).

Another change in the Shi'ite political ethic, a fairly minor one, took place almost imperceptibly in the early decades of the twentieth century. A collection of the practical rulings of Mirza-ye Shirazi (d. 1895), the marja'-e taqlid during the tobacco protest of 1891–2, edited by the champion of anti-parliamentarian traditionalism, Shaykh Fazlollah Nuri (d. 1909), eumerates ten principal ethical duties (*furu' al-din*) (Nuri, 1893:79). The last two, *tavalla'* (friendship [towards 'Ali and the House of the Prophet]) and *tabarra'* (avoidance [of the enemies of the House of the Prophet — i.e. the Sunnis]) had been given currency with the establishment of Shi'ism in Iran, and were emphasized throughout the centuries of Safavid-Ottoman and Qajar-Ottoman warfare and rivalry. Once such rivalry disappeared in the present century, these provisions of the Shi'ite Sacred Law fell into desuetude. They were omitted from the furu' al-din during the reign of the first Pahlavi, Reza Shah.

The ideologues of the Islamic revolution have not restored the elevated status of *tavalla'* and *tabarra'* as furu'. They have, however, reinterpreted these terms in line with the central idea of a purely Islamic theocratic state:

Tavalla' and *tabarra'* mean the friendship of the friends of God and the avoidance of the enemies of God . . . [they are] the foundation of the independence of the Muslims, an independence based on faith and belief which would cause their bondedness to other Muslims and their lack of dependence on the enemies of God (Haddad ʿAdil in *Ettela'at*, 1983).

The devotional love for the House of the Prophet is replaced by the solidarity for the Muslim umma, and the avoidance of the enemies of the Imams by the avoidance of God.

Last but by no means least, we must turn to the topic of martyrdom, prototypically of Imam Husayn in Karbala. The conspicuous use of the imagery of martyrdom and Karbala in the revolutionary activism of recent years should not make us ignore the fact that for many centuries, and especially in the nineteenth century, the tragedy of Karbala constituted an apolitical theodicy of suffering (Arjomand, 1984b:164–6, 240–1). The idea of the martyrdom of Husayn, the Lord of the Martyrs, as vicarious atonement undoubtedly prevailed over its interpretation as the militant assertion of the Shiʿite cause against oppression and tyranny (Enayat, 1982:183).

A religious book from the last decade of the nineteenth century typically illustrates the conception of Imam Husayn as the vicarious sufferer and other-worldly savior: 'The Lord of the Martyrs' ark of salvation is greater than other ships of salvation' (Estahbanati, 1894:341).

A drastic change in the conception of the martyrdom of Imam Husayn set in with the clerical agitation of the 1960s. In 1968, Niʿmatollah Salehi Najafabadi, a student of Khomeini, published the *Shahid-e Javid* (the Eternal Martyr), offering a radically politicized interpretation of the events of Karbala. Diverging from the doctrinal Shiʿite position on the infallible Imams' divinely-inspired knowledge of past, present and future affairs, Najafabadi denied Husayn's foreknowledge of his fate. 'He maintains that Husayn began his movement neither to fulfil his grandfather's foreboding, nor in a reckless mood of defiance, but as a wholly rational and fairly well-planned attempt at overthrowing Yazid' (Enayat, 1982:193), Husayn's martyrdom is thus interpreted as a political uprising against an unjust and impious government and thus the model for Shiʿite political activism.

The book first acquired fame in 1976 when a group said to be disciples of Najafabadi assassinated Ayatollah Shamsabadi, the representative in Isfahan of the apolitical Grand Ayatollah Khoʾi.

After the revolution, the book was reissued with a foreword by Ayatollah Montazeri, Khomeini's designated successor. Khomeini himself has excelled in the glorification of martyrdom, at times attaining poetic and mystical heights.[12] He has enjoined martyrdom for Islam as a religious duty incumbent on each and every individual:

> The preservation of the Islamic Republic is a divine duty which is above all other duties. It is even more important than preserving the Imam of the Age (*Imam-e 'asr*), because even the Imam of the Age will sacrifice himself for Islam. All the prophets from the birth of the universe to the present were sent to strive for preservation of God's words . . . Islam is a divine endowment . . . Its preservation is an inexcusable individual obligation (*vajeb-e 'ayni*) (Rajaee, 1983:70).

The youthful guardians of the Islamic Revolution dutifully acknowledge their eagerness for martyrdom when joining the Corps. This is done in a last will and testament which is published in the newspapers if they attain martyrdom.

NOTES

1. My translation, emphasis added; cf. Algar's translation, *Constitution* 1980:14, 21.

2. Tabataba'i n.d.:V, 398–99, emphasis added. The same traditional Shi'ite view is upheld by less important Qur'an commentaries which appeared in the 1970s. (Thaqafi, 1978:II, 70–73; Najafi, 1979/80:III, 277–81.) Incidentally, the Persian translator of Sayyid Qutb's commentary added a footnote to point out that 'in the commentaries of us Shi'ites, "those in authority" refers to the twelve Imams, may peace be upon them'. (Qutb, 1956/57:44, n.1.)

3. E.g., the late Ayatollahs Mahallati and Ahmad Zanjani, and Ayatollahs 'Ali Tehrani and Murtaza Ha'eri-Yazdi. The opposition of the last two Ayatollahs, who were among Khomeini's favored students, and of Ayatollahs Mahallati and Qumi, who were his close associates in 1963 and were imprisoned with him, must have been particularly disappointing to Khomeini but did not deter him. Of the above-named, Mahallati died in August 1981, and Zanjani in January 1984; Qumi is under virtual house arrest in Mashhad, Tehrani has fled to Iraq, and Kho'i lives there. Shari'at-madari, the most important of the dissident Ayatollahs in Iran, was 'demoted' from the rank of Grand Ayatollah and, despite his subsequent acknowledgement under intense pressure of the legitimacy of theocratic government, was subjected to a campaign of merciless vilification and character assassination, and languished under

house arrest in Qum. Other clerics who share the views of the above-mentioned Shi'ite dignitaries are intimidated into silence or, whenever possible, obliged to declare their support for velayat-e faqih.

4. As we have seen, three Grand Ayatollahs have dissented. Three other maraji'-e taqlid, Golpayegani, Mar'ashi-Najafi, and Shirazi, have accepted Khomeini's superior authority as valiy-e amr.

5. Limitation of space does not allow us to discuss the highly interesting topic of the juristic and judiciary authority of the ulama and the attempts to reconcile it with legislation and codification of the law in the Islamic Republic.

6. *Ettela'at*, 14 Day 1362/January 1983.

7. Friday sermon, 24 Shahrīvar 1361/September 1982.

8. *Ettela'at*, 28 Abān 1362/November 1983.

9. Ibid.

10. One of Khomeini's earliest acts in the Islamic revolution was the revival of the Friday congregational prayer and its full utilization as a political platform. He appointed prayer leaders, *Imam Jom'ehs*, in all large and small towns. The Imam Jom'eh of the town, who is usually also Khomeini's representative in the same town or region, leads the congregational prayer on Fridays and delivers a political sermon.

Ever since the 'demotion' of Shari'at-madari and the full-scale promotion of velayat-e faqih, there have been suggestions, especially by Ayatollah Montazeri, for organizing the Imam Jom'ehs into a centralized national agency. In the second half of 1983, concrete steps were taken to this end. A scheme published in September 1983 envisages a centralized headquarters for the Imam Jom'ehs in Qum, with a hierarchical structure corresponding to the administrative division of the country into province, city, city-quarter, and the rural hinterland of the city. The organization is to be used for the propagation of velayat-e faqih and of Islam, and for strengthening the link between 'the cleric and the layman'. The mosques, under the supervision of the Imam Jom'ehs, are to keep files on every household in their area, distribute essential foodstuffs and gradually absorb all local groups so as to eventually replace the Revolutionary Committee (*Mujahed*, no. 175, 5 Aban 1362). Mosques had already become centers for the distribution of rationed goods, and were collecting information on families living in the areas around them.

Whether the scheme has been officially sanctioned and scheduled for implementation is not known. But it is certainly indicative of the future direction of clerical policy. Since the autumn of 1983, Friday sermons of the Imam Jom'ehs of large and small towns are extensively covered in the daily *Ettela'at*. Predictably, these sermons seek to perpetuate clerical rule by preaching the ideas of velayat-e faqih doctrine. Less obvious perhaps is the prominence of foreign policy issues, especially themes of struggle against American imperialism, and exportation of the revolution. One can only speculate on the effects of such sermons in remote towns, but it is plausible to assume that they make for unprecedented politicization of the youth and for their concern with international politics, which can explain the continual supply of volunteers from such towns for the Mobilization Corps and the army.

So far, the culmination of the effort to organize the Imam Jom'ehs as an essential pillar of theocratic government has been the widely publicized, three-day national Seminar of the Councils of provincial Imam Jom'ehs in December

1983. Nevertheless, in his speech at the Seminar, Ayatollah Montazeri went so far as to envisage — admittedly for the distant future — the unification of the office of governor and Imam Jom'eh, which he considered characteristic of true Islamic theocracy.

11. *Ettela'at*, 7 Shahrīvar 1362/August 1983.

12. As, for instance, the sermon commemorating the martyrdom of Ayatollah Beheshti as a result of the massive explosion at the headquarters of the Islamic Republican Party on 28 June 1981.

REFERENCES

Arjomand, S.A. (1981), 'The Shi'ite Hierocracy and the State in Pre-modern Iran: 1785–1890', *European Journal of Sociology*, 22:40–78.

—— (1984a) *From Nationalism to Revolutionary Islam*. London: Macmillan, and Albany: SUNY Press.

—— (1984b), *The Shadow of God and the Hidden Imam. Religion, Political Order and Societal Change from the Begining to 1890*. Chicago: The University of Chicago Press.

—— (1985), 'The Iranian Revolution in Comparative Perspective', *State, Culture and Society*. 1:3.

Ashraf, A. (1983), 'The Political Significance of Friday Congregational Prayer in Twelver Shi'ism', presented at the annual convention of the Middle East Association of North America.

Baechler, J. (1975), *Revolution*. New York: Harper and Row.

Calder, N. (1979), 'The Structure of Authority in Imami Shi'i Jurisprudence', Ph.D. Dissertation, University of London.

—— (1982), 'Accommodation and Revolution in Imami Shi'i Jurisprudence; Khumayni and the Classical Tradition', *Middle Eastern Studies*, 18:3-20.

Cobban, A. (1968), *Aspects of the French Revolution*. New York: Norton.

Constitution of the Islamic Republic of Iran (1980), trans. by H. Algar. Berkeley: Mizan Press.

Eisenstadt, S.N. (1978), *Revolution and Transformation of Societies. A Comparative Analysis of Civilization*. New York: The Free Press.

Enayat, H. (1982), *Modern Islamic Political Thought*. London: Macmillan.

—— (1983), 'Khumayni's Concept of the "Guardianship of the Jurisconsult"', in J.P. Piscatori, (ed.) *Islam in the Political Process*. Cambridge: Cambridge University Press.

Estahbānātī, Abu'l Hasan (1894/1312Q), *Salsabīl*. Bombay.

Goldstone, J.A. (1982), 'The Comparative and Historical Study of Revolution', *Annual Review of Sociology*. 8:187–207.

Haddad 'Adil, Gh.A. (1983/1362), A series of articles on Islamic political ethics in *Ettelā'āt* in Shahrivar/August-September.

Madani, J. (1983/1362), 'Huquq-e Asasi dar Jomhuri-ye Eslami, in *Sorush*, Nos. 175, 176, 177).

al-Muhaqqiq al-Hilli, Abu'l-Qāsim Najm al-Dīn (1864/1383Q), *al-Muktasar al-Nāfi'*. Najaf.

Muqaddas Ardabili, Molla Ahmad (1966/1386Q), *Zubdat al-Bayān fi Ahkām al-Qur'ān*. Tehran.

Najafi, M.T. (1979-80/1358), *Tafsīr-e Asān*. Tehran: Islamiyyeh.

Naseri, A.A. (1972/1351), *Emāmat va Shafā'at*. Tehran.

Nuri, Fazlollah, ed. (1893), *Su'āl va Javāb*. Bombay.

Qutb, Sayyid (1956/1335), *Dar Sāyeh-ye Qur'an*. trans. into Persian by A. Aram. Tehran: 'Ilmi.

Rajaee, F. (1983), *Islamic Values and World View. Khomeini on Man, the State and International Politics*. New York: University Press of America.

Ruhani, Sayyed Hamid (1982/1360), *Barrasi va Tahlili az Nahzat-e Emam Khomeini*, Tehran: Entesharat-e Rah-e Emam.

al-Tabrisi, Fazl ibn Hasan (1970–71/1349), *Tafsir Majma 'al-Bayān*. Trans. by A. Beheshti. Qum.

Tabataba'i, M.H. (n.d.), *al-Mizān fi Tafsīr al-Qur'ān*. Beirut: al-'Ilmi.

Tabataba'i Yazidi, K. (1912/1300Q), *al-'Urwat al-Wuthqā*. Baghdad.

Thaqafi Tehrani, M. (1978/1398Q), *Ravān-e Javīd dar Tafsīr-e Qur'ān-e Majīd*. 2nd ed. Tehran: Burhan.

al-Tusi, Muhammad Ibn Hasan (1957), *Tafsīr al-Tibyān*. Tehrani, A.B., (ed.) Najaf: al-Matba'at al-'Ilmiyya.

Vezarat-e Amuzesh va Parvaresh (1983/1362), *Binesh-e Eslāmī*. Tehran: Sal-e Sevvum.

References to the newspapers and magazines are given in the text.

131

6

Islamic Arguments in Contemporary Pakistan

Barbara D. Metcalf

The use of an Islamic vocabulary in political discussion in contemporary Pakistan is not unusual in the country's history. What is unusual is that that language has come to dominate all discussion and that no alternative, whether Marxist, liberal, or other, exists as a counter to the dominant ideology. Whether supporter or opponent of the current regime, everyone has learned to argue with Islamic symbols and terminology. The current situation differs dramatically in intensity from the earlier use of Islamic symbols in political discussion in Pakistan. That earlier use of Islamic symbols, hardly surprising in a country created to protect Muslim interests, reminds us that there is no single 'Islamic politics'.

There have been, broadly speaking, three dominant interpretations of what Islamic symbols should mean in Pakistan. The first interpretation made Islam a focus of national unity, not a program for government action. Political leaders in the first decades after independence talked of Muslim interests and rallied the country, above all, by the cry of 'Islam in danger' in relation to India. Pakistan was to be a Muslim homeland, founded to protect business elites; and religious leaders, who had not been central to the movement to found the new state, had no autonomous base of power.[1] Pakistani leaders during the 1950s and 1960s were tied to Western military aid and influenced by American developmental theory. There were, of course, figures who wanted Islamic principles to be more central to governmental concerns. But aside from a commitment that nothing should be undertaken repugnant to Islam and the decision that councils on Islamic ideology should be established to offer Islamic advice, religious issues were never central.[2]

In the early 1970s, a second interpretation arose as the dominant political language turned away from Western Europe and America and identified itself as Islamic and socialist. In 1971 the context of political life had changed dramatically in Pakistan when the civil war between the eastern and western wings led to the establishment of the independent state of Bangladesh. Under Zu'l-faqar Ali Bhutto, the leader with the most popular support of anyone after Jinnah, the loss of the eastern half of the country was weathered with perhaps surprising ease. A more homogenous country came to focus less on its origin as a homeland for Indian Muslims and more on its existence as a Muslim nation on the edge of the Middle East. This image of a Middle Eastern, Islamic identity was fostered by Bhutto's hosting an Islamic conference of heads of state in 1974. It was fueled by the new-found wealth and power of the oil-rich and the desire on Pakistan's part to be identified with, and benefit from, that power. Pakistan called itself the *qila*, or fort, on the eastern edge of the Muslim heartland and offered military expertise and manpower to its fellow Muslims. Migrant laborers provided crucially important foreign exchange and further focused ties to Pakistan's west. Thus two sets of factors influenced a more self-conscious Islamic or Middle Eastern identity: one was internal, the loss of East Pakistan and with it a claim to legitimacy as a South Asian Muslim homeland; and second, an external set of factors, the new-found wealth and power of the oil-rich Muslim states. Bhutto himself was not personally religious, was impatient of the religious leadership, and did not even pay lip service to Islamic standards of drinking, dress, or behavior. But his program for the country was to be called Islamic.

It was also to be socialist, symbolized by the Mao-like uniform adopted by the central leadership. Bhutto's Islamic socialism promised a curb on vested interests in the country and a fairer distribution of resources. It was meant to speak to the discontents of those who had not prospered during the earlier period of growth. Bhutto appealed directly to ordinary people, whose political consciousness and desire for direct involvement in government reached a peak in the early 1970s that had not existed before and has not continued since. As Bhutto felt his position challenged, however, his rule became more arbitrary and his concessions to the very vested interests he had hoped to eliminate more evident. In early 1977 he also made concessions to narrow Islamic interests, notably in a ban on alcoholic consumption and gambling and the establishment of a weekly Friday holiday.

The military leaders under General Zia' ul-Haqq who overthrew Bhutto on 5 July 1977 intended to create stability and order, but, very shortly after establishing themselves, their ambitions grew to use the opportunity they now had to attempt to establish what they called an

Islamic order within the country.[3] Talk of 'Islamic socialism' disappeared overnight in favor of a third interpretation of Islamic symbols, that based on *nizam-i mustafa* ('the system of the Prophet'). Religious leaders still played little role in national politics. Although the *coup* had been supported by an alliance that included the explicitly Islamic party, the Jama'at-i Islami, along with parties of the ulama, that alliance was never an alternative to the military takeover. The alliance was a fragile one, challenging a long-time history of mutual opposition between the classically educated ulama and lay parties like the Jama'at. The formally educated religious leadership in Pakistan had nothing like the independent base of power it developed in a country like Iran. Religious influence within the new regime came from non-clerics, broadly speaking, influenced by the Jama'at, and not from the traditional religious leadership.

This regime benefitted from several years of excellent weather, substantial foreign remittances, and the military aid and stimulus to unity provided by the Soviet invasion of Afghanistan in 1979 (Burki, 1984a). The military in Pakistan is disproportionately large as a result of its historic situation, and the new regime readily established martial law as the fundamental law, with little attention given to individual liberties, fair trial, or freedom of expression. The regime, like the Jama'at, favored the interests of private property. Pakistan is conservative, both socially and in external affairs, more like Saudi Arabia (which has patronized the Zia regime) than Iran. There appears to be little radical opposition within the country, though there are many who chafe at restraints on individual liberty. The greatest challenge to political stability has not been ideological but regional, above all in Sind.

Certain continuities are evident in these three political interpretations of Islam. One is the minor role of the religious leadership, even under the Zia regime. A second is the important influence on the ideologies (and on their longevity) played by external political realities: enmity to India; early dependence, economic and political, on the USA and its allies; growing ties to Middle Eastern oil producers; and support from both other Muslim states and the USA in the aftermath of the invasion of Afghanistan. Third, it appears that, despite the changes in ideology, there has been relatively little change in social relations and in the domination of the landed, business, commercial and military elites. Although both Islamic socialism and the current Islamic reforms speak of the interests of the poor and oppressed and seek to dissociate themselves from the inequities of the early period of growth, neither has created policies to change the pattern of economic distribution or claims to political power. What studies there are confirm a preponderant continuity of the power of the old elites, softened only by unplanned changes like the earnings of migrant workers in the Gulf.

If the newly influential Islamic style in Pakistan, which this essay will explore, is not a vehicle of class interests, what does lend it its current salience? The external influences and internal political changes noted above may have influenced a more self-conscious Islamic identity, but not necessarily the one that has emerged. The question of the pre-eminence of this particular orientation is one to which we shall return after surveying the current movement and the program of the Zia regime in more detail.

ISLAMIC REFORMS: THE NIZAM-I ISLAMI

Throughout Pakistan's history the most serious intellectual challenge to the various regimes has come from the Jama'at-i Islami, an organization long led by the late Maulana Abu'l-A'la Maududi (d. 1979).[4] The Jama'at had its origins before Partition when Maududi, then a journalist and politician, ended a long association with the Jami'atu'l-'Ulama-yi Hind because of its nationalist commitment to co-operation with non-Muslims in order to secure independence. In the early 1930s he established a journal whose target was not political alliance as such but Western culture. His increasingly influential writings sought to show by rational argument the superiority of Islam to any other source of values or guide to behavior.

From 1937 to 1941, as political competition intensified, he directed his writings against nationalism (whether of the Congress or the Muslim League) as one of the most serious threats of Western civilisation to Islam, both because it fractured the *ummat* and because it based political life on alien theories. In 1941, with the demand for Pakistan explicit, Maududi founded the Jama'at-i Islami to embody an example of a disciplined Islamic society. He was influenced in this by the example of both Fascists and Communists in Europe where highly organized minorities, he felt, could influence a whole society. His society, whose members initially lived together, was to be thoroughly Islamic in ideas and conduct. This early opposition to the League discredited the Jama'at in later years in Pakistan; and reminders of that opposition continue to be articulated in controversies today.[5]

When Pakistan became a reality, Maududi, despite his earlier opposition, moved to the new country and soon became the most coherent voice arguing that the state should exist not only to protect

Muslim interests but to embody Islamic principles. The Jama'at founded branches throughout Pakistan to do relief work and disseminate propaganda. The association was feared by early governments and accused of a central role in the anti-Ahmadi riots of 1953 when Maududi, personally deploring the violence, emerged as the spokesmen of the ulama and thus established a reputation of authority. From this time on there were ulama prepared to accept Jama'at leadership on political questions.[6] With the first constitution of 1956, the Jama'at in fact acted as a political party; and since then, when parties have been permitted to exist, the Jama'at has regularly contested elections. It has never had major electoral success, but its influence has been widespread and pervasive in cities and among university students, for whom it has served as a significant source of meaning and identity at a particular stage in their lives. Its influence grew in the early 1970s, in part because of Saudi patronage and support.[7]

With the establishment of the new regime in 1977, members of the Jama'at felt that for the first time their values were being publicly proclaimed at the highest levels and that people they approved of were being appointed to influential roles. The terms that were being used by Zia and others — Islamic system, Islamic economy, Islamic education, Islam as a complete code of life (*mukammal zabita-i hayat*) — all had been honed in Jama'at scholarship and polemics over the years. Even though their ideal of an Islamic state did not permit a military dictator as leader, Jama'at members were prepared to offer their cooperation. In August 1978, Mian Tufail Muhammad, the *amir* of the Jama'at, said that this was 'a golden opportunity for the establishment of an Islamic system which should never be allowed to go unavailed of, (quoted in Mintjes, 1980:48). In that month members of the Jama'at for the first time accepted positions in a federal cabinet. But even after they resigned eight months later, and even when the Jama'at was legally outlawed along with all other political parties, the ideology of the organization continued to be very influential informally.

Despite the widespread publicity and discussion given them, the Islamic changes since 1977 have been deemed 'cosmetic' by critics. An implicit judgement of these policies is given in a document prepared at the request of the Ministry of Finance in April 1980 to recommend basic policies for an Islamic state. The document focuses on ends that are truly Islamic, defining their goal as a better life for more people, moderate economic growth, and social justice. To achieve this goal, the report strongly recommends, for example, a policy of universal education, land redistribution, and limits on inherited wealth. It also argues that a focus on ending interest (said to be a misunderstanding of the meaning of *riba*) and a policy of levying *zakat* would work against the poor, when what is needed is a comprehensive and socially progressive tax policy. These economic recommendations have been largely ignored, although they could have been expected to ameliorate the very low level of social development (as measured by child and female welfare, life expectancy, and literacy) that persists, despite the over-all growth in national product (Burki, 1984b).

In contrast to all this, the Islamic program in Pakistan has called for certain policies, which have been undertaken throughout history by any ruler who wanted to gain religious legitimacy: prohibition of alcohol and gambling, changes in certain taxes (zakat, *ushr*) and in laws related to interest, and changes in the judicial system. Even the taxes and judicial changes, while highly visible, have not had far-reaching impact. The imposition of the corporal *hadd* penalties for certain criminal offenses, for example, has attracted widespread attention, even shock, in the West.[8] Yet they are so limited in application that the current ruler himself has said they will not affect one in a thousand cases; they are those about which the Prophet said it was better for a pious Muslim not to give evidence.[9] Certain shari'a benches and religious courts have been established as a supplement to the existing judicial system to review a limited range of laws. Those associated with the new benches and courts are primarily those qualified to be judges (not the ulama); short courses for them are now offered in the new Islamic University.[10] A federal assembly was appointed, then elected, with only limited power. Although dignified with the title Majlis-i Shura in order to recall the earliest days of Islam, it can only with difficulty be described as an Islamic reform. Every provision and every debate raises, among other questions, sectarian issues, most dramatically so far in the unwillingness of Shi'i Muslims to accept Sunni directives on the alms tax (zakat). A major limitation on change has been the agreement to accept sectarian objections to any Islamic ordinance.

Issues related to women have perhaps attracted more attention than any others, although in fact almost nothing has changed the legal status of women or their opportunities. Women's opportunities are limited less by law than by long-standing customary practices and attitudes, above all those that result in no more than 13 per cent of the female population being literate. The most substantial institutional change has been the establishment of the Women's Division directly responsible to the President within the Cabinet Division in early 1979. It is charged with formulating public policies and laws to meet the needs of women, developing programs to spread female education and employment opportunities, and protecting women's legal and other interests; the division is staffed by women with English, typically foreign, education. This institution exists, however, in an atmosphere that is not supportive of the goals it is meant to achieve.[11]

The general atmosphere, and the encouragement given to those who favor the immurement of women, has created widespread fear about the imposition of second-class civil rights on women, the restriction of opportunities for paid employment, and the enforcement of gender segregation, notably by proposals to create a separate university for women. The phrase that has become current in recent years is *chadar aur char diwari* (the veil and the four walls): an orientation that one side seeks to extend and the other side seeks to resist. The prohibition on women athletes competing publicly in Pakistan or travelling abroad was particularly telling. Also significant has been recurring discussion about female dress and decorum, although in theory such presidential directives as those affecting the dress of civil servants have applied to both men and women.

Two issues affecting civil rights have in particular caused great public concern. One is talk of abolishing the Muslim Family Laws Ordinance of the early 1960s. This law provides certain minimal protection to women in relation to divorce, in consultation before a husband undertakes a second marriage, in securing the rights of grandchildren to inherit, and in procedures for securing rights to maintenance. Recent studies suggest that the actual utilization of those laws has been limited, but they remain a major symbol of women's attempts to secure their own interests, interests they insist Islam has guaranteed but local custom has thwarted. Despite talk to the contrary, the President himself appears to be committed to their protection and an appeal to the Shari'a Court exempted the laws from review on the grounds that they were part of the excluded area of personal law (Carroll, 1982:66).[12]

The second issue that provoked great discussion about the legal position of women took place in the early 1980s over proposed modification of the Law of Evidence. Debate was raised in particular about the proposal to require two women witnesses as the equivalent of one male witness. Those in opposition have argued that the single instance in the Qur'an where this situation seems to prevail is limited to a case on financial matters, where women are presumably less experienced and a second woman is to provide help to the first if needed. The point therefore, it may be argued — if one looks at the essential meaning of the verse — is simply that attention must be given to the credibility and experience of the witness. The Majlis-i Shura, however, recommended that two women be required for each single male witness. The major exception to this was in *hadd* cases (whose legal provisions had already been in force for some time) where no woman could give evidence.

During the debate on this issue in February 1983, a procession of women in Lahore tried to present a petition in opposition to the High Court. The women, some 150 to 200, were attacked by police and riot control squads, and some thirty were arrested. Their protest was led by the Women's Action Forum, an association of women's organizations which seeks to protect women's rights. Women members of the Jama'at and others sharing their views, who had formed their own organization, the Majlis-i Khawatin-i Pakistan, held their own rally and offered their own statement, a mark of the kind of polarization that some expect to continue to grow.

The result of this confrontation, and of others like it, is that, even if there has been no substantial change in the actual laws, there has been far-reaching change in discourse: everyone in public life is forced to think about certain issues, of which the position of women is a central one; and everyone has to address those issues in an Islamic language. This change has taken place in a context of Islamization from the top, not from broad popular demand. Its core support is the military and some segments of the literate urban population. It is instrumental in maintaining an authoritarian regime that seeks to preserve the existing structure of society and itself in power. Yet this ideology is intensely appealing to some segments of the population, and it is the character of that appeal to which we now turn.

ARGUMENTS OF JAMA'ATI ISLAM

The Jama'at has long been known for its extensive publication program of clearly written pamphlets, which are inexpensive and widely distributed. Many characteristics of the movement are evident in even a single pamphlet like the one I shall now examine in some detail to provide an illustration of Jama'at arguments. I shall supplement the arguments of the pamphlet with comments taken from newspaper accounts and interviews that speak to the same issues. The pamphlet is entitled *Three Women, Three Cultures* and was written by Sayyid As'ad Gilani, chairman of the Lahore branch of the Jama'at; and published in 1982.[13] The supplementary comments date primarily from the winter of 1983 and many were stimulated by the dramatic controversy over the protest procession in Lahore noted above.

The pamphlet does not illuminate the systematic political theory of the Jama'at, which is simply taken for granted. According to this theory, the purpose of society is to foster a life obedient to God on the part of individuals, the same obedience that non-human creation embodies automatically, an obedience whose requirements are known to humans through the Qur'an and examples of which are evident in hadith and understood by human reason. Although concerned with the inculcation of individual moral virtues, members of the Jama'at, in contrast to many of the ulama, also insist on the transformation of the social order by political means. Most important to their program is the control of society by the righteous who should wield power in a monolithic state, guided by the advice of people like themselves.

This concern with the over-all social order is evident in the organization of the pamphlet. Thus the 'three women' are not three individuals, but are profiles of what are taken to be the characteristics of women in three different forms of society: the capitalist, the socialist and the Islamic.[14] The capitalist is given more than twice the length of the socialist because the latter is regarded as the 'daughter' of the former; the capitalist system is also more alluring and more dangerous. Each of these cultures shapes what a woman is: it is the political order that is crucial. From this perspective, in contrast to what might be called 'reformist' movements that focus on individual change (like the Tablighi Jama'at and the Deoband movement in the sub-continent), change in the total socio-political environment is given precedence.[15] This concern with the total structure has made the word *nizam*, or system, central to the political discourse in Pakistan today, with the goal being the *nizam-i mustafa*, or, now more commonly, simply the *nizam-i islami*. The current desire for systematization is evident in the on-going discussion about codifying the shari'a and attempting to apply it by formal law to all aspects of life. It is also evident in the assertion, made in this pamphlet as elsewhere, that there is an equivalent to capitalism or socialism in an Islamic system and that that system must be accepted as a whole. 'Whoever adheres to capitalist Western culture or socialist culture can go to its house and pursue it there.'

It is this focus that gives the contemporary movements, responding as they do to the national states and social ideologies of the present century, characteristics that make them, as a Deobandi critic of the Jama'at once said to me, simply 'too modern'.[16] Earlier activists concerned with the state either wanted to place more pious rulers in power or envisaged some utopian community based on Islamic egalitarianism. The ulama in modern times have, like the Jama'at, talked of a return to pristine teachings and of renewal, but their thought about society and politics has been limited to the assertion that they should guide and influence behavior; they expect society to improve if the building blocks of individual lives are fully Islamic. Movements like the Jama'at diverge from such orientations because they want to control the machinery of a modern state themselves. In the internal debate, what defines them is that they deny the authenticity of the medieval schools of law and go directly to the revealed sources, they are *ghair-muqallid* (non-conformist), and can, they maintain, ignore trivia and custom to focus on what is understood to be truly important.

In their thought, however, relatively little attention is given to the economic organization of alternative systems, even though the terms used to describe societies — capitalist, socialist — are economic terms. The currently dominant ideologists in Pakistan are not concerned with far-reaching structural changes to assure economic justice or redistribution; and unlike the Ikhwan al-Muslimun in Egypt and Syria, with which they are often compared, they have not even questioned the legality and morality of private enterprise. In the pamphlet under consideration here, for example, the only possible economic implication of the changes proposed would be to prohibit women from participating in much of the paid labor force. Women would still serve in professional and technical capacities, but only in institutions that serve other women. They would still have higher education, but ideally in separate facilities. It is such issues, relatively peripheral to change in the fundamental structure of society as it now exists, on which these thinkers have dwelt.

A second point, and an important corollary to this dominant concern with the organization of society, is the extent to which positions are formulated against what is called 'Western culture'. That culture must be known, rejected, and kept at bay by impermeable boundaries, whether it is represented by Westerners themselves or by fellow countrymen tainted by exposure to it — particularly those who are seen to have dominated earlier Pakistani regimes. Again this characteristic contrasts significantly with the position of reformists of the Deobandi sort, who argue less with outsiders than with fellow Muslims who are not committed to a program of reform.

Western culture is, however, only partially known and Islamic ideals are often contrasted with the worst of Western realities. An upper-class urban Islamic ideal is also contrasted with a working-class Western reality: in the case of women, leisured urban Muslim women in seclusion are implicitly contrasted either with working-class Western women engaged in unskilled or manual labor or with some vision of 'liberated women'. It is, in fact, descriptions of the West that this particular pamphlet primarily undertakes, for the author hopes to educate his readers who, he believes, are misled by a false picture of Western life. The description, ironically, uses many arguments of Western feminists concerning such matters as crimes against women, wage differentials, and pornography.[17]

The author begins his work with reassurances to those women who are, he claims, the victims of their husbands, becoming Westernized, and who have therefore panicked at the recent discussion of women initiated by the concern with Islamic reforms. These women, the author says, fear what they consider to be a burden of dead teaching to the point that they say, 'Save us from Islam'. But, the author warns them ('our "modern" sisters') that they do not know how Western culture disgraces women. Its first fruit is socialism, which turns women into beasts of labor. 'Shoulder to shoulder' is not strolling along Mall Road or Bunder Road, he warns, but working heavy machines, excavating mines, and driving tractors. In capitalist culture, woman is 'Eve's deprived daughter'. In her youth she is the football of lustful male players. In later years she lives with no husband to hold her hand; no son to serve her, no family to protect her. Her final years bring the torment and loneliness of an old people's home. Women come to bear, the author calculates, three-quarters of the burdens of society.

Women are preyed on and are themselves criminals in such areas as lewdness, sexual deviance, suicide, childhood vagrancy, oppression, theft, and adultery. The three checks on crime are undermined: an inner sense of morality; external punishment (which is replaced by the theory of crime as 'psychological disease' or *nafsiyati marz*); and fear of God's inquisition at the Last Day. To show what happens in a mixed society 'with backward morals', Gilani provides a chart of crimes committed in a single region of the United States during one year, including the number of crimes committed by women. He also gives descriptive examples of what happens in a world with no restraints: women are in the army to amuse men; houses are deserted and hotels and restaurants are full; alcohol and drugs are used and led in the recent past to the 'mixed battalions of hippies' where, as the Urdu has it, 'that was seen which should not be seen'.

'Dating', one of the thirty-odd words in the pamphlet that are considered untranslateable into Urdu, is defined and explained.[18] The bond of marriage is taken so lightly, the author explains, that people have physical relations with scores of others, like animals. The 'fashion' of living together, a form of dating, means that a man can decide he is bored and leave with no responsibility for either the woman or the children. Everything is left to family planners and government orphanages; and one third to one half of the children in Europe, Gilani believes, are now born in these conditions.

The whole notion of 'fashion' in appearance and dress is one more way in which woman is the victim of this materialist, animal world. If a man wishes a woman to be thin, a bizarre notion in a society as poor as Pakistan, she starves herself, even takes poison. This is called 'dieting' and can result in palsy or even death. Women appear in bikinis so that men can be gratified while they themselves remain fully clothed. There are nude clubs and pools, advertisements showing scantily-clad women, sports teams of women watched by men, magazines designed to incite passion. Gilani recalls Allama Iqbal, the modernist poet who is the only thinker the author cites, visiting London early in the century and asking a salesgirl, 'Daughter, why are you here?' Tears came to her eyes and she explained the hard circumstances which forced her to work. Iqbal said, 'This woman should have been the light of a house where she would give true nurture to her offspring; she should not be selling merchandise in a shop.'

Women in the West, far from finding freedom, cannot go out after dark. Police encourage them to carry whistles. Family planning offices work day and night. Women have to learn judo and karate. Women are nothing but shop-soiled 'girl friends'. 'May God grant understanding to those sisters in our country who are fans and flag bearers of this impure culture; and may He protect Muslim women from their shadow!'

Women in socialist countries, 'Eve's daughters deprived of dignity and purpose' lead an even worse life. In these societies marriage is nothing and 'every woman is for every man'. Gilani tells the story of a refugee from Afghanistan whose son returned from schooling in the Soviet Union and wanted to marry his sister! The old man killed his son and fled the country. Under the Soviets, the author explains, animal culture is joined to force.

Again, women suffer most. They do forced labor with no distinction. All wear thick blue clothes and live in barracks. Women do the heaviest work, and their physical and spiritual delicacy is ignored. Frequent abortions leave them barren. Their life is worse than that of animals. Their so-called equality exists only in work and trouble;

they have no role in the governing councils or in any influential positions. All socialist countries are alike, the author says, and he links not only China and the USSR but such an unlikely candidate for socialism as Japan. The picture of the 'West', if factually shaky, is vividly drawn.

Basic to Gilani's argument, then, is, first, the conception of an Islamic system as distinct from the two competing systems and, second, the importance given to describing the inhuman and immoral organization of society in the West. As noted above, the Jama'at has not been led by the traditionally educated. Maulana Maududi, for example, although he wrote extensively on scholarly issues, did not have a proper *madrasa* education, nor did Dr Israr Ahmed, recently a leading spokesman for this orientation, who was trained as a physician in Western medicine.[19] Just as the leadership and organization of the Jama'at differ from the classical pattern, so does the style of writing. These thinkers do not pursue the traditional genres of religious writing, where an essay like this on Western customs would be wholly uncharacteristic.

Certain techniques or approaches make the presentation of this material particularly effective. In the remainder of this essay, I shall identify four points, evident in this pamphlet and in arguments given elsewhere, that are characteristic of the persuasive rhetoric that has been a hallmark of the Jama'at. First, as will have already been evident, the issues chosen are clearly visible ones that arouse highly charged reactions. Some of the intensity of feeling surrounding the topic of this pamphlet, for example, is evident in its opening line: 'Woman is the anchor of our life in society'. The word chosen for this key metaphor, *langar*, not only has root meaning with all its implications of harbor and a steadying foundation, but is used far more commonly to describe the food, sanctified by proximity to holiness, which is offered to the poor and the pilgrim at a saintly shrine. *Langar* is a refuge in a turbulent world. The insistence on the domestic role of women and the importance of limiting women's involvement in public life defines Muslim culture against something alien and also defines a sphere of safety, power, and control.[20]

A second characteristic of the presentation of the argument is the use of deductive logic. Reason here is used to show that Islam is conducive to human life, whereas Western culture makes men less human and more animal. The initial premise is based on Islamic understandings of human nature as distinct from animal nature. Evidence is then deduced from 'facts' about Western societies to show that they reflect and in turn shape the animal elements in humans. The argument is thus taken to be scientific and empirical. The language is logical and deductive, identifying principles, examining their implications, and illustrating them by what might be called a selected reality, although, as noted above, echoing in many cases issues of serious importance to Western feminists.

What is natural and what is revealed are identical. Classic Islamic theory sees man as unique in creation in combining angelic qualities (often summarized in the term *'aql*) which foster rational adherence to a natural law which is also God's revelation, with a lower self (often identified as *nafs*) which is wilful, animal-like, and given to its own irrational appetites. The unique opportunity of humans is to cultivate *'aql* in everyday life so that they live in accordance with their true nature. This theory is not explicit in the pamphlet in hand; it is implicit in its concern with latent animality and the need to control it.[21]

The argument that the Islamic way of life, as understood, is in harmony with nature is a strong one. By nature man is responsible for securing a livelihood for the family, providing for defence, working at industry and agriculture, and organizing social life. Women are responsible for the home and for bearing and nurturing the new generation. When humans thwart this law, they become animals. But the sense of nature as given is not only evident in gender roles. Dr Israr, for example, who, like his sometime mentor Maulana Maududi, had opposed partition, even now insists that the problems of Pakistan are in part owing to the violation of nature effected by the vivisection of the Panjab.

Western ignorance of nature is evident in their development of an alternative theory which substitutes, it appears, a different view of man's created constitution. Darwin's theories are taken to confirm that it is the animal side of humans that Western culture develops. From the late nineteenth century on, it is worth recalling, Indian Muslims were fascinated by Darwinian theories and their implications for Western culture, a fascination epitomized in a couplet of the satirist Akbar Ilahabadi:[22]

Mansur in ecstacy cried. 'I am God';
Darwin's ecstatic cry is, 'I'm an ape'.

And the verse continues with the famous line of Hafez:

The thought of each man is in accord with the capacity of each.

The result of this, the author writes, is that Western philosophy sees man as evolving from animals, and rebelling against oppressive religion, and, in the end, against all religion. Man, free of religion, is animal-like and has no purpose, no feeling or quality of consciousness, no responsibility for his kind.

The author identifies three characteristics observed in the West that confirm this animality. First, Western man has adopted an animal nature because he seeks to destroy everything for the survival of his particular 'herd'. The evidence of this is found in nationalism, imperialism, materialism, and hedonism; there is no conception of world-wide brotherhood. Secondly, Western man has adopted 'such a foolish thought as secularism', an impossible quality for any human conscious of his true nature. Only animals can be secular. Secularism is negated by man's beliefs, feelings, sense of good and evil, and above all his solidarity with his fellows (his *qaum*). Third, Western man has started taking animals as an example for behavior: in clothes, he shows no concern for covering his private parts, in food, he follows no distinction of what is prohibited and forbidden; in human interaction, he has no concept of human etiquette and standards. In the West, the author reports, they have a fashion of eating standing up, like animals. No limits are set in sexual matters. There are no norms of respect for the old or of kindness to the young, no chart of the rights of relatives and neighbors. The human understanding of rights and responsibilities is replaced by force. In such a society, it is the old and the weaker sex who suffer. 'Unable to stalk prey, their value is less in an animal herd.'

Other thinkers, sympathetic to this appraisal of the West, adduce Freudian theories. Dr Israr, for example, argues that Freud shows the basic soundness of the Muslim emphasis on human sexuality. This justifies 'Islamic' reforms controlling access to women; it explains the corruption of Western society where no social program controls the sexual impulses that motivate everyday life. The familiarity of writers with Darwin and Freud, however limited, is a reminder that many of the current spokesmen are not traditionally educated but exposed to secular education or even, as in the case of Dr Israr, educated abroad.

The emphasis on Western animality, logically explicated, suggests the emotive edge to the arguments presented: what could be more feared than such degeneration? It is also one of many elements that fuel fierce anti-American feelings, evident, for example, in Pakistan in the incidents surrounding the burning of the US embassy in November 1979. Western opponents are, at least to some Pakistanis, something less than human.

A third characteristic of the argumentation is that it is bolstered on both sides by authority, by quotations from the scriptural texts of Islam. This element is present in all debate, for when introduced by any one party it has to be answered in kind by the others. In this pamphlet, it is particularly evident in the final section when Islamic society is described and hadith are enjoined to sanction it. This section, based as it is on a reading of sacred authorities, might well be summarized here.

Women in Islamic societies, in contrast to those of the West, are 'Eve's darling daughters', surrounded by comfort, satisfaction, and honor. Islam first put women in a place equal to men, equal in rights, but favored and honored. Because she is physically weaker, a woman has different duties from a man, a difference that is meaningful and purposeful. She is charged with the continuation of the human race.

Women are free of the struggle for survival. They are protected from evil glances, thanks to the veil. An Islamic society follows five rules:

(i) There is no mixed society
(ii) Women avoid going out of the home
(iii) If they need to go out, they do not adorn themselves and use a veil
(iv) They avoid conversation with men who are not related to them
(v) If they must speak, they speak briefly and directly, not gently and sweetly.

These rules produce a different social order (*nizam*) in which the mingling of men and women is limited and protected. These rules, Gilani explains, prevailed until the time of the British, when 'a special service class and the well-to-do' adopted a mental slavery and began distorting the clear orders of the Qur'an and the hadith. When seclusion was observed, he insists, society flourished; when it ended, it declined. Iqbal, quoted again, explained that freedom for women has invariably destroyed human society.

Gilani's list of 'women's rights' is not that of liberals. Islam, he notes, gives a woman the right to private property, to inheritance, and to the marriage portion. She has the right to maintenance. She has the right to leave her husband if he is oppressive or distasteful. She can choose her husband within the limits of modesty. When asked about the differential roles of women and men, the Prophet replied that to manage a house well, keep a husband happy, and behave appropriately was equal to anything men might do. Women are to stay at home; home is the best place for their prayer, it is their field of holy war. All the respect a woman earns (*'izzat, ihtiram*) depends on her attention to her domestic circle. To know the command of Islam is to find well-being, Gilani concludes. The other cultures will disappear, but Islam will last forever.

A fourth and final characteristic of the argument, running like a thread throughout the pamphlet and the debate, is what might be called an argument from status. I choose this phrase rather than 'an argument based on class' because it is necessary to avoid the easy assumption that the argument made has some direct sociological correlative. Gilani speaks of the rich and Westernized as his opponents, but the least reflection will make it apparent that, despite such terms and even the more specific sociological terms he uses, the kind of argument he is making is one that describes a cultural perspective far more than any objective measure of occupation, educational experience, or income. Bhutto, in contrast, made specific appeals to the economic interests of peasants, workers, and the poor, although, in the end, he grew ever closer to the landlords and industrialists who had dominated Pakistan from the beginning (Richter, 1979:553–4). The spokesmen for the *nizam-i mustafa* also speak a language of egalitarianism and seem to denounce the rich — but it is only the rich who do not share their values. There is no element in their program to challenge the existing economic relations in society.

It is possible to make some sociological statements about Jama'at membership. Its leadership has come from academics, students, teachers, lawyers and journalists. Its core supporters are urban and literate, and it has been strong in the universities. It does not include the rural or the very poor. However, it is hard to go beyond these statements. Particularly in the current situation, many are drawn to a Jama'at orientation because the national leadership is known to be sympathetic to it. Pakistan is a society where the elites, and people in general, defer to the authority in power and are likely to be very flexible — or realistic — ideologically. No-one speaks now of 'Islamic socialism', the phrase current only a decade back. Pakistanis have made enormous shifts in the last two decades in the political language they have employed. Those now supporting the government's Islamic policies come from a very wide variety of backgrounds. Some may do so out of expediency, some may be motivated by a desire for order and stability, some may genuinely be committed to the current program or to a vague longing for an Islamic program of any kind.[23]

The appeal throughout the pamphlet is to true Muslims, and against the rich and Westernized. The opposition are summed up by calling them the *apwa* (pl. *apwaee*), treating the English acronym for the All Pakistan Women's Association as an Urdu noun. APWA was founded after Partition as a voluntary organization of privileged women who engaged in a number of welfare activities, initially among refugees and then among the poor generally. APWA has attained international recognition as a social service organization. It is fundamentally conservative in that its programs do nothing to change the structure of society but rather seek to alleviate misery among the poorest people. Recently it has been outspoken in opposition to any talk of government action that would end the Family Law Ordinance or hamper what mobility and public roles are open to women.

Gilani argues that the apwaee have taken up the false European belief that women and men are equal, denying their separate roles as separate wheels of a common enterprise. 'The begums of APWA [*begum* being another loaded term to describe the women of the social elites], whose work is to become second wives of their rich old husbands and to live in luxury and pomp, take up the role of showing off their glitter outside of the house all in the name of "progress" and "equality"' — the English words are used. The serious social work of APWA is thus completely ignored and its members are contrasted to 'innocent Muslim women', 'our God-fearing and good sisters who are obedient in the order of God and the Prophet'. He speaks of a struggle of principle between the voiceless Muslim well-born *shurafa* who are middle-class and the *mutrafin*, defined as capitalists, the well-to-do, and high government servants. It is they who want to turn 'Muslim women' into 'foxes with their tails cut off' like themselves; it is they who will surely be defeated in a pure Islamic struggle, for they are nothing but mongrels. The point of this pamphlet is to show the true face of *sharafat*, of high birth, and to argue that it is not genealogical but moral.

The debate stimulated by the Lahore procession used the rhetoric of class. Women themselves, especially those influenced by the Jama'at, condemned the protesters as 'Westernized and misled'.[24] A hundred ulama in Lahore stated, as reported in *The Pakistan Times*, 17 February 1983, that the women's agitation was 'a proclamation of war against God's commands'; they identified the women as those who 'either belonged to the upper stratum of society who were fond of Western culture and civilisation or were the champions of secularism. . .' Maulana Sami'ul-Haqq Deobandi of Akora Khattak, a member of the Majlis and a well-known correspondent, writing in

Dawn, 20 February 1983, said that the women were not representative 'of the toiling suffering women in the villages' but 'represented
the rich urban and westernized elite'; they were people whose 'influence, wealth and social status were threatened by Islamic social and
legal justice'. In a long signed article in *The Pakistan Times* of 18
February 1983, another columnist, N.A. Khwaja, like the author of
the pamphlet, made APWA responsible for the protest (although
without ever naming the organization); in a phrase neatly combining
Darwinian echoes of the rational theories and the status argument of
the fundamentalists, he dismissed the protesters as 'influential begums
eager to *ape* Western ways' (emphasis added).

As noted at the outset, Jama'at-style arguments have set the terms
of the debate; answers to them have been piecemeal. At best opponents
have tried to deny the appropriateness of the debate, as expressed,
for example, in a somewhat baffled and bemused tone in a letter to
The Pakistan Times of 21 February 1983 by one Lt.-Col. (Ret'd) G.
Dastgir:

> By the grace of Almighty God I was born in a Muslim home like
> any other Pakistani Muslim but during my life of over 50 years
> I have never experienced so much controversy on Islam as I am
> experiencing now for the last 3-4 years. It has almost become a
> matter of routine to read in the Press, see on TV, and hear on Radio
> what is Islamic and what is not. One starts thinking whether our
> ancestors and we have so far been living an Islamic or un-Islamic
> life.

The writer identifies himself as a Muslim, but not with the Islam and
the process of defining Islam current today; he presumably represents
a position that wants religious matters left to individuals and to sects,
and a society that is more open to participation and dissent. In a similar
vein, S.K. Kauser, writing in *Dawn* of 10 February 1983, reviewed
the restrictions on make-up on television, dress, and a separate university, and then asked

> A question stares us all 'why this obsession with women?' Cor-
> rection please . . ., there are other questions: Doesn't the govern-
> ment have better things to do? Aren't there real problems in
> Pakistan? Despite utmost resistance, a thought forces itself out of
> the many queries that whirl within one's mind. Is the victimisa-
> tion of women related to their greater vulnerability? Or is it the
> case that men have become insecure and are willing to use any

means to restore their status quo?

Such writers simply want the issues and, at times, the whole public appropriation of religious symbols, dropped.

Other writers adduce, even if they do not systematically present liberal concepts in their disagreement with the so-called Islamic policies. Those who refuse to accept a limited domestic sphere for women often draw on the language of Western egalitarianism. Here is a letter to *The Muslim* of 20 February 1983:

> Being a working woman and supporting my parents, I fail to fathom why my legal position should be any different than that of any man . . . [The mullas] are not the *thaikadars* of Islam. No one has given them this contract.

An argument of gender equality is thus joined to one of the right of all believers to speak to Islamic issues. The language of Western constitutionalism was explicitly used in the petition of women lawyers to the Chief Justice of the Lahore High Court in speaking of a struggle 'to achieve full and justiciable rights' and to argue that if, as it happens, an oath of a woman is equal to an oath of a man, her evidence must also be equal.

The elite women who are outspoken on issues of their civil rights are also inspired, even if not consciously, by their dominant position in a deeply hierarchic society. They are used to power and respect. An aristocratic woman member of the Majlis cried out indignantly during the debate on the Law of Evidence: 'Am I then worth only half my manservant?' Perhaps no-one would articulate the presumptions behind that statement, but no-one would object to it either.

Most commonly, however, opponents of the current ideology draw on independent interpretations of Islam. Thus the women lawyers in the petition just noted insisted that their position was Islamic and that the advisory Council on Islamic Ideology should be reconstituted with men and women 'able to interpret the true spirit and intrinsic justice of Islam.'[25] Most common, and presumably most effective, are assertions that premise their arguments for women's right not on grounds of ability, necessity, local social structure, or universal rights, but rather on their own citation of Islamic authority.

One of the most eloquent of such interpretations was published in *The Pakistan Times* of 5 February 1983.[26] The author focuses her discussion on the Prophet's first wife, Khadija, and argues that she was a woman in the midst of public life, twice-widowed and managing

151

her own business and family affairs. '[Descriptions of her] reveal a fair-minded businesswoman, with a sense of ethics and confident in her abilities. She had to be informed about business and market trends and to deal with many people. It was because of this, the author argues in detail, that she became an experienced judge of human nature, refused other offers of marriage, identified the superior moral qualities of her employee Muhammad, and married him despite his being 15 years her junior. It was this same acumen and experience — that no woman locked inside a room could ever have had — that gave her the insight to recognize at once the truth of the revelation he brought.' On the occasion of the attack on women in Lahore, the same author wrote of the incident as 'an assault on Qur'anic injunctions that are permanent and binding — the rights of women as human beings'. She also subtly redefined the boundaries of the four walls: 'the Pakistani women have a great responsibility in safeguarding their home, which is Pakistan'.[27] This kind of argument from scriptural authority attempts to see the context and implications of the behavior of personages whom all regard as exemplary.

Other responses based on the texts include general claims to the 'Islamic rights of women'[28], and an insistence that the opposition cannot alone speak for Islam. In a reply to a statement by Dr Israr that he would rather be dead than ruled by a woman, one correspondent wrote in *The Muslim*, 18 February 1983:

> The 'Islam' of these Pakistani Rasputins is but a concoction of alien and pagan beliefs mixed with their own small-time mentality and outlook. There is little patience left among women for their frivolous 'fatwas' on women's dress, women's hairstyles, women's make-up, women's jobs, in fact their total obsession with women . . . Dr. Israr Ahmed deserves to be criticized for his irreverence in deliberately overlooking the example given by our Holy Prophet (Peace be upon Him) . . .

A third kind of response based on authority is a technical one, in which many Pakistanis have become proficient, citing *ayat* and hadiths on specific points. One of the most interesting exercises along these lines was the publication of a pamphlet by a woman, presumably Pakistan's only fully trained female Islamic legal scholar, who was educated by her father and was able to respond in legal detail to the discussion on the Law of Evidence and the Law of Retribution.[29] The pamphlet was written at the request of people associated with the Women's Division, and the scholar herself was reported to have been surprised that her serious, technical legal researches in fact led her to disagree with what was being put forth as Islamic (Idris, 1982).

Such efforts, like the plan of the Women's Action Forum to start classes in Arabic, are meant to counter the common charge that women who oppose these policies are 'not conversant with the teachings of Islam'.[30] Charges against them go beyond that. After the procession in February 1983, groups of ulama informed the women that they were *kafir* and, seeking to strike terror into them, that unless they changed their ways their marriages would automatically be dissolved.

The incident of the attack on the procession made clear the extent to which there was a certain lack of consistency in the position of the petitioning women, a lack understandable in the face of violence, to be sure, but also a lack reflecting the dilemma of trying to speak both an Islamic and a liberal language and yet to avoid what are commonly taken to be the ultimate implications of both. Although insisting on equal civil rights for women, opportunities for employment, and generally lack of restrictions based on gender, even the women petitioning tend to share the general Pakistani assumption that the fundamental role of women is a domestic one and to accept the notion that women deserve particular respect. On this their attitudes coincided with supporters of the fundamentalist position, who disapproved of the petition but also disapproved of the attack: a typical headline, in *Dawn* February 1983, read 'Women's honour to be protected at all costs'. Even the burqa-clad president of the women's wing of the Jama'at student organization, the Jami'at-i Talabat, spoke in public to condemn the lathi-charge and the violence.[31] But support for the women in that sense blurred lack of support for their cause. The women themselves compounded this confusion by bringing a legal charge against the police on the grounds that, as unrelated men (*namahram*) who had laid hands on women, they had violated the principles of *chadar aur char diwari*! The women were, in fact, challenging those principles, but, for short-sighted tactical reasons and, in fact, because of their acceptance of some aspects of women's traditional place, they were prepared to invoke them and thus give them weight.[32]

It is significant, perhaps in the long run decisive, that there is a substantial opposition to the ideology currently dominant in Pakistan. There are new organizations and new groups prepared to interpret Islam. In public however, even if not always in private, it is arguments like the ones of the pamphlet described here that have held center stage.

These arguments, I have suggested, are made persuasive by the choice of a single, rivetting, salient topic that is seen sharply to distinguish Islamic culture from an alien 'other'; by deductive logic and empirical evidence that shows the superiority of what is Islamic in human cultural terms; by citations from authority that legitimize the argument; and by a re-definition of social standing so that Islamic behavior, as defined here, is taken as the supreme marker of superior status. The appeal of this Islamic style, as it is presented here, is overwhelmingly personal and psychological. In this, the position of women and the continuation of the patriarchal family have become the central symbols of order and justice. Such teachings offer a strong assertion of cultural and individual self-worth as defined by Islam and by adherence to a particular interpretation of Islam. As a 'system', it is the equivalent of alien systems, but, in its content, it is not merely equivalent but uniquely superior to all others. It offers not only individual well-being but, ultimately, social well-being by elimination of the injustices and inequities associated with what is defined as the West. In recent years, moreover, such an orientation has enhanced ties to other Muslim states, especially to the Saudi government, which is revered for the sanctity of its holy places and valued for its patronage.

Not all Pakistanis argue this way, not all accept the argument. But this language is dominant in public life today and there is no coherent, fully developed rival language to challenge it, whether couched in terms of Islam, or liberalism, or anything else. Those who accept it do not represent unquestioned 'tradition', but a self-conscious and deliberate reformulation of Islam by people who are literate, often professional, usually urban. They are part of a society characterized by rapid change where educational institutions fail to educate, bureaucracies are corrupt, justice does not prevail, and life often seems to lack dignity. For that society only a new order, in which the position of women is tightly defined, seems to offer hope. The Jama'at, and Islamic groups like them, are not traditional but modern — in their concerns, in their arguments, and, above all, in their goal of monopolizing the symbols and instruments of the modern state to organize a society on principles apart from the other modern systems which they despise; yet fear.

NOTES

1. The classic studies of the background of the Pakistan movement, representing the Indian Muslim and the Pakistani perspective respectively, are Mujeeb, 1967 and Qureshi, 1962. See also Hardy, 1972. For the

position of the religious leadership in the core area of what is now Pakistan, see Gilmartin, 1979.

2. For a survey of these and other aspects of Pakistani history see Sayeed, 1980, Taylor, 1983, and Metcalf 1982.

3. The generalizations about the Zia regime hold as of the time of writing (mid-1986) despite the recent announcement of a civilian government, with Zia continuing as president.

4. For the early history and ideology of the Jama'at see the excellent article by Adams, 1966. The Jama'at currently exists in the two very different political contexts of a presumably Islamicizing military rule in Pakistan and a secular constitutional polity in India. Although beyond what I am able to do, a comparison of the two contemporary organizations would offer an excellent opportunity to investigate how a single movement has changed in two very different contexts.

5. See Mintjes, 1980 for the current re-interpretation of Maududi's position in this period; in this re-interpretation Jinnah becomes more like Maududi and Maududi like Jinnah. In the current debate over the proposed Law of Evidence, discussed below, opponents of the proposal challenge 'these mullas [who] spoke against Pakistan'. (*The Muslim*, 18 February 1983.)

6. The Ahmadi are a highly coherent and successful sect, dating from the late nineteenth century; their beliefs about their founder are said to deny the finality of the Prophet. In 1974 they were declared a non-Muslim minority within Pakistan.

7. Like the Ikhwan al-Muslimun in the Middle East, the Jama'at is in principle opposed to a kingly and feudal regime as un-Islamic. Both movements were drawn to the Saudis, however, because of their Wahhabi origin and because of the magnet of the holy places; the Ikhwan, moreover, found common ground with the Saudis in their shared opposition to Nasser. As the Saudis have used their new-found wealth for Islamic causes, criticism of them has subsided. (See Mintjes, 1980:57.)

8. These are for fornication, theft, gang robbery, drinking, and false accusation of female fornication. Recent work by Daniela Breda, comparing the Hadd Ordinance to the Indian Penal Code, argues that the law was formulated 'through the filter of Western legal ideas'. (In discussions in Paris, May 1986).

9. H. Mintjes, interview with author in Rawalpindi, 20 February 1983. Dr Mintjes has carefully monitored the Islamization program in Pakistan over the last several years. If minimal, there have been, certainly, reported cases of *hadd* penalties, particularly lashing for 'fornication'.

10. Jurisdiction of the Shari'a benches excludes the constitution, fiscal law, Muslim personal law, court procedures, and law relating to financial matters. (Carroll, 1982.)

11. For a more detailed treatment of this and related issues see Maskiell, 1983.

12. Any change would have to be initiated as new legislation proposed by the Council on Islamic Ideology.

13. The final page of the pamphlet lists other publications of the publisher, the Islami Akademi. Three are publications about the Jama'at as indicated by the name *tahrik-i islām* in the title; there is also a biography of Maulana Maududi, as well as one of Imam Khumeini (so named).

14. Western capitalist culture is *sarmayadarana maghribi tahzib* and pagan socialist culture is *mulhidana ishtiraki tahzib*. Each culture is assigned a color: white for capitalist, red for socialist, and green for Islamic.

15. The most widely respected Muslim leader in India today, Mawlana Abu'l-Hasan 'Ali Nadwi, has criticized Maududi and the Jama'at on the grounds that they have distorted Islam by emphasizing political issues to the neglect of acts of worship; all else, he insists, is only a means to them. See his *'Asr-i hazir men din ki tafhim o tashrih* (Lucknow, 1978). This has stimulated a recent debate in India where Nadwi has been answered by S.A. Qadiri on behalf of the Jama'at (See Troll, 1983.)

16. For the development of this argument see Lapidus, 1983.

17. For an example of extensive use of feminist writings, including many articles from the American journal *Signs* (Stanford University), see Ahmad and Sajjad, 1982.

18. The following words, set in quotes in the text, are among the untranslatable terms: fashion, dieting, girl friend, herd, secular.

19. Dr Israr, once allied with the Jama'at but now independent, has opened a school in Lahore and admits only young men who have, like himself, completed university training in some aspect of modern science or technology. (Comments about Dr Israr are based on an extended interview in Lahore, 10 February 1983.) Reflecting the same distance from the madrasas of the ulama, Zia'ul-Haqq has talked of modernizing the madrasas and freeing them from 'the influence of the mullahs'. *Dawn Overseas Weekly*, 8 January 1978 (quoted in Carroll 1982:77.)

20. One can compare the major reformist work on women, the *Bihishti Zewar*, circa 1900, whose genesis also owes something to this desire for a sphere of power and control untouched by political or social intrusions. This book, however, covered all kinds of topics in the religious law and in cultural deportment, meant to assimilate women to the high normative tradition. It was not focused on immurement and it was not written in explicitly oppositional terms.

21. This theory is discussed from many perspectives in Metcalf, 1984.

22. See Russell and Islam, 1974. The reference to Mansur in the verse is to a ninth-century mystic who was executed for his presumed monistic views; the cry referred to, *ana'l haqq*, is known and quoted in many contexts.

23. I am avoiding here the assumption usually made that 'fundamentalists' are to be found among the traditionally educated, the 'lower middle class', people suffering status deprivation or feeling cut off from the benefits of economic growth. Fadwa El Guindi made the same point about the Ikhwan, where at least the student movement 'ranges all the way to the upper socioeconomic class' (El Guindi, 1983).

24. This is one Nazima Ala, speaking for the Jami'at-i Talabat, *The Muslim*, 17 February 1983.

25. *Dawn*, 14 February 1983.

26. Amera Saeed Hamid, 'Women's Role in Society'. The author herself served formerly in the Pakistani foreign service and is now a journalist and researcher. In conversation with her in February 1983, I asked how the Islamization policy, presumably in effect now for some five years, had affected her. She replied very thoughtfully that her own life had not changed in any way at all externally. She and other women and men like herself, however,

had been forced to think about Islam, to learn about their religion in a way that most of those who had been educated in English had never done before. The article discussed here illustrates the fruit of this thinking. One of the most sustained arguments on women's legal rights in accordance with Islam (denying the legitimacy of polygamy and claiming women's right to initiate divorce, for example) is Patel, 1979. The author is herself a lawyer and the book is detailed and meticulous.

27. 'Whither Chadar and Char Diwari?', *The Muslim*, 14 February 1983.

28. For example, Begum Ra'ana Liaqat 'Ali Khan, the articulate and influential widow of Pakistan's first Prime Minister, quoted in *Dawn*, 14 February 1983.

29. The two laws raise parallel implications because of the payment of half the amount of blood money in the case of a woman.

30. A charge made, for example, by the Minister of State for Health and Social Welfare, Begum Afifa Mamdot, the most prestigious woman to have denounced the petitioners who opposed the Law of Evidence (*The Pakistan Times*, 19 February 1983).

31. *Dawn*, 16 February 1983.

32. Nor does the government project a consistent image, as noted above in the discussion of the Women's Division. Here is a small example of that inconsistency in the context of another 'authority' — patriotism. A musical interlude was shown from time to time during 1983 on the state-controlled television in which a singer offered a sentimental song on 'our Pakistan', 'our garden', with scenes of the country flashed on the screen, among them a woman, with head uncovered, gesticulating at a microphone and a woman karate player flinging down what appeared to be a male opponent.

REFERENCES

Primary sources

Dawn (Karachi)
The Muslim (Islamabad)
The Pakistan Times (Islamabad)
Ahmad, Anis, and Muslim Sajjad (1982), *Muslim Women and Higher Education: A Case for Separate Institutions and Work Plan for Women's University*. Islamabad: Institute of Policy Studies.
Idris, 'Atiya (Daughter of 'Allama Khalil 'Arab Ansari) (1982), *Qur'ān wa sunnat aur fiqh-i islami ki roshni men 'aurat ki shahadat aur diyat ka mas'ila*. [The problem of evidence and blood price in the light of the Qur'an, sunna, and Islamic Law]. Islamabad: Women's Division, Government of Pakistan.
Gilani, Sayyid As'ad (1982), *Tin 'aurteen, tin tahzibeen* [Three Women, Three Cultures] Lahore: Islami Akademi.

Secondary sources

Adams, Charles J. (1966), 'The Ideology of Mawlana Mawdudi', in Donald Eugene Smith (ed.), *South Asian Politics and Religion*. Princeton: Princeton University Press.

Burki, Shahid Javed (1984a) '"Pakistan's Sixth Plan: Helping the Country Climb Out of Poverty', *Asian Survey*, 24:400–422.

—— (1984b) 'Economic Management within an Islamic Context', Paper presented to the annual meeting of the Association of Asian Studies, Washington, D.C., 23 March.

Carroll, Lucy (1982), 'Nizam-i-Islam: Processes and Conflicts in Pakistan's Programme of Islamisation, with Special Reference to the Position of Women', *Journal of Commonwealth and Comparative Politics*, 20:57–95.

El Guindi, Fadwa (1983), 'Contemporary Activism and the Current Islamic Debate in Egypt', Paper presented to the conference, Law and Development in the Contemporary Societies of the Middle East, University of California at Berkeley, 28–29 May.

Gilmartin, David (1979), 'Religious Leadership and the Pakistan Movement in the Punjab', *Modern Asian Studies*, 13:485–93.

Hardy, Peter (1972), *The Muslims of British India*. Cambridge: Cambridge University Press.

Lapidus, Ira M. (1983), *Contemporary Movements in Historical Perspective*. Institute of International Studies: Policy Papers in International Affairs, No. 18, University of California, Berkeley.

Maskiell, Michelle (1983), 'The Effects of Islamization on Pakistani Women's Lives, 1978–83', Typescript.

Metcalf, Barbara D., ed. (1984), *Moral Conduct and Authority: The Place of Adab in South Asian Islam*. Berkeley and Los Angeles: University of California Press.

—— (1982), 'Religious Myth and Nationalism: The Case of Pakistan', in Peter Merkl and Ninian Smart (eds), *Religion and Myth in Modern Times*. New York: New York University Press.

Mintjes, H. (1980), 'Maulana Mawdudi's Last Years and the Resurgence of Fundamentalist Islam', *The Al-Mushir*, 22:II, 67–9;

Mujeeb, Muhammad (1967), *The Indian Muslims*. London: George Allen & Unwin.

Patel, Rashida (1979), *Women and Law in Pakistan*. Karachi: Faiza Publishers.

Qureshi, I.H. (1962), *The Muslim Community of the Indo-Pakistan Subcontinent*. The Hague: Mouton.

Richter, William L. (1979), 'The Political Dynamics of Islamic Resurgence in Pakistan', *Asian Survey*, 19:547–57.

Russell, Ralph, and Khurshidul Islam (1974), 'The Satirical Verse of Akbar Ilahabadi (1846–1921)', *Modern Asian Studies*, 8:1–58.

Sayeed, Khalid B. (1980), *Politics in Pakistan: The Nature and Direction of Change*. New York: Praeger.

Taylor, David (1983), 'The Politics of Islam and Islamization in Pakistan', in James P. Piscatori (ed.) *Islam in the Political Process*. Cambridge: Cambridge University Press. 181–98.

Troll, Christian W. (1983), 'The Meaning of Din: Recent Views of Three Eminent Indian Ulama' in Christian W. Troll (ed.), *Islam in India: Studies and Commentaries*. Delhi: Vikas Publishers. 168–77.

7

Seduction and Sedition: Islamic Polemical Discourses in the Maghreb

Jean-Claude Vatin

"Il est difficile de discerner les différences entre ceux qui veulent le pouvoir pour appliquer l'Islam et ceux qui utilisent l'Islam pour accéder au pouvoir."   Maxime Rodinson

PREVIEWS

In North Africa as in many other countries, Islam appears to be an ambivalent force, possessing two contradictory political values: it is a means for strengthening the elite's legitimacy, on the one hand, and a popular instrument for defying that legitimacy, on the other. From the outside, it has been perceived as a new challenge to the West. The Islamic 'resurgence' has appeared as both a regressive and a threatening force. From within, Islam seems to be the only ideology to have endured the tumult of the last two generations and overridden the range of ideologies, from the liberalism and Marxism of the 1950s and the pan-Arabism of Nasser in the 1960s, to local efforts (generated by the increased oil revenue of the 1970s) to blaze an altogether new route through either 'Islamic socialism' or 'capitalist Wahhabism'. Today, a new trend of Islam — as a religion, a culture, a social system — has provided Muslims with an ideology of liberation. It is the sole means to the complete rehabilitation of a civilization, the unique path to self-respecting modernization; thus it is *the* key to authentic development.

In the last several decades, although our knowledge of the evolution of politico-religious thought, of judicial teachings, and of various intellectual debates (from Ibn Khaldun and Mawardi to Abdallah Laroui and Hichem Djait through Ibn Badis and Allal el-Fassi) has increased, our approach to popular Islamic beliefs and rituals has tended toward the superficial, and for a number of reasons.

To begin with, the discourse of the lower classes who gave expression to a revitalized Islam, and who contributed to an ideological and practical revivification of their faith, has only lately become accessible.

Secondly, we lack both the necessary scientific background, and the appropriate tools for comprehending events. With but a few exceptions, the dearth of sound analyses of activist groups and popular movements has prevented us from formulating anything but hypotheses regarding events in the Maghreb.

Nor have we developed the proper terminology. The concepts and the vocabulary forged by the West — *intégrisme*, fundamentalism, nativism, Islamic activism — have been obviously less than adequate. Recourse to the ambiguous term 'Islamism' in the present paper is yet another demonstration of the perplexity of scholars who want to study 'revitalization movements' and 'revivalist ideology'.

Still another difficulty arises from the assertions by certain scholars of Islam that there can be no such thing as an 'Islamic resurgence' because Islam has *always* been central. The invocation of religion in times of crisis has always been characteristic of Islam, especially when its followers have felt threatened by an often hostile Western world. If there does exist a 'resurgence', it is only in Western or more generally foreign minds.

However, just because Islamic resurgence has always been a salient feature of Muslim civilization it does not mean that we must conclude that each period of religious awakening has had the same origin. [1] Furthermore, it is exasperating to hear that there are no new phenomena in the Islamic world. Is it not more a case of foreign scholars' renewed attention and journalists' sudden concern for religious matters, as rooted in either economic or political interests?

However, one must object to the formula according to which religion has always been the key factor in the Muslim community. One need not delve deep into history to see the reduced role of Islam in the struggle for national independence in North Africa. At the end of the colonial period, the Muslim cultural and religious code did not underpin the resistance, whatever governments and official commentators may have later claimed.

In the case of Algeria, for example, the ulama were said to have infused the nationalist discourse with religious slogans and Qur'anic quotations. At that time all political movements (most of which had secular programs) had to submit to the terms of the ulama's requirements. Although certain traces of this trend can be found in the nationalist literature, there is considerable evidence that Islam did not in fact provide the ideological foundation of the war. Clearly, although Algeria was in the throes of a crisis, this was not a case of Islamic 'resurgence'.

Today, with independence an established reality, the language of politically articulate groups has truly changed; today, the political discourse *is* replete with Islamic slogans and symbols.

The overlapping of politics and religion in the Islamic world is an obvious and long-standing fact. In the last generation, however, a (subtle) inversion has occurred. Whereas just after independence it was the political elite which strove to control the popular base through the terms of Islam, in the last several years the people themselves have seized the terms and concepts of their religion in order to counter both the power and the specious appeal of the government.

The polemical discourses of the Maghreb to which we shall now turn cast in high relief this recent trend.[2]

THE POLEMICAL DISCOURSES: 'ISLAMISM' OBSERVED

Two 'objects', each of them serving to distinguish a type of instrument for political mobilization, will allow us to observe 'Islamism' in the making. A comparison of these two ideological productions, one drawn from the Moroccan, the other from the Tunisian literatures, should help draft a more elaborate typology of Islamist groups.

Examining two discourses

In Morocco, between 1979 and 1981, Abd Assalam Yassin was editor of *Al-Jama'a*, a review which extolled the virtues of the Prophet Muhammad and glorified the 'original' Islam. At that time *Al-Jama'a* was one of the best periodicals issued by the 'Islamists' in North Africa. In Tunisia, a group calling itself *al-Ittijah al-Islami* published another review, *Al-Ma'rifa*, which asked for a democratic reappraisal and was censored by the local governments.

From appeal to revolution

In 1979, A. Yassin published, in French, *Revolution à l'heure de l'Islam* (Revolution at the time of Islam) in his home-town of Marrakech. He called it a '*book of appeal*' as well as a 'book of combat'. He might also have called it a book of controversy for he strove deliberately to counter official Islam and, indirectly, the Moroccan monarch and his fellow ulama.

The author, born in 1928, was a bilingual school teacher before becoming a primary school inspector. He has served numerous

162

prison terms, since he sent a public letter to the sultan, more than a decade ago, entitled 'Islam or the deluge'. Since then, he has been the most likely candidate for intellectual leader of the Moroccan religious opposition. He presents himself as the product of a renewed Islam, of a cultural force rising from the ashes in the Arabian desert of a catalytic power restoring the Arabs' historical pride and political strength. He is, by his own account, a Muslim moralist, a religious thinker, not a politician.

The stated purpose of Yassin's essay was to define both the 'Islamic ideal', as well as the 'Islamic method' (*minhaj*), which would, by means of a re-reading of the Qur'an and a re-evaluation of Muhammad's teachings, induce the Islamic revolution.

The issue was, he wrote in his preface, 'to islamicize modernity not to modernize Islam'. In order to address it, he forebore to inform his readers of current events in 'Islamdom' (the Muslim world). Rather, he provided them with intellectual arguments and theoretical weapons. He wanted to help his co-religionists to find 'the right path' to a new era, to what he himself called 'the prophetic way'.[3]

The Islamic society has been de-islamicized, he suggested. Imported systems of reference, ways of life, foreign ideologies were responsible for social and moral 'disorder'. Islamic peoples, he commented, had been subjected to continuing injustice and they remained oppressed elites whose culture owed more to both East and West than to Islam. Occidental liberalism had produced only corruption, which had led to a leftist revolution, followed by the dictatorship of a state bourgeoisie. Thus the citizenry had been pulled by revolutionary and counter-revolutionary cycles, both of which were completely alien to the Islamic personality and tradition (Yassin, 1979: 29–30).

The 'great challenge' was to put an end to such destructive practices so that independence could be attained and the Islamic Order introduced. 'The Islamic revolution', Yassin wrote, 'whether as a short- or long-term goal, commanded attention as the only alternative . . .' to what he calls *jahiliya* (ibid.:30). This term he defines as: a world governed by ignorance, violence and selfishness; a world with no spiritual principles whatsoever. Jahiliya has, since the time of the Prophet, been a threat to the umma (ibid.:13,33). Today, according to Yassin, it has invaded 'our markets, our universities, our way of life. It is both the source of inspiration and the dispenser of technology. It is the master of our destiny'.

The only weapon which can be successfully used to fight jahiliya is jihad; but jihad as action not violence. It is less a battling with the enemy than the active supporting of 'education and political action until jahiliyan ideas and habits have been completely defeated' (ibid:14). As opposed to the jahiliyan revolutionary formula which proclaims 'Let us take power in order to change all structures', the Islamic formula reads: 'Let us fight on two battlefronts at the same time, that of education and that of politics, in order to modify the relationships between man on the one hand and God, his fellow-creatures, and nature, on the other'. Jihad is no longer an uprising of religious partisans who prepare for the holy war, as most Orientalists and Western observers have claimed. Rather, it is an on-going religious pedagogy, a sustained cultural effort toward mobilization.[4]

What kind of non-military, non-violent, weapons will jihad employ? First, it must appeal to those virtues (*muruwa*) of 'courage, generosity, straightforwardness' (ibid.:19) which represent the key elements of the community of believers' moral and spiritual strength. It must also appeal to fraternity and *shura* (deliberation and political choice) (ibid.:153). In other words, jihad will be based on the Muslims' essential qualities: on their remarkable capital of precepts, their moral code, their historical experience. The Islamic world will be saved through Islam.[5]

As for the Islamic order, it will be restored after the 'Islamic man' is changed; after an ethical transformation of society is effected.[6] And the masses will embark on this 'revolutionary' change under 'the firm leadership of Islamic elites' (ibid.:69).

What Yassin prescribes, in this context, is a '*marching force*', as distinct from a forced march (ibid.:66–7,167). The double metaphor is meant to emphasize the gap between Marxist practices of authoritative mass mobilization, and the Islamic cultural jihad as defined by the author. Whatever the means used by the Muslim community to aggregate itself, its main target is the political apparatus, especially its leader(s).

Although Yassin does not devote a special chapter to the problems of political legitimacy, he has provided certain clues which can be used as a guide. In Chapter One, 'To Renovate Islam', he wrote:

In Muslim history, usurpation was, and still is, one of the causes (if not the main one), of the jahiliya's penetrating into the Islamic society. All future renewal of Islam depends on the kind of answer we will find, as well as on the attitude that we will have towards this phenomenon. If the discourse's illegitimate character is not clearly made known as *the* taint of Muslim history for almost fourteen centuries, we'll remain blind to it, to our present and future as well (ibid.:16).

In the following chapter 'To Rush to the Top', the author returns to the point:

> Since the caliphate democracy, which brought to power the first caliphs, has been reduced to royal dictatorship, from the time of Moawiya and his successor until now, the prince's will has not corresponded to the people's will (which has been suppressed) (ibid.:63-4).

Nasser's military defeats and final economic failure, for instance, may be attributed to a charismatic leadership which failed to unite the people in accordance with both popular demands and the 'Islamic energy' (ibid.:64). The record of Marxist oligarchies, liberal democracies and military regimes in the Third World, he adds, was no better.

Implicit in such statements is that revolutionary Islamic regimes must replace the illegitimate regimes which have been in control in the Muslim world. Yassin describes the new society at length. In essence, Islamic democracy will introduce a system governed by the wise, not the sly (ibid.:226).

The new rules will rest on three elements: the restoration of Justice through Law (the Islamic code); the re-establishment of morals through education; the revival of *hisba* (the power to control).

The institutions of the proposed Islamic government, as defined on pages 227 and 228, may be summarized as follows:

(a) the body known as the 'Appeal', which will have authority regarding Islamic political morality;

(b) the Imam, the executive who will be elected by the 'Appeal' body and who will be responsible to it;

(c) the *hisba* assemblies, in charge of policy implementation at all levels, from the remote village to the capital;

(d) the courts, which will remain independent, provided they meet the 'Islamic' requirements.

Islamic democracy means representation (i.e. elections at each stage), responsibility, control and thus sanction. Political participation and majority governance are the rule (ibid.:145). All this may appear to be a copy of Western democracy colored by the recent Iranian experience, but it is the Islamic 'code' which makes the difference. When we look more closely at the kind of state which is expected, it is apparent that after revolutionary Islam takes over, the state apparatus will be stronger than ever. Since: 'as soon as the Islamic power rests on Islamic bases, everything will have to be rebuilt' (ibid.:139); because morals will be revolutionized under the protection of the law (ibid.:167); because of the need for economic development, social transformation and international independence. But the change will not become truly Islamic until institutions of the (former) disorder are freed, and leave the way open for man to be God's true follower (ibid.:168). At this final stage God's total and original sovereignty (*hakimiyya*) will have resumed.

No bloodshed, a progressive conquest of people's hearts and minds achieved before taking power, Yassin's revolution sounds benign. In fact, however, even in *Révolution à l'heure de l'Islam* (written for a foreign public) various remarks supporting the Iranian uprising and the new regime of the *faqih* demonstrate that the Islamist Moroccan thinker had found a model in the Iranian experience. He had longed for such a revolutionary movement which would precede a catalytic series of Islamic explosions.[7] Moreover, stylistically, his contributions in several issues of *Al-Jama'a* have proven that his language can indeed be tough and his revolutionary goal violent.

Looking at Moroccan society, Yassin observed that, despite formal independence, the country was still not free of foreign influences. Colonialism persisted, he claimed, as evidenced by the fact that the population continued to think in Western terms, and that atheism remained dominant. In an instant, his half-tone discourse became sour, and his criticism bitter.

Where is Islam today, he lamented? 'Does it lie in our democratic political system which has been the source of all disorders weakening our society?' 'Can we find it within either despotic laws which have kept us under control, or in our economic system which has never ceased to make the poor poorer and the rich richer?' (*Al-Jama'a*, 4:13). Yassin argued that there was no visible proof that, in spite of its official sanction in the constitutional text which made it the religion of state, Islam was still alive.

> Today, renegades, sinners and drunks happen to govern this country, while true believers are forbidden to practice their religion. Politics, economics as well as their management have been the monopoly of a class utilizing them for its own ends. God's precepts have been thrust aside. Shall we keep quiet regarding these unfair sanctioned rights?

In the old days powerful Islamic states were built thanks to an exemplary combination of the sword and the *da'wa*. Yesterday, Saudi Arabia's builders still used both elements. Today, the da'wa people have no right to express themselves, they are not allowed to talk, nor to work. That explains why 'Morocco has become a brothel after Beirut's destruction' (*Al-Jama'a*,5).

The program for Moroccan Islamists follows, almost naturally, after this denunciation. It outlines several steps: to unite all *jama'at al-da'wa* in the country; to prepare believers to rid themselves of the jahiliyan attitudes and practices; to take power and elect a *faqih*, the consequence of which will be: that if the king (*malik*) continues to consider himself the commander of the faithful (*amir al-muminin*), he shall no longer be God's legitimate representative (*khalifat* Allah).

Islam and democracy

Unlike the Moroccan example, the Tunisian example we have selected requires some preliminary remarks. If Yassin is an exception in Morroco where the number of 'Islamist' movements is limited and government's control very tight, the Tunisian *al-Ittijah-al-Islami* (Movement of the Islamic Tendency, often referred to in the French press as the MTI) is a more complex and better organized structure, enjoying well-known, if limited, popular support.[8]

Its literature, produced by a group of authors, has largely appeared in periodical form: in *El Mujtama'*, in *El Habib*, and especially in *Al-Ma'rifa*, (a journal first published in 1970, whose audience increased gradually before it was banned by the government in 1979).[9] Moreover, the movement has received official recognition, which almost reached the level of institutionalization when its leaders considered transforming the MTI into a political party before the 1983 elections.

Yet another distinction from Yassin's trend turns on sources of inspiration. Islamic thinkers of the past have been less frequently quoted by Tunisian 'Islamists'. Among them, contemporary men like the Egyptian Sayyid Qutb, the Iraqi Bakr El-Sadr, and the Iranian 'Ali Shari'ati have been referred to as well as the founder of the Ikhwan in Egypt, Hasan al-Banna, the traditionalist Pakistani scholar, Maududi, or the Iranian faqih, Ayatollah Khomeini. The Iranian revolution has been partly responsible for the growing politicization of the movement.[10]

Finally, while Yassin has been more preoccupied with morals and politico-religious pedagogy, the editors of *Al-Ma'rifa* have demonstrated that they are additionally interested in practical issues, in economic and social problems.

The majority of *Al-Ma'rifa*'s articles have stressed a two-fold divorce. One consists of an open parting with the official Tunisian ulama. The other is an explicit break with whatever comes from 'the West'. Elements of the texts, then, demonstrate that essential precepts, as continually repeated by official Islamic scholars, have become pure incantation. If words such as *salat, zakat*, and *umma* have lost their meaning, it is because those who give them currency are only paying lip service to a religion.

Once Islam was a great civilization of statesmen, scientists, and philosophers. Now, it is a mosaic of nation-states, some of which are governed by elites whose primary concern is to bring their own country under Western influence. Instead of Islamic communities being ruled by Islamic principles, we observe leaders who, in the name of Islam, imprison and even execute their co-religionists. Despots and atheists have joined forces to suppress Islam, through their armies, their currencies, and their ideologies.

According to this literature the dependency of Tunisian society is nowhere more sharply revealed than in the patterns of ordinary life. People have become selfish, greedy, immoral. They drink, smoke, cheat and swear. They are hypocritical. They practise the five daily prayers, but only perfunctorily. In short, they flout the body of Qur'anic precepts. Muslims are, however, reminded that there is still a way out, by retiring within oneself for a while and examining the causes of one's moral decay. The true believer will soon realize that he should break his unlawful habits and illuminate for others another way of life.

This process will prepare Muslims for mass mobilization, and for participation in the fight to revivify Islam.[11] This implies a national code which will put an end to imported rules and rites.[12] In a later stage, the umma will be re-united. To reach this final stage, Tunisians are referred to the works of the modern Islamic activitists, Hasan al-Banna, Maududi, Khomeini, whose conduct is also an object of imitation. The language is simple, the message is clear, and the whole discourse is disturbingly familiar.

If the elite has been so Westernized as to become entrenched, how then can it be dislodged? If the answer is not explicit in *Al-Ma'rifa*, it can be inferred from a text of one of the leaders of the MTI movement, Rashid el-Ghannushi. In his book published in 1982, *Da'wat ila al-Rushd* (An invitation to the age of reason)[13] el-Ghannushi speaks of 'The Islamist movement and modernization'.[14]

For el-Ghannushi, political power carries germs of totalitarianism. He sees two cases within one transitional period, in which great risks of extremism prevail. First, whenever the cosmopolitan (Westernized) ruling elite feels threatened by the Muslim masses with which it is culturally at odds, it is likely to suspend public liberties, and to tighten its political control. To stay at the top, however, it needs allies

168

as well as clients, so it recruits them from among other social strata and extends some of its own privileges to them. It also requires foreign support, which is offered through financial and economic agreements, making the national market increasingly dependent on the international (Western-controlled) market. Ruling elites thus become an instrument of repression within an Islamic country, while they themselves are manipulated by an external force.

A second occasion for violence arises when the masses (and their leaders) attempt to overturn the ruling elites. In this situation they are tempted to dispense with legality and replace an oligarchic pro-Western dictatorship by a popular Islamic dictatorship. This, remarks el-Ghannushi, should be avoided. The leader of the MTI suggests that it is not the restoration of the old model of the Islamic state which is desirable; rather one should strive for the building of a political society capable of solving the problems of the time.

The final Islamic goal is democracy, with all the strengths which have been nourished through the Western historical experience of freeing itself from political bonds and absolute monarchies. Those specific qualities (equality, liberty) will, of course, be implemented within a Muslim context. They will allow Islam to become truly revolutionary.[15]

Comparing notes

The two 'Islamist' discourses, the Moroccan and the Tunisian, have much in common. Indeed, there are many similarities between the arguments of the MTI and Yassin. Both proceed from a criticism of the current situation in their country. Both have concentrated on the 'modernization' process which has led to virtual alienation. In their attempts to borrow technology from the West and ideology from the East, the two communities have become completely estranged. Money (the Western disease) and myth (the Marxist disease) have destroyed them. Having abandoned their religious principles, they have lost their way. This is the jahiliya syndrome.

Hence the introduction of a reversal, with the 'original' Islam as a source of inspiration. Both Al-Jama'a and Al-Ma'rifa have followed precedents, such as the Ikhwan at the time of al-Banna in Egypt or certain Pakistani ideologues more recently; they have speculated about the best way to return to a creed which could then be rebuilt into a mobilizing ideology. Finally, they have outlined the most suitable means for selecting and installing a legitimate government.

At this stage, the two discourses must be categorized separately, not so much because Yassin is more utopian than his fellow reformers, but because his means for reaching the goal are so different. Shaykhs Rashid al-Ghannushi, 'Abd al-Fatih Muru, Salah-eddin Jursh and Hassan Ghudbani, have a far more legal attitude than their Moroccan colleague. They have attuned themselves to that which is political to the point of having considered transforming the association into a political party. When one recalls their rejection of Shaykh Mestaoui's offer to enter the Neo Destour party in the 1970s, their sudden conversion is all the more striking.

For the MTI, the Islamic discourse has become a political discourse, through which participants have criticized the regime. For them, Bourguibism — as an ideology of transformation through 'modernism' — has proven its inadequacy. Like an old coin, it should be withdrawn from circulation. Further, the official Islam of the *Mufti el-diyar al-Tunisiya* and the imams of the state-run mosques (whose legitimacy is rooted in the nationalist period) is said to be invalid. However, the politico-religious discourse advocates neither a complete political turnover nor a popular uprising. If the MTI's leaders offer a counter-culture, or perhaps even a counter-society, they do not suggest a counter-state. They believe they can attain power through legal means. They also hope that the present state apparatus, once in better hands, will be capable of transforming the country. They want power for themselves, but they are ready to limit themselves to pressure tactics in the hope of a formative role.[16] Meanwhile, despite the prince's disloyalty to Islam, he remains beyond reproach.

Yassin's goal, by contrast, is far more radical. Starting from the same premises as the Tunisian 'Islamists', and sharing their stereotyped and conservative views of the origins of the current decadence, he has nevertheless reached a different conclusion. His is more a discourse of de-legitimization than of political criticism. The king's power has lost its legitimacy because the sovereign no longer meets Islamic requirements. He himself is an obstacle to the constitution of a purified society. Here, Islam takes precedence. Through the Qur'an and the shari'a, it is the code upon which economic modernization and social transformation must be based. There can be no compromise, whether ideological or practical, with capitalist recipes or Marxist expedients. Nor, even in the long term, will the 'Islamists' come to terms with the Moroccan monarchy. What follows is a complete rift with the political establishment, which leads to a counter-society, as in the Tunisian case, but also to a counter-state, however illusory.

Yassin, however, does not campaign for an immediate political turnover. As noted, he is more interested in changing hearts and minds through his personal teaching (da'wa) than in popular mobilization (*haraka*), which entails the risk of civil war (*fitna*). He does not recommend a regicidal solution such as that of the al-Jihad who assassinated President Sadat on 6 October 1981. However, his ultimate ambition, the election of an Imam, does imply that the king should be deposed.

Here we find an important element which will help us to compare different 'Islamist' movements. That is, the relationship between 'Islamists' and politics may be appreciated in terms of the movements' own expectations. Hence, we should ask ourselves several questions. Which 'Islamists' wish to remove themselves from the political arena, and have decided to limit themselves to moral condemnation or ideological criticism? Which, on the other hand, focus on engaging in political battles? Which are more intent upon mobilization by means of puritanical slogans; and which capitalize on legal provisions in order to change the system from within? Finally, which groups aim to launch revisionist political programs *competing* with those of the state and which have programs of total *rupture* with the established order?[17]

The question of rupture brings us back to those archetypal (if not archaic) distinctions between legalism and violence, liberalism and totalitarianism, which run the length of historical Islam. We must, however, differentiate between religious and political discourses within the same 'Islamist' groups. Some are religiously conservative yet still capable of expressing views which run, politically, from the mild to the tough. While others, religiously progressive, tend to be politically tough. But the religious and political parameters, and their sub-variables, must be introduced if we are to judge 'Islamism' today.

In the aforementioned cases, we considered two discourses of the traditional type, based on similar judgements but leading to different practical conclusions. Let us now turn to those other Maghrebi groups which have developed more progressive arguments.[18] To all appearances, the progressive Islamists share their conservative co-religionists' perceptions. For them, the propagandistic aspect of the da'wa rests on the same Islamic principles: the purity of life, the necessity of proselytes practising what they preach, the invitation to re-unite the umma according to the Muhammadan model. References to Islamic philosophers, political thinkers and martyrs, are often identical. Even the progressive movement's recommendations to launch campaigns to restore Islamic values may echo that of their conservative counterparts.

However, when we examine more closely the progressives' own

interpretation of the Islamic code, we find slogans with clear socialist and Marxist connotations. Moreover, their aim is not to re-create the Muslim city of the Prophet; this ideal is an illusion. The progressives' concern is to construct a *new Muslim city* which would answer Muhammad's needs, were he alive today. They aim toward a new type of equality, a new form of solidarity, inspired by the Islamic dogma. Consequently, they are less intent on the purification of the umma through eliminating foreign influences, than on the *development* of the umma by means of instruction in adapting themselves to circumstances, and developing practical solutions to contemporary problems.

This has a direct impact on the type of state and government that the progressives recommend. Because the focus is shifted from an imitation of the past to an adaptation to the new, political power may be seen as the affair of man not God. *Islam* through the Qur'an is the basis: it is a cosmogony; and as such, it is immutable. *Islamic thought*, on the other hand, is a historical production, liable to change. It is an interpretation by man of the word of God. The conclusion is that the form and selection of government, as well as the administration of a community, should respond to the requirements of our time.

Er-rai, a periodical expressive of these progressivist views, and the works of Hichem Djait, offer a discourse whose logic radically diverges from that of the Movement of the Islamic Tendency.[19] This difference between Islamist groups, i.e. between 'leftists' and 'rightists', is also found in Algeria, and to a lesser extent, in Morocco.

RELIGIOUS DISCOURSES, SOCIAL DEMANDS AND INVESTMENTS OF THE POLITICAL SPHERE.

Our formal conclusion may be summarized as follows: i) the religious discourse has permeated the political discourse; ii) it is by means of social demand that the Islamic code has been made legitimate; iii) it is due to the down-grading of the state's image that the political sphere has been infused with 'Islamist' phraseology.

Looking at the social strata in the Maghreb today, it is apparent that — as in Egypt since 1954 and in the rest of the Middle East since 1967 — a new society has emerged. Political elites and popular spokesmen manipulate a populist ideology which employs a vocabulary highly charged with Muslim references. This is so partly because the political elite itself has changed; most significantly in Algeria, to some extent in Tunisia, and to a lesser degree in Morocco.

The three Algerian presidents since 1962 and their clients have been the representatives of a world which has become different socially as well as culturally. They belong to a social stratum which is less influenced by and oriented to the West than was the political elite of the 1930s—1950s. Furthermore, their social support now requires more than a simple change in 'style' by political hierarchies. Members of the 'new' upper middle class — which has developed through both the process of modernization and the extension of the state apparatus — might once have been satisfied by a dual system of formal Islamic slogans at the national level and a completely secularized life on their own plane. However, this duality has become increasingly difficult to maintain because, with improved education, far more people are now able to make themselves heard. The number of 'cultural beneficiaries' having increased, the social uprising has elevated a larger part of the middle class; and its members in turn tend to impose their own more popular code, a code closer to the 'Islamicate', a code which is at odds with *cultural* double talk and the *political* double game.

It is also this intermediary group which has proclaimed that if liberalism and Marxism have not fulfilled the extravagant hopes attached to them since World War I, 'Third Worldism' has also failed to provide an alternative ideology. The lower middle class more than any other social group has been tempted to return to that fecund (and culturally more 'authentic') source of messianic and utopian hopes: Islam and its rich political heritage. The Islamic tradition, whether *great* (that of the umma) or *little* (that of nations, ethnic groups, cultural minorities, local collectivities), has been called upon as a last resort.

Turning to the urban and rural masses, one sees numerous indications of the Islamic religion's being a catalyst in the forming of cultural and social collective identity. 'Islamism' responds to unexpressed needs: it is a complete subsuming of all activities, whether economical, social or political, under *one single system of reference*. The understanding is that a return to basic structures and norms would create cultural stability, as people would share in the same permanent religious stock. Problems of economic development, and social upheaval have produced more than a general unease concerning the future of each population. The state's difficulties in reaping the anticipated fruits of modernization have increased popular doubts about the slogans and policies — the very creed — of government for the last decade.

Unable to keep its promise, the state no longer monopolizes social attention. If the 'Green March' in Morocco has once again hoisted Hassan II into the saddle, events since then, such as riots in Casablanca in 1981 and in several other cities in January 1984, as well as the war of attrition with the Polisario in the western Sahara, have dampened Moroccans' political enthusiasm. If Bourguibism was once a political ideology of adaptation, it is no longer regarded as such. The riots of January 1978 proved that political institutions were still useful channels for popular discontent; the confrontation took place between the trade unions, the UGTT and the government. Five years later, with slogans of their own, crowds took to the streets with local leaders who belonged to no official organization. In Algeria, the splendid illusions of the 'industrializing industrialization' have vanished and many believe that the state will not provide everyone with jobs, education and social protection. The political elite's self-legitimizing discourse of the 1970s, based on a mixture of tradition (Islam) and modernity (development), has already been openly questioned.

Classical political intermediary forces, namely ruling parties, are state instruments more than they are citizen representatives. Opposition groups have been banned or bought, and the functions of trade unions and national organizations have been eroded.[20] Parliaments and local assemblies have provided governments with as many relays as they needed to convey their messages and to ensure that policies as defined in the capitals were implemented. But they are no longer able to channel public resentment and popular demands. Nor have Islamic institutions done any better. The ulama have become governmental agents ever ready to confirm by *fatwa* the government's action or intent. In Morocco, they have regained some of their prestige and have been assembled into an official body by a king eager to use them as protection against popular attacks expressed in religious terms.[21] Imams, muftis and scholars appointed to Islamic councils or other neo-religious bodies, have also been manipulated by governments, anxious to demonstrate that Islam was the official religion, i.e. that it was a religion to be imposed upon the people according to rules determined by the top political echelon.

The state language has been changed in order to regain its control over civil society. It has thus been injected with Islamic references of a new type, in order to cut off the enemy's supplies by borrowing its own arguments. Religiosity has been everywhere praised, if not fostered. Governments have given evidence of their religious concern. In Tunisia, Premier Muhammad Mzali has tried to undermine the 'Islamists',[22] when he announced measures which were tailored to the Islamists' expressed wish, at the beginning of the Ramadan

Deal with Your Clients' Doubts, Reservations and Objections (DROs) to Giving Up Awfulising Attitudes and Acquiring Non-Awfulising Attitudes

Dealing with your clients' DROs to surrendering an awfulising attitude and acquiring an alternative non-awfulising attitude instead will help prevent your clients from grossly exaggerating the negativity of an adversity and the dire consequences of doing so. The following is the most commonly expressed client doubt in this area:

> My awfulizing attitude shows that what has happened to me is tragic while the non-awfulizing attitude makes light of this tragedy. Therefore, if I surrender my awfulizing attitude in favour of the non-awfulizing alternative, I am making light of what is tragic about my life.

In the following excerpt, the therapist breaks down a non-awfulising attitude into its component parts to show the client that their doubts about surrendering their awfulising attitude in favour of its alternative non-awfulising attitude are misconceived.

Therapist:	What's your reaction to working towards adopting the attitude, 'It's very bad to be diagnosed with diabetes, but not awful', rather than the idea that 'It's awful to be diagnosed with diabetes'?
Client:	I'm not keen.
Therapist:	Why?
Client:	Because it minimises the tragedy for me of getting diabetes.

DOI: 10.4324/9781003423348-90

Therapist: OK. Can I make an important distinction between the terms 'tragic' and 'awful' as they are used in REBT?

Client: OK.

Therapist: 'Tragic' refers to something that has happened in your life that is highly aversive and which has changed your life for the worse, but has not irrevocably ruined it. Although the event is 'tragic', you can transcend it and go on to live a life with some meaning and happiness. 'Awful', on the other hand, means that something has happened to you that has irrevocably ruined your life which you cannot transcend. As a result, your life is devoid of meaning and the possibility of happiness. Does that make sense to you?

Client: Yes.

Therapist: So, holding a non-awfulising attitude enables you to acknowledge that being diagnosed with diabetes is tragic, but not awful according to the distinction that I have just made.

Client: So, from what you say it seems that the non-awfulising attitude helps me to come to terms with the tragedy of my diagnosis and to get on rebuilding my life, whereas holding an awfulising attitude means that I think that my life is over and there is nothing that I can to do rebuild it.

Therapist: Exactly.

Client: Then, can you help me to acquire the non-awfulising attitude please?

Therapist: Sure.

By carefully articulating the components of a non-awfulising attitude, the therapist helps the client to see that such an attitude does not make light of tragedy. Indeed, it helps the client to acknowledge that a tragedy has happened to them, but gives them hope that they can rebuild their life. On the other hand, the client is helped to see that their awfulising attitude turns a tragedy into an end of the world experience which they can never get over. Consequently, the client period in the summer of 1982.[23] President Chadli has had mosques built and has had the Islamic university of Constantine opened at last. In Morocco the king can still profit from his religious heritage as commander of the faithful. All the leaders' calculations may be disappointed, however, as popular demands may increase faster than expected.[24]

'Islamist' thinkers and populist imams have understood a two-fold phenomenon very well: the religious popular demand, on the one hand, and the decrease in the state's legitimacy, on the other. First, they have observed the intensity of the *religious demand* and the basis of integration and consensus it enjoyed. They have also noticed that this demand was related to a change of mentality and opinion. A general anxiety had set in, and they saw a means to set the people's minds at ease. Not through a theologically sophisticated discourse, but rather through a simple set of rules related to clothing, devotional practices, campaigns against alcohol, women's behavior, the use of the Arabic language, among others. 'Islamist' proselytes found supporters among students first, and especially among those certain of a degree at the end of their university 'career' but uncertain of gainful employment afterwards. They succeeded in gaining solid backing within the faculty of sciences and, strangely enough, among women. From there they extended their influence toward the petty bourgeoisie, a social group anticipating practical profit from its recent access to culture through public education, and a traditionally poor sector which felt more deprived than any other economic minorities of its chances of scaling the social hierarchy.

The 'Islamists' felt that, in spite of the failure of 'Islamdom' in the world, the 'Islamicate' still existed, and that Islam, as a religion, a faith, a way of life, was powerful enough to capitalize on and even to rebuild the image of the Islamic state. However, their movement of religious reconquest could not be limited to individual morals and behavior. At a certain point, the re-islamicization of social life would have to extend to public life (Etienne, 1983). Encroachments on the state's ideological territory would soon follow. Their counter-culture, itself a basis for a counter-society, would seriously threaten the leadership.

'Islamist' activists have realized that they could nevertheless run the risk of confronting the official ideology. They believed that the image of the state as the great supplier was waning. They knew that they could rely on the tradition of a politically utopian 'Islamism' as well as on millenarian movements and messianic trends always ready to challenge political leadership on religious grounds. The politico-religious messiah has never been far from people's minds. He is still the promised religious and political liberator of the oppressed, the one who could restore social justice and public liberty, the one who could purify political power, recreate internal peace and drive out the infidels.

Such expectations have not been reflected in collective opinion in the Maghreb. However, the 'Islamists' could count on critics emphasizing the *de facto* secularization of Tunisia and Algeria as well as the moral 'deviation' of the monarch in Morocco. No doubt the Iranian revolution was able to nurture this sentiment for a counter-Sultan in Islamic-oriented governments.

'Islamist' popular leaders saw beyond that. They were attuned to the practical implications of this recently revealed breach between the state apparatus and civil society, and the consequent erosion of the latter's confidence in the former. They perceived a *legitimacy gap* and understood that the state was no longer master of either *national identity* or *Islamic solidarity*. Thus a utopian definition of an improved political system could be drawn and presented to Muslims who had already realized that the universalist pretentions of the West were outdated.

The models of the Islamic state, which have been promulgated in sermons and writings, vary greatly. Some have emphasized the original system built up by the Wahhabis in the Arabian peninsula, praising the 'martyrs' who attempted to seize the Grand Mosque in 1979. Others have focused on the Shi'i uprising and recommended a revolutionary government such as that of the Ayatollah Khomeini in Tehran. Few have proposed the Qaddafian *Jamahiriya* as an alternative, in spite of the *Green Book* and the financial support that the Libyan leader is said to bring to opposition groups in North African countries. Some approach the extreme of an Islamic despotism, while others seek a revolutionary government. There is a vast spectrum of possibilities between what Paul Vieille and Zouhair Dhaouadi (1982) called a 'formalist Islamism' (which 'is akin to fascism, and takes hold of the imagination of the disinherited, before turning it against them'), and the 'Islamism of intelligence', which returns people to their roots in order that they may adapt to reality.

Maghrebi 'Islamists' are not yet sufficiently powerful either to be recognized political brokers or to wage battles openly. They are unable to win a significant proportion of votes even were there to be genuinely free elections and multi-partism. Political authorities retain the power to crush them, to jail their local leaders, to ban their literature and restrict the access of their preachers to mosques. They also lack their ultimate weapon, that is, a new *Islamic thought* (juridical-theological) on which they could draw in order to construct an *Islamic state* geared for the twenty-first century. They have yet to be provided with a wholly revised version of the Islamic city.

NOTES

1. Although mosques may have been used as centers of political resistance over the generations (as demonstrated by the attack in 1979 on the Grand Mosque in Mecca), in each case the causes and effects were different.

2. In his almost exhaustive bibliography on contemporary Islam in the Maghreb, Shinar (1983) does not mention studies dealing with this new trend, before 1978.

3. Cf. also *Al-Jama'a*, 9:95. The words 'prophetic way' echo the Egyptian Islamic thinker, Sayyid Qutb, whom Nasser had executed. The title of Qutb's pamphlet (1964) may be translated 'Blazing the trail', or 'Marks on the route'.

4. Jihad is a combination of what the Prophet called a 'minor fight' (war) and a 'major fight' (a permanent effort undertaken for man to 'become morally and spiritually better'), ibid.:19; and cf. 67-68. But Yassin also declares (ibid.:25) that military and political fighting (jihad in the first sense) 'is imperative to restore Islam'.

5. 'The Islamic recovery must aim high and big; it is necessary to restore Islam as a saver while unifying the Muslim community.' Ibid.:73.

6. 'One must revolutionize morals under the banner of the law.' Ibid.:167; cf. also 168.

7. Explicit in the 'Epilogue', ibid.:273. See also *Al-Jama'a*, 5:13ff.

8. The MTI emerged in February 1981, when there were incidents in Lycées and other secondary schools. Police reports cited the MTI as the principal instigator, an allegation which the group rejected. At that time the leaders were prepared to transform the MTI into a political party, profiting from the 'pluralist' opening created by the Tunisian government.

9. In 1979 it was estimated that *Al-Ma'rifa* published 25,000 copies.

10. See the article on 'The leaders of the modern Islamic movement', *Al-Ma'rifa*, 4 (April 1979):13–21.

11. On this aggressive policy, see *Al-Ma'rifa*, 8 (September 1979).

12. *Le Monde*, 7 July 1979.

13. Paris, MTI Presse

14. Published separately earlier. el-Ghannushi was sentenced to a ten-year prison term. He was freed, with sixteen other Islamist activists, after President Bourguiba had pardoned him, on 3 August 1984.

15. A good study of Tunisian 'Islamist' movements has been made by the Tunisian journalist Belhassen (1979). See also Tessler, 1980; Camau, 1981, and Ben Achour, 1981. Belhassen, 1981 presents interesting views on Islamic women. Cf. also Hermassi, 1984, Duteil, 1983, and Burgat, 1984.

16. Hassan Ghudbani also attempted to create the 'Islamic party of the shura'.

17. The word 'rupture' is used by Yassin himself, in one of the headings in Chapter I (1979:32), and in a heading in Chapter III ('volonté des ruptures') (ibid.:106).

18. The *mouvement islamique progressiste*, in Tunisia, is a much smaller group than the MTI. Its leaders, together with those of the MTI, were arrested in July 1981 (after a government-appointed imam in M'saken had been ousted and replaced with a popular imam), for 'actions likely to disturb public order and to violate the security and freedom of citizens'. Tried by a Tunis court, most of those arrested (about a hundred) were sentenced to prison terms. Some were freed in August 1984 (see note 14). Another Islamist movement, calling itself the Islamic Liberation Party, has developed even more radical tendencies. Thirty of its members were arrested and sentenced to lengthy prison terms on 23 August 1983; none were among those pardoned a year later.

19. See *Er-rai* of October and November, 1981, for instance. The essay in the 20 November issue ('For a progressive conception of Islam') gives a clear view of what comes of mixing revolutionary and Islamic ideals.

20. The extraordinary conjunction of the reduction of the UGTT trade union to political slavery after the riot of 26 January 1978, and the impact of the Iranian revolution one year later, is responsible for the sudden audience for the 'Islamists' in Tunisia.

21. See, for example, the Congress of the Ulama in Ujda in 1979, and the *dahir* (royal decree) of 1981 creating ulama councils at the regional level. Instead of putting popular demands before the sovereign (one of their traditional missions in Morocco), ulama now satisfy themselves with reinforcing the monarch's legitimacy. This explains why popular imams and local Islamic leaders of low social status have been able to assume the traditional function of representation. See Leveau, 1981.

22. The French idiomatic expression '*couper l'herbe sous les pieds de quelqu'un*', with reference to governmental action towards Islamists, has been used by Premier Muhammad Mzali (who was still Minister of Education at the time). See the interview with him in *Jeune Afrique*, 960 (30 May 1979):71–77. He was later accused by political opponents within the party of using the Islamist trend as well as demagogic propaganda for Arabization in order to become Prime Minister himself.

23. In 1979, Tunisian Premier Nouira, his ministers, and the politburo of the PND all outbid the Islamists in the use of Islamic concepts. Later, they tried to minimize their influence and ridicule their enterprise. Finally, they openly criticized them, declaring their undertakings were dangerous, then illegal. They banned their periodicals (such as *al-Moujtama'*) and took legal action against its editor.

24. Governments have had three successive strategies during the past ten years, which have followed the Tunisian pattern mentioned in the previous note: i) using 'Islamists' as shock troops to counter Marxist or leftist groups; ii) cutting the ground from under Islamic extremists by borrowing their vocabulary and demonstrating the religious 'rigor' of the state; and iii) taking action against the Islamists and jailing their leaders.

REFERENCES

Belhassen, Souhayr (1979), 'L'Islam contestataire en Tunisie', *Jeune Afrique*, 949: 62–84; 950:65–68; 951:89–92.
—— (1981), 'Femmes Tunisiennes Islamistes', in Christine Souriau (ed.), *Le Maghreb Musulman en 1979*. Paris: CNRS, 77–94.
Ben Achour, Yahd (1981), 'Islam perdu, Islam retrouve', in ibid., 65–75.
Burgat, Francois (1984), 'Intégristes: la voie Tunisienne', *Grand-Maghreb*, October:61–63.
Camau, Michel (1981), 'Réligion politique et réligion d'état en Tunisie', in E. Gellner and J-C Vatin (eds), *Islam et Politique au Maghreb*. Paris: CNRS, 221–30.
Duteil, Mireille (1983), 'L'intégrisme au Maghreb: la pause', *Grand-Maghreb*, November.
Etienne, Bruno (1983), 'La vague Islamiste au Maghreb', *Pouvoirs*, 12:155–76.
el-Ghannushi, Rashid (1982), *Da'wat ilā al-Rushd*. Paris: MTI Presse.
Hermassi, El Baki (1984), 'La societé Tunisienne au miroir Islamiste', *Maghreb-Machreq*, January-March:39–57
Leveau, Remy (1981), 'Islam et contrôle politique au Maroc', in E. Gellner and J-C Vatin (eds.), *Islam et Politique au Maghreb*. Paris: CNRS, 271–80.
Qutb, Sayyid (1964), *Ma'alim fi-l tarīq*. Cairo: Maktaba Wahaba, also (1973) Beirut: Dar al-Shurruq
Shinar, Pessah (1983), *Essai de Bibliographie Sélective et Annotée sur l'Islam Maghrébin Contemporain, Maroc, Algérie, Tunisie, Libye (1830–1978)*. Paris: CNRS.
Tessler, Mark (1980), 'Political change and the Islamic revival in Tunisia', *Maghreb Review*, January-February: 8–19.
Vieille, Paul and Zouhaïr Dhaouadi (1982), 'Pour une approche anthropologique de l'Islamisme', *Peuples Méditerranéens/Mediterranean Peoples*, 21:199–211.
Yassin, Abd Assalam (1979), *La révolution à l'heure de l'Islam*. Marseille: Presses de l'Imprimerie du Collège.

8

The Response of Muslim Youth Organizations to Political Change: HMI in Indonesia and ABIM in Malaysia

Muhammad Kamal Hassan

INTRODUCTION

The position of Muslim non-political (party) organizations *vis-à-vis* the state ranges from violent confrontation to unapologetic insubordination, depending on the nature and objectives of the respective organisations and the policies of the government. In Malaysia and Indonesia, Muslim youth organizations have been asserting their Islamic identity in different ways since the world-wide resurgence of Islamic consciousness of the 1970s, against a background of two contrasting political contexts.

Since the early 1970s the Indonesian state has moved in the direction of greater military control, with a systematic program for the depoliticization of Islam. This paved the way in the 1980s for the controversial policy which allows no ideology but the state ideology of Pančasila as the sole *raison d'être* for both political and social organizations.[1] The decade of the 1970s was the era of the rise of the Army to supreme authority, with the 'Functional Group' organization GOLKAR as its political wing, as well as of the drastic decline of Islamic political influence. Even the one party political organization allowed to represent Islamic interests, the *Partai Persatuan Pembangunan*, was manipulated in such a way as to make it virtually impotent as a political force in the 1980s.

As the Army sought to replace the ideologically-oriented political system of the pre-1965 days with the program-oriented politics of national development, Muslim political leaders in this predominantly Muslim country pressed for the return of democratic conditions as spelled out in the 1945 Constitution. Their demands were denied by the military leaders, and a major political transformation was achieved by the Army in the name of Pančasila Democracy (cf. Samson,

1972, 1973; Ward, 1970; Hindley, 1971, 1972). Many Islamic youth organizations, in sympathy with their elders, were against the process of depoliticization of Islam in Indonesia. But there was little they could do apart from helping the remnant Islamic forces in the last two controlled general elections, which served only to entrench the position of the army-backed GOLKAR and the military control of the Indonesian state. The HMI (*Himpunan Mahasiswa Islam*, Association of Islamic Students), the largest and oldest Muslim university student organization in the country, however, was in favor of program-oriented politics as advocated by the army government, and this led to a period of tense and unfriendly relations between its leaders and the Muslim groups who strove for the political advancement of Islam. The power-holders in the military and the influential secular elites were quite favorably disposed to HMI's independent position and its espousal at this time of 'secularization' as a solution to Indonesian Muslim problems.

The discourse on secularization as represented in the early 1970s by Nurcholish Madjid and the so-called 'Renewal Group' became a highly controversial issue within the Muslim community and brought discredit to HMI as a whole (Hassan, 1982:78–140). Other Muslim youth and student organizations were opposed to the idea and rallied behind the disillusioned veteran political leaders of the Muslim community. The tension between the secular power-holders and the ostracized Muslim leaders has prevailed until the present day, as issue after issue has drawn the two groups further apart. The most serious issue in the 1983–85 period was the attempt by the government to make Pančasila, once and for all, the sole ideological basis for all organizations — political or other. It is in this political context that we observe a change in the mood and behaviour of HMI, a change that may take the Muslim youth of Indonesia, moderates as well as radicals, into yet another era of tribulation and uncertainty. This essay attempts to examine the changes in the contemporary Islamic discourse of two Muslim organizations — HMI in Indonesia, and by comparison ABIM in Malaysia — in the context of changing political trends.

THE MALAYSIAN CASE

The context in Malaysia offers a striking contrast to that of Indonesia. Here the fortunes of Malay versus non-Malay ethnic politics have a direct impact on the decline or progress of Islam. Malaysian politics prior to the 1969 race riots was a politics of compromise between

Malay nationalist leaders in UMNO (United Malays Nationalist Organization) and their non-Malay counterparts in similar ethnically-bound political parties (Means, 1969; 264–84; Funston, 1980, 1981). The alliance of these parties ruled Malaysia after Independence in 1957 on the basis of mutual co-operation in order to meet the needs and aspirations of each ethnic group. The politics of Islamic political supremacy was championed only by an opposition party, PAS (Pan-Malayan Islamic Party), but this did not pose a threat serious enough to topple the government in the general elections. However, the election results of 1969 showed that, in spite of defeat, PAS had obtained a large share of the Malay votes, which alarmed UMNO leaders. The ethnic riots which followed in the wake of the elections caused government leaders to form a National Front coalition of several parties, including (for a time) PAS. The status of Islam as the 'official' (but not the established) religion of Malaysia was thenceforward greatly enhanced by the creation of an Islamic Affairs Division in the Prime Minister's Department, and the establishment of the Faculty of Islamic Studies in the National University of Malaysia, the National Committee on Islamic Affairs, the Islamic Education Division in the Ministry of Education, the Islamic Religious Council of the Federal Territory, the *Dakwah* Foundation of Malaysia, and the Islamic Teachers Training College, in addition to the building of new schools and improvements in the pilgrimage facilities for Malaysian pilgrims to Mecca.

The decade of the 1970s in Malaysia coincided with the rise of the *da'wa* (Islamic proselytization) phenomenon, marked by the mushrooming of private Muslim organizations for the purpose of spreading the message of Islam to Muslims and non-Muslims alike (Mohammad Abu Bakar, 1981: 1040–59: Nagata, 1980: 128–41; Kessler, 1980: 3–11; Funston, 1981: 167–89; Lyon, 1979: 34–45). In addition to the existing PERKIM (Muslim Welfare Organization) led by the ex-Prime Minister of Malaysia, Tunku Abdul Rahman, there arose in the early 1970s three important nation-wide organizations — the Darul Arqam, the Jamiah Tabligh and ABIM (Angkatan Belia Islam Malaysia, Islamic Youth Movement of Malaysia) — besides a number of Muslim student organizations in the colleges and universities. The most important and influential Muslim youth (and da'wa) organization is ABIM, which advocates the idea of Islam as a comprehensive way of life and as providing the answers to all human problems in the political, economic, social and cultural spheres.

The government in the 1970s viewed the da'wa phenomenon with some degree of apprehension, while the growing popularity of

ABIM, led by its charismatic leader Anwar Ibrahim, worried the power-holders in UMNO and the secular elites. Several disgruntled PAS supporters joined ABIM and later rose to positions of leadership, raising the eyebrows of several government leaders who felt that ABIM, in spite of its non-political stance, would eventually only help to serve the interests of PAS. Its rise was considered detrimental to the political interests of the National Front, and UMNO in particular.

As a result, ABIM had to bear the brunt of the establishment's wrath and suspicion from its creation in 1971 till the end of the decade. In 1982, Anwar Ibrahim, who had been a vociferous and credible critic of the establishment, sparked off a wholly unexpected political furor by joining the Mahathir-Musa administration, a move which baffled friends and foes alike.[2] The new administration of Dr Mahathir, unlike its predecessors, adopted a conciliatory and accommodating attitude towards da'wa and even proclaimed its desire to promote the 'inculcation' or 'infusion' of certain 'Islamic values' (*penerapan nilai-nilai Islam*) in the administration. This major shift in the UMNO leader's public stance and subsequently in official discourse on Islam, and Anwar Ibrahim's joining the Mahathir administration, gave ABIM its first major crisis, shaking the movement to its very foundation (Mauzy and Milne, 1983).[3] The ABIM leadership, in the face of strong opposition from within the membership and severe criticism from PAS, managed to save the organization from paralysis by formally and publicly reiterating its critical as well as its 'non-partisan' stance. Inwardly and in private there is a readiness among the leaders to review ABIM's past, admit some mistakes and operate in 'a more mature way'. Without Anwar Ibrahim, ABIM is nevertheless still critical of some government policies and efforts to implement them, but with a greater willingness to 'understand the realities'. While ABIM is presently pursuing a more mature policy of coping with changing socio-political realities — partly because of changes in its perception of the sincerity of the highest political leadership — other organizations such as PAS and certain groups of Malaysian students at home and abroad have deliberately opted for an uncompromising and rejectionist attitude towards the Mahathir administration and UMNO. This has given the impression to some cynical observers that, owing to the outwardly positive and generally accommodating attitude of the government towards the so-called 'resurgence of Islam', ABIM has for the moment assumed a less radical posture.

Anwar Ibrahim's dramatic decision to join UMNO and the government, in spite of his colleagues' attempts to make him change his mind, exposed ABIM for the first time to serious criticisms from within its ranks and without. Anwar's arguments that he could play a more positive role for the sake of Islam through active participation in UMNO under Dr Mahathir's leadership, now that Mahathir is seen by him as truly and sincerely committed to the promotion of Islamic projects in Malaysia, were received by many ABIM members with great scepticism and dejection. Some went to the point of declaring that the move could not be justified or defended by principles of shari'a, and that there was no known precedent in the ancient or modern history of genuine Islamic movements, including al-Ikhwan al-Muslimun in contemporary Sudan. For Anwar, the UMNO-backed government, which he used to criticize on Islamic grounds, had changed its position on several issues under Mahathir's leadership. He is said to have felt that UMNO itself could be made more favorably inclined towards Islamic goals if it were properly exposed to Islamic ideas and visions by Islamically committed individuals working from within. He did not choose to join PAS, although he had been looked upon as a potential leader of PAS and had enjoyed good relations with some PAS leaders, not only because he disagreed with the propagation of the idea of *kafir-mengkafir* (branding UMNO as a *kafir* organization) in some PAS circles, but because he felt that there was less scope in PAS for a truly universal appeal that would cut across racial and cultural boundaries in a multi-ethnic society. Naturally, some PAS-inclined members of ABIM as well as his friends in PAS were grievously hurt and shocked by what was felt to be an implicit betrayal of the *umma*'s confidence in Anwar's potential as the future political leader of Malaysia's Islamic movement. ABIM's central leadership failed to dissuade Anwar from changing his decision and finally saw no other alternative but to 'let Anwar go'.

The immediate effect of the ABIM leadership's acquiescence in Anwar's defection was to make it unpopular in the eyes of many disgruntled and alienated followers. Its credibility was questioned by these dissidents and for the first time it had to face hostile criticisms from some sections of the membership. For the first time in ABIM's history, the rallying cry of 'Allahu akbar!' was used to show indignation *against* the leaders, at the 12th annual conference held in August 1983.

Against the unceasing, if isolated, dissatisfaction discernible at the grass-roots levels, and in an attempt to restore the confidence of ABIM's members and supporters throughout the country, Siddiq Fadil, the new president who succeeded Anwar, stressed loudly and clearly in two successive conferences that ABIM's principles and visions had not been in the least compromised by the trauma of Anwar's departure. Siddiq's voice, which represents the collective conscience of the central committee, is most significant for he not only understands Anwar deeply but has always been very critical of the government on Islamic issues. The 'General Guidelines for the Direction of the Struggle' (*Garis-garis Besar Haluan Perjuangan*) which he declared at the 1982 conference, as well as 'Responding to the Challenge of the Era of Resurgence' (*Menyahut Čabaran Abad Kebangunan*) delivered at the 1983 conference, explain ABIM's cherished goals, convictions and aspirations as the all-embracing Islamic da'wa movement which regards itself as 'the spokesman of the umma'. The 'General Guidelines' set forth (Fadil, 1982:2–4, 15–25, 26–7, 30, 31, 32, 39, 45–7, 59):

(a) the aim of establishing Islam as a divinely prescribed way of life in all aspects of human life;

(b) the stages of comprehensive Islamization, beginning with the development of the individual, the family, the umma, the Islamic state, the Islamic world and the Islamic Caliphate;

(c) the true solution to the issue of disunity within the umma as given in *sura* Al-Nisa: 59;

(d) the main strategies for developing a generation of God-fearing youth, the proper methodology of da'wa education, reform and jihad in all its forms;

(e) the idea of Islam as inclusive of politics, though, as ABIM is not a political party, 'its political role is not cast in the form of a political party which focuses on the struggle for power . . . For the supporters of the Islamic movement, political party considerations should not transcend the interest of the Islamic movement';

(f) ABIM's willingness to co-operate with other groups in matters which are beneficial to Islam and the umma;

(g) the assertion that Malaysia's plural society should not be used as an excuse for not fully implementing Islamic teaching;

(h) the need to replace secular development with Islamic development which is based on the development of man as God's creature and vice-regent on earth;

(i) the goal of complete Islamization, not in bits and pieces ('*Islamisasi tempelan*') patched upon an unislamic fabric; however, useful projects such as the Islamic University and the Islamic Bank are acceptable if they are implemented according to the wishes of the umma, with the caveat that an Islamic Bank is really not a great achievement since it can be established even in the midst of secular financial institutions, as is the case with the Islamic Bank in Luxemburg;

(j) the fundamental rights of man including freedom of expression and association, in the face of the perpetuation of the infamous Internal Security Act of 1960 and the Societies Act (amended) of 1981;

(k) the need to 'return to Islam'; not 'Look West' or 'Look East' but 'back to the Qur'an and the Sunna'.

The call for 'complete Islamization' and the affirmation of the Islamic unity of religion and politics in Siddiq's speech are in consonance with ABIM's traditional stand even during the presidency of Anwar Ibrahim. Perhaps Anwar Ibrahim, as Minister of Youth, Sports and Culture and later as Minister for Agriculture, will find the exuberance and eloquence of Siddiq rather irksome though not unbearable, for in a sense he is listening to his own voice — in the past. He could not, however, take exception to Siddiq's strongly worded criticism of the Islamization program of the Mahathir administration which Anwar is helping to popularize, for he knows full well that Siddiq is only being faithful to the goals of ABIM. In doing so, ABIM's credibility as an independent Islamic movement is maintained, although the die-hard cynics refuse to budge from their opposition stand. It is true that some ABIM leaders have reviewed their position vis-à-vis the Islamic Revolution in Iran and that the ABIM leadership is trying to keep at arm's length from the fire of PAS wrath by harping on its independent and non-partisan nature, with its own methodology and vehicle, da'wa. The call for a more mature approach in da'wa, which translates into a more tolerant attitude towards 'the ignorant society' at large, coincides with Anwar's plunge into UMNO politics and lends itself to the facile conclusion that the plunge has a causal relationship with the maturing process in ABIM.

Upon closer analysis of Siddiq's speeches and private conversations, the maturing process appears to be a genuine development. ABIM's senior leaders have been at the helm of the organization since their university days, and today many are nearing, if not already above, forty years of age. The obsession with rhetoric is receding with age and experience, and the fascination with slogans supplied by the literature of international Islamic movements such as the Ikhwan and the Jama'at-i Islami has faded somewhat in the harsh light of complex particularities, which are in no way envisaged in those popular Middle-Eastern or Pakistani texts written for a quite different audience. Hence Siddiq's 'Response to the Challenge of the Era of Resurgence' is an admission of the futility of endlessly pursuing generalities (*'umumiyyat*) and solidarity-making. There has been a surfeit of general statements on the suitability of Islam as a way of life for all times and climes; what is needed, says Siddiq, in Malaysia's own context today, is an attitude of problem-solving which calls for the ability to formulate concrete and specific programs relevant to the realities of the contemporary Malaysian situation (Fadil, 1983:10–13). This is indeed a radical departure from past discourses, coming from an 'old' ABIM leader whose devotion to the ideals of an orthodox Islamic movement has never waned, but whose sensitivity to the complexities of the local scene has also been sharpened in the process, at the cost of the loss of some popularity among his admirers.

THE INDONESIAN CASE

If the Malaysian situation may be perceived as the gradual strengthening of Islam's official position by an administration of Malay nationalist leaders who have recently come out openly in favor of 'the inculcation of Islamic values in the administration' and the establishment of certain Islamic social and economic institutions (the Islamic Bank, the International Islamic University and Islamic Insurance), the Indonesian situation presents a contrasting picture of greater consolidation of military power with the corresponding elimination of meaningful Islamic influence in the state. The series of political and administrative steps designed to promote Pančasila as the only permissible ideology governing the political behavior and action of all groups — now a *fait accompli* — followed by its acceptance as the basis of all social (i.e. non-political party) organizations, are seen by many Islamic leaders and intellectuals as obvious attempts to prevent any possible resurgence of Islam and communism as the two major socio-political forces in Indonesia which could challenge the army domination.

Despite the distressing and discouraging political atmosphere, Islam is still attractive to many Muslim youths and students. A network of non-official independent youth groupings associated with mosque activities (*Ikatan Remaja Masjid*) has emerged in the 1980s to give a glimmer of hope for the preservation of Islam as a way of life for the younger generation. The HMI also has not been unaffected by the reassertion of Islamic consciousness but, as a student organization which traditionally espouses loyalty to the Indonesian nation, it has never been associated with Islamic resistance, radicalism or fundamentalism. However, recent political developments and the apparent failure of the regime to achieve 'a just and prosperous society' as spelled out in the 1945 Constitution have alienated a number of HMI members and leaders in Jakarta, Yokyakarta, Bandung and Medan. The Pančasila issue began in August 1982, when President Suharto urged that all socio-political forces, particularly political parties, should accept the state ideology as their sole principle. This statement led the national and strongly government-controlled People's Consultative Assembly (MPR) to resolve in March 1983 that the two existing political parties and GOLKAR must make Pančasila their sole principle. Regarding social organizations, it was explicitly declared that a law concerning them would be promulgated. At the time of HMI's fifteenth congress in late May 1983, that law had not yet been framed, but the authorities expected social and student organizations, including HMI, to indicate their willingness to adopt Pančasila as their sole basis.

HMI stuck to its erstwhile principle of Islam as the basis of the organization. It was significant that, during the Congress, the proddings of the State Minister for Youth Affairs, Abdul Ghafur, an HMI alumnus, were brushed aside by the delegates in a wave of spontaneous Islamic fervor, and that women delegates were not allowed entrance unless they wore the Islamic headdress or *jilbab* — a new phenomenon in HMI's history. As a consequence of this adamant posture, many of HMI's proposed conferences and training programs were denied permits by the local police and the military authorities. HMI's firm stand, followed in September 1983 by the arrest of Tony Ardie, a former leader of the Jakarta branch, for allegedly inciting hatred and hostility toward the establishment, which became a major issue in the press, indicates that the authorities cannot take traditionally moderate youth organizations such as HMI for granted. Under the circumstances, it would take more than gentle persuasion to make HMI leaders accept the Pančasila policy without protest. Some HMI alumni are not happy that HMI is resisting government pressures, but the gradual hardening of its Islamic stand and a change in the Islamic discourse — much to the dissatisfaction of many accommodationist Muslim politicians — may urge those alumni to review some of their former attitudes and rationale for renewal (*pembaharuan*) of Islamic thinking in Indonesia. Many had joined the band-wagon of the New Order and turned their backs on the past political struggle of Islamic groups, in favor of Indonesian nationalism. But if secularization was hailed by prominent HMI members in the 1970s as the savior of the Muslim umma, today the idea of Islam as purely a personal and private religion is no longer popular.

HMI is openly critical of state development programs and the processes of political manoeuvering that go on in the name of Pančasila Democracy. It has consistently expressed its concern for social justice and the plight of the poor masses, under a development strategy that is viewed as the unfolding of *dependencia* with Indonesia acting as the periphery to the capitalist (OECD) center. It has voiced its criticisms in speeches and publications against unemployment, poverty, corruption, bureaucratic control and misuse of political power. But as a university student organization, HMI does not, unlike ABIM (which is a da'wa movement of Muslim youth), try to transgress the limits of action imposed by the authorities. Individual members, however, may sometimes act on their own initiative to appear more vocal or more critical than others. HMI aspires to 'the development of a just and prosperous society' but it always stresses that the steps taken should be *proporsional dan konstitusional*'. Its behavior has been guided by its constitution, and by official documents which explain further its aims and objectives. One such document, the NDP or *Nilai-Nilai Dasar Perdjuangan* (Fundamental Values of the Struggle), published by HMI in 1971, is an important ideological discourse prepared by Nurcholish Madjid to explain HMI's Islamic foundation, and it has served as a guideline in its understanding of Islam. The thrust of the NDP is a humanistic Islamic conception of man and society based on a liberal interpretation of *hanif, fitra* and *khalifa*. There is no discussion at all of the place of shari'a in Islam and if there is a reference to God's law (*hukum Allah*), it is always meant as God's law in nature and history (*sunna Allah*), not the Islamic penal and civil laws. This type of discourse coincided with the emergence of the so-called 'Renewal Movement' in the 1970-72 period. In the final analysis, the message of 'Renewal' was the secularization of society and the state, in which Islam was to be viewed as nothing more than a personal and private religion (Hassan, 1982:105–15).[4] It is perhaps not surprising that numbers of thoughtful members of HMI, like Ahmad Wahib and his friend Djohan Effendi, discussed in the chapter by Johns in this book, left the organization at this point.

That was more than a decade ago. Today there are HMI members who feel that the NDP should be revised, if not altogether replaced by the more current trend of understanding Islam as a complete way of life based on *'aqida* (uncompromising credal monotheism), shari'a (divine law) and *akhlaq* (ethics). A former president of HMI, H. Ahmad Zacky Siradj (1982:5), claimed in February 1982 that, ever since it was established, HMI had taken Islam in a total sense as a source of inspiration for every action:

> In this respect, Islam is not understood only as a spiritual teaching, but as a system of life from which emanate *fitri* and *hanif* teachings. This involves not only the life eternal but mundane living.

The scope of Islam, drastically reduced in the short-lived secularist discourse and temper of 1970–72, seems at the present moment to be regaining its original dimension in the perception of many HMI members. This is attributable to many factors — the influence of a wider da'wa consciousness, within and without HMI, the disenchantment with military control, the rapprochement with respected Muslim leaders of the older 1945 generation, the spread of Islamic literature stressing the unity of 'aqida, shari'a and akhlaq, and finally the impact of events in the Muslim world. The firm and defiant stand of HMI at their May 1983 congress (*Tempo*, 4 June 1983; *Progresif*, 1983) should be viewed against the above background, which was in no way envisaged by Muslim youths in the early 1970s. They were under the impression that the New Order would be a liberating and humanizing agent of change, a socio-political force that would deliver the cherished goal of 'a just, prosperous and democratic society in which the people [*rakyat*] reign supreme'. Thus, the 1983 congress was seen by some observers as a test of HMI's commitment to Islam.

In a July 1983 article entitled '*Batu Uji Komitment Kita Terhadap Islam*' ('A touchstone of our commitment to islam'), Lukman Hakiem (1983), an HMI leader from Yogyakarta, reported that an HMI alumnus had complained about the current Islamic fervor in HMI, saying that

> one of the reasons for the decline of HMI today is that HMI activists are people who are too busy engaged in public speeches and moving from one sermon to another. They are more active in various mosque activities in comparison to student activities.

Why should HMI be confined only to the campus and campus politics and ignore the problems faced by the umma, asked Lukman. It had accepted the principles of Pancasila as a state ideology in its constitution, but had made Islam its foundation, and the defence of this Islamic

190

foundation was absolutely essential, he said. Today, more and more young people were seeking Islam not through formal organizations. Many were searching for religion and, if Muslim organizations abandoned Islam, they would be abandoned by young Muslims.

Lukman revealed that prior to the 1983 congress, HMI leaders had reviewed the cadre training system which had been in operation so far.

> We all agreed to change completely the cadre training system. We want to give a sharper Islamic dimension to our training, because we do realize that ultimately, whether we like it or not, in the light of Peter L. Berger's observation that the major world ideologies are in process of collapsing, not only will Islam become an alternative world ideology, it will be imperative. Islam is absolutely necessary for well-being in this world and in the hereafter. (Hakiem, 1983:7).

This new mood in HMI, which is rooted in the basic assumption that Islam is more than just a system of worship and that it cannot be divorced from the state, is bound to create more problems for the organization and individuals associated with it in their relationship with the state authorities. Already official permission has been withheld for some student organizations to hold special meetings and programs. Whether or not HMI will continue to resist pressures from above remains to be seen. To be sure, HMI is not the only student organization which has not yet indicated its desire to change its 'organizational principle', but if the government does finally come up with a law requiring the adoption of Pančasila as the only principle even for social organizations, there is bound to be a lot of disquiet and restiveness. However, state and military power are so powerfully entrenched that it is unlikely that any major confrontation between the government and Muslim groups will take place, similar, as one commentator (*Far Eastern Economic Review*, 11 August 1983) had said:

> to those which blew up when the government sought to introduce a secular marriage law in the early 1970s, raise the position of Javanese beliefs in the mid-1970s or change the tradition of closing down schools during the Muslim fasting month in 1980.[5]

CONCLUSION

The present political situation in Indonesia in which the army reigns

supreme has alienated not only the old leaders of the '1945 generation' as represented by the 'Petition of 50' some years ago, but also
the younger generation of Muslims (Awanohara, 1985). The alienation has affected even the HMI, which in the early 1970s was under
the sway of the 'Renewal Group's' ideas of secularization. The failure
of the regime to realize the aspirations of the critical younger and
older generations at a time of worldwide resurgence of Islamic consciousness has restored the Muslim faith in Islam not only as a personal religion, as stressed in the secularization discourse, but as a
comprehensive socio-political program. The HMI leadership of the
1980s began to emphasize the idea of Islam as a complete way of
life, and many individual members have sought a more radical
expression of their commitment to Islamic tenets.

For some, HMI's ideological guidelines, as represented by the
Nilai-Nilai Dasar Perjuangan, are no longer adequate. They feel there
is need for their replacement by a more forthright and comprehensive Islamic discourse. The HMI as a whole is therefore receptive
to increasing Islamic pressure from within and without, but it has maintained its independent nature and continues to foster its links with
nationalistic peer groups and the fundamentalist undercurrent.
Together, these form a part of a public dissent against the increasingly authoritarian establishment which, in the name of Pančasila
Democracy, officially proclaims that the goal of New Order national
development is the 'development of the total man'. At the beginning
of the New Order era the official rhetoric won the support of the
Muslim younger generation, but in the 1980s they began to realize
that Islam is better endowed than the state for the holistic development of man, society and culture. This realization presents Islamic
youth groups with a dilemma. The new and larger Islamic discourse
demands a greater degree of commitment and activism, but such
activism is being severely curtailed, and in some recent cases even
ruthlessly suppressed.

It is interesting to note that in the Indonesian situation the holistic,
fundamentalist and radical discourses are emerging against the
background of the de-islamization of the PPP, the only party which
can claim to represent the interest of the Muslim umma but one which
has recently experienced a crippling internal crisis. In the Malaysian
situation, it is the Islamic political party PAS, now openly championing
the cause of a non-accommodating Islamic political struggle, which
seeks nothing less than a complete implementation of the shari'a.
ABIM, which aspires to a similar goal, has not, to be sure, abandoned
its commitment to the holistic Islamic world-view, but, being an

independent non-partisan Islamic youth organization, open to both PAS and UMNO supporters, it views the present socio-political situation as inhospitable, if not wholly unconducive, to the strengthening of Islam in the country. Whereas in the past the government's leaders were hostile towards ABIM's influence in the spread of da'wa, today under the Mahathir administration, the government appears to be willing to support a process of gradual and non-destabilizing institutionalization of Islam. Under the circumstances ABIM is cautiously evaluating Mahathir's idea of 'infusing Islamic values in the administration', without abandoning its own demand for a consistent and unfragmented implementation of Islamic teachings. This new attitude of 'critical appraisal of what is good and beneficial for the umma and a firm rejection of what is bad' is no doubt consistent with its own nature as a da'wa organization which does not contest for political power in the country. But in the eyes of PAS and some organizations struggling for the establishment of nothing less than an Islamic state, such an attitude is interpreted as ambivalent and a capitulation to the pragmatic schemes of 'Islamic cosmetics' designed by 'the *Taghuti* system'[6] to postpone indefinitely the development of the Islamic state by winning over its opponents. They refuse to take the bait, as it were, and call upon Muslim youths and students to reject the administration's gestures of Islamic good-will, on the ground that the Islamic system can never truly grow out of the essentially secular, capitalistic and nationalistic system, notwithstanding the power-holders' declaration of good intentions.

As far as ABIM is concerned, the Mahathir-Anwar combination may be seen either as a new experiment in the process of Islamizing Malay nationalism, or a reverse process of pragmatic Malay nationalism co-opting Islamic elements in an effort to contain and domesticate the worldwide Islamic upsurge. Whether or not the new trend in Mahathir's administration can stand the test of time, ABIM's leaders see some signs of positive attitudes and the opening up of new opportunities for the progress of Islam in Malaysia's precarious and delicate socio-political balances. If the new trend towards the promotion of particular Islamic values and institutions continues to gain wider official support, it will be safe to assume that ABIM will be more inclined to play a constructive role. ABIM will, in effect, be called upon to produce more and more concrete specific programs which not only conform to Islamic principles but, more importantly, fit into the plural context of a rapidly changing Malaysian society. This, then, will be the real test of the ability of Muslims in the Islamic movement to solve contemporary problems, not on the theoretical level but in the context of down-to-earth realities. If, on the other hand, the trend proves to be nothing more than a clever political device to lead Islamic elements into a false paradise, then not only will ABIM assume a radical posture *vis-à-vis* the state but Islamic groups of divergent methodologies may eventually be forced to coalesce into an alliance directed against the state, in terms of the Islamic system versus the 'Jahiliyya Taghuti System'. Then the Islamic movements, including ABIM, will take inspiration from Qur'anic guidelines concerning the proper steps to be taken in any religious and ideological conflict. For in the Islamic movement's repertoire of methodologies and strategies, the contingencies of both conflict and peace in human relations are provided for.

In the Malaysian case, ABIM is at present availing itself of the methodology of *islah* (reform of society), *ta'awun'ala'l-birr* (cooperation for good ends), *silm* (peace) or *musalaha* (reconciliation) as demonstrated by the Ikhwan in Sudan, whereas in the Indonesian case perhaps the stage is being set, albeit in an unco-ordinated manner, for the methodology of *jihad fi sabilillah* (struggle in the way of God) against what is perceived as the embodiment of tyranny and the arrogance of military power hostile to the progress of Islam. In both cases, the choice of these methodologies and their relevant discourses has been dictated primarily by the behavior of the state *vis-à-vis* the resurgence of Islamic assertiveness and identity at home as well as abroad. It appears that, when the state acts beyond the limits tolerated by religion, the Islamic discourse assumes a defiant posture, but when the state adopts a more sympathetic attitude towards religious progress, the defiant discourse becomes more conciliatory.

NOTES

1. The doctrine of Pančasila, expounded by the late President Sukarno, founder of the Indonesian republic, combines five tenets — belief in God, humanitarianism, social justice, democracy based on consensus and representation, and national unity.

2. On Anwar Ibrahim in UMNO, see 'The Position of Islam in Malaysia' *The Star*, 10 April 1982; 'We Need Better Dialogue', *The Star*, 17 January 1983; Morais, 1983; 'Anwar: Judge Us by Our Actions', *The Star*, 9 May 1983. See also 'Islam's Rising Cry', *Asiaweek*, 24 August 1979:21–24, 29–31, and *Far Eastern Economic Review*, February 1983:14–15.

3. On government response to the Islamic movements in Malaysia, see 'Preaching Moderation', *Far Eastern Economic Review*, 3 March 1983:20–25.

4. An important influence in this 'secularization' argument was Harvey Cox's *The Secular City* (1965), which defines secularization as 'the libera-

tion of man from religious and metaphysical tutelage, the turning of his attention away from other worlds and towards this one'. Cf. Hassan, 1982:108.

5. For a Hartford Seminary Foundation Ph.D. thesis by an Indonesian pastor sympathetic towards HMI, see Tanja, 1982. Criticism of this is to be found in Sitompul, 1982.

6. *Taghut*, a false god, a tempter to error.

REFERENCES

Awanohara, Susumu (1985), 'Indonesian Politics: The Islam Factor', *Far Eastern Economic Review*, 24 January:26–31.

Crouch, Harold (1981), 'Indonesia', in Mohammed Ayoob (ed.), *The Politics of Islamic Reassertion*. London: Croom Helm, 190–207.

Fadil, Siddiq (1977), *Kebangkitan Ummat: Kenyataan dan Harapan*. Kuala Lumpur: Yayasan Dakwah.

—— (1982), *Garis-Garis Besar Haluan Perjuangan*. Kuala Lumpur: ABIM.

—— (1983), *Menyahut Cabaran Abad Kebangunan*. Kuala Lumpur: ABIM.

—— (1984), *Dāʿī: Pembina 'Aqidah Pembangunan Ummah*. Kuala Lumpur: ABIM.

Far Eastern Economic Review (1983), February:14–15; March 1983:20–25; 11 August:38.

Funston, John (1980), *Malay Politics in Malaysia. A Study of United Malays National Organization and Party Islam*. Kuala Lumpur: Heinemann Educational Books, Ltd.

—— (1981), 'Malaysia' in Mohammed Ayoob (ed.), *The Politics of Islamic Reassertion*. London: Croom Helm, 167–89.

Hakiem, Lukman (1983), Batu Uji Komitment Kita Terhadap Islam (stencilled).

Hassan, Muhammad K. (1982), *Muslim Intellectual Responses to 'New Order' Modernization in Indonesia*. Kuala Lumpur: Dewan Bahasa dan Pustaka.

Hindley, Donald (1971), 'Indonesia 1970. The Workings of Pantjasila Democracy', *Asian Survey*, February:116–18.

—— (1972), 'Indonesia 1971. Pantjasila Democracy and the Second Parliamentary Elections' *Asian Survey*, January:56–68.

Kessler, C.S. (1980), 'Malaysia: Islamic Revivalism and Political Dissaffection in a Divided Society', *Southeast Asia Chronicle*, 75:3–11.

Lyon, M.L. (1979), 'The Dakwah Movement in Malaysia', *Review of Indonesian and Malayan Affairs*, 13:2.

Mauzy, D.K. and R.S. Milne (1983), 'The Mahathir Administration in Malaysia: Discipline Through Islam', *Pacific Affairs*, Winter:617–48.

Means, G.P. (1969), 'The Role of Islam in the Political Development of Malaysia', *Comparative Politics*, I:264–84.

Morais, J.V. (1983), *Anwar Ibrahim: Resolute in Leadership*. Kuala Lumpur: Arenabuku Sdn. Bhd.

Natsir, Mohd. (1982), 'Tolong Dengarkan Pula Suara Kami'! *Panji Masyarakat* (Jakarta), 21 October:2–4.

Noer, Deliar (1982), 'Asas Tunggal Partai', *Kompas*. 25 October:4.

Pančasila Sebagai Azas Tunggal (1983): Dewan Dakwah Islamiah Indonesia.

Progresif (1983), 2, Year I, July-August.

Revival of Islam in Malaysia: The Role of ABIM. Kuala Lumpur: ABIM, n.d.

Risalah: Juru Bicara Ummat (1981). Kuala Lumpur: ABIM.

Samson, Allan (1972), 'Islam and Politics in Indonesia', unpublished Ph.D. Dissertation, University of California, Berkeley.

—— (1973), 'Indonesia 1973: A Climate of Concern', *Asian Survey*, February:159–65.

Siradj, H. Ahmad Zacky (1982), *Pidato Dies Natalis Himpunan Mahasiswa Islam Ke-XXXV*. Jakarta: HMI.

Sitompul, Agussalim (1982), *HMI Dalam Pandangan Seorang Pendeta* (a critique of Victor Tanja's book on HMI). Jakarta: Gunung Agung.

The Star (1982), 10 April.

—— (1983), 17 January.

—— (1983), 9 May.

Tanja, Victor (1982), *Himpunan Mahasiswa Islam*. Jakarta: Sinar Harapan.

Tempo (1983), 4 June; 19 November.

Part Three

Change and the Individual Voice

9

Authority and the Mosque in Upper Egypt: The Islamic Preacher as Image and Actor

Patrick D. Gaffney

The jural and theological tradition of classical Islam contains a considerable literature dealing with mosques as places of public assembly and religious cult. From the beginning of Muhammad's foundation of a community in Madina, where the courtyard of his own house became the first mosque, the inherent authority associated with the place of prayer and weekly muster has been plainly recognized. During his life the Prophet himself supervised all activities carried out there and when he was absent or indisposed he specifically delegated temporary responsibility of such leadership to an assistant, most notably Abu Bakr, who later became his first successor or caliph. Furthermore, the Prophet explicitly regulated the establishment of other sites as mosques, even to the point of ordering the destruction of unauthorized buildings such as the 'mosque of opposition', *al-masjid al-darar* discussed in the Qur'an (IX:107 ff.) ('Masdjid', *Encyclopaedia of Islam*, 1936; Calverly, 1925:ch:IV, V).

Given the great importance attached to mosques in the first centuries of Islam, it is hardly surprising that the theme has reappeared in recent discussions of both practical and theoretical interest. Among those most persistently engaged in this pursuit are reformers who view the mosque as the point of departure for an overall revitalization of Muslim society (Mahmud, 1976).

In modern Egypt, efforts to promote general socio-political improvement by reforming the mosque as a center of communal religious practice must be understood within the context of wider historical currents. For one thing, Egypt's colonial experience, although it lasted longer than that of many Arab lands, was never one of direct European rule or even a single country's domination. As a result, the decisive steps in the process which led to the elimination of the traditional economic structure supporting mosques were initiated by the Muslim rulers beginning with the great Muhammad 'Ali (1805–48). Among other means employed by Muhammad 'Ali and his successors to consolidate state power and to centralize its administration, were measures that effectively appropriated *waqf* properties and placed the dependent mosques under a civil bureaucracy (Baer, 1969:79–92).

In addition, the development of modern educational, legal, and commercial systems caused the increasing marginalization of the traditional religious elite, the ulama (Crecelius, 1972:167–210; Marsot, 1972:149–66). In short, the autonomy and scope of religious institutions in Egypt has steadily shrunk before an expanding state apparatus, a process which reached its climax in the 1960s under President Jamal Abdul-Nasr. At that time, not only was Cairo's Azhar University, the last great bastion of conservatism, purged and restructured to assure its dependence on secular power but, in reaction to stirrings from remnants of the Muslim Brotherhood, comprehensive laws were passed for the strict regulation of all religious and social organizations.

As a consequence of this history, no mosque in Egypt can function in any formal sense apart from a defined relationship to the state. Similarly, no Islamic preacher delivers a Friday sermon without an implied form of political as well as religious authorization.

Another current that has marked the character of mosques in modern Egypt stems from a concern for Islamic orthodoxy in both doctrine and ritual. These motives were certainly prominent among such influential writers and teachers as Muhammad Abduh (1849–1905) and Rashid Rida (1865–1935) whose views are well known, but they were also behind the activities of many less intellectually oriented organizers. One representative of this applied dimension of the *salafiyya* movement (literally, return to the way of the ancestors) was Shaykh Mahmoud Muhammad Khattab al-Sibky (1858–1933). He founded in 1913 what has since become a national network of mosques with related social facilities, whose official title is the Shar'ia Co-operative Society of Followers of the Qur'an and Sunna of Muhammad. Their declared purpose is to support the construction and staffing of mosques where practice conforms to the authentic teachings of Islam as found in the Qur'an and Sunna (Berger, 1970:119). It bears mentioning, in passing, that the Muslim Brotherhood in its early phase was cast in a similar mould, although the vision of its charismatic founder Hassan al-Banna (1906–49) clearly included more political aspirations (Heyworth Dunne, 1950:31–55; Mitchell, 1969:47).

Within this general climate of reform, a zeal for ritual and moral purity on the part of neo-traditionalists coincided with the disapproval of ignorance, superstition and wasteful enthusiasm by the nationalist and liberal thinkers. Both groups, therefore, supported government policies designed to suppress the dramatic displays associated with popular Sufi devotions and to bring these fraternities under the control of state agencies. This gradual process, together with the breakdown of the guild system and the erosion of clan and village solidarity which had provided the strength of Sufi orders, was virtually complete by the beginning of the twentieth century (Gilsenan, 1967:11–18). A by no means minor effect of this course of events was the reassertion of the mosque as the only approved and legitimate institution for public religious expression. Thus, today in Egypt, one finds that certain heads of Sufi *turuq* are integrated into the state-subsidized religious establishment, some holding positions as preachers. This also means that the characteristic relationship of a Sufi *shaykh* with members of the fraternity has also changed to resemble more closely the rapport of other Islamic preachers to their congregations (de Jong, 1978:111).

In addition to the pressures of secularization and reform upon the character of mosques in contemporary Egypt, there is a regional factor. Broadly speaking, Upper Egypt has always been somewhat isolated, conservative and xenophobic. Its inhabitants tend to be poorer, less educated, and more closely bound to a tribal ethos than the similar peasant population of the Nile Delta, who have benefited from the proximity of more Europeanized cities and the Suez Canal. In Upper Egypt, therefore, the transformation of mosques began later and it has been less thorough, but the preacher has none the less emerged as the principal figure of authority.

Finally, the changing shape of mosque practice in Egypt, and especially Upper Egypt, must be seen in the light of the relationship between religion and nationalism. In brief, the nineteenth-century mercantile economy that caused the direct intrusion of world market factors upon the Egyptian peasantry served also to create new forms of centralization and tighter bonds of dependence of the rural sectors upon exterior power centers. Nationalist leaders who blamed European governments and entrepreneurs for this state of exploitation were quick to play on distinctions of religion. Furthermore, by the time of World War I, when the Nationalist Movement began to win popular rural support, not only had mosques become a rallying point for anticolonial protest, but the appeals that mixed modernization and reform had succeeded in stirring still more primordial sentiments. Marshall Hodgson remarks (1974:285), for instance, on the toning down of the 'more emotional and much of the more collective side of religion' in the village cultural life of this period, with the result that 'as emotions were withdrawn from cult, they were invested in politics'. This observation of a high convertability between the values of religion and politics underlines once more the place of the Islamic preacher. Correspondingly, it signals the reason for the increasing official attempts to regulate the use of this ritual authority.

At the beginning of the modern period, the Islamic sermon or *khutbah al-juma'*, which forms part of the congregational prayer at the Friday noon ceremony, had become ossified into a fixed formulary recitation. In some rare instances where the preacher or *khatib* was a man of classical learning, this oration might be more elaborate, as Edward Lane indicates (1836:93–5) in his description of preaching in the Azhar district of Cairo in the 1830s. But more normally, and certainly for Upper Egypt, if the sermon was not omitted, it typically consisted of a short text of rhyming prose taken from a medieval source. Often, the same verses were repeated each week, even while their actual meaning would be lost on the illiterate listeners and perhaps on the one preaching as well.[1]

In reaction to this illiteracy among preachers and this fossilization of ritual, Muhammad Abduh and others proposed education and administrative schemes designed to modernize the sermon and to upgrade the quality of mosque leadership. Their efforts resulted in a movement that sought to revitalize the sermon, transforming it into a new idiom that would provide a relevant and informed address, spoken in vernacular Arabic and serving to enlighten and direct Muslim consciences (Rida, 1931:630). Also, from the start, this revival of Islamic preaching merged freely with strains of modern political awareness. This fusion of Islamic and patriotic values continues as Malcolm Kerr neatly summarizes (1975:44):

the dominant, explicitly political movements of the twentieth century in the Arab world — nationalism and socialism, eventually personified by Nasser — have not been altogether secular phenomena, even when their appeals and discussions leave religious terminology behind. Rather, there has been a transposition of religious symbols into secular ones, concealing an underlying continuity of psychological concerns and cultural issues.

In a similar pattern, the ideological converse of this transposition is also common. Note, for instance, how many militant Muslim groups encode their ardent, if somewhat confusing, political agenda in a strictly religious language. Saad Eddin Ibrahim (1980:433), who interviewed a number of Islamic extremists in prison after their arrest under President Sadat, points out that their socio-economic views closely resembled a moderate socialism hardly distinguishable from that of the British Labor Party or Abdul Nasr

> but any suggestion to that effect invariably produced an outraged response. Islam is not to be likened to any man-made doctrine or philosophy. It would be more acceptable if we were to say that British socialism resembled Islam. In fact, some of them have attributed Mao Tse-tung's success in China to his emulation of Islam, rather than to his adherence to Marxism.

What is revealed here is the familiar phenomenon of a single flexible repertory of symbols invested with meaning at different levels of social and cultural reference. This condensation of the sacred and the secular into one elastic vocabulary is particularly well known in Islam, and it is only intensified by an enduring sense of crisis. Under such conditions of increasing tension, the semantic potency of these abstract symbols mounts and consequently a ritualized setting is required for their effective and creative manipulation. Ritual supplies a circumscribed and diminished frame of reference because it separates ordinary language and gesture from the partial or diffuse contexts of everyday usage. Within the culturally construed setting of the sermon, an exceptional mode of discourse becomes possible that concentrates attention on a unity of the ideal and the real which is normally shattered in day to day experience. Moreover, since ritual, if it is effective, refracts societal dynamics, its force is generated only through the action of certain recognized persons. In other words, the right publicly to define the meaning of shared symbols and to interpret inter-subjective experience by means of them is not arbitrary. Rather, it is the privilege and the responsibility of a designated role, in this case, the preacher, to conjoin and expound the relationship between categories and values that are at once public and private (or sectional). Thus, rightful access to ritual leadership implies authority of itself as Victor Turner suggests (1977:146) in pointing out that

> the person or party who controls the assignment of meaning to religious or political symbols can also control the mobilization efficiency their central position has traditionally assigned to them.

THREE TYPES OF PREACHER

The variety of Islamic preachers found in the mosques of Upper Egypt reflects the diversity of social forms and cultural preferences among the population. Since preaching is a corporate event, it only occurs in conjunction with the appearance of a certain kind of association which might be called a mosque congregation. Mosques too acquire proper identities due to their location in certain quarters or neighborhoods, historical associations and an assortment of physical factors such as size, style, and decor. But most important of all in the identity of a mosque is the question of how it was established, and, usually closely linked to this, by what resources it continues to function. Here, then, a triangular interaction is involved, with the mosque itself providing a symbolic focus, while the preacher serves as a ritual specialist, and spokesman for the congregation of participating worshippers. All these elements combine to form the context for what is pronounced as the text of the preachment. The raw verbal content of a sermon cannot be properly understood apart from its setting, its speaker, and its hearers, which together constitute a system of reference.

In Upper Egypt, we can distinguish between three types of preachers that have crystallized historically into separate though not exclusive images of ideal types, representing compatible aspects of Islamic authority. Such a typology, following Weberian usage, exists as a conceptual abstraction that perceives a this-worldly rationalization of other-worldly sacred values. Each type derives its legitimacy from the particular way it qualifies 'pure' charisma, or, in Weber's terms, from the way it 'proves itself', which indicates that each corresponds to a certain form of social organization.

The first type is the 'saint' or *wali* whose authenticity is expressed as personal *baraka*, which is not seen as a talent or skill but rather as a 'mode in which the divine reaches into the world' (Geertz, 1971:44). Living, or more normally dead, he is conceptualized as an intercessor and wonder-worker, a familiar conduit for divine force and blessing. Classically, the *wali* complex is most fully realized in the localized Sufi order, where the moral bonds of kinship or community and the saint's spiritual favor essentially coincide. Often, the wali is honored as a special patron, and devotion can include practices characteristic of magic and fetishism.

The second type is the 'scholar' or *'alim* whose authority derives from his knowledge or even his personification of the Law, *Shari'a*, which he preserves and applies. Traditionally, the 'alim has embodied the prestige of the classical Muslim civilization, particularly in its jurisprudential aspect, and it was his function to legitimate the exercise of political power. The ulama were teachers, judges, managers of charitable endowments, and counsellors in public and moral affairs. More recently, since secularization has deprived this clerical class of their monopolies of legal and educational institutions, the 'alim survives as a remnant in only a few places, most prominently as the shaykh of a mosque, where certain residual attributes of the former elite are still honored, notably the Azhari education.

The third type is the reformer or inspired activist who has figured historically as a 'holy warrior' or *mujahid*. Whereas, classically, this 'knight' assumed his task in conquest, defense and governance, today the image is more closely associated with the claims of modern lay movements, such as the Muslim Brothers and its successors, who strive to establish *al-nizam al-islami* in the modern world. Until their recent suppression, this ideal was most publicly asserted in Upper Egypt by student groups which called themselves *al-jama'a al-islamiya*. The vision of this 'Islamic Society' included not only claims to superior doctrinal and ritual purity, but also forceful demands for moral conformity extended to all areas of civil life. The basis for this authority does not lie in inspiration or learning, but in the capacity to defend and enforce.

Needless to say, this typology represents an abstraction, for, ethnographically speaking, actual preachers are more complex and malleable than the analytic artifice. None the less, it is worth noting that there is a similar three-part classification that roughly corresponds to this one in the official categories that define the legal structure of religious organizations in Egypt. Two of these types of authority are under the Ministry of Waqfs, while the third area of competence falls under the Ministry of Social Affairs. Within the Ministry of Waqfs, a clear and consistent administrative division separates one bureaucracy which is responsible for all that has to do with the system of government-subsidized mosques from a second bureaucracy charged with the administration of Sufi orders and their public activities. The third class of organizations, which are somewhat more diffuse, are called 'voluntary benevolent societies' (*al-jama'a al-khairiya* or *al-jama'a al-diniya*) and they are supervised by a special division within the Ministry of Social Affairs (Berger, 1970:92).

MINYA

The research I conducted on preachers in the mosques of Upper Egypt was concentrated around the city of Minya or, to give it its proper name, al-Minya al-Fuli. I resided there for eighteen months during 1978–79. Although the site has been inhabited since early antiquity, the city as it stands today, some 250 kilometers south of Cairo on the western bank of the Nile, is largely the result of modern urbanization. At its core, traces of the original village are clearly discernible, now surrounded by various stylistically distinct products of various late nineteenth and twentieth century building booms. Also interesting is the shape of the city, with its roughly 250,000 residents, which runs in a long relatively thin urban sprawl for several kilometers along the river bank and incorporates into its northern and southern expansion other distinct pre-existing villages. The city serves as the capital of one of the five governorates of Upper Egypt, which means that regional directorates of civil and military administration are situated in it. Likewise, it provides all the other usual services of a provincial metropolis to the largely rural population of the surrounding hinterland.[2]

There are approximately fifty substantial mosques in the city of Minya as well as scores of smaller places of prayer of various sizes and degrees of permanence. But only at about twenty mosques, and these would be the largest, is there a regular Friday noon prayer which includes the formal sermon. Of these, I shall single out two for discussion, chosen because they are among the most prominent and because they represent what is locally understood as the two contrasting types of religious institutions. One of these two mosques is considered old, although the current building is very recent since it has been completely renovated by the Ministry of Waqfs in a style that conforms to their prescriptions for a 'cathedral' mosque. It is a greatly enlarged and enhanced version of what had been a mosque built around a *zawiyya*, a saint's tomb shrine, which probably dates from the early seventeenth century. The saint here honored is a wali who resided and died in Minya, known as Shaykh al-Fuli, who has since become the patron of the city and the most highly regarded wali in the region, at least as measured in terms of popular devotion and public expenditure. The present mosque also enjoys a magnificent location as it is set off slightly from the surrounding buildings and overlooks the Nile at that juncture of the city where the original pre-modern village meets the straight streets of the first nineteenth-century expansion. The second mosque represents a newer form of religious institution, and dates from the late 1960s. It was founded by a retired school teacher on an abandoned lot used as a dumping ground, as part of a voluntary benevolent society which was meant to provide certain social and charitable services. It is situated on the western side of the city on the west side of a large canal which had formerly been a sort of natural boundary, although since the 1950s the area has grown into a large popular quarter. Also, this mosque is strategically located adjacent to the major automobile and pedestrian bridge over the canal, and very close to the major bus terminal.

The people of Minya discriminate in practice between only two categories of mosques, defined in opposition to each other. In the local view, mosques are understood either to belong to the 'government', i.e. *masjid hukumi*, or to be 'popular', i.e. *masjid ahali*. Although this difference is framed historically in terms of their financial dependence, today the most significant distinction is given in organizational terms, as a stated contrast between two types of preachers. A government mosque is one that is headed by a professional *imam* who is an Azhar graduate with all that this implies. He is appointed and paid by the Ministry of Waqfs and is identified with its large local bureaucracy, where scores of administrators, inspectors, clerks and engineers handle all details related to these mosques and their personnel. A popular mosque, on the other hand, functions as a component of a voluntary benevolent society whose primary purpose is to provide its members with mutual assistance or to dispense specific charitable services according to the terms of its charter. The president of such a society oversees its administrative affairs, and usually, as is the case here, where the society also includes a mosque, he serves as its imam and preaches the Friday sermon.

The voluntary benevolent society in the form described here is a modern phenomenon of a protean character. In 1900, records indicated that there were 65 such societies in Egypt, almost all of them located in Cairo and Alexandria. In 1949, there were 1,401 and by 1960, there were 3,195. By 1978, there were probably double this figure throughout Egypt, and perhaps a hundred in Minya alone. But by no means all of these societies are religiously motivated, for, in fact, most are chartered with straightforward social and philanthropic objectives, such as assisting in different aspects of education, health care or recreation. The remarkable proliferation of these voluntary benevolent societies can be traced to many causes, but certainly one of the foremost is that such groupings have become, for all practical purposes, the only legitimate basis for any regular formal association in Egypt. Thus, as far as mosques are concerned, the founding of a voluntary benevolent society has evolved as the most available legal mechanism for Muslims to form an enduring congregation where they can be assured that their place of prayer will remain in their own hands and that their preacher will be a man of their own choosing. The policy of the Ministry of Waqfs has long been to expand its network not by original construction so much as by the incorporation of already existing facilities into its operations. It is only the exorbitant expense of providing for the maintenance and personnel of the nation's estimated 40,000 mosques that has forced the Ministry to limit the number it actually regulates to approximately 6,000. When the Ministry does take over mosques, however, as it continually attempts to do depending on budget allotments, it purposefully chooses those that are the best established and most heavily used. Hence, without a recognized legal independence to protect them against such eventual absorption, mosques which have been built by local initiatives can be easily brought into government control by the decision of local administrators of the Ministry of Waqfs.

Despite the array of differences and variants between these two institutions, the preachers in both cases can be described in terms of two sets of functions, a ritual role and a mundane, professional identity. But in neither case can the individual totally separate the two dimensions, for the voice from the *minbar* or 'pulpit' is also heard as that of a functionary, a countryman, a neighbor, who occupies a place in the wider social world. It is this double function that invests the preacher with credibility and gives a sermon its pragmatic context. The sermon is a symbolic representation of that which the preacher and ultimately the congregation seek to realize in the realm of moral action. He serves therefore as an image and an actor. He is at once the point of articulation for fixed and sacred ideals and the focus for conduct in a changing human world where interests are in conflict and intention does not suffice for results. The efficaciousness of a preacher's leadership hinges in large measure on his ability to bring consistency to this image and actor relationship. He must preserve this double focus, for should he abandon the tension, by radically isolating his two-fold functions or by attempting to eliminate one or the other, he would deprive the ritual of its dialectical character. The preacher as pure image would ultimately reduce his performance to empty formalism, whereas the preacher as pure actor would lead to sermons of purposeless fantasy. On the other hand, to collapse the two foci together would confound metaphor with reality and thus undermine the essential distinction between subjective and objective experience, opening the way to the distortions of magic and millenarianism.

SHAYKH 'ALI

The Azhari preacher, whom we shall call Shaykh 'Ali, should be treated first because he represents that form of religious authority that is socially and culturally most explicit. Because his role is more institutionalized he embodies a wider range of idealized assumptions. It is largely by contrast with this conventional figure that our second example takes its meaning. Several major attributes of his position have already been indicated, such as the 'cathedral' character of the mosque, its association with the eponymous wali, Shaykh al-Fuli, and its full incorporation into the national system overseen by the Ministry of Waqfs. What must be added, however, is that this superimposition of bureaucracy upon *baraka* has not accomplished the easy integration of these two modes. Rather, it is the preacher who, as chief administrator of the complex and as its ritual specialist, is expected to bring these disparities into harmony.

Shaykh 'Ali is in his late forties and is a native son of the region of Minya. He resides at present in his ancestral village a few kilometers north of the city. This fact of indigenous origin is of extreme importance in Upper Egypt, not only for the general comfort of the person concerned, but as a basis for genuine acceptance by others, for Sa'idis (the slightly tainted term for Upper Egyptians) are proverbially suspicious of outsiders and notoriously stubborn in their dealings with rationalized officialdom and its agents (al-Hakim, 1947).[3] Also, it is exceedingly rare to find senior Azhari preachers here with local origins, for there have been very few of the past generation who completed the Azhar curriculum in Cairo and, of those who did, even fewer returned to employment in the mosques of the provinces. Consequently, numerous government mosques in the district are without regular preachers, for qualified men are not available. And the great majority of Azhari shaykhs who do occupy posts in Minya are very young recent graduates who come from the Delta, where religious education is far more developed and the status of a mosque preacher has traditionally been higher. Virtually all of these migrant preachers regard their appointments as a temporary displacement, an inconvenience to be endured until an opening becomes available near their native town, where some of them have left wives and families living. Others are postponing marriage until a more permanent assignment is offered. The most ambitious, of course, aspire to posts in Cairo itself.

Shaykh 'Ali's age is also of importance, because it marks him as a member of the generation whose early adulthood coincided with the high tide of the Revolutionary era and who now dominate the controlling offices in the public sector. Specifically with regard to his role as preacher, his age also indicates that he is a graduate from the 'old' Azhar, that is, the University Mosque, as it is now romantically conceived in its pristine form, previous to its thorough overhaul and relocation by Abdul Nasr. Since that watershed, it is the popular view that its great professors have been dismissed, its curriculum has been altogether diluted, and its standards have been considerably lowered. Now, it is said, this religious training only attracts candidates who are barred entrance to other colleges because of their poor academic performance. The sign of this debasement is that almost none of these new preachers know the Qur'an by heart, which is still considered the prerequisite of all religious learning. Interestingly, the Azhar has recently opened a branch of higher studies in Assiut, 130 kilometers south of Minya, where, according to popular opinion, the quality of education is even more retrograde. In sum, therefore, local perception accords Shaykh 'Ali the distinction of a rare antediluvian 'alim who is furthermore 'one of us', with its underlying implications of familiarity and influence. It might also be noted that the position as head of al-Fuli went unoccupied for some time before this particular Shaykh was appointed.

All Azharis and *a fortiori* all modern reformers attest that the cult of a wali is heterodox, and most young Azharis in Minya urge its active suppression. Some have gone so far as to keep the doors to shrines locked or to have the cenotaph removed altogether. But Shaykh 'Ali pursues a compromise. He tolerates the popular devotional practices that daily enliven the shrine of Shaykh al-Fuli, but he delegates supervision of the tomb and associated activities to subordinates. He is greatly assisted in this double attitude by a convenient spatial separation of the symbols. For in this particular case the customary saint's tomb is not located inside the mosque proper but apart in a cupola shrine, with a veranda and colonnade connecting the two structures. The shrine has one door leading towards the mosque itself and a second door opening to the street outside, which means that entry and exit can be made without encroaching on the mosque. Thus the large numbers of peasants who constitute most of the wali's devoted following, and, of course, women, who normally never go into mosques, can be accommodated without involving the Shaykh personally. He carries out his functions in the mosque and maintains his small office (which has the only telephone of any mosque in the city) on the opposite side of the shrine complex.

Every Friday and on great feast days excitement around the

shrine runs high and the traffic in and out of the tomb chamber reaches mob proportions. On these occasions, social distance and a modicum of order is maintained by the shrine's attendants who are strategic-ally stationed at the doorways. Then, during the actual prayer and sermon, the shrine is closed and, with that, the crowds diminish. There can be no doubt that the central appeal of the mosque for these visiting villagers and the numerous similarly oriented city-dwellers is the wali. The weekly ceremony that they share is not the formal prayer and sermon but the miniature *mawlid* festival that springs up around the building for a few hours each Friday, when musicians, dancers, Sufi perfume-vendors, hawkers of sweets and other curiosities converge, mix, and soon after quickly disperse. Shaykh 'Ali avoids being seen in the midst of this exuberance, but takes no measures to discourage what he concedes to be the misguided pious enthusiasm of the uneducated. Also, after the Friday service, when most of the con-gregation have departed, he permits an old-fashioned Sufi *dhikr* to be held on the veranda between the shrine and the mosque, a conces-sion allowed by no other Azhari preacher in the city.

It should also be noted that Shakyk 'Ali's monthly income is regu-larly supplemented by a share of the donations that are deposited in the alms-box set beside the saint's tomb. This cash, along with money from the resale of gifts in kind, principally jewelry and meat, is counted once a month by a delegation of eight that includes the top administrative staff of the local Ministry of Waqfs office. All of them receive a special bonus, graded to their rank, for these book-keeping tasks. The rest of the proceeds are then divided, with three-fourths going to the Ministry of Waqfs, and the remaining fourth allotted by a complicated formula to the employees of the al-Fuli mosque. The total monthly intake varies between £E500 and £E700. The preacher's share is just over 4 per cent which means that Shaykh 'Ali gets roughly £E25–30 a month in addition to what is already his considerably monthly salary of £E72. (By comparison, the starting salary of an Azhari preacher was set at £E30 a month, which is approximately $42.) Needless to say, the idea of benefitting from practices which are condemned as unorthodox is roundly criticized even by those Azhari officials who participate in the collection of these donations and accept their share.

In addition to being a cult center for *fellahin*, the al-Fuli mosque attracts another distinct group which regularly attends the Friday prayer and identifies with its second, related aspect. This group, smaller in number, is dominated by the urban gentry, including pro-perty holders, merchants, middle to high functionaries and some youth who share similar traditional bourgeois values. They are drawn to this mosque because of its self-evident status as the local embodiment of historical continuity and a politico-religious synthesis. There are older and larger mosques in the city, and mosques more richly adorned, but this one enounces a 'classical' heritage, and its ritual is conducted with the appropriate marks of amplitude, such as the services of a professional Qur'an chanter. The ritual grandeur attempted here takes the great centers of Muslim civilization as its model. It is the same highbrow style displayed in broadcasts of Friday prayer or in familiar photographs from the Egyptian press. It is the local religious showplace to which notables can bring their cosmopolitan cousins and colleagues who might be visiting the city. Also, the Ministry of Waqfs use this location for the events they sponsor on religious holidays, or for the occasional guest speaker. General civic ceremonies, such as congratulatory assemblies for public officials, are also held here. Finally, it is to this mosque that the governor of the province comes from time to time, arriving, typically, at the last minute in a flourish of limousines and jeeps, accompanied by his guards and entourage. And this same select dignity was affirmed most conspicuously in December 1978, when President Sadat made a rare visit to Minya, at the end of which he attended the Friday prayer at this mosque, on which occasion the service, including the sermon, was transmitted live over the national radio.

Shaykh 'Ali's personal manner is formal and reserved, with a cordiality expressed in the liberal courtesies of traditional hospitality. His social self and his ritual role are closely bound together, as shown most clearly by the fact that he wears the distinctive Azhari uniform at all times. His sermons are delivered in the florid, classical *fusha* (ampleness) of the trained and well practised religious orator. Although they are given without any notes, their content is highly structured and correctly punctuated with the prescribed verbal formulae that signal introduction, internal division, and conclusion. These stately homilies are gracefully interlaced with illustrative citations from the Qur'an and the *hadith* and they are of typical Azhari brevity, no longer than 15 or 20 minutes, whereas sermons in popular mosques can often continue for an hour or more. In addition to these tokens of Islamic refinement in the sermon, there are similarly indicative embellishments of the ritual prayer such as a sung response to the imam's rubrical exclamations — a feature known as *al-balagha*.

Thus, Shaykh 'Ali projects the image of a double identity that fuses elements from the traditions of the wali and the 'alim. He unites the two constituencies of his congregration — one by active and the other by passive gestures, into an assembly that is meant to reflect the unified community (*umma*) and the nation. He speaks in this dual capacity as protector of the patron saint and as spokesman for the orthodox religion by raising the level of discourse towards a lofty height of generalization and inclusion. He achieves this elevation by making maximal use of what Victor Turner (1967) calls the 'polysemy' or 'multi-vocality' of the focal symbols of each complex, which in the abstract greatly overlap. He plays down the judgemental or exclusionary tendencies of the reformist context by avoiding drawing attention to the confusions of modern history and the existential limits imposed by competing structures. He does not appropriate to himself the baraka of the wali, nor does he presume to exercise the jurisprudential prerogatives of an 'alim, but rather he allows his own personality to be absorbed into an image that dramatizes their memory. He incorporates a generalized conception of their historical authority. In other words, he forges a synthesis that emphasizes the force of the ritual role which greatly constrains his relevance as a social actor. What he imparts, as a result, is a vision of common action that is more closely identified with the liminal rather than the ethical dimensions of religion. Participation in the saint's blessing and fulfilment of the Shari'a legalism are presented as concentrated upon ritual action rather than upon specific worldly activity or moral behavior. For Shaykh 'Ali, image and actor meet in his position as a proper civil servant in a society where religion is officially institutionalized and the charge over its practice is entrusted to clerical professionals. The proper task of the mosque and the preacher is to provide for the public exercise of religion within these circumscribed structures. Hence his purpose is properly to complement and not to oppose secular authority located in other functionally specific institutions.

An example from the sermon rhetoric of Shaykh 'Ali that illustrates how he interprets his authority in terms of ritualized religious duty rather than concrete moral action can be seen in his manipulation of the term *amn* or 'security' in the sermon he preached in the presence of President Sadat already noted, which I was able to record from the radio. The preacher first proposes a metaphoric parallel that equates contemporary society with the community of believers of Madina where the Prophet first established his polity. Shaykh 'Ali then cites three promises of security made to those who believe, playing on the common semantic root for belief and security, that is, *amuna*, 'to believe'; *iman*, 'belief'; *amina*, 'to be safe, secure'; *amn*, 'security, peace'. The community is first promised dominion over the earth and its resources, for, he says: 'God made men to love

213

work in agriculture that security of nutrition (*amn al-ghadhi*) might be realized and that every living creature might obtain all its needs'. These remarks are made against a background of political strife and controversy surrounding the heavy subsidies that keep the prices of food staples low, subsidies that Sadat has sought to withdraw. In January of the previous year, the announcement that the subsidies were being lifted brought widespread rioting and the government reversed its policy and reinstated them. But at the end of the same month in which this sermon was preached, the original plans were partially reasserted, by the elimination of support for cigarettes and gas while leaving food prices unchanged. The idiomatic expression rendered here literally as 'security of nutrition' is the Egyptian Arabic equivalent of the complex of ideas and feelings known as the 'green revolution', which is one of the terms Sadat and his spokesmen use when they speak English. The phrase constitutes a slogan and it is ubiquitous in public political rhetoric.

The sermon continues:

> The second promise is the consolidation of religion. This is realized in the security of nutrition and the security of industry, for any nation (umma) independent in its materials will need no other besides itself as it takes steps to build and construct and promote the progress of work toward welfare in the afterlife as well as welfare in this world . . .

Here appears the explicit religious echo, then substantiated by Qur'anic citations, of Sadat's frequently repeated call for new industries and for more aggressive exploitation of untapped natural resources. The official line at this time was full of rosy anticipation of the imminent prosperity that was guaranteed to result from an eventual peace with Israel, friendship with America, and the recovery of the oil fields in the Sinai. In the next section of the sermon, the logic that condenses 'faith' and 'security' into one analogy is even more explicit:

> The third promise is the establishment of (the nation's) full security in the possession of its religious faith. It shall fear God alone, for how shall it fear a creature when it has with it the power of the almighty Creator who responds to dangers when he is called and who uncovers evil. For God, exalted be he, entrusted to the Quraysh two blessings, the blessing of nourishment in hunger and the blessing of security in fear. . . .

214

In essence, the accomplishment of God's promises is assured by man's full faith in them. This faith, in turn, is explicitly demonstrated in the ritual expressions that are most precisely religious as a collective task and destiny.

SHAYKH HASSAN

The second preacher under discussion is thoroughly a layman who, in theory, conducts ritual functions only incidentally by virtue of his position as president of a voluntary benevolent society which has a mosque as one of its facilities. He is sometimes but not consistently addressed or referred to with the honorific title of 'shaykh', so for our purposes we shall call him Shaykh Hassan. He is about the same age as Shaykh 'Ali and also a native of the immediate vicinity. Shaykh Hassan was long respected as a school teacher before he was recently promoted to the influential post of Director of Public Relations at the provincial office of the Ministry of Education. His formal education was entirely secular, although, like many of that period, he attended a traditional *kuttab* for a time as a child after school hours. When he speaks of the religious education of his youth, however, he claims to be an autodidact whose great source of enlightenment was *The Life of Muhammad* by the great liberal intellectual and social reformer, Muhammad Husayn Haykal. He went on to advanced studies at what was then the British Teachers' College in Assiut, where he specialized in English.

Unlike the vast majority of more recently trained language instructors in Upper Egypt, Shaykh Hassan is quite fluent. This unusual competence, given his relatively modest class background, has brought him to the attention of the Provincial Governor's office. He is called upon as a translator on occasion, and he sometimes hosts English-speaking dignitaries on touristic outings to local attractions, Pharaonic or technological. Through his office, he is daily involved with teachers and administrators in schools throughout the region and with officials in other bureaucracies, which provides him with a valuable network for keeping abreast with affairs in a variety of realms. Not surprisingly, he is sometimes called upon by the police or involved parties to act as an intermediary in the traditional forum for settling feuds called *majlis al-sulh*.

Shaykh Hassan took over the task as preacher of this mosque only very recently, although he had long been an occasional preacher in some other popular mosques, notably the small room set aside for religious functions at the local Teachers' Club. He was elected to the presidency of the benevolent society only in January 1978 upon the death of his father, who had founded the society and had served as its preacher. Shaykh Hassan's father, who had been a primary school teacher, was best known for his long involvement with the Muslim Brothers, for which he was imprisoned on several occasions. In 1965, when Abdul Nasr carried out the last of several purges directed at the Muslim Brothers, Shaykh Hassan was also arrested, although he was released after a short internment. The obvious link to his father and his own experience of persecution for Islam have provided the preacher with an evident prestige among the younger generation of fundamentalists who have idealized the martyrs of this earlier era and who strive to rekindle their struggle. At times in his sermons, Shaykh Hassan makes discretely oblique allusions to prisons, or oppressors of Truth, the meaning of which is transparent to his hearers.

The approximate coincidence of Shaykh Hassan's promotion in the Ministry of Education and his assumption of ritual and administrative duties at the benevolent society has greatly enlarged his exposure as a lay religious leader. While he had already been active as a speaker at assorted groupings in Minya, he was now being called on by more august forums. A crowning achievement was an invitation to appear on a nationally televised talk show called 'This is Islam', which was broadcast in April 1979. Here, interestingly, the uneven relationship between the two offices, the secular and the religious, was revealed when the host introduced him most elaborately as a senior regional ministry functionary, and quite secondarily as the head of a benevolent society. In fact, still more telling, the host mistakenly introduced him as the head, that is, the Director, of Minya's office of the Ministry of Education.

The physical character of the setting for the ritual also gives important indications about the effect Shaykh Hassan is attempting to achieve. First, the mosque proper is rather small in scale and simple in its adornment. Its pulpit, for instance, is not the elaborate wooden minbar with stairs leading to an elevated platform, often adorned with five carving and decorous curtains. It is simply a low platform, like a small podium with a primitive railing, painted white. But even so, Shaykh Hassan avoids such a symbolic association, for it is his custom to preach while seated on the floor, which is covered with mats rather than carpets, facing his congregation and using a microphone. The crowd that assembles here on Friday for the prayer and sermon is too large to fit into the mosque, although their number could easily fit into the mosque of al-Fuli. Here the overflow is accommodated on mats set up outside beneath loud-speakers that carry the words of the preacher.

In a technical legal sense, Shaykh Hassan's mosque exists as a modest ancillary aspect of a benevolent society whose primary purpose is charity and mutual aid. This particular benevolent society is named 'ilm wa-imam ('Science and Faith'), although it is virtually never called that except by the preacher himself in certain formal references. Rather, it is called after its preacher, 'the mosque of Shaykh Hassan' or sometimes, reflecting previous usage, that of his father. The proper name is a familiar slogan featured centrally in the 'October Paper' in which President Sadat, in 1974, outlined the goals of his regime, including his progressive, pluralist change of direction and his 'open door' to capitalist investment.

In theory, this mosque of the Science and Faith Society, like other of this 'popular' type, exists essentially for the use of the members of the society, although non-members who desire to join in their prayer would certainly not be excluded. This membership is legally defined in terms of a regular monetary contribution to a common fund which maintains its facilities and supports its various activities. The fact of the matter is, however, that very few of the several hundred who attend the Friday prayer at the mosque with any frequency are members in this strict sense, and in practice membership is an extremely loose category. There are certain specific services supposedly provided for the benefit of members, but these services are conceived as also available to the poor who may need them, or others who may have some less direct reason to be associated with the benevolent society, most probably stemming from family or local bonds rather than ideological commitments. One service offered by the benevolent society, and, in the eyes of many, its most significant one, is a food co-operative, the major feature of which is the sale of meat. The meat in question is that of the gamousa, the indigenous water buffalo, whose slaughter was at this time strictly regulated by the government. Meat prices are expensive and fixed officially, although there is a great deal of manipulation by butchers in order to obtain higher rates in the form of tips for better cuts or for holding some quantity back from the rush which often exhausts the limited stock. The benevolent society has some kind of arrangement, which frequently malfunctions, whereby 'members' can order meat in advance and then purchase it at a discount. Sometimes seasonal produce will also be available. Practically speaking, however, no supplies of anything are dependable at this co-op and quality fluctuates greatly so that, when there is an overabundance of perishable goods, the operators are only too happy to sell to whoever can pay. Consequently, householders tend to rely on regular merchants or the market and the co-op seems to spring to life only on Fridays, when occasionally shipments of fruit or vegetables are brought in to take advantage of the crowd gathered for the prayer. At such times the preacher announces the availability of these items or other special sales at the end of his sermon.

Other facilities associated with the Society include low-cost dormitories for students, a primary medical care clinic, and meeting rooms used for such things as supplementary school lessons near to examination time or as workshops for sewing or doing simple repairs.

Attendance at this mosque is in general more selective than the heterogeneous and frequently non-resident group at the mosque of al-Fuli. Those who attend are males from middle- and lower middle-class backgrounds who share a fairly high degree of formal education. The congregation also includes some students and a good number of young graduates, such as teachers, engineers, and clerks, who have not yet married. It can be assumed, for instance, that the members of the congregation will consider themselves by local standards relatively *au courant* with national opinion and world affairs. Consequently, Shaykh Hassan often makes elliptical allusions to items that have recently appeared in the press, to passing styles or public personalities, always carefully measuring his words to impart recognizable comments upon controversial questions with only indirect inferences. As an 'independent' preacher, he is expected to be provocative and critical, but he must avoid explicitness on matters of high religious (including sectarian) and political sensitivity, lest he compromise his impartial stance, which would not only risk alienating some of his listeners, but perhaps subject him to pressure from disapproving civil authorities.

Disparities in status and socio-economic origin are strongly played down at this mosque and equality is displayed, as seen, for instance, in the customary simple dress of the congregation and the absence of preferential seating. Shaykh Hassan often expounds on this egalitarian theme and he reproaches other mosques for honoring notables or official dignitaries with special entrances and front-row places at prayer. This stress on brotherhood, however, masks an implicit recognition of the positive value of hierarchy (of which he too is a beneficiary), as is displayed in the ways in which the preacher manipulates the symbols of social rank. On one particularly striking occasion, Shaykh Hassan interrupted the main theme of his sermon to discourse on the need for modesty and economy on the part of the wealthy and high officials who are too often attached to pomp and habits of conspicuous consumption. Then, moving from the abstract to the concrete, he proceeded to compliment in glowing terms a certain district supervisor who was 'anonymously' present. Although he did not name the man, he identified him quite elaborately with references to his post, his residence, and numerous specific achievements of the man's career. He then went on to indicate in a sort of guessing game approximately where within the mosque, in what row and on what side, this 'anonymous' guest was sitting, all the time lauding the man for his lack of ostentation. In this way, Shaykh Hassan obeys the convention that forbids him to single out anyone by name, but calls at least as much attention to the subject as he could have accomplished by a formal introduction. He frequently indulges in such verbal manoeuvres.

Shaykh Hassan bases his authority on his commitment to reform and action, which implies his freedom from those influences that have compromised the 'official' preachers and turned them into the mouthpieces of the state. Hence, it is a point of high significance, and therefore much trumpeted abroad, that he performs ritual services without remuneration. With his income from his government post, he is hardly in need of another salary, although he clearly receives a certain sum justified as 'expenses' from sources within the benevolent society. Furthermore, others who contribute time and services to activities of the benevolent society also conceptualize them as 'voluntary' although here too there is manifestly regular material benefit received for these services. Likewise, on an ideological level, all who are associated with the benevolent society, including the preacher, assert their independence from government support. But more accurately, it is a matter of degree, for both money and goods, originating directly or otherwise in several official agencies, including the Ministry of Waqfs, the Ministry of Education, and the Ministry of Social Affairs, are sought after and accepted by the benevolent society.

The mentality which depicts the government mosque and the popular one as an alternative pair has recently been complicated by the appearance of a third point in the compass, namely groups representing the new wave of fundamentalist Islam. As was noted earlier, Shaykh Hassan is considered outspoken in comparison to the Azhari preacher, for he dares to comment with stark relevance and critical judgment on local and national foibles. But in the late 1970s, as the conflict between Sadat and militant Islamic groups, some with open foreign support, began to escalate, the battle of words spread to the pulpit. In Minya, this provocative position was represented by zealots from among the student Islamic Society, who moved from merely preaching in their own assemblies to begin preaching in certain small mosques near the university where no Friday prayer had been customary. One effect, however, was to trigger a version of the competitive process that Michael Hudson (1980:16) refers to as the 'outbidding' of 'claims to Islamic legitimacy' which pressed Shaykh Hassan either to sharpen his own repudiation of established religion or risk being condemned as part of it.

Amid such a climate of escalating dissent, however, this skilful strategist took a middle course, in which he attempted to respond to their aggressive drive towards extremism by selecting themes in his sermons with a double meaning. First, he would signal broad approval of their intentions and objectives by talking at length on the important role that 'youth' (the code term for members of *al-jama'a al-islamiya*) played in the earliest days of Islam. Long sections of many sermons consisted of accounts from the life of the Prophet, involving incidents in which he entrusted to youth the responsibility for leadership in combat, for mission work (da'wa) and for government. Among them are stories that pit the idealistic young converts against the callous and greedy Meccan aristocrats, or narratives of combined expeditions in which the young outshine the veterans. But then, in the running commentaries which this preacher always provides in the midst of the episodes he recounts, he turns these stories into mirrors of behavior at a different level. He avoids altogether the triumphant climaxes and concentrates, often with exaggerated self-consciousness, on what he isolates as the excellent personal manners of the Prophet, on the way that Muhammad not only exhibited in his own behavior the consummate perfection of courtesy, patience, generosity and kindliness, but how it was precisely these qualities that he rewarded in others, not their capacity to intimidate or to excel in violent confrontations. His emphasis is on reason, *'aql*, and proper moral conduct, *'adab*, in tacit opposition to what is locally called *'asabiya*, roughly, 'fanaticism'. Small groups of these student activists had begun to launch disruptive demonstrations, such as praying the evening prayer on a busy bridge so as to cause massive traffic jams; or picketing the gates to the campus on the day the Camp David Accords were signed, so as effectively to close the university; or a break-in shortly after Khomeini returned to Tehran that attempted to seize and occupy the City Hall in order to claim Minya also for Islamic governance. So Shaykh Hassan matched them with sermons that dwelt on the moderation, tolerance and meekness of precisely those same early Islamic heroes who are most extolled for their military achievements, such as

Khalid ibn al-Walid and ʿAmr ibn al-ʿAs, or ʿUmar ibn al-Khuttab and Muʿāwiyah, who also exemplified the perfection of good government, in tacit contrast to the current regime.

At the same time, this lay preacher constantly reiterates the scientific basis for Islamic ritual practices. He encourages resort to the daily prayer, for instance, as a method for relieving psychological tension, and he likes to quote remarks from British doctors who he says have demonstrated this finding. His sermon rhetoric often touches on the scientific breakthroughs of the day, as reported in the popular media, such as test-tube babies, space travel, or sophisticated telecommunications, as ways of infusing his remarks with perspectives of a modern changing world and its compatibility with belief. He demonstrates a similar modernist outlook by the fact that he avoids all tokens of religious dress; nor does he wear a head covering. He presents himself in nothing more formal than the standard tunic and trousers combination that are universally worn by men of his station. Although he has a moustache, he refuses to grow a beard, which serves locally as the deliberate emblem of affiliation or sympathy for the cause of Islamic fundamentalism.

Interestingly, this preacher also adapts the diglossia of Arabic in Egypt for his own purpose in the sermon in an extraordinary way. He does not speak entirely in the pure classical Arabic of the Azhari, nor does he use the rousing colloquial speech of the popular actor, as do the militants in their more or less demagogic addresses. Rather, he employs a masterful mixture, frequently switching between the two levels, sometimes for quick qualification, extrapolation or exclamation, sometimes for longer disquisitions, all of which can give the remarkable effect of two voices and dramatic movement. He manages to mesh the ponderous authority and eloquence of the idealized idiom, like a talking book, with the familiarity, freshness and humor of everyday banter. As has been said, he typically structures his sermons around texts recounting episodes from the life of the Prophet, but intermingled in them is all manner of academic or gossipy comment, which may seem full of digression, but in retrospect is plainly part of a sort of jig-saw *Gestalt*. At times, he presents a single long passage from the *Sira*, at other times, he strings together an assortment of isolated incidents, for he preaches from notes, and the text of the book(s) is before him as he quotes it. All these narrations are designed to infer a contrast with contemporary situations.

In one sermon, for instance, Shaykh Hassan built upon texts that told of the consultations held by early Muslim leaders before deciding on a plan for any attack or campaign. They are depicted as calling in experts and charting all the contingencies, and as having the safety of the soldiers and the welfare of their families as their highest priority. This sermon followed shortly after the incident at the airport in Cyprus in February 1978, when a number of Egyptian commandoes lost their lives in a tragic and thoroughly bungled rescue attempt. Hijackers who objected to Sadat's rapprochement with Israel had kidnapped *al-Ahram* editor Yusef al-Siba'i, who was eventually killed in the fracas after the Cypriot National Guard opened fire on the Egyptians. The hijackers surrendered unharmed. But even while the focus of the preacher's remarks was unmistakable, buttressed as it was with pellucid geographical allusions to early Muslim sea battles around islands in the eastern Mediterranean, the shaykh extended his innuendo to include carelessness and wastefulness, neglect and irresponsibility in planning and administration at lower levels, including locally, where he spoke of the 'demon of *rutin*', meaning the inefficiency and immobility of 'routine' or bureaucratic inertia, wastefulness and mediocrity.

Another theme with numerous variations draws on stories illustrating the accessibility and frugality of the early Caliphs and their eagerness to see justice served beyond any self-interest. Shaykh Hassan explains, without any need to be explicit, how they declined to spend funds on lavish public ceremonies, they wore no elaborate military uniforms, invested in no colossal monuments, and occupied no great palaces. Such remarks clearly rebound upon the national elite, but he likewise presses the examples into service as critical of more immediate extravagances, such as expensive weddings, costly advertising gimmicks, or the hypocrisy of giving lavishly decorated Qur'ans as ceremonious presentations while leaving their contents unstudied. Nor does he hesitate to condemn what is considered the permissiveness of mixed-sex parties, the unscrupulous hoarding or black-marketeering of shopkeepers, and the lack of public spirit and professional solicitude among professionals such as teachers or doctors. He also makes disapproving comments with regard to traditional religious practices, such as the celebration of the Prophet's Birthday, the belief in a wali's miracles, or the allowing of women in funeral processions. But the tone of these condemnations always maintains an undercurrent of respect and a willingness to pursue discussion. This open attitude is perhaps seen most fully in the Shaykh's practice of inviting anonymous questions in the form of 'letters' which he answers publicly at the end of some sermons.

The image Shaykh Hassan projects as a preacher can be seen as an idiosyncratic combination of a modern lay 'alim and a *mujahid* dedicated to moral reform. But it is a composite of social and religious authority which lacks a certain degree of stability and unity. Shaykh Hassan attempts to overcome this implicit inconsistency with regard to his ritual role by his many measures designed to minimize the emotional potency of the religious symbols involved, and to diffuse their marked sacred connotations into the discourse of a community meeting, an academic lecture, or admonitions regarding social priorities. The fact that Shaykh Hassan concentrates his preaching around biographies of the Prophet and other secondary materials and very seldom even quotes the Qur'anic text, except for some of its most stylized phrases, suggests an apt metaphor for the distance he maintains from the crucial core of the collective spiritual value system. This preference for human history over the sacred word is replicated in an emphasis upon moral and individual action over communal and specifically religious expressions of Islam.

But this insistence that 'aql and adab constitute the supreme categories for belief and action is also undermined by his need constantly to redefine them in terms of religious symbols whose meanings in relation to the larger community extend well beyond the boundaries of this balanced middle ground. This preacher's attempt to construct a convincing liberal interpretation requires him to compete with two increasingly polarized and highly publicized extremes, and the opposition between them has caused a decline in the collective appeal of a discriminating center. Shaykh Hassan's reluctance to exploit the *liminal* and emotional potency of ritual symbols has its benefit in an avoidance of their inflation through unharnessed enthusiasm. His casual and sober tone discourages rash actions and escapism. Yet this movement toward rationalization, and the emphasis on the subjective aspects of ritual, poses certain disadvantages as well.

The essential premise of this preacher's ritual role stems from the presumed mundane and practical character of the benevolent society. But as its religious dimension, evidenced by the mosque itself, has grown to dominate all other activities, to the point where it forms the exclusive attraction for most of its congregation, the symbolic context of the ritual role has also changed. The assumption that the weekly prayer and sermon constitute a ceremonial renewal and consolidation for those engaged in a concrete collective enterprise is no longer valid. Those drawn to this mosque can be more accurately described as largely otherwise uncommitted individuals for whom the qualities Shaykh Hassan displays as a preacher are virtually indistinguishable from the qualities he represents as a social actor apart from this position. As a result, the benevolent society, which has its stated

223

function in the application of concrete religious principles within a bounded face-to-face social organization, has been largely transformed into an institution which has ritual as its major, and for most its only, shared experience.

This subtle transition into a community of ritual rather than a community of action represents a certain impoverishment of the religious symbols, however, for their underlying function is not to unify at the highest levels of cultural inclusion, but to articulate opposition. By resisting the centripetal force of the ritual itself, by asserting his identity as actor upon the image of the interstitial religious mediator, Shaykh Hassan reclaims in the pulpit the weight of his secular prestige, but only at the price of narrowing the breadth and depth of reference carried by the symbols he invokes. His ritual authority is no longer validated by collective achievements of structural change, hence his critical and practical posture with regard to the culture-affirming religion of the establishment is either a fiction or it is substantiated by an ideology of opposition to other centers of religio-political power. What is being generated, in short, is a nascenty sect, the stirrings of a separate self-justifying institution that does not aspire to unify the diverse and stratified segments of a whole society, but to create a cohesive new self-understanding of a particular interest group that is recent and restless.

NOTES

1. Taha Hussein's masterful memoir of his youth (1948) describes well the customary use of classical Arabic with minimum comprehension.
2. See Hill, 1979: 2–8, for a helpful discussion on the difficulties of distinctions between urban and rural in contemporary Egypt.
3. Al-Hakim's classic of modern Egyptian fiction recounts the experience of a magistrate who is assigned to a post in Upper Egypt. The problems of integrating into the society as a lawyer are reminiscent of the difficulties faced by these preachers on district assignment.

REFERENCES

Baer, Gabriel (1969), *Studies in the Social History of Modern Egypt.* Chicago: University of Chicago Press.
Berger, Morroe (1970), *Islam in Egypt Today: Social and Political Aspects of Popular Religion.* Cambridge: At the University Press.
Calverley, Edwin Elliot (1925),*Worship in Islam: Being a Translation with Commentary and Introduction of al-Ghazzali's Book of the Ihya' on the*

Worship. London: Luzac and Company Ltd.

Crecelius, Daniel (1972), 'Nonideological Responses of the Egyptian Ulama to Modernization' in Nikki R. Keddie, (ed), *Scholars, Saints, and Sufis.* Berkeley: University of California Press.

Geertz, Clifford (1971). *Islam Observed: Religious Development in Morocco and Indonesia.* Chicago: University of Chicago Press.

Gilsenan, Michael D. (1967) 'Some Factors in the Decline of Sufi Orders in Modern Egypt.' *The Muslim World.* 57: 11–18.

al-Hakim, Tawfiq (1947); *Maze of Justice*, trans. A. Eban. London: Harvill Press.

Heyworth-Dunne, J. (1950), *Religious and Political Trends in Modern Egypt.* Washington D.C.: Published by the Author.

Hill, Enid (1979), *Mahkama! Studies in the Legal System, Courts & Crime, Law & Society.* London: Ithaca Press.

Hodgson, Marshall, G.S. (1974), *The Venture of Islam.* Vol III. *The Gunpowder Empires and Modern Times.* Chicago: University of Chicago Press.

Hudson, Michael C. (1980), 'Islam and Political Development', John L. Esposito (ed.), in *Islam and Development: Religion and Sociopolitical Change.* Syracuse University Press, 1–24.

Hussein, Taha (1948), *The Stream of Days: A Student at the Azhar.* trans. by H. Wayment. London: Longmans, Green and Co.

Ibrahim, Saad Eddin (1980), 'Anatomy of Egypt's Militant Islamic Groups: Methodological Note and Preliminary Findings', *International Journal of Middle Eastern Studies,* 12: 423–53.

de Jong, F. (1978), *Turuq and Turuq-linked Institutions in Nineteenth Century Egypt.* Leiden: E.J. Brill.

Kerr, Malcolm (1975), 'The Political Outlook in the Local Area', in Abraham S. Becker (ed.), *The Economics and Politics of the Middle East.* New York: American Elsevier Publishing Co.

Lane, Edward William (1836, rep. 1978), *Manners and Customs of the Modern Egyptians.* The Hague: East-West Publications.

Mahmud, 'Ali 'Abdul-Halim (1976), *Al-Masjid wa-Altharahu fi al-Majtama' al-Islami.* Cairo: Dar al-Ma'arif.

Marsot, Afaf Lutfi Al-Sayyid (1972), 'The Ulama of Cairo in the Eighteenth and Nineteenth Centuries' in Nikkie, R. Keddie (ed.), *Scholars, Saints, and Sufis.* Berkeley: University of California Press, 149–66.

'Masdjid', *Encyclopedia of Islam,* (1936).

Mitchell, Richard, P. (1969). *The Society of the Muslim Brothers.* London: Oxford University Press.

Rida, Rashid (1931), *Tarikh al-Ustadh al-Imam al Shaykh Muhammad 'Abdu.* Vol. 1. Cairo: Matba'a al-Manar.

Turner, Victor W. (1967), *The Forest of Symbols: Aspects of Ndembu Ritual.* Ithaca: Cornell University Press.

—— (1977), 'Symbolic Studies', in B. Siegel et al. (eds), *Annual Review of Anthropology.* Palo Alto: Annual Reviews, Inc.

10

Three Islamic Voices in Contemporary Nigeria

Allan Christelow

To speak of Islam in Nigeria is to speak of a large and rapidly growing community — it is commonly estimated that well over 50 per cent
of Nigeria's approximately 100 million citizens are Muslim. It is also
to speak of a complex phenomenon in which an intensely unitarian
religion interacts with an unusually wide array of political, ethnic,
historical, and economic factors. The unitarian quality of Islam is made
salient in the North of Nigeria by still vital memories of the founding
of an Islamic state, the Sokoto Caliphate, in the early nineteenth century. The writings of the leaders of the Sokoto jihad — Shaykh
Usuman dan Fodio, his brother Abdullahi, and his son Muhammad
Bello — remain a source of inspiration to many Muslims in Nigeria
(Last, 1967; Hiskett, 1973; Martin, 1976). The North also encom-
passes Sokoto's Muslim rival to the east, the Sultanate of Bornu.

When the British established the frontiers and the political structures of modern Nigeria in the early 1900s, they amalgamated the
strongly Muslim far north with radically different societies to the
south. In the Southwest, the Yoruba had a strong political tradition
of their own, and both Islam and Christianity had established roots
among them by the beginning of the colonial period. The major ethnic
group of the Southeast, the Ibo, proved strongly receptive to Christianity, and especially to Catholicism. Both of these groups had a long
head start over the North in the field of modern education. The
minority groups inhabiting the broad Middle Belt of Nigeria have been
proselytized by both Muslims and Christians, and the process of
change from traditional to universal religions is still going on there,
in complex interaction with economic, political, and cultural factors.
In discussing Nigerian society in the 1970s and 1980s, another unit
of analysis has to be taken into consideration — the flow of immigrants
from neighboring countries into Nigeria, and from the Nigerian

countryside into the cities. As Paul Lubeck dramatically demonstrates in chapter 4 of this book on the 'Yan Tatsine uprising, the religious outlook of the predominantly young male immigrants can be strongly affected by their often acute economic problems.

Since independence, Nigeria has fluctuated between rule by civilian political parties and by the military. From 1961 to 1966, and again from 1979 until the end of 1983, there was a civilian government, dominated by the parties which represented the conservative northern elite, who drew their power and influence from their control over the traditional political structures of the emirates. These parties were, in the earlier period, the Northern People's Congress (NPC), and, in the later, the National Party of Nigeria (NPN). The main focus of opposition was among the Yoruba, a large majority of whom supported first the Action Group, and then the Unity Party of Nigeria (UPN). The Ibo-based political parties tended to hedge their bets, vacillating between alliance with and opposition to the northern elite.

Notwithstanding the famous NPC slogan of 'One North', the northern elite parties' domination at the federal level was heavily dependent on support from areas which were only partially Muslim, or even heavily Christian, in the Middle Belt, and in the non-Ibo area of the Southeast. Within the heavily Muslim far north, the NPN had two serious rivals, the People's Redemption Party (PRP) based in Kano state, and the Great Nigeria People's Party (GNPP), which was based in the Northeast. While the latter had its origins in the historical rivalry between Bornu and Sokoto, the PRP reflected primarily a class division — the opposition of the *talakawa*, or masses, to the office and land controlling elite, the *masu sarauta* (Paden, 1973; Zartman, 1983).

Thus, when we come to discuss the revival of Islam as a political force, a central theme of many of the papers presented in this volume, we must bear in mind that Nigerian politics involves a peculiarly complex web of alliances and oppositions, and that, while the North has a rich heritage of Islamic politics from the Sokoto jihad, the dynamics of contemporary Nigerian politics have created pressures towards a separation of religion and politics. Further, the older generation of Nigerian politicians can recall how the religious effervescence of the mid-1960s contributed to tensions leading to the secession of the predominantly Christian Ibos, and the tragedy of the civil war of 1967–70.

This paper is a presentation of three different examples of Islamic political thought in Nigeria, each of which, in a different way, reflects the tensions of this complex situation. All three thinkers discussed are nationally known figures, with access to the print and other media, so it might well be seen as a study of Islam among the elite. In contrast, Paul Lubeck's paper can be seen as a study of Islam at the popular level, and the phenomenon which he analyzes can be seen as reflecting the failure of these elite thinkers to create an Islamic political vision which fully and effectively addresses the problems of Nigeria in the 1980s.

Given the extent and nature of those problems, however, it needs to be said that the task is a monumental one. The response of Islamic thinkers to them has been by no means static and uniform, or tradition-bound. The examples discussed below are indicative of important changes which have taken place in the last decade. In the late colonial and early Independence periods, the relationship between Islam and the sphere of modern politics had been largely an indirect one. Religious symbols were invoked for the purposes of garnering votes or obtaining patronage, and they could have an important role in working out a redefinition of community. But as far as their discourse and modes of thought were concerned, they remained largely insulated from one another.

Just as Muslim religious figures had once prepared charms for pagan chiefs, so they could perform similar services for modern educated politicians. In this situation, no coherent rationale seemed to be needed on either side, only some assurance of the effficacy of the relationship, and a harmonious meshing of definitions of authority and community. Such a relationship seemed quite compatible with the complex web of alliance and opposition in Nigerian politics.

But circumstances have changed dramatically in Nigeria during the years of the oil boom and the Second Republic, from 1974 to 1983, and the most far-reaching changes have come in the North. Here, the once powerful traditional rulers, the emirs, had been stripped of most of their formal powers by the military regime in the late 1960s. And the introduction of Universal Primary Education (UPE), beginning in the mid-1970s, had near revolutionary effects in this region where only a tiny minority had attended modern schools up until now, while far more youngsters had attended traditional Qur'anic schools (Muhammad, 1980; Clarke, 1979). These changes combined to create an electorate more literate in the languages of modern politics, English and Hausa. And it was an electorate who sought a new basis of authority. Yet many of them — perhaps to justify their own acceptance of modern innovations — would want this new basis to be shaped from, or at least clearly consistent with, the established value system of Islam. Hence we have witnessed, since the mid-1970s, a burgeoning of new Islamic political discourse.

The central concerns of this discourse have been the two most essential problems in Nigerian public life: pluralism and corruption. In grappling with these problems, Islamic political thinkers find themselves faced with a severe contradiction. On the one hand, if Muslims are to prevail in federal politics, Islam needs to be reconciled to a pluralistic system, run within a secular political framework. On the other hand, the unitarian tradition of the Sokoto jihad, with its stern sense of moral rectitude, stands as an obviously attractive remedy for the problem of corruption.

This situation is illustrated by the position of the NPN in the Second Republic. The party was closely identified with the northern elite, whose traditional basis of legitimacy derived from their descent from the Sokoto jihad leaders. Yet to maintain their position as the dominant party, they had to act as defenders of what was widely perceived as a pluralistic and corrupt *status quo*. The populist PRP often identified itself with the jihad's spirit of reform and justice, and yet the PRP leaders realized only too well that to succeed at the national level, they would have to join forces with largely non-Muslim southerners.

The net result of these political equations is that an Islamic political party is not a viable proposition in Nigeria, as it seems to be in some countries in South and Southeast Asia. Nor, to date, does there exist in Nigeria a centrally controlled Islamic bureaucracy, such as one finds in such diverse settings as Algeria and Indonesia.[1] Without a party structure, or central bureaucratic control, Islamic discourse, at the national level, has tended to become embedded in diverse institutions, above all in the media, the educational system, and the courts.

It will thus be a contention of this paper that, in order to understand Islamic discourse in Nigeria at the national level, particularly that which appears in national newspapers, one needs to look at the institutional background of the writer. This is by no means to say that this national institutional discourse has replaced that of the local religious teacher, the *mallam* (Hausa) or *alfa* (Yoruba), but it is certain that national institutions have increased considerably in importance since the beginning of the 1970s, and yet little attention has been paid to them by scholars interested in Islam.[2]

In this essay, I shall be looking at the discourse of three Nigerian Islamic thinkers, and interpreting it in terms of their institutional background and experience. The first is Abubakar Mahmud Gumi, who is a man of the mosque and its extensions, the Islamic organization, and, most importantly, the radio. He usually expresses himself in Hausa. In his case, I shall concentrate on a published interview, since this best conveys his media style. The second thinker is Ibraheem Sulaiman, who is a lecturer in one of Nigeria's modern Anglo-American-style universities, Ahmadu Bello University in Zaria, at the Institute of Administration. His published work is nearly all in English. The third thinker, Abdulmalik Bappa Mahmud, comes from the Muslim court system, where he serves as a state grand *qadi* (judge). He writes both in Hausa and in English.

Nearly all of the writing which I shall be considering comes from the same newspaper complex, *The New Nigerian/Gaskiya Ta Fi Kwabo* of Kaduna,[3] but it will be clear that there is no strictly defined house orthodoxy. Rather, these newspapers tend to serve as a forum for a variety of interest groups, most of them loosely aligned behind the NPN. No other Nigerian newspapers devote as much space to Islamic discourse, and indeed most southern papers eschew religious discourse altogether. The only other important newspaper in the North, *The Sunday Triumph*,[4] is linked to the NPN's local populist rival, the PRP, and insofar as it discusses religion, is concerned with criticizing the NPN's manipulation of religion for political purposes. *The New Nigerian* editors themselves are well aware that identification of a political party with Islam can be a political liability in Nigeria, as well as an advantage. Thus the English language *New Nigerian* carries only a limited amount of Islamic discourse, most of it quite mild in tone. The Hausa language *Gaskiya* carries much more Islamic discourse, some of it quite polemical in character.[5]

However, the rough rule of thumb about no religious polemics in English is not so rigorously applied in the recently established (1981) *Sunday New Nigerian*, which carries a regular column by Ibraheem Sulaiman. This change can be seen as a reflection of the burgeoning of Islamic political discourse in the universities, where Sundays are a day of rest and of even more avid newspaper reading than usual.

Two of the thinkers discussed are identified with movements. Gumi is a leading light in the movement called Izalatul Bidia wa Ikamatul Sunna (The Removal of Blameworthy Innovations and Establishment of the Orthodox Tradition), usually referred to simply as 'Izala'. This is a Wahhabi-influenced group dedicated to moral reform, and to combating the influence of the Sufi tariqas. Ibraheem Sulaiman is associated with the university-based Muslim Students Society, and has been a major contributor to the MSS magazine, *The Radiance*. But, as a rule, discourse in newspapers avoids direct identification with movements. I would suggest that this is not simply to avoid identification with the actions of more flamboyant elements who may allegedly be connected to these movements, but also because the

230

thinkers' primary identities lie with their institutional positions (in Hausa parlance, their *sarauta* (see Smith, 1960:6–7)) rather than in a movement.

ABUBAKAR GUMI AND THE DEFENSE OF THE STATUS QUO

Abubakar Gumi is one of the best known Nigerian Islamic spokesmen, and one of the most controversial. He was a close associate of the Sardauna of Sokoto, Sir Ahmadu Bello, working with him, when the Sardauna was Northern Region Premier, to create a framework of centralized Islamic institutions in the region. Up until the 1950s, Islamic institutions in the North had been run almost entirely on a local emirate basis, and the controversial character of Gumi has as much to do with his representing the intrusion of central authority into local affairs as it does with his being identified with the 'conservative northern oligarchy'. He served as Grand Qadi of the Northern Region, and was a founder of the Jama'atu Nasril Islam, which attempts to serve as a sort of umbrella organization for various Islamic groups (Paden, 1973:183–4).

Since the dismantling of the Northern Region in 1967, Gumi has not held an official government position, and he has emerged as the foremost spokesman of what could be termed conservative Islamic reformism in northern Nigeria, maintaining his base at Kaduna, the old regional capital. He is very active in preaching and organizing, and has wide international contacts. But he is probably best known to Nigerians for his talks on Radio Kaduna, which, along with *The New Nigerian* and *Gaskiya*, was part of the old Northern Region media complex. He is renowned for his polemics with the Sufi tariqas, whose strongest base is in Kano, but this is an issue which the print media steer clear of, and is extraneous to the questions being treated in this paper.

Gumi is closely identified with the NPN, and with the argument that this party should be identified with Islamic interests. In fact, if he is often thought to imply this, he does not directly say it. What he does say is at once simple and complex. He urges all Muslims to vote for Muslim political candidates. The implication of this is not necessarily that one should support the NPN, but rather that one should not support southern Christians, such as Azikwe (Ibo, leader in the Second Republic of the Nigeria People's Party), or Awolowo (Yoruba, leader of the UPN). If one reads Gumi's position in this second, literal way, one finds that he has put his finger on an important operative principle of Nigerian politics. Northern Muslims form the largest single block in Nigerian politics, but a great many of them opposed the NPN. However, many of those in the two northern opposition parties, the PRP and the GNPP, balked at the idea of a strong alliance with a southern party, and this issue led to serious rifts in both of them. In contrast, southern minority groups and factions have no qualms about supporting the NPN if it offers them a tangible advantage.[6] Gumi did not create these facts, but likes to point them out.

The real vulnerability of Gumi is not his identification with the NPN, but with the political process itself, and with the *status quo*, as emerges in the following interview with a journalist from *Gaskiya*.

Concerning the Mixing of Men and Women in Registration and Voting: the views of a Mallam Interviewed by Adamu Yusuf [1982]

Allah has his power as in the days of old. It is the business of all of us to provide food for our hungry families. And as for those who don't have any work, they have to move in search of it. We are voting for politicians in 1983, so problems are going to arise. At that time, they are going to bring many promises to the masses of the whole country.

Now some of the people are saying that they are not going to allow their women to go and mix with men. And there are those who say about the whole thing, 'Cats are howling'. They are not going to get into this nonsense, because they feel that when politics begins they will get nothing at all. Well, having said this, our correspondent had an interview with . . . Shaikh Abubakar Gumi, who needs no introduction, since everybody knows what a famous mallam he is . . . Here is how that discussion went:

Gaskiya Ta Fi Kwabo: God bless you. What about the legality of men and women mixing together, especially as the time of elections draws near?

Alhaji Abubakar Gumi: Well, it is said that if the Muslims rest, the unbelievers [*kafirai*] will make war on them, so it is a duty for men and women to arise and take up arms. If a woman takes up arms, isn't there a mixing of the sexes in this situation? You see why the Muslims are not oppressed! Well, [by analogy to this], it is correct to cast a vote.

Now since this will be beneficial to oneself and, moreover, beneficial to the Muslim community, it is Satan who prevents them from going out. It is not like going to a party where men and women mix, as at a wedding party or a naming ceremony. Doesn't one say that *kamun ango* [seizing of the bridegroom — a Hausa tradition] is permissible? All those who do not see what is going to happen in this matter, it is a pity, for it is this [voting] which benefits Muslims. It is Satan who persists in saying that the bringing together of men and women in the polling place is not appropriate. I want you to see that this is the word of Satan. As long as a man's wife covers her body properly, well, there's no problem. If you hear somebody say that this is a gathering of men and women, we don't want it, this is Satan who urges the unbelievers, men and women, to oppress the Muslims.

I personally will go out with my wives, with our children following. If this is not done, even to the point of letting unbelievers predominate, then what is our position?

Gaskiya Ta Fi Kwabo: God bless you. Well, what appeal do you make to the men to let their women go to vote?

Alhaji Abubakar Gumi: I appeal to them in a harsh voice to know their religion. This religion, if you do not protect it, it will not protect you. This is what makes me say that politics is more important than prayer. If a man does not say his noon prayer, he acknowledges [the seriousness of] this, and [so] he does not apostasize. But if he acknowledges [the seriousness] of politics, and yet he does not vote, unbelief comes to him. I hope you see the difference! With politics, one stands for prayer and worship together, whereas prayer is only part of this.

With politics, one protects men's blood and their well-being. With politics, one protects the wealth of men, and their belongings, and also one's kinfolk and associates, and whatever one cares about. With politics, one protects the manliness of men, so if you say that you won't do it, who is going to protect us? Pagans who don't even know whether or not they are Muslims? Because of the importance of what confronts you, will you not make an effort not to lose it? Well then, one does politics. It is a necessity that every man takes his women and children above the age of eighteen to register so that we can predominate over the non-Muslims.

Gaskiya Ta Fi Kwabo: Some people I see take refuge in saying that since the first time they voted, they were not given what they needed, so they are not going to take the trouble to vote, since they are just being taken advantage of.

Alhaji Abubakar Gumi: What sorts of needs do they expect to be met? Do they want someone to give them money? The one who is given money for a vote, or the one who says that when someone gives him money, then he will vote for a Muslim, well this is unbelief [*kafirci*]. Because of this, I call on men, that is Muslims, to study in order to know their religion. If they don't study it, they won't become enlightened. Many people assume that politics is none of their business, that instead it is the work of soldiers or police, which is a big mistake, because this is the way life is.

If you give up politics, you give up religion. It is necessary that you make your children do it. Then everything that has been said will make you progress. If you fix that which must be fixed, then you will progress with it. May God help us all to vote for the right thing.

Gaskiya Ta Fi Kwabo: God bless you. If we look around, we find that there are politicians who make many promises to the masses for their votes. Then, if they are elected, they don't remember the promises, much less fulfill them. What do you do about that?

Alhaji Abubakar Gumi: What promises? Among the politicians, there are some who might say, if you vote for him, he will give you an [electric] fan. Well, because he says that if you vote for him, he will give you a fan, but if he doesn't give it, then are you going to say that you won't vote for a Muslim?

Gaskiya Ta Fi Kwabo: God bless you. Now how do you explain why one should go out and vote?

Alhaji Abubakar Gumi: What the politicians do is to try to protect the laws of Allah which he gave us. They make an effort to protect them according to their ability. If they do this, they cater to our needs. What do the masses need? Does one not protect their well-being? He [the average man] knows how to go to his farm and raise a crop, to take care of his wives and family. After that, what is he looking for? Here are the roads that have been built. If he has something to sell or wants to buy something, he gets a ride [to the market]. There are police taking care of the roads. Well, after all this, what does he need? For someone to give him a fan to cool his house?

Gaskiya Ta Fi Kwabo: God bless you. So now I understand that you are appealing to the masses to unite to obtain progress by voting well, especially if it is for the sake of religion.

Alhaji Abubakar Gumi: Very true, absolutely necessary. He who refuses his duty to vote refuses his religion completely. May God protect us.

Gaskiya Ta Fi Kwabo: Thank you very much, may God help the people to understand.

Alhaji Abubakar Gumi: Yes, thank God.

The occasion for this interview was the voter registration campaign taking place in August 1982, one year before the national elections which were to sweep the NPN back to power, albeit briefly. Women first voted in northern Nigeria in 1979, and so the question was still a fresh one in the region with the approach of the 1983 elections. One should bear in mind that since the NPN appealed to the more conservative Muslims, the possibility of its male supporters keeping their womenfolk at home posed a serious potential problem. At the same time, the question of women going to the polling place posed an ostensibly religious issue, and so it was the one political matter which a religious leader or a traditional ruler could comment on in the media without opening himself up to the charge of political partisanship. Also, it should be pointed out that, historically, discourse concerning women's rights has been the preserve of the NPN's populist rival, the PRP (under the First Republic, the Northern Elements Progressive Union, or NEPU).

The question of women voting is of concern to all classes of people, and not just to a learned elite, who are the usual audience of newspaper articles. It is not simply that everybody over the age of eighteen is eligible to vote: everybody is concerned with, and can easily grasp, questions about proper social comportment. Gumi's style is one very much suited to this wide audience. It is oral and didactic, with simple, emphatic arguments, usually repeated with a slight variation to make sure that they get across. It is a style with strong roots in traditional Islamic teaching and preaching, and which has been skilfully adapted to electronic amplification on radio sermons and talk shows.

The most interesting thing about the way in which Gumi develops his arguments is his interweaving of new, contemporary Islamic themes with older, locally rooted Islamic tradition. The image of women fighting alongside of men to defend the faith is, one suspects, a reflection of images from the Iranian revolution (and more broadly the new Islamic activism), of the *chador*-clad woman cradling the Kalashnikov. And too, there are clear traces of Khomeini's ideas in the proposition that 'politics is more important than prayer' (*siyasa ta fi muhimmanci da salla*). What Khomeini actually says is that 'protecting Islam is more important than uttering prayers or fasting' (Enayat, 1983:170). The twist which Gumi adds is to equate *siyasa* — meaning here participation in present-day Nigerian politics — with protecting Islam.

The question of men and women mixing is one which goes back to the time of the Sokoto jihad, when the open mixing of the sexes in frivolous, non-Islamic celebrations was part of the religious backsliding against which Shaykh Usuman dan Fodio inveighed (Last, 1967; Hiskett, 1973). Against this background, there is an obvious problem facing anyone who wishes both to uphold traditional Islamic values and to justify the mixing of the sexes. There is a sort of liberal, modernist reading of the Sokoto jihad literature which points to Shaykh Usuman's strong support of his daughter's education (Boyd and Shagari, 1978). But Gumi eschews this sort of approach. He attempts instead what one might call a sort of transvaluation of values, identifying the image of mixing in voting with the image of jihad, that is, with a set of values well known in northern Nigeria for the condemnation of public mixing of the sexes. One can suggest that the Iranian revolution, and the rise of the new Islamic activism, helped to stimulate this transvaluation of values.

However, while Gumi evokes images from the militant heritages of Iran and Sokoto, he puts them to work in defense of the Nigerian political *status quo*, which has little to do with either. 'Siyasa' in contemporary Nigeria means boisterous, free-wheeling party politics, and contracts for the party stalwarts, not revolutionary commitment. And 'Satan', as far as Gumi is concerned, is not international imperialism, or godless bolshevism, but rather the parochial, traditionalist, suspicious-of-the-world-beyond-the-village mentality of the very people whom he is addressing, or else those within Nigeria who might contribute to or exploit that mentality.

The journalist Adamu Yusuf puts Gumi on the spot by asking him to respond to the problem of political disillusionment. Why bother to vote for any politicians if they are all corrupt and full of empty promises? Here Gumi's response is quite far from either the Sokoto jihad or the Iranian revolution, but strikes one as more in tune with the classical Islamic political theorist al-Mawardi, whose ideas gave an underpinning of legitimacy to a waning Abbasid caliphate. Gumi asserts that the legitimacy of established political authority derives from the upholding of the sacred law, and he even seems to qualify this for the Nigerian situation, suggesting that all that one needs to do is to uphold the law 'according to one's ability'. Other than that, all that one can expect of politicians is to build roads and to put policemen on them. In short, he deals with the problem of disillusionment by suggesting that the fault lies with those who are naive enough to accept the illusions in the first place, and that the only significant question in Nigerian politics is which community dominates the national political scene.

His method of argument by analogy is one which is firmly established in orthodox Islamic thought, and it contrasts sharply, as will be seen, with the style of a younger Islamic thinker in the modern university system. But his basic argument is a distinctly awkward one, since the value system to which he subscribes hardly lends support to the basic proposition that women should have the right to vote. What he is saying in effect is that, while there would be no reason for women to vote in a homogeneous Muslim society, Muslim women should be made to vote because Nigeria is a pluralistic society. Though not mentioned in his discussion, the Nigerian Constitution of 1979 sets the basic framework of political discourse in Nigeria, and Gumi, unlike some younger activists, accepts this framework. What he seems to be doing in this interview is struggling to reconcile a liberal and secular constitution with conservative Islamic values. In order to do this, he borrows the potentially very radical image of women participating in the struggle to defend the faith. In order to neutralize the radical implications, he qualifies the principle of women's political participation with the injunction that the man should lead his women to the polls, and enlighten them as to whom they should vote for.[7]

IBRAHEEM SULAIMAN AND ISLAM IN THE MODERN UNIVERSITY

The university lecturer Ibraheem Sulaiman has an altogether different audience from that of Abubakar Gumi. Writing lengthy essays in English, he addresses mainly university students, whose education has given them a wide exposure to Western social and political concepts. His sources of inspiration are eclectic. They include Sayyid Qutb, Ibn Khaldun, Muhammad Asad, and Solzhenitsyn.

One can find a resemblance between the works of Sulaiman and those of 'Ali Shariati. But there is a more striking resemblance in style and themes to the works of the Algerian writer Malek Bennabi, whose most important works were published in the late 1940s and early 1950s. Like Sulaiman, Bennabi wrote (at that time)[8] in a European language, and for a largely student audience, in a newspaper (the moderate Ferhat Abbas's *La République Algérienne*), and in a Muslim student magazine *(Le jeune musulman)*.

The themes which Bennabi and Sulaiman develop are quite similar: the corrosive effects of the colonial experience on Muslim values and personality, the intellectual and moral weakness of contemporary Muslim society, the dangers of imitating Western ideas and culture. Both look to the Qur'an for insights on how to understand the contemporary Muslim plight. Islam is presented as a third way between the failed ideologies of capitalism and communism. Both affect a sort of religious-political purism, disdaining the compromises of established leaders, yet they see fit to publish their works in the press of what would be termed, in their respective contexts, 'moderate' parties.[9]

Both Bennabi and Sulaiman combine an intense Islamic idealism with a search for an understanding of historical pattern. In doing so, they constantly confront this problem: if the final and complete message has been received, why does the community which has accepted it suffer such great historical reverses? Both writers cite Ibn Khaldun extensively, but neither has that thinker's concern for economic and political realities. Their reading of Ibn Khaldun is a moralistic one, one might say Toynbee-esque.

One also finds in Sulaiman's work a more mystical approach to historical analysis, with strong traces of the influence of Sayyid Qutb, who saw history as a constant struggle between *'al-nizam al-islami'* and *'al-nizam al-jahili'*, the Islamic order and the order of ignorance. Sulaiman writes:

We see history as the struggle between Islam, on the one hand, and what is not Islam on the other, that is, the struggle between Justice and Injustice, between Truth and Falsehood, between Discipline and Corruption, between Belief and Rejection. (1982).

But he gives this approach a particular inflection, emphasizing above all the truth/falsehood dichotomy, and arguing for the *inevitable* triumph of truth:

As we glance through the pages of history, we see that always falsehood mounts unto the surface of history, roaring, screaming, creating social dramas; its men known for making a noise, telling lies, and spreading disorder, all in the effort to overwhelm the Truth, and confuse its nature. Soon it fades away, and is cast off as rubbish, the fact that its agents have created great political expressions notwithstanding. But Truth moves on. (ibid.)

The sense of the inevitable triumph of truth runs against the sense of urgency and the penchant for voluntarism which one finds in Sayyid Qutb and his followers (Ajami, 1983:22–30). And the mention of 'great political expressions notwithstanding' suggests perhaps a surreptitious acceptance of some elements of the system being condemned.

A clue to this ambivalence can perhaps be found in Sulaiman's analysis of Nigerian history. Whereas Sayyid Qutb could find a substantial audience for his condemnation of the foreign, corrupted monarchy established by Muhammad 'Ali, the ineffectual Wafd, and the failed dreams of Nasr, Sulaiman cannot deal so lightly with the Muslim heroes of Nigeria, Sir Ahmadu Bello, Sir Abubakar Tafawa Balewa, Sa'adu Zungur, Murtala Muhammad, and Aminu Kano. With the exception of the first, resented by many for his heavy-handed political methods, all are widely respected in northern Nigeria. With the exception of the last, they all died martyrs' deaths.[10] Sulaiman finds himself obliged to give them all a measure of praise for their ideals, before turning to the condemnation of their methods. The Northern Region premier, Sir Ahmadu Bello, worked through 'the dirty secular political institution'. Murtala Muhammad, the most popular of Nigeria's military rulers, a man with a strongly Islamic image, made the mistake of using 'the corrupt military complex'. Aminu Kano indulged in secularism. Only the poet and intellectual, Sa'adu Zungur managed to stay above the vulgar fray (Sulaiman, 1980; 1982b).

As to the external enemies of the truth, Sulaiman finds two: colonialism and zionism. The colonial experience he sees as a sort of temporary deviation from a true, authentic historical project:

colonisation is a falsehood in itself, and its legacy, however powerful it may appear, is nothing but a false expression. So this mighty expression is bound to be cast off on the shores of history as mere scum which must eventually vanish (1982a).

This statement might be read as reflecting the northern Nigerian experience of indirect rule, where the colonial impact was a relatively superficial one. (Such a statement would be altogether out of place in the writings of the Algerian Bennabi, for instance.)

Colonialism, for Sulaiman, is primarily a political falsehood. When he moves into the sphere of ideas, it is 'zionism' which is the dominant falsehood. It must be emphasized that Sulaiman uses the term in a complex and original, if not sharply defined, sense. He does not equate zionism with the Jews or with Israel, though the latter would be an illustration of the concept of zionism, and one might expect a mutual sympathy between Israelis and other 'zionists'. Sulaiman's key statement on zionism is this:

Human thought must be freed from the inhibitions created by the zionists who have sponsored their own sons to imprison universal thoughts into parochial cages in almost every field of endeavour (1981).

Again, a few paragraphs later, 'zionism' is clearly used in relation to the intellectual sphere, in reference to

> the intellectuals who are drunk with the opium of zionist-inspired ideologies, and who are so appallingly ignorant of their own environment that they are not fit to be members of the society they claim to fight for.

This lambasting of zionism for being parochial and cosmopolitan at the same time is not easy to decode. One might suggest that in the Nigerian context it refers to the image of a southern intellectual, who is both highly specialized technically and attached to an ethnic identity, on the one hand, and yet at ease with Western speech, dress, thought, and life-styles, on the other. Islam represents the polar opposite of this: the insistence that technology and scientific thought be subordinated to universal religious values; and identification with a universal, but non-Western, community. If this interpretation is correct, 'zionism' is used as a sort of code word for a complex idea which is difficult to articulate, but it is not simply a structural prop, lacking all content (Rousillon, 1982).

When one places this reading in the Nigerian context, one is reminded of an old problem: the fear of Northerners that better educated, more ethnically conscious Southerners might come to dominate the country. The use of the term 'zionism', while it introduces some confusing, tangential issues, puts the issue on a more abstract plane, so that it is not an actual ethnic identity which is called into question, but rather the phenomenon of ethnic elitism, and its correlate, disdain for the less educated, less sophisticated Muslim.

Whereas Abubakar Gumi understands Islam as the value system and basis of identity of one of Nigeria's competing communities, Sulaiman tries to detach it from any particular communal basis, to present it as a universal as opposed to a particularist solidarity, as an ideology relevant to all Nigerians. 'Islam', he writes (1981), 'offers the best and most reliable possibility for Nigeria to secure the total and all embracing freedom it requires to become a nation in earnest.'

While in this sense Islam is the *antithesis* of ethnic particularism, a basis for a 'transethnic identity' (Paden, 1973), it is the *counterthesis*, or rival, of Marxism. It would be most accurate to portray the rivalry as being between Islamic nationalism and Marxist nationalism, a debate not so much over ideologies as over what ideological inflection to give to a sense of nationalism shared by almost all educated young Nigerians.

For Nigerian students, the appeal of Islam, as Sulaiman projects it, is that it gives them a sense of being able to affirm their own intellectual identity. Sulaiman cites, with considerable feeling, a famous statement by the Waziri Junaidu of Sokoto, comparing the Sankore, the Islamic university of Timbuktu, with the Western-style universities of modern Nigeria. The latter are, said the Waziri, 'a cultural transplant whose roots lie in another tradition'. And he went on: 'I speak for many of my countrymen when I say that, unlike the Sankore, our universities appear to belong to us only in their location and their name' (cited in Sulaiman, 1982b).

The alien origin of Marxism is, in one sense, a source of vulnerability. But in another, it is an advantage, since this allows it to be more effective as an agent of transethnic integration. One peculiarity of the Marxist nationalist-Islamic nationalist rivalry in Nigerian universities is that the Marxists tend to place a great emphasis on foreign policy, especially African liberation movements, while Islamic activists concentrate more on internal social issues. The explanation is perhaps that the Marxist analysis of imperialism allows it to emphasize its transethnic appeal, whereas an Islamic international issue, such as Palestine, tends to arouse antagonisms within Nigeria. Islam's widest popular appeal is as an antidote to political corruption and social conflict.

This appeal is presented most easily where Islam can be identified with a sense of universal morality, for instance on the road question. Sulaiman sees this as an illustration of how Nigeria's development plans have been concerned solely with infrastructure, as opposed to human development. The roads are first and foremost a source of profit to corrupt ministers and party-stalwart contractors. And once built, 'good roads are immediately taken over by armed robbers and indisciplined drivers' (1982b).

In presenting specifically Islamic responses to social issues, two problems can arise: how to avoid identification with traditional, conservative, anti-modern attitudes, which have little appeal to students; and how to address the apprehensions, doubts, or antagonism of the non-Muslim.

The first sort of problem comes up in dealing with the question of begging, and the closely related one of Qur'anic schooling since traditionally Qur'anic students support themselves in part by begging. This question has received a great deal of attention from Islamic student activists, who have put forward proposals for integrating independent Qur'anic *mallams* into a centralized institutional system

(Dayyabu, 1982). But in the case of Sulaiman, while he goes on at great length about the disintegration of Nigerian Muslim society, he seems to avoid dealing with concrete institutional proposals. To do so would carry him into the very traditional terrain of hadith and legal scholarship, and away from the task of building Islam into a national ideology.

The second problem — addressing the apprehensions of non-Muslims — arises with the question of law. Sulaiman speaks of the growing frustration of all Nigerians with crime and violence, asserting that there is

> an undeclared concensus on the fact that Islamic law is the most effective legal order in existence, and its record of success in minimizing, or even eliminating crime, and in integrating human society, in instilling discipline and social consciousness, has never been matched in history. (1982b)

He notes the lower crime rates in Muslim areas of the country, and then asks: 'Is this not enough to convince us that if we want a better society, we should give Islamic law its supremacy?' The important point here is to establish the relevance of Islam to problems at the national level, a task which is essential to presenting it as a counter-thesis to Marxism.

However, there is an ambivalence in Sulaiman's position which comes out in his treatment of the university question, for he seems to suggest autonomy for the four universities of the far north, Zaria, Kano, Sokoto, and Maiduguri (ibid.), so that they can become properly Islamic universities.

Given the immense obstacles to implementing a program such as his in Nigeria, Sulaiman's tendency is to put off implementation into the future. He says (1982e), 'we envisage in the next one or two decades, the continuation of the process of decay, and even the acceleration of the process of disintegration'. In his gloomy assessment of the situation, he effectively distances himself from the more activist current among the Muslim students, the most interesting expression of which has been the refusal by a group of Islamic activists in Sokoto schools, many of them women, to sing the Nigerian national anthem.[11]

In terms of style of argument, there is an interesting contrast between Sulaiman and Gumi. Whereas Gumi argues by analogy, such as between jihad and electoral politics, leading his listeners from an old, widely accepted proposition about what constitutes correct

242

behavior to a new one, Sulaiman has a penchant for the metaphor and the parable which are used not to determine correct behavior, but as a tool for giving a religious underpinning to a reading of history. The metaphors are frequently of an organic character, about the inevitable process of growth and decay (1982d), or chemical, the process of separating the pure from the impure (1982a). He frequently makes use of parables from the Qur'an which demonstrate the impermanence of worldly happiness and prosperity, and condemn those who take it for granted (1982c). The taking of good things for granted, the attitude of human vanity, is linked by Sulaiman to the Qur'anic concept made popular by the Iranian revolution, corruption on earth, citing Qur'an 2:11: 'And when it is said to them: "Create not corruption on the earth", they say, "We are promoters of peace"'. Sulaiman comments at length on the early verses of the *Sura al-Baqarah* (2:8–20), where the theme of vanity is linked to man's dependence on God for his ability to perceive. It is God who gives and takes away the light — of fire (2:17) or lightning (2:19–20) (1982h).

The metaphor of light for knowledge is a widely recurring one in Sulaiman's work, and in the imagery of the Muslim Students Society. As noted earlier, the magazine of the Society's Ahmadu Bello University, Zaria branch, is called *The Radiance*. The emphasis on this metaphor is perhaps best explained by the fact that one is dealing here mainly with university students, many of them the first in their families to have modern schooling. Knowledge is the key to their hopes for advancement, but their knowledge (and ultimately, their power) needs a religious base to be accepted as legitimate in their own society. For the earlier generation, represented by Abubakar Gumi, modern learning had a much more limited role, and the elite which he represented had claims to traditional legitimacy.

In the Qur'anic metaphor, light is continually associated with God's omnipotence and the need for man's humility. And light, according to Sulaiman, should be distinguished from fire: the angels were made from light, whereas the prideful Iblis was made from fire, and stands for moral and intellectual decadence, which is the product of false, secular learning.[12] Prometheus, in this scheme of things, would find no sympathy.

Connected with the emphasis on religious knowledge is a continual insistence on the importance of moral factors in historical change, and the rejection of 'materialist' strategies of development. 'Materialist achievement', Sulaiman writes (1982g), 'is of no avail to a nation that has set itself on a path towards a bad end, since decadence and disintegration is a moral, not a material, factor.'

The appeal for a thoroughly Islamic education needs to be understood in the context of the Nigerian educational system, where the North has long lagged seriously behind the South in modern schooling, while it has maintained a vigorous traditional system of Qur'anic schooling. Moreover, in the North, while the British often paid lipservice to the need for reconciling traditional and modern learning, they generally treated Islamic education with a policy which might best be termed benign neglect (Hubbard, 1975). If the North has been able to catch up in the production of educators and administrators, it still lags far behind in the production of scientists and technicians, with many places in the science faculties of the North being taken by southerners, for lack of qualified northern students. Thus the situation is quite different from the Middle East, where technical students often form the prime recruiting ground for Islamic activists.

While Ibraheem Sulaiman attempts to gauge his discourse to a national framework, setting forth Islam as a solution to national problems, it is still strongly conditioned by what is primarily a northern problem. In the universities of the far North, the problem of reconciling the world of faith and that of scientific knowledge is still a quite real one. And so, Sulaiman's discourse hesitates between national revolution and local involution.

ABDULMALIK BAPPA MAHMUD ON ISLAM, LAW, AND AUTHORITY

Abdulmalik Bappa Mahmud is the Grand Qadi of Bauchi State, and his judicial experience appears to have affected him in several ways. He is often critical of his fellow Nigerian Muslims, but not in the despairing, bleakly pessimistic way of Sulaiman (1982f). It is rather the chiding criticism of the judge, who sees every day a procession of human weaknesses and foibles.

It is also a position in which he often has to deal with the realities of Muslim-Christian or Muslim-traditional religionist relationships in day-to-day life, in a state which straddles the mainly Muslim North and the religiously mixed Middle Belt. He points to several verses in the Qur'an which state clearly that there is no compulsion in religion, that a Muslim's duty is rather to warn and admonish the non-believer, who, should he reject the warning, will be called to account for this in the hereafter (1982a, citing Qur'an 2:256, 50:45, 88:21-2). He underscores the Qur'an's message of tolerance among peoples of the book, and states that, in his experience in the courts, he has handled numerous cases between Muslims and non-Muslims where the non-Muslims turned out to be in the right.

Whereas Gumi assumes a lack of trust between religious communities, and Sulaiman is preoccupied with defining the identity of Muslims in a Western-style, secular educational system, Mahmud has the dignified, serene sense of self-confidence which one often finds in the older generation of Nigerians. To him, Islam is the best religion, the Qur'an the completion of God's revelation, and so it should be natural for Muslims to be tolerant and respectful towards non-Muslims who bear no malice toward them or their faith.

He even sees this illustrated in the prohibition on Muslim women marrying Christian men, while it is acceptable for a Muslim man to marry a Christian woman. The Muslim man, he argues, would respect his wife's prophet, since he is recognized by the Qur'an, but the Christian husband might curse his wife's prophet (1982c).

As a Muslim judge in a country strongly influenced by the Anglo-Saxon legal tradition, Mahmud is very much concerned with the question of rights, and has written a long, three-part essay on the question of rights in Islam. He gives the British due credit for having guaranteed basic human rights in 1688, the French in 1789, and the Americans in 1791, before humbly suggesting that Islam was over a thousand years ahead of them. As for the question of human rights in Nigeria, he mentions the Westminster-style Constitution of 1963, but seems to pass over in silence the Constitution of 1979, with its American-style presidential system, whose demise (in January 1984) few Nigerians seem to regret (1982a).

A consistent theme in Mahmud's writing is his rather skeptical attitude toward the power of the modern state, and his sense that rights involve not simply guarantees of material well-being, but also guarantees against the oppression of the state. The best illustration of this is his section on 'freedom of flight from authority' (1982b), which upholds the duty of Muslims to take in those fleeing from oppression and injustice in another country. And he extends this to cover the right to migration of those who cross borders in search of education, or simply in order to make a living. Mahmud does not venture any specific examples; as a man of law, he is concerned above all with abstract principles. The passage which I am citing was written before the mass expulsion of 'illegal' immigrants in 1983, but the popular xenophobia behind the expulsion was already present, and one can read Mahmud's statement as a sharp criticism of such sentiment.[13]

Mahmud is particularly vehement in his condemnation of the arbitrary use of state power in the economic sphere, especially in land questions. He presents his critique in the form of a long-term historical analysis, in which he points an accusing finger clearly at the illiberal British colonial authorities, who sought to prop up their rule by giving free reign to the powers of traditional rulers. Islamic law had served to protect property rights, and to act as a check on the arbitrary authority of the emirs and their hangers-on. He reports that after the arrival of the British:

> Indirect rule made some emirs and chiefs so powerful that they discarded following Islamic law, and proceeded to cheat their subjects. It went to the extent that a person was not even aware of his right of ownership of his house, let alone his farm. (1981a).

The justification for such policies offered by Lord Lugard, chief architect and publicist of Indirect Rule in Nigeria, was that it was designed to protect the poor illiterate Hausa peasant from the exploitation of rapacious coastal natives. But the chief practical effect (and one suspects that it was intended) was to make that very peasant all the more helpless against the whims of his emir.

Since independence, Mahmud argues, the consistent theme of the Land Tenure and Land Use laws has been to reinforce the arbitrary powers of the state, at the expense of both the northern peasant and the southern interloper. Nowhere is the abuse of power so keenly felt and resented as in the question of expropriation for the building of roads, public institutions, and irrigation projects. Compensation is often slow, and the process subject to corruption and inefficiency — which hurt the user-occupier — and to political manipulation, which can greatly enrich the agile and politically influential speculator.

Under Islamic law, Mahmud argues, the situation would be quite different:

> a governor or constituted authority has no power to acquire land belonging to people, unless they voluntarily consent to sell it, just as exemplified by the Messenger of Allah, P.B.U.H., by the purchase of the land on which he built his mosque at Madina, at the cost of 20 dinars. (1981b).

It is interesting here to compare Mahmud's historical analysis with that of Sulaiman. On the one hand, the analysis is similar, that the Nigerian state represents, in effect, a continuation of the colonial state. But Mahmud is not concerned with heroes or martyrs or international conspiracies. He is concerned with the question of power, and how to place limits on the abuse of power. Implicitly, he suggests that the colonial experience destroyed the limits of power inherent in the Islamic system, and thus he condemns the colonialist for negating the values of his own culture.

By setting the colonial experience in this perspective, Mahmud, in a subtle and skilful way, appeals to all Nigerians, as he does when he suggests that the southern trader and the northern peasant both suffer injustices from the tyranny of the state. By shifting the focus from who has power in the state to how to prevent the abuse of power, he establishes a basis for strengthening the unity of Nigeria as a society, and, at the same time, affirming communal values.

Mahmud has also written extensively on zakat, the Islamic charity tax. Just one year after the 'Yan Tatsine uprising in Kano, there was a conference on zakat at Bayero University in Kano, bringing together figures ranging from Mallam Aminu Kano, the inspirer of Kano's populist religious tradition, to Shaykh Nasiru Kabara, head of the Qadiriyya tariqa.[14] The timing of the conference reflected the sense among Kano Muslims that they needed to close ranks, to find an Islamic response to the social problems which had contributed to the 'Yan Tatsine disturbances exactly one year earlier. For this occasion, Mahmud prepared a detailed statement on Islamic law regarding zakat, how the tax rate is calculated, and to what categories of people it is to be disbursed (1981-2; Gwarzo, 1982).

Though he does not address it, the zakat question could lead to a quandary for Mahmud. For, according to the law, as he seems to interpret it, zakat is to be paid to the state. Is the same state which deals abusively with land and immigration questions to be trusted with the collection and distribution of the sacred charity tax? It is this sort of question for which Mahmud's quite traditional approach does not give a satisfactory answer.

CONCLUSION

A convenient ground-rule for the comparative discussion of Muslim societies might be stated thus: first one needs to explain the diversity — the patterns and nuances of local politics and religious demography, economic and social structures, the educational system, and the structure of religious institutions. Only when this has been done can one go on to developing an understanding of aspects of interconnectedness and commonality.

Politics and religious demography are particularly important for the comparison of Nigeria with other cases presented in this volume. Most of the cases discussed involve countries where there is a strong predominance of Muslims in the population, and thus where one can assume a strong potential for Islamic political expression. The scholar's interest is focused on relations between Islamic movements and the state, and there emerge a wide range of possibilities: revolutionary seizure of state power by the religious leaders (in Iran); control and manipulation of religion by the state, leading to a marginalization of religious activists (in the Maghreb, and to a degree in Egypt and Indonesia); and co-optation or collaboration (in Pakistan and Malaysia).

In Nigeria, religious diversity and the patterns of political alliance have given the state a strongly secular character, and to question this secularism is to question the very basis of the Nigerian polity. Yet, if the Nigerian state is secular, Nigerian politics often take on a religious coloring, and in the North, there is a strong tradition of religious politics going back to the Sokoto caliphate. Also, there is no clearly articulated national ideology, such as Pančasila in Indonesia: the Nigerian state is not only secular, it is non-ideological. The initial resolution of this problem, in the First Republic, was to confine religious political expression to the regional level. While the regional structures have been abolished, their traces remain in the Muslim court system, and in the Kaduna media complex, the respective bases of Abdulmalik Bappa Mahmud and Abubakar Gumi. Both of them accept the secularism of the Nigerian state by keeping it at a distance, and seeking to prevent it from interfering with the affairs of Islam.

In Ibraheem Sulaiman, we find an attempt to promote Islam as a national ideology, but he cannot adopt the procedure of the Islamic ideologist in such settings as Iran or Tunisia, who says, in effect, this is what we believe, therefore let us practise it. Instead, he must develop an argument for it being the best ideology, in terms of results, and the most authentic and national ideology for Nigeria, and he does not seem entirely convinced of his own case, leaning at times towards the regionalization of ideology.

Another source of differences between Muslim countries lies in the organizational structures of religion. We are all now well aware of the importance of the autonomy of the Shi'ite ulama in Iran, and it is useful to contrast this with the strong control of the state over religious affairs in the Muslim countries along the Mediterranean littoral, but also to note that in both cases one finds centralized, national, religious structures. The element which made possible this centralization was the *awqaf* religious endowments — which all around the Mediterranean were seized by central governments in the process of modernization. This element was absent in Nigeria, where religious specialists were instead dependent on the support of local rulers or communities or on their own resources. Even within the caliphate there was no centralized religious institution to speak of: it was the emir, or local ruler, who had the most important role in managing religious affairs, and this situation was generally reinforced by the British. There are no national or regional-level religious institutions in Nigeria, and periodic proposals to create a national ministry of religious affairs are met with widespread opposition. Yet religious discourse has become embedded in various national institutions, particularly the media, the schools, and the courts, and no discussion of change in Islam can be separated from the question of change in these institutions.

By far the most important changes are occurring within the educational system. Above all in the North, the rapid spread of modern education has made possible the diffusion of new ideas and a breaking down of the insulation between national and local levels. But as Lubeck's paper shows, it has also contributed to provoking a new popular Islamic radicalism among those displaced by the expansion of the new system (traditional Qur'anic teachers) and those not included in it, especially rural immigrant Qur'anic students.

When we look at the discourse emerging from the student movement, as represented by Ibraheem Sulaiman, we find the most evident area of commonality between Nigeria and other areas of the Muslim world today. But this commonality of discourse has to be read within the diversity of conditions. For one thing, there is no prospect for dialogue between this movement and the secular Nigerian state. For another, Marxism or a '*marxisant*' African-style socialism exercises a strong attraction for many young Nigerians, especially since the ideological niche of an authentic socialism has not been preempted by an existing corrupt, repressive regime, as it has been in many parts of the Arab world and Asia. Having no prospect of entry into national politics, and facing strong ideological competition, an integralist Islamic ideology in Nigeria can lead to an embittered, inward-turning rejectionism.

But if common phrases take on different meanings and inflections in different settings, one can find elements of commonality in looking at the questions of the relations between Islam and politics, and between Islam and non-Islamic systems of belief and thought.

Bringing Islam into politics everywhere means the possibility of being caught out on compromises, of being accused of hypocrisy or opportunism. While this is a very old theme, the much greater importance of the modern state in social and economic life makes more difficult a position of aloofness toward politics on the part of religious spokesmen. This creates pressures — felt especially by young and well educated Muslims — not to use Islamic values simply as a basis for justifying or criticizing political action, but to forge Islam into an ideology to guide political action.

The momentum and character of social change in the last decade, especially rapid urbanization and the spread of modern education, has created a favorable terrain for this development. Rapid change has a way of accentuating the importance of traditional values and identity. But to raise Islam to an ideological plane is to call into question old relationships of tolerance between religious communities, something especially important in Nigeria; and it is to place Islam in direct competition with other ideologies, namely, various forms of socialism and nationalism. Here the essential question is whether Islam can generate an ideology adequate to the needs of a modern, complex society, or whether, to gain adequacy, it needs to be combined, explicitly or implicitly, with one or more of its modern secular rivals. Further, do those in search of an ideology expect it to be revolutionary and unitary, or to be part of a spectrum of competing ideologies?

Finally, at least in the case of Nigeria, there is a question as to whether the search to give political expression to Islam will be contained within established institutions, the preserve of the educated elite, or whether an important role will be taken by popular leaders whose terrain is outside of established institutions, whether traditional or modern. Given the diversity of discourse at the elite level, and its apparent inability to come fully to terms with Nigeria's complex problems, and given Nigeria's increasing economic difficulties, one can suggest that popular, anti-establishment alternatives will at least not disappear.

NOTES

1. The 'Yan Tatsine disturbances in Kano in December 1980 sparked off numerous suggestions for a ministry of religious affairs, and there seemed to be serious plans afoot for this in the last months of the Shagari administration (late 1983), but there have been no indications that the military regime intends to carry through these plans.

2. With the exceptions of Muhammad, 1980 and Clarke, 1979.

3. *Gaskiya* was begun during World War II to rally opinion for the Allied war effort. It now appears three times a week. *The New Nigerian* was established by the Northern Region government, and began publishing, six days a week, in early 1966.

4. *The Sunday Triumph* began publication in 1981. By 1983, there was an episodic 'daily' edition.

5. Articles in *Gaskiya* were cited by witnesses before the Datti Ahmed Committee of Inquiry into the 30 October 1982 disturbances in Kano as a 'cause' of religious turbulence among secondary school students. See *The New Nigerian*, 19 November 1982.

6. A key base of support for the NPN in 1979 was the minority states of the Southeast, Rivers and Cross River. The surprisingly strong showing of the NPN in the Yoruba areas in 1983 may have been owing to a widespread calculation that the best way for Yoruba politicians, especially those at odds with local UPN machines, to reach power at the national level was through the NPN with its 'zoning' system of rotation by region for the choice of its presidential candidate.

7. The second figure interviewed, Abubakar Abdulkarim, carries this a step further to argue that one should vote for candidates who will enforce laws which keep women in their proper Islamic role.

8. After 1965, most of what Bennabi published was in Arabic, in keeping with the Algerian policy of Arabization.

9. Bennabi was critical of the Algerian Association of Reformist Ulama's decision to commit itself to alliances with political parties in the late 1930s and again in the late 1940s.

10. Sa'adu Zungur suffered from tuberculosis. He died in 1958. Ahmadu Bello and Abubakar Tafawa Balewa were both killed in the *coup* of January 1966. Murtala Muhammad was assassinated in February 1976. Aminu Kano died of natural causes in 1983.

11. The Sokoto incidents occurred in May 1981.

12. Sulaiman, 1982. There are shades of 'Ali Shariati here.

13. The 'Yan Tatsine disturbances in Kano in December 1980 were widely blamed on foreigners, and prompted many calls for measures against illegal aliens.

14. The final statement of the conference appeared in *The New Nigerian*, 5 February 1982.

REFERENCES

Ajami, Fouad (1983), 'In the Pharaoh's Shadow: Religion and Authority in Egypt', in James Piscatori (ed.), *Islam in the Political Process*. Cambridge University Press, 12–35.

Boyd, Jean, and Alhaji Shehu Shagari (1978), *Uthman Dan Fodio, The Theory and Practice of His Leadership*. Lagos: Islamic Publications Bureau.

Clarke, Peter B. (1979), 'The Religious Factor in the Development Process in Nigeria: A Socio-historic Analysis', *Genève-Afrique*, 17:45–65.

Dayyabu, Abdulkarim (1982), 'Fadada Ayukan Kwamitin Masallacin Juma'a na Jami'ar Bayero Zai Taimaka (Broadening of the Activities which the Bayero University Mosque Committee is Going to Help)', *Gaskiya*, 20 April 1982.

Enayat, H. (1982), *Modern Islamic Political Thought*. London: Macmillan.

Gwarzo, Dr Hasan (1982), 'Zakka a Musulunci (Zakat in Islam)', *Gaskiya*, 9, 11, 13, and 16 February 1982.

Hiskett, Mervyn (1973), *The Sword of Truth*. New York: Oxford University Press.

Hubbard, J.P. (1975), 'Government and Islamic Education in Northern Nigeria', in Mervyn Hiskett and Godfrey Brown, (eds), *Conflict and Harmony in Tropical Education*, London, 152–67.

Last, Murray (1967), *The Sokoto Caliphate*. London: Longman.

Mahmud, Abdulmalik Bappa (1981a), 'The Use of Land Under Islamic Law, Part I', *The New Nigerian*, 25 May.

—— (1981b), 'The Use of Land Under Islamic Law, Part II', *The New Nigerian*, 27 June.

—— (1981–82), 'Zakat in Islamic Law', *The New Nigerian*, 18 December 1981, 8 January and 5 February 1982.

—— (1982a), 'Bayani Kan Hakkin Dan Adam a Karkashin Shari'ar Musulunci (An Explanation of the Rights of Man Under Islamic Law) Part I', *Gaskiya*, 3 April.

—— (1982b), 'Bayani . . . Part II', *Gaskiya*, 6 April.

—— (1982c), 'Bayani . . . Part III', *Gaskiya*, 8 April.

Martin, B.G. (1976), *Muslim Brotherhoods in 19th Century Africa*. Cambridge: Cambridge University Press.

Muhammad, Akbar (1980), 'Islam and National Integration Through Education in Nigeria', in John Esposito (ed.), *Islam and Development*. Syracuse University Press, 181–206.

Paden, John (1973), *Religion and Political Culture in Kano*. Berkeley: University of California Press.

Rousillon, Alain (1982), 'Science moderne, Islam, et stratégies de légitimation', *Peuples Mediterranéens*, 21:117–135.

Shariati, 'Ali (1980), *Marxism and Other Western Fallacies*. Trans. R. Campbell. Berkeley: Mizan Press.

Smith, M.G. (1960), *Government in Zazzau*. London: Oxford University Press.

Sulaiman, Ibraheem (1980), 'Exit From a Critical Century', *The Radiance*. 2:8–15.

—— (1981), 'Islam: Source of Total Freedom for Nigeria', *Sunday New Nigerian*, 20 December.

—— (1982a), 'On Truth and Falsehood', *Sunday New Nigerian*, 24 January.

—— (1982b), 'Nigeria: Two Decades of Independence', *The Radiance*. 3:8–16.

—— (1982c), 'On Instability', *New Nigerian*, 25 April.

—— (1982d), 'The Fall of Nations', *Sunday New Nigerian*, 30 May.

—— (1982e), 'Conclusion to the Fall of Nations', *Sunday New Nigerian*, 15 August.

—— (1982f), 'The Quranic Message', *Sunday New Nigerian*, 27 August.

—— (1982g), 'The Moral War', *Sunday New Nigerian*, 29 August.

—— (1982h), 'Nigeria: Change or Decadence', *Sunday New Nigerian*, 3 October.

Yusuf, Adamu (1982), 'Game da Cudanyar Maza da Mata a Wajen Rajista ko Zabe (Concerning the Mixing of Men and Women in Voter Registration and Voting)', *Gaskiya*, 10 August.

Zartman, William, ed. (1983), *The Political Economy of Nigeria*. New York: Praeger.

An Islamic System or Islamic Values?
Nucleus of a Debate in
Contemporary Indonesia

A.H. Johns

Muslims in Indonesia face a variety of issues in considering how and on what terms they are to respond to the modern world. For the secular educated middle classes especially, there are various issues which need to be resolved. They relate to the interpretation of the Qur'an; the relevance and authenticity of many *hadith*; the place of the Islamic community in a pluralist society; and the manner and degree of the implementation of the Shari'a.

In many respects the last is central. The broad Sunni attitude to the Shari'a is succinctly expressed in Robert Brunschvig (1967:9):

> In classical orthodox doctrine, Muslim Law (*Shari'a*), which is ethico-juridical, is based, in the first place, on sacred texts that need no justification. In the absence of a notion of natural law, and in the negation of ethical or rational values that impose themselves upon God, or which God imposes on Himself, or which may be inherent in Him, the revealed or inspired datum, a divine phenomenon, is *a priori* exempt from the demands of rationality which rightly manifest themselves with regard to human laws.

The issues are recognised, and the diversity of response ranges from a radical fundamentalism to the most tolerant ecumenism. Nevertheless, Indonesia, although the most populous Muslim nation in the world, with a population over 90 per cent Muslim, so far from being a Muslim state is distinguished by the vigorous religious pluralism entrenched in its social and political structure and its cultural life.

The public stance of Islam in Indonesia, however, has a decidedly fundamentalist character. The vocal Muslim leadership is concerned that legal force be given to Islamic norms of behaviour. There are pressures on women to dress with Islamic modesty, moves to restrict the sale of alcohol, and to close down casinos. Two recent events deserve special mention. One, in 1973, was the successful mass protest by Muslim students who occupied the Parliament building and prevented the passage of a marriage bill that would have reduced the authority of the religious courts and permitted a form of civil marriage; the other, in 1981, was the issue of a *fatwa* condemning Muslim attendance at Christmas celebrations. Such events are symptomatic of a groundswell of intense religious fervor, which Muslim leaders are able to mobilize if it appears necessary to exert pressure on the government, either to protect the position of Islam within the state, or to ensure that in crucial areas of family life, Islamic ethico-religious norms have, for Muslims, the force of law.

Such Islamic ideologues have a readily recognizable style of public address. There is the triumphalist theme: Islam is coming into its own. Indeed, the more radically inclined see the Iranian revolution as nothing less than a divine cultural revolution. Yet paradoxically, Muslims are also presented as facing desperate odds. They are locked in battle against powerful foes. Turning points and last ditches abound. Ever present is the danger of the thin end of the wedge. Specific enemies are pin-pointed. Single causes for complex problems are diagnosed. It is, for example, frequently alleged that Christians have a representation in senior government positions greater than is justified by their proportion of the population, a situation for which Snouck Hurgronje is held to be personally responsible. This, in turn, is presented as the reason why the government disregards the wishes of the Muslim masses, and is reluctant to implement the Shari'a.

The method of argument is crude: it divides the world into a 'them' and an 'us', and is decorated by frequent references to various publications, now available in the Indonesian language, such as *The Protocols of the Elders of Zion*, the pseudo *Gospel of Barnabas*, and Maurice Bucaille's *The Bible, the Qur'an and Science*.

Behind this persona, however, is an extraordinary variety in the understanding and practice of Islam, ranging from that to be found in the various syncretist folk traditions to the individualist eclecticism of the Western-educated intellectual elite. This latter constitutes a small but potentially creative minority. Its members find the prevailing public stance an inadequate response to the challenge of the modern world and see in it and its activities the arrogance of a clerical class, greedy for power, and attempting to impose its human idea of God and Islam by political means.

AHMAD WAHIB

Normally it is not in the nature of such an elite to make headlines.
In 1981, however, the publication of a journalist's diary made such
individualist ideas of religion a matter of public debate. The journalist was Ahmad Wahib. He was born in Sampang, Madura in 1942.
He grew up in a strongly religious environment. His father was head
of a *pesantren* (a traditional religious school) and a well-known personality in his district. He was an independent-minded man, who took
the reformist ideas of Muhammad Abduh seriously. He removed from
his house ancestral cult objects associated with Madurese folk traditions, such as spears, *keris*, amulets, and books of spells. He disregarded time-honored beliefs about good and bad days, and deliberately
began to build a new house on a day magically unauspicious. Equally striking, he had his son educated in the government secular school
system. He was moreover the first person in his district to send his
daughter to a government school, and the first to have her married
without *adat* ceremonies. Thus Wahib was in a position to absorb
much of the pesantren lifestyle and ethos, to learn about religious controversy and to garner a body of ideas that he was to develop in his
own way.

He graduated from the mathematics streams of senior high school
in 1961, and enrolled in the Faculty of Mathematics and Physics at
Gajah Mada University in Yogyakarta. Although he eventually
reached the final year of the course, he never completed his degree.

He was a committed Muslim, and soon after settling in Yogyakarta
he became an active member of the Gajah Mada branch of the *Himpunan Mahasiswa Islam* (HMI), the Islamic Students' Association.
It was a courageous act. The early 1960s saw the intensification of
the political struggle between President Soekarno, radical nationalist
groups, and the Communist Party of Indonesia on the one hand, and
the Army, supporters of the banned Masyumi (the political wing of
the reformist movement), and various smaller parties, on the other.
There was heavy political pressure on Muslim associations. The HMI
nevertheless was strongly anti-Soekarno and anti-communist. Wahib
became a member of its 'inner group' and took part in the discussion
of basic policy issues in resistance to this pressure, such as, for
example, whether the HMI should concentrate its efforts on
'ideological development' or 'program orientation'. The discussion
of such issues, as Muhammad Kamal Hassan's paper in this volume
attests, generated an interest in more general questions, such as what
was meant by the term 'Islamic ideology'? Was Islam, in fact, an

ideology? How could a political ideology be formulated for the Indonesian Muslim community? What was the position of Islam *vis-à-vis* secular ideologies such as democracy, socialism and Marxism? Such concerns were consistent with Wahib's family upbringing.

Yogyakarta, however, is one of the most intellectually and culturally rich cities in Indonesia, and it was to leave its mark on Wahib's personal development. It is a city of educational institutions. The University of Gajah Mada for historical reasons has a great national appeal and attracts students from all over Indonesia. But there are other schools and colleges, both private and government, which exercise a similar appeal. These include the Catholic Education Institute, Sanata Dharma, the private Islamic University, Universitas Islam Indonesia, and the State Islamic Institute, Sunan Kalijaga. The ethnic variety among the tens of thousands of students, the presence of various religious traditions, and the extraordinary measure of religious tolerance characteristic of the Javanese of Central Java have resulted in a remarkable openness between religious traditions and an uninhibited social mingling between people of very diverse backgrounds. This impressed Wahib deeply.

More specifically, there were two circumstances that were to have a decisive formative influence on him. One was the local Jesuit community with which he became acquainted at a Catholic student hostel where he lodged. The other was his participation in the meetings of a discussion circle organized by a Professor at the Sunan Kalijaga Institute and former Minister of Religion Dr Mukti Ali, who had studied at McGill University in Canada. These meetings were not open to the public, hence it was known by the English name 'Limited Group'. Its purpose was to provide a forum for the uninhibited discussion of basic religious issues.

Mukti Ali says of the group that it attracted a wide variety of participants, and regularly invited guest speakers from various walks of life, both Indonesians and foreigners. It discussed issues important for Indonesian Muslims within a framework that could be productive of new ideas. Often difficult theological issues were raised, and the views put forward were often unorthodox or provocative. [1]

Wahib's decade in Yogyakarta was one of the most turbulent in Indonesian history. It saw the collapse of the economy and the rise of political tensions that came to a climax with the attempted Communist *coup* in 1965. The crushing of the *coup* was followed by the mass killing of tens of thousands of suspected Communists in Central Java alone, and led to the establishment of the so-called New Order under General Suharto. It was a terrifying period that left deep psychological scars on many who lived through it.

It was no doubt a combination of all these elements — his home background, adjustment to a new environment, with the consequent dramatic broadening of his horizons, political and personal pressures, and the appalling slaughter in the wake of the attempted *coup* — that contributed to a profound shift in Wahib's understanding of Islam and which led him to resign from the HMI on 30 September 1969. It is probably not a coincidence that this date was the third anniversary of the launching of the attempted *coup*.

In 1971 Wahib left Yogyakarta for Jakarta to look for work, and eventually found employment as a cadet reporter for the weekly news magazine, *Tempo*. He attended philosophy classes at a private institute for the study of philosophy founded by a Javanese Jesuit. At the same time he took part in various discussion groups, and set about drafting an ambitious program for the discussion of theology, politics and culture within a single frame of reference. He was killed in a traffic accident on the evening of 30 March 1973.

THE DIARY

His diary was discovered after his death. He had started to keep it, albeit intermittently, when he arrived in Yogyakarta in 1961. The entries increase in detail and earnestness around 1966 and, from the end of 1968, they frequently take the form of mini-essays on various aspects of cultural, religious and political life in Indonesia. It was edited by his friend and associate in the HMI, Djohan Effendi, who resigned from the organization with him on the same day and for the same reasons. The entries selected for publication are divided among four broad topic headings — Religion, Politics and culture, Student life and Personal quest.

For our purposes, those entries relating to religion are of primary importance. One of Wahib's key ideas is set out in an entry of 15 July 1969:

> In fact I am of the view that were the Prophet Muhammad to return to this world, and to observe those parts which are developed and those which are not, and see the kinds of ideas that human beings now have, I am sure he would withdraw from circulation many of the hadith that are now, generally speaking, taken literally by his followers and replace them by new ones.

On 22 August 1969 he was to write:

> Quite frankly, I would like very much myself to meet the prophet Muhammad and invite him to live in the 20th century and to give his answers. I have little confidence in those people who are called his heirs.

The word heirs is advisedly chosen. Wahib is alluding to the well-known *hadith*, 'The ulama are the heirs of the prophets'. His remark is tantamount to a rejection of the Islamic establishment.

Later on 29 March 1970, he is to write a scathing indictment of the ulama

> Behold how the ulama attempt to impose specific laws on mankind. Alas, the fact is that here they spread abroad only the words of the Law, and make little effort to understand and analyse the human problems to which it is addressed. What possibility is there, by such means, to transform the Law into an interior awareness . . . The result is rather the reverse. People increasingly shun the laws they formulate. To what extent do our ulama — not to speak of being experts — have any appreciation at all of anthropology, sociology, culture, science, politics and the like?
>
> In my view, our leading ulama, such as Hasbi, Muchtar Jahja, Munawar Cholil and the others, have no right to lay down the law on matters of morality and government. How can they make the right decisions when they have no grasp of the issues in human society and the like? They do nothing creative. They are just beginners at the task of interpretation.
>
> As far as I have seen, the language our ulama use in their preaching is very deficient. They are so poor in the use of language they are incapable of putting into words the meaning of God's utterances — their language is like a desert . . .
>
> So far from using their imagination [to bring a message to the deepest recesses of the human heart], they are suspicious of anyone else who attempts to do so. They regard the utterances of God as positive law, and regard any attempt to give a deeper expression of their meaning of formulations as forbidden.

Yet in rejecting the ulama he is fully aware that he has to face for himself the problem he believes they have failed to address, namely, how to translate a message, from beyond time and transcending every limitation, into a form appropriate to a particular time and place, without being untrue to or unworthy of its divine uncreated original.

259

Thus on 28 March 1969 he wrote:

> I do not yet understand what Islam really is. So far I only understood Islam according to Hamka, Islam according to Natsir, Islam according to Abduh, . . . and frankly I am not yet satisfied. What I seek I have not yet found, not yet discovered, and that is Islam according to Allah, who made it. How can I do so? By direct study of the Qur'an and the Sunna? I can try. But others may think that all I get will be Islam according to myself. Never mind. The important thing is the conviction in my sound mind that the understanding I achieve is Islam according to Allah. This is what I have to be sure of!

So why has the necessary translation not been made? What needs to be done?

On 17 January 1969 he wrote:

> We Muslims are not yet able to translate the truths of the teaching of Islam into a program that can be realized. There is a need for the *ultimate values* of Islamic teaching to be translated into the conditions of today. This is not realized. . . . This is why we are always left behind in our attempts to achieve anything, and tend to be exclusive.

His diagnosis of the problem is that the leaders of the Muslim community are playing with words and formulas and are out of touch with reality. This isolation from reality leads to a defensiveness, arrogance and fear, which in turn make it impossible to distinguish between idea and reality. And it is impossible to be creative without a perception of the necessary tension between idea and reality.

On 8 March 1969 he attempts in his own way to get to the heart of the problem:

> What ought to be is that the philosophy of Islam is universal and eternal; the reality is that it is continually changing — which simply indicates that the philosophy of Islam is not yet perfect. Never mind! We strive to get as close to perfection as possible. Thus it does not matter that there is one philosophy according to Mawdudi, another according to others. Uniformity of opinion throughout space and time is difficult to achieve, even though it ought to exist. It doesn't matter. Let it be. But even if we don't agree on it, what at least is the philosophy of Islam according to ourselves? Are not we ourselves the young thinkers of Islam? As to which is the true

religion, the problem is the same. There ought to be only one religion. The reality is there are many sorts of religion. Every religion has to feel that it is God's religion. That it is the one that is universal and eternal.

This leaves him with no alternative but to accept pluralism, as he puts it in a passage of extempore free verse on 16 August 1969:

For us theist and atheist can gather together,
Muslim and Christian jest together,
Artist and athlete freely associate,
Unbeliever and devout be close friends,
But pluralist and anti-pluralist can never meet.

In 1970 he reflects again on the narrow defensiveness of Muslim thinkers, as in an entry of 10 April of that year:

A defensive attitude, always concerned to justify itself arises because (i) of the immaturity of the Muslim community that has only recently escaped from oppression by other peoples, and (ii) because the process of reciprocal adjustment [to the new situation] still leaves the Muslim community regarding itself as a minority besieged on all sides.

Attacks on the Muslim community have made Muslims feel defensive. This defensive attitude has made them more exclusive, and because of this, to feel all the more under siege.

The remedy, total freedom of thought, not restricted by the formulations of religious doctrine, he had already suggested on 17 July 1969:

I believe that those who do not exercise freedom of thought are wasting the most valuable gift that God has given them, namely the mind. I pray that God will guide those who do not use their minds to the full. Yet I realize that anyone who does exercise freedom of thought indeed seeks this restlessness. His restlessness leads him to reflect on all kinds of matters, above all on basic issues, attempting to take a stand on intellectual objectivity alone.

At the same time he recognizes that there is an unavoidable contradiction between accepting his religion as revealed truth and the exercise of absolute freedom of thought. This he admits in an entry of 9 March 1969:

> In fact, all this time we have not been exercising freedom of thought. Whenever we set out to evaluate anything, we start out from the assumption that the teaching of Islam is good, and that all other ideas are below it, and inferior to it.

He tries to come to terms with the problem making a frank acknowledgement:

> Sometimes my heart tells me that in several respects, the teaching of Islam is bad. Thus God's teachings in several respects are bad, and several of the teachings of men, that is, great men, are far superior. It is my unfettered mind that speaks, a free mind that struggles desperately to bring itself to dare to think as it wills, without fear of incurring God's anger. It is only because of my belief in the existence of God, and that the Qur'an is truly from God, and that Muhammad is truly a perfect man, that in the final analysis I still believe that Islam in its totality is good and perfect. It is only my mind that cannot grasp this perfection.

He perceives that attempts to reconcile the claims of each can lead to intellectual dishonesty. This, he points out in the same entry, is likely to be the besetting sin of the Muslim who:

> attempts to see the truth of social ideals from without (Islam) and then automatically spreads them as though they were Islamic ideals. He has the intellectual ability to be convinced that the ideals from without Islam are good but because he does not have the courage to say that these ideals are better than those to be found within Islam, he has no alternative but to claim that they are in accordance with Islam.

Thus the faults and flaws that reason discovers in Islam must be acknowledged with a scrupulous honesty. As he writes on 8 June 1969:

> Now is the right moment for me to try to promote a democratic attitude even though I am not of the opinion that Islam is not completely democratic. I frankly admit that in this matter I am, up to the present, not a complete Muslim. I am not going to pretend to deny that I reject the ruling of an Islamic law that a Muslim who does not pray should be punished.

262

I believe that one of the characteristics of a democrat is not to inflict psychological terror on anyone who disagrees with him.

Three days later, i.e. on 11 June 1969, he makes a further plea for total honesty:

I do not want to be hypocritical, to put on a show of being holy and the like. Any attempt to conceal the possible influence of one's sub-conscious is simply pretence, and I do not want to put on a pretence, least of all to fellow human beings. Neither in respect of matters relating to the Law of God, nor of those relating to the HMI, do I want to be hypocritical.

In the same entry he indicates that his plea for freedom of thought is thorough-going, to be applied as consistently in political as in religious matters:

. . . in a seminar yesterday, I openly criticized the government's prohibition of communist lecturers from giving classes and lodged a protest at the resolution passed by the MPRS [Majelis Perwakilan Rakyat Sementara — People's Provisional Assembly].

He saw a particularly insidious form of intellectual dishonesty among Muslim intellectuals in the use of *a priori* judgements, and the tacit application of a double standard. This he explains at length on 3 August 1969:

We intellectuals must always take care to maintain as our basic principles: [argumentation] *a posteriori*, and a single standard, especially those of us brought up in an Islamic socio-cultural environment.

No matter how pointed our criticism of the *general attitude* of the community, we should never fall into the error of judging anything *a priori* wrong any more than of judging it *a priori* right. We must genuinely be able to avoid making use of a double standard, a double standard that takes the side of the Muslim community or that of the non-Muslim community.

It is well for us to remember that to say *assalam alaikum* need not necessarily be Islamic; to recite the Qur'an so loudly that it can be heard far and wide, need not necessarily be Islamic; to write using the Arabic script need not necessarily be Islamic; to put on a show of sincerity or religious devotion need not necessarily be

Islamic; to lace one's conversation with verses of the Qur'an need not necessarily be Islamic; to invoke blessings upon the prophet when making a speech need not necessarily be Islamic. Likewise to denounce a girl for wearing a head shawl need not necessarily be modern; to make light of the importance of the ritual prayer need not necessarily be modern; to defend atheism, to reject formalism . . . to criticize the Islamic community, to defend those who dance in the western manner need not necessarily be modern.

These are matters in which we must exercise much care in case we fall into the trap of making a show of being Islamic, or a show of being modern.

This does not mean that *a priori* I do not approve of people who always say *assalam alaikum*, write using the Arabic script, lace their conversation with verses from the Qur'an etc. Likewise it does not mean that I do not approve of those who denounce the wearing of the headshawl, attack the Muslim community, reject formalism and the like. The important thing in exercising freedom of thought, is to free ourselves from the tyranny within ourselves. We have to dare to free ourselves from two tyrannies: the tyranny of pride, pride at being supposedly genuinely Muslim, sincere or modern, or intellectual, or moral, or pure or authentic and the like, and the tyranny of fear, at being supposedly conservative, atheistic, out of date, unbelievers, Mu'tazilites, disoriented, ideologically weak, suspect as to faith, secularist, westernizing and the like.

There is a passion in this last entry. 'Atheistic . . . an unbeliever, a Mu'tazilite, disoriented, ideologically weak, suspect as to faith, secularist, westernizing, are part of the catalogue of abuse used by traditionalist Muslims to denounce suspect liberals. There is little doubt that such terms were hurled at Wahib himself, and it was such denunciation and abuse that eventually forced him to resign from the HMI.

It is clear that the ferment of ideas, and the desire for a genuine renewal, that he saw or thought he saw in the HMI — the organization on behalf of which he expended so much energy — had been illusory. Just as the ulama had let him down, so had the organization from which he expected so much, and for which he had expended such efforts.

Nevertheless, he tries to assess honestly the strengths and weaknesses of two other Islamic organizations that he got to know well in Yogyakarta, the Muhammadiyya, a reformist association founded in 1912, and the Nahdatul Ulama (N.U., Ar-Nahdat al-'ulama, Renaissance of the Ulama), an organization of traditionalist ulama founded in 1926 in response to the inroads into the Islamic community made by the reformists. His remarks in the entry of 23 June 1970 are penetrating, even if his conclusions, that the traditionalists are more adaptive than the reformists, may at first sight appear paradoxical.

> Has the Muhammadiyya succeeded in its efforts to wipe out what it calls 'innovation and superstition'? As far as the 'innovation and superstition' resulting from the teaching of the N.U. is concerned, the Muhammadiyya can be said to have succeeded. But in coming to terms with the 'innovation and superstition' that is the product of Indonesian culture itself, and has become institutionalized as such in the traditional customs of the people, the Muhammadiyya has run into difficulties. It wants to eradicate them but does not enjoy the necessary cultural superiority. It makes its attacks alright, but does not have available a new, 'clean' culture, [to replace what it wishes to destroy].

On 6 June he had written:

> It has of course to be admitted that the stand taken by the Muhammadiyya against innovation in worship and religious ritual has much value. But it must also be admitted that this attitude contains conservative elements, which at times degenerate into reaction. . . . [There are indicators which show that] the N.U. is more appreciative of culture [than the Muhammadiyya]. It has an awareness of the value of change. The content of change may be true or false, and the conservative attitude (which rejects change) is at least safe from the possibility of error. So were this readiness of the N.U. [to accept change] to be invested with an honest, intelligent and democratic approach to issues, one might expect a far brighter future for it than for the Muhammadiyya. . . . In culture, whether we like it or not, we need innovation in abundance. For no activity, including religious rituals, carried on by people within a cultural tradition, can exist, naked, unencumbered by ties of cultural innovation. Rituals are necessarily performed in the context of a culture, and it follows from this that the 'antagonistic attitude to cultural innovation in the performance of religious rituals' displayed by the Puritans of Islam [the Muhammadiyya] must be reviewed.

Wahib's break with the HMI caused him bitter pain. He had worked for it and in it from 1961 to 1969, becoming one of its senior members. On 30 September 1969, he resigned from it. It was a decision that he did not reach easily. On 14 August he wrote in his diary four pages of free verse, expressing his dedication to it, the reasons for his incompatibility with it, and his grief at leaving it. That the verse sounds horrendous in my English translation should not disguise his sorrow at ending a profound commitment to the organisation:

The HMI is not simply a tool that can be exchanged
 for another tool;
The HMI is not simply a conduit which can be exchanged
 for another;
It is as though the HMI has become our soul;
It is in our veins and our pulse;
It is in our mirth;
It is in our grief;
It is in our raunchiness;
It is in our childishness;
The HMI has drawn from and fills our veins.

The reasons for the parting of the ways were complex. From Wahib's point of view, the organization did not tolerate pluralism even in the understanding of Islam, and wished to impose a tight internal discipline. Doubtless the organization too had its views; they can be discussed elsewhere.

The day Wahib and his friend Djohan resigned, 30 September 1969, Wahib noted in the diary:

May the leadership of the HMI, reflect not on Djohan and Wahib who have left, but rather on the *reasons* why there are now activists who leave it . . . Two people departed publicly on 30 September 1969 . . . actually they had left, silently, long before.

Indeed, on 21 March he had written:

When [my colleagues such as] Salman Karim or Imaduddin and their friends say that people such as myself and Djohan have no right to be in the HMI they are not all that wrong. Because the line that the HMI has followed, especially from early 1967 up to the present, i.e. mid-1969, Djohan and myself as a matter of principle cannot accept. Djohan and myself regard it as out of date, reactionary and primitive. During all this time we have really been in the opposition.

'Reactionary and primitive' are strong words. They are uttered out of Wahib's conviction that the attitudes of HMI were tantamount to a sell-out to what it most vehemently condemns, as he writes on 22 August 1969:

There you have it! We have tacitly accepted secularism, even though we loudly denounce it.

Djohan Effendi put the matter more explicitly in his letter of resignation. He claimed:

A closed attitude and a blind *a priori* fanaticism which is now poisoning the Islamic community make it impossible for it to accept a healthy inspiration from modern knowledge, and the result is disastrous.

And of some of the activities of the HMI he said:

We are guilty of living by a double standard . . . We often think of the *aqidah* [the Creed] as the foundation of our life and struggle, but forget that the *aqidah* is not to justify the means but to purify the means. The HMI has too long and too deeply been involved in the activities of practical politics, which have forced us to face dirty practices. This challenge we have met by preparing our cadres to treat practical politics as an arena of confrontation of political forces by giving them theories and strategic-tactical principles. We have taught them that politics/policy is not a matter of true or false/right or wrong, but a question of victory or defeat. We have infiltrated our activists into other organisations, such as the PKI to carry out our mission, to achieve our goal, and for that, they have had to be two-faced . . . The PKI has failed physically in its attempt to defeat us, but has succeeded in destroying our moral fibre . . . these tactics have now been used for individual purposes within the HMI . . . they put victory above truth . . . we must stick to a single standard . . . consciously . . . or unconsciously we who have for so long been opposing secularism and denouncing Machiavelli have in practice surrendered to secularism and become good followers of Machiavelli. (Effendi, 1969[2]).

Thus the only repository left for trust is the individual, on whom, in the last resort, the responsibility for the search for truth must lie.

This was the direction in which Wahib's thoughts were moving when on 8 September 1969 he wrote:

God, I want to ask whether the standards set by your religion are fixed or changing. God, just what is it in your teaching that is really fundamental, which cannot change, which has to be a guide for the development of standards in society?

I believe it is no longer right to include Ijma' [consensus] in the array of sources from which the Law is derived, an array which includes the Qur'an, the Sunna and Ijma' [Wahib omits the fourth source, Qiyas]. In a world which is rapidly changing, and in which individualism is becoming increasingly prominent, the Qur'an and the Sunna are enough. Let everyone understand the Qur'an and the Sunna in their own way.

Now then, as the standards that apply in society develop, so the laws of Islam must develop. The *haram* and *halal* of today cannot be the same as the *haram* and *halal* of three or four centuries ago, let alone what they were when the Prophet was still alive. Therefore there must be many hadith of the Prophet and even verses of the Qur'an itself which no longer apply, simply because they are no longer necessary, and the harm that was once feared (and to avoid which they were promulgated) no longer exists, due to the new standards that now apply in society.

I am aware that changes in moral standards will certainly bring about changes in the possibilities for the occurrence of harm and benefit that they allow. Because the Law of Islam, in my view, takes as its point of departure matters relating to harm and benefit, moral laws in Islam must also change *pari passu* with changes in the moral standards of society. Well then, will not this situation cause confusion and even conflict within Islamic circles, because it appears that there is no legal certainty? Yet confusion and conflict are commonplace enough, and do not need to be avoided, for they are symptomatic of a society in movement formulating better values . . . (Only those who are active in creating, using every opportunity to best effect in the dynamic of society, can serve as guides for society).

For Wahib, clearly, conformity and stagnation are the real enemies of Islam. He therefore denounces (8 June 1969) the 'fanatics' who are bent on creating a unified Islamic community:

Those fanatics for unity who are behind Persami KMI, PPI, PPUI [the acronym and abbreviations stand for Muslim organizations] are of the opinion that unity of the Islamic community is a critical issue, and therefore has to be achieved as a key to the solution of other problems. They do not realize that there are many matters that have to be hotly debated. Therefore, for me, now is not the time for the unification of the Muslim community, whether in the form of federation, confederation or joint secretariat . . .

In my view, at this stage, every Islamic organization should follow its own path.

I believe that to set up unification of the community as an ideal is a great mistake.

Wahib's ideal as a Muslim and an activist is to urge individuals to come to terms with Islam in the way that is most fruitful and meaningful to themselves as individuals. This he sees as a process of 'secularizing' Islam, i.e. bringing it into the world, not secularizing society. Thus he envisages the state adopting a neutral attitude towards religion for the sake of religion, not in order to avoid any contamination between religion and the state. Superficially, he concedes, this may not be much different from the philosophy of the Western secular state. In orientation and intention, however, he claims, the difference is profound. It makes it possible for individuals to achieve through their own efforts a genuine realization of Islām in the modern world.

To achieve this 'secularizing' of Islam, there needs, in his view, to be an understanding of the words of the Qur'an and the Prophet in a way appropriate to modern times. We have seen how he has dropped Ijma (consensus) as one of the sources of Law. Since he does not even mention Qiyas (analogy), this leaves only two sources out of an original four, the Qur'an and Hadith, and these two, in fact, he sees not as sources of Law, but as historical sources for the 'history' of Muhammad, both consisting of words uttered by him (either the divine words put on his tongue by the angel Gabriel, or his sayings as a man). Muhammad, then, is given a higher status than the Qur'an revealed to him. Other sources for the history of Muhammad that he suggests derive from conditions in Arabia during his life-time, and what can be learned of its systems of government, economic life, role in international relations, cultures and social customs, climate and physical geography, alongside the personalities of the Prophet and his companions, and much else besides.

By these means the Qur'an and hadith are set in 'the total historical and social context' of Muhammad's time, thereby highlighting not dead formulas but the life of Muhammad and the teaching that he spread.

These ideas are set out in the entry of 17 April 1970. To continue, in his words:

> Well then, this correction [of orientation] enables us to avoid formalism, because our prime task is now the problem of how we can transfer ideas which actually are from Muhammad (originating from God) into a variety of other situations. What we have to achieve in this transference after carrying out *ideation*, is a process of transformation. How is this transformation to be made? It requires a great deal of knowledge of such disciplines as sociology and others. The more complex a society, the more difficult it is to carry out this transformation, and because of this, the greater the need for the support of such disciplines in order to discover an '*adequate re-interpretation of the normative image*'.
>
> I believe that by positing the history of Muhammad and his struggle as the source of Islamic teaching, Muslim humanity becomes involved in the task of *historical direction* in attempting to discover from this history of Muhammad a clear source [of wisdom] for our time. In this task of *historical direction* the spiritual and intellectual activity of Muslim humanity can find voice. Only by carrying out this task as well as possible and understanding the task of *historical direction* as a Call from God, and at the same time a visitation from Him to ourselves (*direct communication with God*) is it possible to understand Divine Revelation in its full sense, i.e. that a divine revelation is also made to us, in addition to the greatest revelation, the Qur'an, made to Muhammad.

This may be seen as a development of the ideas expressed in an entry of 15 July 1969.

> I do not agree with the ways in which people interpret verses of the Qur'an. I see that scant attention is paid to the *asab al-nuzul* [circumstances of revelation], or the spirit of the time when verses were revealed. I truly hate the rape of verses of the Qur'an and words of Hadith in the way they are explained. Never mind, I will follow my own path.

He then gives an example of a verse thus abused, in such injunctions as to speak the truth: 'Even if the unbelievers hate it, even if the polytheists hate it.[3]

Verses such as these, he continues, are used by rabble-rousers to inflame the feelings of the masses:

> They are not sufficiently aware of the differences that exist between the situation at the time of the Prophet and that of our age. At the time of the Prophet, the followers of the Prophet were totally good, and the believers totally evil. But today, our followers are part good and part evil and our opponents, too, part good, part evil. Might not the spiritual constellation be different? Might it not be the case that materially we too in part are unbelievers, although formally professing Islam. Thus to make use of such verses is no longer appropriate.
>
> Were we to return to the [spiritual] constellation at the time of the Prophet, then we would have the right to make use of these verses. Now we do not have that right.

Thus, if in 1969, among his reasons for resigning from the HMI was revulsion at the use of the Qur'anic verses in an exclusivist, rabble-rousing way, by 1971 he was attempting to set up a framework for interpretation of the Qur'an and hadith within which all his intellectual problems could be solved, whether concerning the formulation and implementation of Islamic Law, the example of the Prophet, or the phenomenon of religious pluralism in general.

In fact early in 1970 he was groping his way towards a personal understanding of *fiqh* (Islamic jurisprudence), which on 24 January 1970 he understands as the 'secularization' (i.e. a realization) of Islamic teaching in the context of a particular time and place. He writes:

> In my view, the Qur'an and Hadith were *fiqh* in the lifetime of the Prophet Muhammad. This was the first *fiqh* in the Muslim community. The Qur'an therefore is the product of a 'secularization' of Islamic teaching at the time of the Prophet. The agent [the 'secularizor'] is God himself. And hadith, I believe, is also the product of a 'secularization' of Islamic teaching at the time of the Prophet. The agent in this case is Muhammad.
>
> Because of the status [of these formulations] as the first *fiqh*, they have a special place far above other formulations of *fiqh* that succeeded them. Because we do not know for certain the primal will of God and the Prophet, and the primal [pre-eternal] *fiqh* which encompasses all places and times, has not been 'translated', this first *fiqh* is at once the highest and most authoritative source [of

knowledge of the will of God and the Prophet available to us].

Because of this, if subsequent *fiqhs* have merely the status of explanations, or 'interpretations derived from the use of reason' and the value of something 'the development of which deserves a hearing' the first *fiqh* has the status of 'phenomena', in the sense that we should seek the ideals behind these phenomena; it therefore has the value of something, the ideals of which have to be explored.

Certainly there are many verses of the Qur'an and many hadith which are the product of a 'transmittive' or 'transmigrative' or 'translative' secularization because they have an authority that extends over all time and space. Others, however, are the result of a 'transformative secularization' [i.e. require transformation] in space — Arabia, and in time, the 14th century [A.H.]. For these latter, the process of ideation is very urgent. . . .

Thus, it is not religion which has to adapt itself, but *fiqh*.

Wahib was to return on several occasions to this problem of the traditionally central role of Law in Islam, as for example, on 30 July 1970.

In my view, the Law of Islam does not exist. What does exist is the history of Muhammad, and from it let everyone of us draw his own lessons concerning his relationship with God and his fellow human beings. The history of Muhammad is the source of the religion of Islam. But Islam itself is not the only guide that can answer questions arising in Muslim life, whether they concern the individual or the community.

In case there is any doubt as to what this implies, on 7 November 1970 he writes in a lengthy passage:

Taking the history of the Prophet as a source means that Muslims have to make an abstraction [from what they discover in this source] and make a comparison between this and its historical setting. In this way the relationship between a Muslim and the Prophet Muhammad can be creative. Therefore not every word and deed of Muhammad has to be imitated. We regard him as a good model (*uswa hasana*) from whom we must learn much. A complete picture of this good model is in his history.

THE DEBATE

Reading this diary is like listening to one end of a telephone conversation. We do not know how Wahib's ideas were received in the HMI, what response he provoked, or how he fitted in with its policies over the years that its entries were written. Likewise, we do not know the course taken by the discussions in which he took part at the 'Limited Group' meetings. Some of his views could certainly have given rise to anger and heated debate. Indeed, they caused pain and a sense of guilt to himself, as though he were disobeying God by questioning his Laws. Thus he exclaims (9 June 1969):

God, understand me!

God, how can I accept your laws without first having doubts about them? Therefore, God, be understanding if I still have doubts about the truth of your laws. If you do not like this, give me such an understanding of them that my doubts vanish, and I be swiftly brought from the level of doubt to that of acceptance.

God, are you angry if I speak to you with a free mind and heart, the mind and heart that you yourself have given me, with a great capacity for freedom: God, are you angry if the mind, with the capacity for knowledge, that you have given it, is used to the limit of that capacity?

God, I long to speak with you in an atmosphere of freedom. I believe that you hate not only hypocritical utterances but also hypocritical minds, minds which do not dare to reflect on the ideas that rise within them, minds which pretend not to know their own thoughts.

His persistent questioning of himself on so many issues left him at times with a feeling of desolation, emptiness and uncertainty, as on 29 November 1969:

I do not know whether I am under a curse to be thinking in this way, to be involved in questions that can never be settled.

Is it possible that all this is going to plunge me into an eternity of wandering? Ah, thousands of issues arise in my heart. Hundreds of questions spring up in my mind, and no answer can be found to them. Alas, there is no-one who understands that such a turmoil cannot possibly be resolved from within myself.

Yet on another, later occasion, he could write in all simplicity of a dream in which he saw Mary, mother of Jesus (31 December 1969):

> Last night I dreamt I met with mother Mary. She was dressed in white, and her face so full of holiness, impressed me deeply. She smiled and gazed at me, and her loving look brought me comfort and happiness. I myself am not a Christian, so I do not know why I found such peace and inner tranquility while face to face with her. Could I ever know such peace in daily life? I long for her, she who is full of wisdom, whose gaze is gentle and tender; every expression of her personality fills me with wonder and reverence.

There is much besides in the diary which deserves careful reading and reflection. By any criteria it is a remarkable document. It represents Wahib's dialogue with himself on a wide range of issues: religion in the widest sense of the word, Indonesian politics and culture, student life and his own restlessness. Such introspective writing and self-exposure is rare in Indonesia, even in a diary. In fact, to find an equivalent self-scrutiny and self-exposure, one has to go back to the letters of Kartini (1964) written in Dutch to Dutch friends between 1900 and 1904. Not only this, it reveals a perception of the self virtually unknown in Indonesia: the self as something essentially provisional and incomplete, struggling to come into being. This is the significance of what he wrote on 1 December 1969, perhaps still in the wake of the trauma of resigning from the HMI.

> . . . I am not Hatta, not Soekarno, not Shahrir, not Natsir, not Marx, and not anyone else either. Indeed . . . I am not even Wahib. I am becoming Wahib. I am seeking, continually seeking, on the way towards, trying to become Wahib. Truly, I am not I. I am becoming I, am continually in process of becoming I. Only in my death agony will I be I!

And this self, still coming into being, endures the pain of emptiness, as poignantly expressed in his mystically tinged prayer of 18 January 1973:

> Lord, if this spiritual emptiness I feel can be the beginning of a new insight into your secret self, then plunge me deeper into this emptiness so that I may the more single-mindedly search for its meaning.

The faith behind the prayer is as rare in Indonesia as his perception of his self: the faith that can accept doubt as a component of faith. Thus on 15 October 1969 he asks himself:

How, indeed, can people be ordered to give a willing assent to the belief that God exists, if they are not allowed to consider the possibility of the truth of the 'belief' that God does not exist?

Perhaps he has experienced in his own way what Unamuno experienced when he wrote:

Those who believe that they believe in God, but without passion in their hearts, without anguish of mind, without uncertainty, without doubt, without an element of despair even in their consolation, believe in the God Idea, not in God Himself.

Certainly he represents an experimental mode of faith seeking understanding which is new for Indonesia. New, but not totally unknown, for the Sumatran poet Amir Hamzah in the 1940s had occasionally achieved similar insights (Hamzah, 1954).

In several respects the ideas that Wahib explores in the diary would be disconcerting to mainstream Muslims, even though he says nothing that could be taken to question the traditional doctrine of the inspiration of the Qur'an, the authenticity of the corpus of hadith, or even the historical reliability of the early biographies of the Prophet. The Qur'an still has a unique position as a revealed book, albeit that Muhammad, as the most perfect and wisest of men, is accorded a higher status than it. Yet Wahib's personal solution to the problem of the modernization of Islam is radical enough. He has reduced the four traditional sources of the Law, the Qur'an, Hadith, Ijma and Qiyas to one, a source that he calls 'The History of Muhammad'. The Qur'an and hadith are simply, though not exclusively, components of the corpus of material that constitutes this source. His procedure is to examine traditional Islamic teachings in the light of the answers he gets from the questions that he puts to this material. If questioned concerning the validity of a particular rule, he would ask what were the conditions during the time of Muhammad that led either the Qur'an or Tradition or Muhammad's example to indicate the appropriateness of that rule to the good of the community. If no parallel existed between the age of the Qur'an and modern times, the rule might be disregarded. If there was a parallel, but conditions had changed, then the intention behind the rule might be realized equally well by other means, for human values, expectations and circumstances in the twentieth century had changed in a way inconceivable to the Arabs of the seventh century.

The character of the contemporary world as represented in Indonesia, Wahib has argued, renders irrelevant any idea of authority vested in an Islamic state to impose Islamic law. An Islamic government should do no more than provide the conditions in which Muslims, without prejudice to other communities, can work out for themselves the best way of realizing Islamic values in a particular time and place. Muslims accordingly have no claim to special privileges in a plural society. Moreover, as democrats they are bound to accept, respect, and enter into dialogue openly with every other group. Wahib believes that, in the modern world, this is the challenge Islam faces, and if it accepts it, it will receive by divine inspiration the guidance it needs.

From reading the diary it becomes clear that the point of all Wahib's questioning is to liberate the spiritual values of Islam from formulations that have lost their meaning. He shows great perceptiveness, and argues with a keen intelligence. Nevertheless, his lack of formal training in the Islamic disciplines is at once evident. Despite his home background, he was, albeit in the best sense of the word, an amateur in religious thought. His knowledge of Arabic was slight, he knew little of fiqh, even his familiarity with the Qur'an and hadith was limited. On the other hand, he had the advantage that his intellectual formation was not moulded by the study of fiqh. He was thus all the more free to respond as an individual in a pluralist society, to the humanistic, poetic and spiritual appeal of the Qur'an; to see his own Faith, no matter how deeply he loved it, as one among a rich and diverse world of religious traditions. In a very real sense he is an 'outsider' with an educated sensitive mind who, while deeply committed to the Islamic tradition, looks at its salient features, and decides for himself what he will regard as central and what peripheral. From his remarks on the Law, it is clear that he had rejected its traditional foundation as summarized by Brunschvig in the quotation at the beginning of this chapter, and made it subject to history and reason.

His approach, he admits, is individualistic. The results may be equally so. After all, the question 'What would Muhammad have done in such and such a situation? can very easily become: 'what would I do were I Muhammad?', or even 'what would Muhammad have done had he been me?!'

The sources of his ideas are eclectic. His notions of the character of scripture in Islam appear to reflect his long and sympathetic association with the Jesuits of Yogyakarta. He clearly looks on the Qur'an and hadith as justifying their authority by the contribution they make to knowledge of Muhammad the man: what is central is not the revealed book, but the person the book reveals.

It is difficult to see other than a Christian source for this paradigm. Even so, Wahib uses the paradigm in his own way: not to lead to an encounter with a personal saviour, or to discover the self-manifestation of God in human form, but as a means of circumventing the great edifice of *fiqh* developed through the centuries, and codified into the four schools of Law. At the same time, his ideas show emphases that may well derive from the Lahore wing of the Ahmadi movement:[4] a rejection of the authority of the ulama and of ijma, a readiness to re-interpret the text of the Qur'an, a reliance on reason and the understanding of human history and society derived from a study of the social sciences; an inclination to withdraw from the political arena, a distaste for violence, and a strong mystical undercurrent that allows the possibility of a direct inspiration from God to the individual. None of these emphases is exclusively Ahmadi; indeed, disillusion with political life was a natural reaction of many to events in Indonesia in the 1960s. Certainly no single one of them would be grounds for considering him an unreliable member of the Muslim community: they were shared by such great figures as Sir Sayyid Ahmad Khan and Iqbal. But Wahib had Ahmadi friends, and in any case, the Lahore Ahmadis, a highly educated minority group, had had a presence in Yogyakarta for many years. They had had influential supporters, such as H.S. Tjokroaminoto, founder of the Sarikat Islam, and had at times worked together with the Muhammadiyya. Doubtless many of the ideas in the diary emerged during the meetings of the 'Limited Group' in which Wahib took part between 1967 and 1971.

CONCLUSION

It is difficult to estimate the significance of the diary as a contribution to the multiple voices in world Islam. There is no doubt as to the interest it aroused in Indonesia: it sold ten thousand copies in six months (July-November 1981), and provoked at least five hundred pages of reviews and comments — some favourable, others hostile.

How widespread was the influence of the 'Limited Group', which perhaps served to generate many of Wahib's ideas though not thereby responsible for them, is difficult to say. Certainly there was more than one such group. That this one is so well-known is due to the chance factors of Wahib's death, the existence of the diary, the intervention of an editor, and its publication. It is also thanks to the diary that we know that, when Wahib went to Jakarta, the counterparts of the Yogyakarta 'Limited Group' discussions took place there. But this tells us nothing of the subsequent role or influence of other participants in Mukti Ali's group, though one may safely conclude there is a multiplier effect at work.

The fact that the book has attracted so much interest simply proves that its ideas fell on fertile soil. In part, this soil was the Western-educated intelligentsia, an elite for whom the language of the Friday sermon held little appeal. But ethnic Javanese, whether those educated in the Javanese court tradition or the peasantry, have long had a rather condescending attitude to Islamic Law, the ulama, Muslim activists, and the exclusive claims of Islam generally. To such it presents a very acceptable understanding of Islam, one which does not reject cultural and religious values from without Islam. Its success perhaps testifies to the degree to which religious pluralism is established in Indonesia. The publication did not cause civil disturbances, it was not banned. One might query how it would have fared had it been published in Malaysia or Pakistan.

Wahib could not, of course, have foreseen the Iranian revolution, and the seizure of power by a revolutionary fundamentalist movement in Islam, bent on inaugurating a divine cultural revolution with the Qur'an as its guide in place of the little red book. Nor did he realize that his highly individual understanding of Islam, without the safeguards, the checks and balances of centuries of traditional *fiqh* — which gave the Nahdatuly Ulama the flexibility and adaptiveness he admired — could be turned on its head, and put to far more effective use, by the radicals. The point is made clearly in an article of Mangol Bayat (1983):

> The Qur'anic verses quoted by radical Muslims to justify their activities have acquired a specific interpretation mediated through the revolutionary ethos. To prior generations these verses had a traditional meaning and a historical context. For contemporary radical groups who view the Qur'an as a revolutionary document for all time, that traditional meaning has been dropped . . . thus neo-normative Muslims, unencumbered by the traditional, historical, linguistic and philological interpretations of the past . . . allow specific verses to address each individual and society in their existential moment.

And these are the very verses that Wahib regarded as 'transformative', needing to be transformed, not 'transmigrative', passing across space and time — verses such as in *sura 3, Al Imran*, verse 28, 'Let not the believers take unbelievers as close associates instead of believers'. When the choice and interpretation are left to the individual, it is the individual's attitude of mind, not tradition, that is to be decisive.

Of course, there are limitations and even *naïvetés* in Wahib's writing. Reference has already been made to the grammatical mistakes in his citation of Qur'anic verses. It is likewise clear that, despite his frequent references to *ijtihad*, he had no acquaintance with the complex treatment of the concept in fiqh. Nevertheless, there is in his ideas integrity, generosity, and a profound personal consistency. And, after all, such ideas are not limited to Indonesia. There are many Islamic modernist intellectuals, especially though not exclusively from the Indian sub-continent, who see Islam not as a system of Law, but as a revelation of spiritual and human values. They regard those parts of the Qur'an revealed at Mecca as of universal significance, those at Madina as having only a local, Arab application.

It is impressive to see the appearance of such a modern educated Islamic elite in Indonesia, passionately committed to the religious values of Islam, yet giving generous recognition to the pluralist reality of the society in which they live. It is in the nature of things that the efforts of such aspirant reformists should arouse the ire of conservatives and fundamentalists more than downright disbelief.

Thus Professor Rasjidi (1982), writing in the periodical *Kiblat*, remarked bitterly that the publication of Wahib's diary was a dark page in the history of Indonesian Islam under the New Order. It was a page he saw lightened by the appearance of a work by a French surgeon, Maurice Bucaille, *The Bible, the Qur'an and Science*, a half-baked mish-mash of pseudo-science and pseudo-exegesis, translated into Indonesian by Rasjidi himself. If it is in such a direction that many of the Muslim intellectual establishment need to look to find intellectual illumination, the freshness and vitality of Wahib's mini-essays, and the persistence of his questioning, needs no further justification.

NOTES

Special thanks are due to Mr Djohan Effendi of Jakarta for making available to me much of the documentation on which this essay is based.

1. The background information given here, and all quotations, are from Effendi and Natsir, 1981:1–16.

2. I am indebted to Dr H. Feith, Department of Politics, Monash Univer sity, for showing me a copy of Djohan Effendi's letter of resignation.

3. It may be observed that this is not a Qur'anic verse, but a combination of the last phrases of verses 32 and 33 respectively of *sura* 9, *al-Tawba*. In addition the words he cites in the form *kafirin* (unbelievers) and *mushrikin* (polytheists) should be *kafirun* and *mushrikun*.

4. The reference is to the adherents of the Ahmadiyya movement founded by Mirza Ghulam Ahmad of Qadian in the Punjab. The Mirza died in 1908, and when his son succeeded him as second *Khalifa* in 1914, the movement split in two, Khwaja Kamal ad-Din and Maulvi Mohd. 'Ali seceding to form what is known as the Lahore party, the original group being the Qadian party. The most important difference between the two groups was that while the Qadian party regarded the Mirza as a Prophet (a claim that, in the light of the explicit Quranic description of Muhammad as the last of the Prophets, was clearly heretical), the Lahore party looked on him mainly as a reformer.

REFERENCES

Bayat, Mangol (1983), 'The Iranian revolution of 1978–79: fundamentalist or modern?', *Middle East Journal*, 37:30–42.

Brunschvig, Robert (1967), 'Logic and Law in Classical Islam in G.E. von Grunebaum (ed.), *Logic in Classical Islamic Culture*. Wiesbaden: Otto Harrassowitz.

Effendi, Djohan, and Ismed Natsir (eds.) (1981), *Pergolakan Pemikiran Islam. Catetan-arian Ahmad Wahib*. Jakarta: LP3ES.

Hamzah, Amir (1954), *Nyanyi Sunyi*. Jakarta: Pustaka Rakyat.

Kartini, Raden Ajeng (1964), *Raden Ajeng Kartini. Letters of a Javanese Princess* (transl. A.L. Symmers, introd. H. Geertz). New York: Norton Library.

Rasjidi, H.M. (1982) 'Pergolakan Pemikiran Islam' (Intellectual Ferment in Islam), *Kiblat*: Vol. xxix, No. 16: January: 1.

Glossary

abangan (Indon.) term used to refer to less rigorous Muslims in Indonesia.

ādab cultivated or learned in a moral and ethical sense, exhibiting the classical religio-social virtues

adat (Indon., from Arabic *'āda*) tradition, custom; *adat desa*, village custom.

akhlāq ethics and morality.

alfa (Yoruba) local religious teacher.

'ālim (pl. *'ulamā'*) learned man; in particular one learned in Islamic legal and religious studies.

Allāhu akbar Allāh is most great.

amīr secular ruler; a military commander; other leaders by extension; *amīr al-mu'minīn*, Commander of the Faithful. Cf. *emir*, in Nigeria.

'āmmī commoner.

'aqīda (pl. *'aqā'id*) the Islamic creed or articles of faith.

'aql reason, reasoning, intelligence.

ashrāf gentility; esp. among Indian Muslims, those who trace their lineage to the Prophet Muhammad, his Companions, or to the Mughal or Pathan (historic) ruling classes.

astāna (Bengali, from Sanskrit) community house.

ayāt a sign; a verse of the Qur'ān.

bahas (Bengali, from Arabic *baḥth*) debate, discussion.

baraka blessing; divine force or favor, associated esp. with saints or relics.

begum (Urdu) lady, queen, title used for Mughal women.

bid'a innovations; actions in disagreement with the practice established by the Prophet Muhammad's example or that of the early Muslim community.

burqa' (Urdu; Ar. *burqu'*) mantle covering a woman from head to foot except for the eyes.

čandi (Indon.) temple.

chādar (Urdu) mantle covering the body from head to foot: *chādar aur chār diwārī*, the enveloping mantle and enclosure within four walls — reflecting the ideal for women of some Pakistani ideologists. Cf. Iranian *chādor*.

čikal bakal (Javanese) first-founding ancestors.

da'wa call, propagation, proselytization. Cf. *al-da'wa ilā al-tawḥīd*, the call to unitarianism of the 'Wahhabis'.

dhikr recollection of God, often through the repetition of specific formulas associated with one or another Sufi *ṭarīqa*, q.v.

dīn faith, religion; *dīnī*, pertaining to the sacred as distinct from the secular. Cf. *siyāsa*.

dukun (Indon.) priest; traditional healer.

emīr see *amīr*.

etteqātī (Ir.) syncretic.

faqīh (pl. *fuqahā*) scholar of Islamic law; jurist.

fatwā (pl. *fatāwā*) formal legal opinion, issued by a qualified jurist.

farā'id fundamental duties of the Islamic faith.

fiqh Islamic law, as set out by the jurists (*fuqahā*).

fiṭra man's innate character of attachment to God; original state of the soul, characterised by purity.

fitna civil strife, dissension.

furū' positive law.

fusha elegance, ampleness (e.g., of speech, address).

ghair muqallad non-conformist, opp. of *muqallid*, q.v.; and see *taqlīd*.

ḥadd (pl. *ḥudūd*) fixed limit, boundary; fixed punishments for certain crimes mentioned in the Qur'ān.

ḥadīth (pl. *aḥādīth*) reported words, deeds, and occasions of tacit approval by the Prophet Muhammad, based on the authority of a chain of reliable transmitters.

ḥajj the Meccan pilgrimage, and the rites there; *ḥājj, ḥājjī*, one who has performed the pilgrimage.

ḥākimīya sovereignty.

halal approved.

ḥanif one who professes the true religion.

ḥaraka movement, popular mobilization.

haram forbidden.

hijra migration, strategic withdrawal, used esp. to refer to the Prophet Muhammad's withdrawal from Mecca to Madina in 622 C.E., from which year dates the Muslim, *hijrī*, lunar calendar.

ḥisba the power to control.

hukum Allāh (Malay) laws of God.

'ibāda (pl. *'ibādāt*) ritual duties, including ablutions, prayer, almsgiving, fasting, pilgrimage to Mecca, reading the Qur'ān, and recollection of God.

'īd festival; *'Īd al-Adhā*, Feast of Sacrifice (during *hajj*); *'Īd al-Fiṭr*, festival marking the end of the fasting month.

ijmā' consensus, usually of the learned.

ijtihād the use of individual reasoning.

imām leader; in the context of the mosque, the leader of ritual prayer; *imām jom'eh* (Ir.), Friday prayer *imām*.

iṣlaḥ reform of society.

isnād the chain of transmitters of authentic tradition (cf. *ḥadīth*).

jāhilīya pre-Islamic time of ignorance; *jāhilī*, ignorant.

jihād striving, effort; *jihād fī sabīlillāh*, striving in the way of God, if necessary war in this cause.

julāhā (Bengali) weaver.

juma', jam' week, or gathering: therefore the Friday, weekly congregational prayer.

kāfir unbeliever in the Islamic revelation; cf. *kafirai*, in Nigeria; and *kafir-mengkafir* (Malay), to accuse someone of being an unbeliever.

keris (Malay), dagger with wavy blade.

khalīfa successor, deputy; by extension, man as God's trustee on earth.

khaṭīb preacher, the person who delivers the Friday sermon (*khuṭba*, c.v.) at the noon prayer of assembly.

khuṭba sermon; in a larger sense, any public address or homily: *khuṭba al-juma'*, the Friday sermon delivered at the noon prayer of assembly.

langgar (Indon.) prayer house.

madrasa school, often associated with a mosque.

Mahdī the expected, divinely guided leader.

majlis al-ṣulḥ council of peace, or settlement.

malik king, sovereign.

mallam (Hausa, from Arabic *mu'allim*) religious teacher.

marāji'-e taqlīd (sing. *marja'*) (Iranian), sources of imitation.

masjid mosque; *masjid ahāli*, popular mosque in Egypt, supported by voluntary contributions, as contrasted with *masjid ḥukūmī*, under government control and subsidized by the state.

ma'ṣūm infallible.

mawlid birthday celebration, esp. *Mawlid al-Nabī*, Prophet's Birthday.

minbar pulpit, usually a stylized wooden construction with steps leading to a platform from whence the Friday sermon is delivered.

modin (Indon. from Arabic *mu'addin*, often anglicized as *muezzin*) prayer caller, and by extension a general mosque functionary.

mujaddid renewer.

mujāhid one who engages in *jihād*, c.v.

mujtahid one qualified to undertake an effort to form a legal opinion, in Islamic jurisprudence.

muṣālaḥa reconciliation between Muslim social groups.

muqallid follower, one who adheres to a particular school of law.

murū'a virtues.

muwahhidun unitarians, those who insist on the oneness of God.

nafs the lower or 'animal' faculty of the human soul, as opposed to the 'angelic' faculty.

niẓām order, system: *niẓām-i Islām* (Urdu), the Islamic system; *niẓām-i mustafa* (Urdu), the system of the Prophet (used as slogans in contemporary Pakistan); *al-niẓām al-jāhilī*, the system of the age of ignorance.

panchayat (Hindi) village council.

pembaharuan (Indon.) renewal.

pesantren (Indon.) religious boarding school of traditional kind (cf. *santri*)

pīr (Urdu) spiritual mentor, teacher of the Sufi Path.

punden (Javanese) burial shrine.

puthi (Bengali) literally, book or manuscript; term used for all Bengali literature of the early and middle periods, and in the nineteenth century associated with a literature created by semi-literate Muslims in a mixture of Bengali, Arabic, Persian, and Urdu.

qādī Islamic judge, magistrate.

qiyās analogy.

rahbari (Iranian) leadership.

rakyat (Malay) people, citizens, the masses.

ribā usurious interest.

sābiqi (Bengali, from Ar. *sābiq*, antecedent) traditional Muslims in Bengal, 'syncretists'.

Sa'īdī someone from upper Egypt, country bumpkin.

Salafīya term used to denote the reform movement founded in Egypt in the late nineteenth century, and its extensions elsewhere, derived from the word for ancestors or forefathers.

ṣalāt Islamic ritual prayer, to be performed at five prescribed times daily.

santri (Indon.) someone who has attended a *pesantren*, or religious boarding school, and by extension any zealous Muslim.

sarauta, masu sarauta (Hausa) the office- and land-controlling elite in Nigeria.

sawah (Malay) wet-rice land.

sayyid lineal descendant of the Prophet Muhammad.

shahāda the Muslim confession of faith: There is no God but Allāh, and Muhammad is His Prophet.

shahīd witness for the faith, hence a martyr.

sharī'a the totality of the exoteric revelation of Islam; Islamic 'law'.

sharīf (pl. *shurafā*, *ashrāf*, q.v.) someone who is distinguished, or high-born.

Shī'a Muslims holding to the rights of 'Alī and his descendants to leadership of the community; the minority of Muslims in contrast to the Sunnī, q.v.

shirk associationism, polytheism.

shūrā consultation, arrangements for collective deliberation and political choice

siyāsa worldly affairs, politics.

silm peace in society.

sunna 'the trodden path'; the normative practice of the Prophet Muhammad and the early community, embodied in the *hadīth* (q.v.) literature.

Sunnī that majority of Muslims which accepts the authority and validity of the actions of the whole first generation of the community; *cf. Shī'a.*

sūra chapter of the Qur'ān.

surau (Malay) young and unmarried men's houses in Minangkabau, more generally prayer houses.

tabarra (Iranian) avoidance of the enemies of God.

ṭāghūt a false god, a tempter to error.

ta'āwun 'alā'l-birr mutual co-operation for the good of society.

tajdīd renewal; cf. *mujaddid.*

talakawa (Hausa) the masses or commoners in Nigeria.

taluqdār (Urdu) petty land-owner.

taqīya dissimulation of one's faith.

tarekat (Indon.) see *ṭarīqa.*

ṭarīqa (pl. *ṭuruq*) Sufi brotherhood or order.

tavalla (Iranian) friendship to the friends of God.

tawba repentance.

ulū'l-amr those in authority.

umma the Islamic community.

'ushr a tithe levied on agricultural products.

ustāz (Urdu) teacher.

uṣūl al-fiqh science of Islamic jurisprudence.

vālī (Iranian) governor.

velāyat-e faqīh (Iranian) theocratic government.

velāyat-e amr (Iranian) governing authority.

walī a saint, in the Sufi tradition.

waqf (pl. *awqāf*) endowed property designated in Islamic law as held in trust for the benefit of the community.

wilāya authority, sovereign power.

zakāt mandatory alms-tax on accrued wealth.

zamindār (Urdu) revenue-collecting agent of the Mughal state.

zāwīya shrine, usually associated with a saint's tomb.

Index

abangan 33, 42
Abbas, Ferhat 237
Abduh, Muhammad 200, 202, 256, 260
Abdullahi dan Fodio 45, 226
ABIM *see* Angkatan
Abraham 120
Abu Bakar 62, 199
Acheh 35
adat 37-8, 68
'Adil, Haddad 118, 123, 127
Afghanistan 134, 143
African religion 69, 105
Agam 38-9
Ahmad Khan, Muin-'ud-din 39-40, 42
Ahmad Khan, Sayyid 277
Ahmadis 136, 155; Lahore wing 277
Ahmadu Bello University 9, 230, 243
Ahmed, Israr 144-5, 156n19
Ajisaka myth (Aji) 62-4, 66, 68-71, 77
Akhbari 113, 119-20
Akora Khattak 149
al-Ahram 222
Al-Jama'a 162, 166-7, 169
Al-Ma'rifa 162, 167-9, 177n9
Ala, Nazima 156
Aladura African Churches 69
alcohol, prohibition of 38, 66, 133,
    137, 175
Alexandria 207
Algeria 7, 17, 229, 237, 239;
    independence struggle 161;
    'Islamists' 172-6
'Ali Khan, R.L. Begum Ra'ana Liaqat
    157n28
'Ali, Mawlana Basharat 40
'Ali, Mawlana Karamat 42
Ali, Mukti 257, 278
All Pakistan Women's Association
    (APWA) 149-50
almsgiving 89-92, 101-2
    see also ushr; zakat
al-'Amili, Makki 125
Amlashi, Ayatollah Rabbani 123
'Amr ibn al-'As 221
Angkatan Belia Islam Malaysia (ABIM)
    7, 181-7; present situation 192-4
Ansari, Shaykh Murtaza 116
Appeal, the 165
al-Aqdasi, Shaykh Jibril b. 'Umar 45
'aqida 190, 267
'aql 145, 220, 223
Arabia 4, 35-7, 62, 176, 267, 279
Arabic 40, 43, 46, 153, 175, 202, 221,
    224n3
Arabs 19, 43, 75, 163, 172; pan-
    Arabism 160

Ardabili, Mukaddas 115
Ardie, Tony 188
Asad, Muhammad 237
Assiut 210
al-Azhar 8, 40, 47, 200, 202, 205-12
    passim

Balewa, Sir Abubakar Tafawa 239
Bali 54-6, 66, 69, 73
Bandung 188
Bangladesh 133; *see also* Bengal
el-Banna, Hasan 167-8, 200
baraka 8, 204
Bauchi State 244
al-Bayan. Majma 115
al-Bayan, Zubdat 115
Bayero University 99
Beheshti, Ayatollah 130
Beirut 167
Bello, Sir Ahmadu 231, 239
Benevolent Societies 207-8, 217-18,
    223
Bengal 4, 18, 22-3, 34, 36, 39-42
Bennabi, Malek 237-9
Berber 43
Berger, P.L. 191
Berque, Jacques 32
Bhutto, Zu'l-faqar Ali 133, 148
Bihishti Zevar 156
Birni 86
Bloch, Marc 27
Bondo 44
Bornu 226-7
Bourghibism 170, 174
Braudel, F. 21
Britain 112, 203, 221; British
    colonialism 39-41, 90-1, 147, 226,
    244-7
Bromo, Mt 55
Brunschvig, R. 254, 276
Bucaille, M. 255, 279
Buda 5, 53-77; conversion 67-76, *see
    also* conversion; festival *see* karo;
    final decline 53, 66-7; mythology
    see Ajisaka; pre-colonial 55-7; *see
    also* Java; religion: 'world' and
    'traditional'; Tengger
Buddhism 75-6 *see also*
    Hindu-Buddhism
Bukari 104
al-Bukhari 45, 94
Bulum-Ketu 86

Cairo 13, 45, 48, 49, 200, 202, 207,
    209
Calcutta 40

calendrical occasions 37, 43, 46,
    105; *see also* Mahdism
Caliphs 165, 222
Camp David 220
capitalism: denounced 169-70, 237;
    mercantile-colonial 90-3; semi-
    industrial 83, 91-104; 'Wahhabi'
    160; *see also* West, the
Casablanca 174
Catholicism 80, 257
centralization; Islamic authority 117-19,
    129, 231, 249, *see also* faqih; state
    91, 99, 112-13, 248-9
chadar aur char diwari 138, 153, *see
    also* women
Chadli, President 175
China 58, 144, 203
Christianity 17, 21, 70, 80, 91;
    Christians in pluralist states 226-7,
    231, 244-5, 255, 261, 274; *see
    also* Catholicism; Jesuits; religion
class differentiation *see* socio-economic
clothing 38, 143, 146, 221; restrictions
    147, 150, 175, 188, 221
coffee, effects of introduction 23, 38,
    57-9, 90-1
colonialism 21, 38-41, 57-9, 90-1, 199,
    237-41 *passim*, 247; *see also*
    Britain; Netherlands
communism 135; *see also* socialism;
    Marxism; Indonesian Communist
    Party
Congress, the (Indian party) 135
conversion, religious 5, 17, 22, 24,
    53-77; and 'world' religion 67-76;
    disenchantment with 'traditional'
    religion 72-6; historical background
    see Buda; Java; Horton's experi-
    ment 69-71; *see also* religion;
    socio-economic
cooperatives 217-18; *see also*
    benevolent societies
Copts 13
courts *see* juristic; Shari'a
Cox, H. 194n4
cults, local *see* shrines
Cultures 34
Cyprus 222

Dacca 48
Darul Arqam 182
Darwinism 145-6, 150
da'wa 7, 8, 47, 166-7, 171, 182,
    185-6, 189, 220
Dawn 150, 153
Delhi 48
democracy, Western: approved 167-8,
    262; democracy, islamic 165;
    denounced 166; *see also* pluralism;
    West, the
Deoband 140-1
Deobandi, Maulana S.H. 149

Derrida 33
Dinka 24
Dir'iya 35
Djait, Hichem 160
Dobbin, C. 37-8
Dudhu Miyan 41
Durkheim 24, 70, 94

East India Company 39-41
economic factors: over-emphasis
    criticized 16; *see also* socio-economic
education 67, 154; effects of greater
    access to 21, 27, 104, 173, 228;
    indoctrination 122; madrasas 156
    see also mallams; Qur'anic
    students; mosque 218; serving *jihad*
    163-4; universities 182, 220, 244,
    255; *see also* al-Azhar; Islamic
    Universities; Sulaiman, Ibraheem;
    women 141, 236
Effendi, Djohan 189, 258, 266, 279
egalitarianism 42, 141, 148, 151, 218
Egypt 8, 13-14, 141, 167, 172,
    199-225; benevolent societies
    207-8, 217-18; militants 219-21;
    nationalism 201-3; orthodoxy
    200-1, 213; 'popular' mosque
    217-24; regional differences 201,
    209, 224n1; state control 199-200,
    248; 'state' mosque 207-15;
    typology of preachers 204-5; *see
    also* Muslim Brotherhood; Nasser;
    Sadat
El-Habib 167
El-Mujtama 167
elections, women participation 232-7;
    see also women
Er-rai 172
Ettela'at 118, 122, 123, 127, 129, 130
Evidence, Law of 138-9, 151-2, 155-6

Fadil, Siddiq 184-7
Family Laws Ordinance (Pakistan),
    138, 149,
faqih, velayat-e 115-17, 119-24; abroad
    166-7; as new article of Shi'ite
    faith 121, 123-4; objections to 119,
    128-9; *see also* Imamate
Fara'idis 23, 36, 39-43, 45-6
Faridpur 40
fascism 135
el-Fassi, Allal 160
fatwa 42, 174
feminism 142, 145
feudalism 27
fiqh 271-2, 276-8
Fodio *see* Usuman; Abdullahi
Foucault, Michel 2
France 112-13, 245
Freud 146
Friday holiday 133, 211, 218
Fronde, the 112

Fulani (Fulbe) 43, 86, 91; Fulani Jihad 36, 43-7, 87, 226, 235; *see also* Sokoto
al-Fuli, Shaykh 206, 210, 218
funerary rites 66, 222
furu 'al-din 126
Futa Toro 44
Futa Jalon 44

Gajah Mada University 256-7
gardawa see Qur'anic students
Gaskiya Ta Fi Kwabo 230, 232-4
Geertz, Clifford 19, 33, 72-5
Ghafur, Abdul 188
el-Ghannushi, Rashid 168-70, 177n14
Ghudbani, Hasan 170
Gilani, S.A. 139-49 *passim*
GNPP *see* Great Nigeria People's Party
Gobir 44-5
GOLKAR 15, 180-1, 188
Golpayegani, Ayatollah 129n4
Gombe 86
Goody, J. 26
Gospel of Barnabas 255
Great Nigeria People's Party (GNPP) 227, 232
al-Guindi, F. 156n23
Gulf, the 135; Gulf war 121, 128
Gumi, A.M. 9, 229-30, 240, 242-3, 248; discourse 231-7

hadd penalties 137, 139, 155
hadith: disregarded 242; in ritual 212; social issues 94, 140, 147, 152; studies 35, 45; validity questioned 254, 258-9, 268-9, 271, 275
Ha'eri-Yazdie, Ayatollah 128n3
Hafez 145
hajj, the 47, 61, 67, 182; communications through 34, 36, 43; corruption 100; politicization 125; *see also* Hijaz; Madina; Mecca
Hakiem, Lukman 190-1
Hamid, Amera S. 156n26
Hamzah, Amir 275
Hassan II, King 14, 22, 162, 167, 170, 174, 176
Hassan, Shaykh *see* sermon
Hausa 34, 36, 91, 231-2; Fulani *jihad* 43-5; language 9, 85, 91, 228-9
Haykal, Muhammad Husayn 215
Hijaz 34, 35-6, 43
hijr 45
al-Hilli, Muhaqqiq 116
Himpunan Mahasiswa Islam (HMI) 7-9, 181, 187-92; and Ahmed Wahib 256, 258, 263-6 *passim*, 271, 273; Islamic resurgence 189-91; resisting Pančasila 187-9; secularism accepted 189, 192
Hindu 15, 40-2, 67, 69
Hindu-Buddhism, Javanese 54-5, 62, 66, 68, 76; *see also* Buddhism; Bali
hisba assemblies 165

Hiskett, M. 36
historical change, conceptualization 20-1; *see also* Islam — effect of changing
HMI *see* Himpunan
Hodgson, M. 18-19, 201
Hopi 73
Horton, R. 69-72
Hudson, M. 220
Hurgronje, Snouck 255
Husayn, Imam 127
Hyde, L. 33

Ibn Badis 160
Ibn Khaldun 160, 237-8
ibn Sa'ud, Muhammad 35
Ibo 226-7
Ibrahim, Anwar 83-6, 193
Ijma' 268-9, 275, 277
Ikhwan al-Muslimun *see* Muslim Brotherhood
Ilahabadi, Akbar 145
Imamate: Khomeini acclaimed as 'Imam' 120; Moroccan discourse 165, 171; reinterpretation 117-18; *see also* centralization; *faqih; taqlid* theory of infallibility 113, 115-16
imam jom'ehs 122-3, 125, 129-30
India 13, 62, 145, 279; and Pakistan 132, 154-6; the 'Indian Mutiny' 41
Indonesia 3, 13; colonial rule *see* Netherlands; communists' slaughter 53, 256-7 *see also* Indonesian Communist Party; education 257; fundamentalism 22, 254-5, 278; Malaysia compared 187, 194; national ideology 15, 73, 192, 229, 248 *see also* Pančasila; pluralism 73, 254, 278-9; youth organizations *see* Himpunan; Wahib, Ahmad; *see also* Bali; Java; Madura; Sumatra
Indonesian Communist Party 53, 66, 187, 256, 263
industrial relations 85-7, 91-7
interest, abolition of 137
Iqbal, Alama 34, 143, 147, 277
Iraq 128n3, 167
Iran 3, 5, 6, 13, 35, 111-31, 134; the Constitutional revolution 126; *see also* monarchy; Mohammad Reza
Iranian Revolution 83, 111-31; Constitution 111-12, 117-18; defined as traditionalist 111; deviation from Shi'ite tradition 112-22 *passim, see also* faqih; Imamate; influence on Islamic world 6, 13-14, 22, 165-6, 176, 186, 235-6, 243, 255, 278; *see also* centralization; Khomeini; pluralism; politicization; Shi'ism
Islam: approaches to discourse 33-47 *passim*, 55, 84; authority *see* legitimacy; capacity for self-renewal 18; claims of superiority

145, 154, 203, 238, 262;
depoliticized see Pančasila;
secularism; state; diversity 1,
19-20, 31, 33, 47-8; effect of
changing circumstances 4, 20-3,
33, 258-76 passim 279; holistic
view — as complete code of life 8,
122, 136, 140, 154, 173, 185,
189-92; human condition — Islamic
view 10, 145, 164; ideal and
method (minhaj) defined 163; Islam
or 'islams' 19-20, 47-8; Islamic
'resurgence' 160-1 see also
'Islamists'; Law see fiqh; Law;
Shari'a; neo-Marxist view 79-85;
'radio Islam' 9, 22, 212-13 see
also media; reinterpretations 152-4
see also hadith; Qur'an; revivalist
movements see reformists,
Wahhabi; ritual see mosque;
prayer; sermon; and see religion;
Shi'i; Sunni
Islamic Socialism 133-4, 148, 160
Islamic Universities 137, 175, 185,
187, 241-2
'Islamists' 6, 14, 22, 27, 161-77; and
democracy 167-9; compared
169-72; political discourse 172-7;
progressive 171-2; revolution urged
162-7; see also Iranian Revolution;
legitimacy; Jama'at-i Islami;
politicization; Wahhabi
Islamization 5-7, 42, 139, 155n9, 163,
185; and see conversion; da'wa;
politicization
Isfahan 127
isnad 34
Israel 214, 239 see also Camp David;
Palestine
al-Ittijah al-Islami (MTI) 162, 167-70,
172, 177n8
ijtihad 123
Ivory Coast 36
Izala 230

Jago 56
jahil 14, 19, 162-4, 194; jahiliya
syndrome 169
al-Jailani, 'Abd al-Qadir 45
Jakarta 4, 48, 188, 238, 278
al-Jama'a 162
al-jama'a al-islamiya (Egypt) 205, 220
Jama'at-i Islami 134-6, 139-41, 144,
148-50, 153-4, 155-6, 186
Jama'at al-da'wa 167
Jama'atu Nasril Islam 231
Jamiah Tabligh 182 see also Taglighi
Jama'at
Jami'at-i Talabat 153, 156
Jami'atu'l- 'Ulama-yi Hind 135
Japan 113, 144
Java 4, 33, 53-77; coffee introduced
57-9; colonial period 58-65;

conversion 25, 53 see also Buda;
conversion; cultural unity 19;
Madurese migrations 57-61;
mythology 22 see also Ajisaka;
pre-colonial 55-7; regional
differences 68; religious tolerance
257-8, 278; see also Buda;
Indonesia; Tengger
Jerusalem 121
Jesuits 257-8, 277-8
Jews 239
Jibril b. 'Umar 36
jihad 49n9, 83, 87; and Iranian
Revolution 125-6; Fulani (Sokoto)
36, 43-7, 87, 226, 235; Padri 38;
political 163-4, 177n4, 185; women
232-6 passim, 242; see also
martyrs
al-Jihad 171
Jimeta 86
Jinnah 133, 155n5
Johnson, N. 23-4
Junaidu, the Waziri 241
jurisprudence, Islamic, exercised 38;
see also fiqh; law; Shari'a
juristic (judicial) authority and system;
in Pakistan 137; Shi'ite 113-14,
119, 121, 122; see also centralization; pluralism; Shari'a; ulama
Jursh, Salah-eddin 170

Kabara, Shaykh Nasiru 247
Kaduna 86, 105, 230-1
Kano 48, 85-106, 231, 242, 247; see
also mallam; Nigeria; Qur'anic
students; 'yan Tatsine
Kano, Aminu 239, 247
Karbala 127
karo festival 53, 63-6
Kartini, R.A. 274
kawi, Mt 55
Kembar 65
Khadija 151
Khalid ibn al-Walid 221
Khalwatiya 45
Khaz'ali, Ayatollah 119
Khilafatists 32
Kho'i, Ayatollah 119, 127
Khomeini, Ayatollah 111, 114-15,
117-23, 125, 127-8; in Islamic
world 155n13, 167-8, 176, 220,
235; his students' roles 114-15,
127, 128; allegedly performing
miracles 120; successor 121, 128;
see also faqih; Imamate; Iranian
Revolution
khutba see sermon
Khwaja N.A. 150
Kiblat 279
Kidal 56
al-Kurani, Ibrahim 34

Lagos 99, 104

Lahore 139, 140, 149, 151-2; *see also* Ahmadis
land laws 113, 114, 137, 246
Lane, E. 202
Latin America, theology of liberation 80
Law, Muslim 165-6, 272, 276; four sources 268-9, 275, 277; primary and secondary commandments 124, 279; *see also* Shari'a; juristic
legitimacy, of authority — of ruling elite: Islam used to delegitimize 14, 23, 98, 164-5, 167, 170, 175 *see also* 'Islamists'; *jahil*; monarchy; State; Islam used to legitimize 83-4, 137, 162, 170, 172-6 *passim*, 236 *see also faqih*; politicization religious authority: typology of preachers 204-5, 220, 222; *see also* ulama
Lenin 33
liberation, theology of 80-2, 160
Libya 176
Life of Muhammad 215
literacy 26
local cults 72, 76 *see also* Buda; religion; scale; shrines; syncretism
London 100, 143
Lucknow 155
Lugard, Lord 246
Luxemburg 186

Madina 34-5, 45, 47, 199, 213, 246, 279; *see also* Mecca
Madura 58-9, 61, 65, 70, 256
Maghreb, the 3, 6-7, 35, 248; *see also* Algeria; Morocco; Tunisia
Mahallati, Ayatollah 128
Mahathir, Dr 183-4, 186, 193
Mahdism (messianism, millenariarism) and urban unrest 83, 85-6, 97, 105-6; in Iranian Revolution 113, 119-21; 'Islamist' movements 173, 174-5, 208; *see also* calendrical occasions
Mahmud, Abdulmalik Bappa 9, 230, 244, 248; discourse 244-7
Maiduguri 86, 242
Maitatsine (Alhaji Mohammed Marwa) 86-7, 97-8, 105-6; *see also* 'Yan Tatsine
Madjid, Nurcholish 181, 189
Majapahit 54, 56, 68
Majlis, the (Iran) 120, 121
Majlis-i Shura (Pakistan) 137, 139, 149, 151
al-Makki, Shaykh Tahir al-Sunbal 40
Malang 55, 61-5 *passim*
Malaysia 7, 9, 18, 33, 248; Indonesia compared 187, 194, 278; youth organizations 181-7, 192-4
Mali 43
mallams: in pre-colonial Kano 87-9; prior to Fulani Jihad 44-5; social unrest after oil-boom 5, 85, 94, 97,

104, 229, 241 *see also* Qur'anic students
Mannheim 21, 25
Mao 133, 203
maraboutic 21, 24
Mar'ashi-Najafi 129n4
Mardin, S. 26
Marrakech 162
marja'iyyat 122-3
martyrdom 121, 125, 127-8, 176, 239
Marwa, Alhaji Mohammed *see* Maitatsine
Marx, Karl 81-2, 84
Marxism: denounced 169-70, 173; materialist dialectic approach to Islamic social forces 79-85; practices borrowed 164, 172, 240; seen as threat 242, 249; *see also* Socialism, Communism
Mary, mother of Jesus 13, 274
Mashhad 128
Masyumi 256
Mataram 56-8
Maududi, Maulana A.A. 6, 135-6, 144-6, 167-8
al-Mawardi 160, 236
Mecca: Ajisaka myth 62-3; Grand Mosque 176, 177n1; Laws contrasted with Madina's 279; meeting place for scholars 22, 35-6, 38, 41, 45, 47; Muhammad's 220; praying in direction of 105; *see also hajj*; Hijaz
media 22, 125, 128, 216, 229-31 and *see* 'radio Islam'
Meshkini, Ayatollah 123
Mestaoui, Shaykh 170
Minangkabau 36-9
Mindanao 36
Minhaj 163
Minya 206-8, 210-20 *passim*
Miskin, Hajji 38
Mohammad Reza, the Shah 113-19 *passim*, 125, 126
Mo'men, Ayatollah 124
monarchy, 14, 21, 155n7, 165, 167, 170-1, 176, 178n21
Montazeri, Ayatollah 128, 129, 130
Monthly Review 80, 82
Morocco 7, 9, 14, 21-7 *passim*; 'Green March' 174; 'Islamist' discourse 162-7; new Islamic emphasis 174-5; Tunisia compared 169-72
mosques: centres of community control 129n10; in factories 94-5; Islamic discourse 47-8; and Islamization 64-5, 67; 'state' and 'independent' mosques 8, 14, 205-9, Shaykh 'Ali's 'state' mosque 207-15, Shaykh Hassan's 'popular' mosque 217-24; youth organization 187; *see also* prayer; sermon
Motahhari, Ayatollah 118, 123

Mu'awiya 165, 221
Mughal, the 39-40
Muhammad, the Prophet, 116, 147,
    151-2; Ajisaka myth 62-4, 69;
    appearing in visions 45; biography
    as inspiration 151-2, 162, 220;
    descendants of *see* Sayyids; in ser-
    mons 212, 223; mosques 199, 246;
    role of women 147, 151-2;
    teachings inducing revolution 163,
    171-2; ultimate authority 116, 258,
    269-70, 272, 275-6
Muhammad al-Raj 45
Muhammad 'Ali 200, 239
Muhammad Bello 45-6, 49n8
Muhammad, Mian Tufail 136
Muhammad, Muhsin al-Din
    Muhammad *see* Dudhu Miyan
Muhammad, Murtala 239
Muhammadiya 65, 264, 277
mujadid 46
mujahid 205, 222
mujtahids 114, 123, 125
Muru, 'Abd al-Fatih 170
Muslim Brotherhood (Ikhwan al-
    Muslimun) 141, 167, 169, 184,
    194; in Egypt 14, 200, 205, 216
Muslim League (India) 135
Muslim, The 151, 152
muwahhidun 35, 39, 43, 45-6
mythology 22, 62-4, 71, 77n7, 243 *see
    also* Ajisaka
Mzali, M. 174, 178n22

Nadwi, Mawlana Abu'l- Hasan 156n
Nahadatul Ulama (NU) 264-5, 278
Najafabadi, N.S. 127
Nan Rinceh, Tuanku 38
Nan Tua, Tuanku 38-9
Naqshbandiya *tariqa* 35 *see also* Sufi
Nasser, A. 160, 165, 202-3, 239; suppress-
    ing 'Islamists' 14, 177n3, 200, 216
National Party of Nigeria (NPN) 101,
    227, 229, 231-2, 235
nationalism: competing with Islam 135,
    146; fusion and transposition 15,
    201-2; Islam focus of national
    identity 8, 23, 67, 132, 176, 193,
    240-2; *see also* Pančasila;
    secularism; state
Nejd 34, 35-7, 43, 46
Neo Destour 170
Netherlands: the Dutch in the East
    Indies 39, 57-9, 64-6
New Nigerian, The 230
Nigeria 3-6, 8, 79-107, 226-51; civil
    war 86, 92-3, 104, 227; colonial
    abuse 246-7; compared to Islamic
    states 248-50; constitution 245; cor-
    ruption 98-104 *passim*, 229, 236,
    239, 241, 246; crime 100, 242;
    diversity 226-8, 240, 247-8; educa-
    tion 104, 228, 244, 249 *see also*

Qur'anic students; 'Islamist' view
    of history 238-9; pluralism 229,
    237, 240, 248, 250; pre-colonial
    87-90, *see also* Bornu; Fulani;
    Sokoto; Qur'anic students and
    industrial labor compared 85-7,
    91-7; socio-economic consequences
    of oil-boom 5, 83-7 *passim*, 91-4
    passim, 98-104; the 'moral
    economy' 87-90, 97-104 *passim*;
    typology of discourse 8-9, 229-31,
    240, 242-3, 246
Nigerian Elements Progressive Union
    (NEPU) 97
Nile Delta 201, 209
nizam-i mustafa (nizam-i Islami) 6,
    134-5, 140, 147-8
Northern People's Congress (NPC)
    205, 227
Nuer 24, 73
Nuri, Shaykh Fazlollah 126
Nursi, Said 26

oil: effect of oil-boom on Islamic
    revival 133-4, 160; nationalization
    111; socio-economic consequences
    of oil-boom 5, 83-7 *passim*, 91-4
    passim, 98-104
Ottomans 36, 114, 126

padri 25, 36-9, 43, 46
Pahlavi 115, 126 *see also* Mohammad
    Reza
Pakistan 3, 132-56; 'Islamic socialism'
    133-4; Islamization 5-7, 135-9;
    Jama'ati arguments 139-54; women
    laws 138-9; Zia regime 135-5; *see
    also* Evidence, law of; *hadd*;
    Jama'at-i Islami; women
Pakistan Times, The 149-50
Palestine 23-4, 241
Pan-Malayan Islamic Party (PAS)
    182-6 *passim*, 192-3
Pančasila 7, 15, 180-1, 248; origin
    194n1; resisted 187-90; *see also*
    Himpunan; Indonesia
Panjab 145
partai Persatuan Pembangunan (PPP)
    180, 192
People's Redemption Party (PRP) 95,
    101, 227, 229, 232, 235
PERKIM 182
petroleum *see* oil
pluralism: juristic authority (Shi'ite)
    117, 122-3, *see also* centralization;
    faqih, Shi'ism *taqlid* religious 71,
    171, 233-6, 254, 278-9, *see also*
    secularism
Polisario 174
Political economy of meaning, defini-
    tion 16
politicization: control of symbols 203;
    Islamic ethic 120, 123-8, 141, 171,

233-6; see also Iranian revolution;
  'Islamists'; Jama'at-i Islami;
  legitimacy; Shi'ism
prayer: and politics 121, 231-6 passim
  see also imam jomeh; politicization;
  'radio Islam'; clashing with
  industrial discipline 93-5; Friday
  congregational 41, 59, 125, 129n10
  see also mosque; sermon; salat
  (daily prayer) 38, 67; Wahib's
  273-4; 'Yan Tatsine 105
Priangan 58
'primitive' societies 24, 33, 71 see also
  local cults; religion; scale
Prophet, the see Muhammad
Protocols of the Elders of Zion 255
Prussia 113
puthi literature 42

Qaddafi 47, 176
Qadiriya 36, 40-1, 45, 247 see also Sufi
Qajar 125, 126
el-Qashashi, Ahmad 34
Qum 48, 119, 123, 129n10
Qumi, Ayatollah 119, 128n3
Qur'an: appeal 276; in ritual 48, 92,
  199, 212, 221, 223; militancy 27,
  163, 243, 278-9; political authority
  115-16, 128n2, 185; primary
  authority 31, 170, 186; revelation
  of God 14, 18, 140, 172; relevance
  today 9, 26, 237, 254, 268-9, 275,
  277; social issues 42, 94; study 88
  see also mallams; Qur'anic students;
  Wahhabism 38; women's role 147,
  152; see also; hadith; Muhammad
Qur'anic students (gardawa) 5, 85-91,
  94-5, 98-106; compared to
  industrial labour 94-5; effects of oil-
  boom 98-105; the 'moral economy'
  87-91; radicalism provoked 85-7,
  105-6, 241, 249; see also mallams;
  talakawa; 'Yan Tatsine
Quraysh 214
Qutb, Sayyid 128n2, 167, 177n3, 237-8

Rabbani, Amlashi, Ayatollah 123
Radiance, The 230, 243
Rahman, Tunku Abdul 182
'radio Islam' 9, 22, 212-13
Ramadan 59, 174, 191
Rasht 125
Rasjidi, H.M. 279
rationalization, religious definition 74
reformers 9, 17, 22, 75, 141, 199,
  256; typology of 205; see also
  Deoband; 'Islamists'; mujahid;
  Wahhabi
religion: and the individual 76;
  assumed a receding force 13-15;
  rapprochment with the left 80;
  three conceptual elements of r's
  political economy 20-7; 'world' and

'traditional' (small-scale) religions
  5, 23-5, 54, 67-76, 226, 'sense of
  sacredness' 72, 'the local context'
  73-6, see also conversion; Buda;
  local cults; socio-economic
Retribution, Law of 152 see women
Rida, Rashid 200
Riyadh 35
Ricklefs, M.C. 54-7 passim
Rodinson, M. 7, 32, 160
Russell, Bertrand 32
Russia see Soviet Union

sabiq 42
Sadat, A. 14, 171, 203, 212-14, 217,
  219; peace initiative 214, 220, 222
Sadduqi, Ayatollah 120
Safavids 113, 120, 125, 126
Sahara 43
Sahel 43-4
Salafiya 47
salat see prayer
Sampang 256
Sankore, the 241
santri 59
Sarbidaran 125
Sarikat Islam 277
Sa'uds 35
Saudi Arabia 125, 134, 136, 154, 166
sayyids 113
scale: element of religion's political
  economy 23-5; small-scale religion
  see religion
secularism 146, 149, 176, 181, 189,
  192, 194n4, 227, 239, 248-9, 267;
  'secularizing' Islam 269-71; see
  also nationalism; pluralism; state
Senegambia 44
sermon, Friday 8, 47-8, 125, 129,
  200-24; al-balagha 212; and the
  state 125, 129n10, 200; double
  function 8, 208; fixed formula
  47-8, 202; Shaykh 'Ali's 212-14;
  Shaykh Hassan's 218-24; typology
  of preachers 204-5; see also
  mosque; prayer
Shagari 98, 104
Shah, the see Mohammad Reza
Shamsabadi, Ayatollah 127
shar'ia 31, 268-9, 275; and authority
  124, 170, 213; courts 38-9, 137-8;
  implementation 6, 189-92 passim,
  255; superiority claimed 242; see
  also juristic; law
Shariat Allah, Hajji 36, 39-42, 45
Shari'at-madari, Ayatollah 119, 121,
  128-9
Shari'ati, Ali 167, 237
Shattariya 38
Shi'ism: antagonism toward Sunnis 126,
  137; changes in political ethics
  124-8; contrasted with Sunnism
  113, 114, 134; furu' al-din (ten

principal duties) 126-7; revolution
in 6, 111-12, 123; transformation
of theory of authority 115-24
Shirazi, Ayatollah 129n4
Shirazi, Mirza-ye 126
shrines, local 8, 21, 40, 204, 206,
210-11, 222; *see also* Buda; local
cults; syncretism; *wali*
shura 118
al-Siba'i, Yusef 222
al-Sibki, Shaykh Mahmud M. Khattab
200
Sind 134
al-Sindi, Muhammad Hayya 34, 45
al-Sindi, 'Ab'ul Hasan 45
Singasari 56
al-Singkeli, Abd al-Ra'uf 34
Siradj A.Z. 190
Sivaism 54, 76n2
slave trade 91
Smith, W. Robertson 17
socialism 133, 140, 143-4, 160, 165,
203, 237; reassessment of religion
80; *see also* Islamic Socialism;
Marxism; trade unions
socio-economic factors: influencing
conversion 37, 58-60 *see also*
coffee, *surau*; influencing 'Islamist'
movements 148-51, 166, 173, 175
see also egalitarianism, oil; influencing 'Wahhabism' 22-3, 37-42
see also *zamindars*; influencing
urban insurgence 97-104; small-
scale religions 73
Soekarno 256
Sokoto 45, 87-9, 226, 229, 231, 235,
241-2 *see also* Fulani
Solzhenitsyn 237
Sorush 118, 121-2
Soviet Union 134, 143-4
Spain 21
state power 3, 83-4, 248; and human
rights 245-6; control of Islam 200,
247; coopting Islam 172-6 *see also*
Pakistan; Indonesia and Malaysia
contrasted 7-8, 187; seized by islam
5, 112-14, 163 *see also* Iranian
Revolution; *see also* centralization,
Islamization, legitimacy, nationalism,
pluralism, secularism
Sudan 43, 105, 184, 194
Suez Canal 201
Sufi (*turuq*) 26, 35-7, 40, 43, 45-7,
49n5, 56, 64, 204-5, 211;
suppressed 201, 230-1; *see also*
Khalwatiya, Naqshbandiya, Qadiriya

Suharto 257
Sulaiman, Ibraheem 9, 230, 237, 246,
248; discourse 238-44
Sumatra 4, 23, 34, 37, 68, 275; *see
also* Minangkabau
Sunan Kalijaga 63, 257
Sunday Triumph, The 230
sunna 31, 46, 186, 268-9, 275
Sunnism: antagonism towards Shi'ism
126, 137; contrasted with Shi'ism
113, 114, 134, 248
Surapati 57
surau 37-8
syncretism 42, 105 *see also abangan*;
sabiqi; shrines
Syria 141

tabarra 126-7
Tabataba'i 115-16, 128
Tabataba'i Yazdi, Kazim 125-6
Tablighi Jama'at 140; *see also* Jamiat
Tabligh
al-Tabrisi 115
Tabriz 119
Taha Hussein 224n1
talakawa 85, 89, 91, 97; *see also*
gardawa
taqiyya, denounced 126
taqlid, marja'-e 111, 114, 117, 122,
125, 126
tariqa, turuq see Sufi
tavalla 126-7
tawba 41
Tehran 120, 123, 125, 176, 220
Tehrani, Ayatollah 128
Tengger 4, 54-5, 57-60, 63-5, 68, 76
see also Buda; Java
Theravada Buddhism 75
'Third World' 47, 79, 165, 173
Tibyan 115
Timbuktu 241
Tjokroaminoto, H.S. 277
Torodo 44-5
Toynbee 238
trade unions 94-5, 97, 174, 178n20
Troeltsch, E. 17
Trunajaya 57
Tuareg 44-5
Tumpang 61
Tunisia 7, 177-8, 248; coopting
'Islamism' 172, 174-6; 'Islamist
discourse' 162, 167-70
Turen 63
Turkey 13, 26
Turner, V. 203
al-Tusi 115

ulama: Shi'ite 6, 111-23 *passim*, 129n5, 248; Sunnite 26, 248; authority questioned 9 *see also* Wahib; coopted by state (Maghreb) 161, 162, 167, 174, 178n21; in Pakistan Islamization 6, 134, 136, 141, 149, 153, marginalization in Egypt 200, 204-6, 222; *see also* legitimacy

Umar 62

United Malays Nationalist Organization (UMNO) 182-6 *passim*, 193

United States 125, 129, 132, 134, 142, 146, 214, 245

Unity Party of Nigeria (UPN) 227, 231

universities *see* education; Islamic universities

urdu 142-3, 149

'ushr 41, 137; *see also* almsgiving

Usman 62

Usuli 116-17

Usuman dan Fodio 36, 45-6, 49n8, 226, 235-6

Valéry, Paul 2

velayat-e faqih see faqih

Wafd, the 239

al-Wahhab, Muhammad ibn 'Abd al- 34-5, 45

'Wahhabi' movements 4, 9, 22, 34, 35-47; Nejd 35-7 *see also* Fara'idi, Fulani, Padri; validity of term 4, 34, 47; 'Wahhabi'-influenced 160, 176, 230

Wahib, Ahmad 9, 189, 256-89; background 256-8, 276-7; diary 258; *hadith* relevance questioned 258-9, 268-75 *passim*; 'Limited Group' 257, 277-8 *see also* Himpunan; secularism urged 268-9; the debate 273-7

wali cult 204, 206, 210; *see also* shrines

waqf 200, 205-12 *passim*; and centralization 249

warfare 36, 166; *see also jihad*

Weber, M. 24, 55, 72-4, 204

West, the; cultural oppression 114, 135, 160, 163, 166, 167, 170, 237; immorality claimed 144-6, 169; inadequacy of terminology 74, 161, 164; politico-economic dependence 132, 134, 169, 189; resisting Western education 104, 241; West's reaction to Islam 135, 160;

Westernized intellectual 112, 168, 278; women compared 139-43, 147

Western Sahara 174

women 6, 137-54; education 141, 236; elections 232-7; equality 137-9, 149-53; political participation 175; socialist women compared 143-4; western women compared 139-43, 147; woman's role 147-9, 249n7; *see also chadar*, Family Laws, Evidence, Law of

World Bank 101

'Yan Tatsine 5, 8, 86-7, 104-6, 247; *see also mallams*; Nigeria; Qur'anic students

Yassin, 'Abd Assalam 162-7, 177n4; compared 169-71

Yazd 120

Yazdi, Kazim Tabataba'i *see* Tabataba'i

Yazid 127

Yogyakarta 188, 256-8, 264, 277-8

Yola 86

Yoruba 226-31 *passim*

youth organizations, Muslim 7, 180-95; Indonesian 181-7; Malaysian 187-95; *see also* Angkatan, Himpunan

Yusuf, Adamu 236

zakat 41, 65, 67, 137, 168, 247

zamindars 39-42

Zanjani, Ayatollah 128

Zaria 242-3

Zia 'ul-Haqq 133-8

Zionism 239-40, 255

Zungur, Sa'adu 239

Zuwo, Alhaji Sabo Bakin 101

For Product Safety Concerns and Information please contact our EU representative GPSR@taylorandfrancis.com Taylor & Francis Verlag GmbH, Kaufingerstraße 24, 80331 München, Germany

Printed and bound by CPI Group (UK) Ltd, Croydon, CR0 4YY

08/06/2025

01897007-0010